Sexuality, Morals and Justice

Sexuality, Morals and Justice

A Theory of Lesbian and Gay Rights Law

Nicholas Bamforth

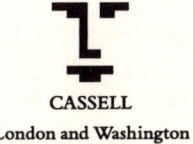

CASSELL
London and Washington

For a catalogue of related titles in our
Sexual Politics/Global Issues list please write to us
at the address below.

Cassell
Wellington House
125 Strand
London WC2R 0BB

PO Box 605
Herndon VA 20172

© Nicholas Bamforth 1997

All rights reserved. No part of this publication may be reproduced or transmitted in any form or by any means, electronic or mechanical including photocopying, recording or any information storage or retrieval system, without prior permission in writing from the publishers.

First published 1997

British Library Cataloguing-in-Publication Data

A catalogue record for this book is available from the British Library.

ISBN 0 304 33145 7 (hardback)
     0 304 33147 3 (paperback)

Front cover photographs
Top: 'Protest against censorship in the arts', Metropolitan Museum, New York City, 1989 © Ellen B. Neipris; Centre: 'Supporters of the Oregon Citizens' Alliance advocate anti-gay legislation', Portland, Oregon, 1992 © Donna Binder; Bottom: 'OutRage! demonstrate at the 25th anniversary of the Sexual Offences Act', London, 1992, © Denis Doran.

Designed and typeset by Ben Cracknell Studios
Printed and bound in Great Britain by Biddles Ltd, Guildford and King's Lynn

Contents

	Preface	vii
1	Themes	1
2	Injustice under Law?	22
3	Understanding Lesbian and Gay Rights	64
4	Justifications: Their Nature and Operation	107
5	Justifications for Prohibition or Restriction	148
6	Justifications for Legal Protection: Immutability, Respect for Privacy, and Liberationism	196
7	Justifications for Legal Protection: Equality and Beyond	235
8	The Limits of Law and Law Reform	272
	Bibliography	294
	Table of Cases	304
	Index	307

Preface

In a society which claims to respect individual liberties, the moral legitimacy of any law will depend upon whether a sound, principled justification can be found for it. A law which lacks such a justification is likely to be open to easy political attack, thereby undermining its effectiveness. As a consequence, those who advocate the introduction of new laws which seem likely (at least initially) to be morally controversial, need to make sure that they are advancing a coherent justification for the reforms they desire.

This book seeks to find a coherent justification for 'lesbian and gay rights'-based law reform measures relating, for example, to an equal age of consent for homosexual and heterosexual intercourse in the UK and the prohibition of discrimination because of a person's sexual orientation. Without adequate justification, such measures are bound to appear illegitimate and are unlikely politically to succeed. In the USA, for example, hard-won reforms have persistently been attacked by 'New Christian Right' groups as unfair 'special rights' for lesbians and gays – a claim which can only be rebutted by offering an adequate justification for the measures concerned.

I will suggest that an adequate moral case for law reform cannot be made using arguments based on respect for privacy, sexual liberation, or the idea that a person's sexual orientation is predetermined. The currently popular claim that law reform measures are justifiable in the interests of equality also contains many weaknesses. In consequence, I will argue that when properly considered, 'equality' is best seen as a label for the social result towards which law reform measures are supposed to work. The true justification for such measures is, however, one based on ideas of autonomy and empowerment. Social and legal hostility towards members of sexual minority groups will be difficult to overcome even with such a justification: without it, the task is likely to prove still harder.

An earlier version of chapter 3 was presented at the 1995 'Legal Queeries' conference at Lancaster University; earlier versions of chapters

4 to 7 have been presented as seminar papers at Essex University, Nottingham University and University College London; and an earlier version of chapter 8 was presented as a paper at the 1994 W.G. Hart Legal Workshop, and later published under the title 'Human Rights, Sexual Orientation and the Social and Legal Effects of Law and Law Reform' in *Understanding Human Rights* (London: Mansell, 1996), edited by Conor Gearty and Adam Tomkins. I am grateful to the participants in all these seminars and conferences for their comments and, in the case of chapter 8, to the Institute of Advanced Legal Studies and to Mansell for permission to reproduce the material in amended form.

Most of the research and writing for this book was carried out while I was a lecturer in the Law Faculty at University College London, from 1994 to 1996. I should like to express my thanks to the Faculty for providing a challenging environment in which to work, and to Ann Tucker and Helen Ghosh for secretarial assistance. At Cassell, Steve Cook, Roz Hopkins and Charlotte Ridings skilfully coaxed the work along. Finally, I am deeply indebted to the many friends and colleagues who were kind enough to offer opinions on drafts, to pass me information which I would not otherwise have seen, and to cheer me up when progress seemed slow. I would particularly like to thank Peter Bartlett, Richard Gardiner, Andrew Le Sueur, Helen Reece, Carl Stychin, Bill Swadling, Beth Thornburg, John Walters and, most of all, Nick Turner.

Nicholas Bamforth
February 1997

1

Themes

Some people are morally *offended by the suggestion that they should treat someone who is not kin as if he were a brother, or a nigger as if he were white, or a queer as if he were normal, or an infidel as if she were a believer. They are offended by the suggestion that they treat people whom they do not think of as human as if they were human.*

— Richard Rorty[1]

We have been the silent minority, the silenced minority – invisible women, invisible men. Early on, the alleged enormity of our 'sin' justified the denial of our existence, even our physical destruction. Our 'crime' was not merely against society . . . but 'against nature'. . . . Long did we remain literally and metaphorically unspeakable. . . . That time is over. . . . Gay people are coming out – and moving on – to organized action against an oppressive society.

— Jonathan N. Katz[2]

Introduction

During the last forty years, demands for law reform have assumed a central role in political campaigns organized by and on behalf of lesbians, bisexuals and gay men in Britain, Canada and the United States.[3] It is unsurprising that this has been so. The law – especially the criminal law – is one of the major devices of social control used in all three societies to regulate or condemn those who engage, or desire to engage, in sexual acts with people of the same sex.[4] The removal of long-standing criminal laws which prohibit or which try to restrict such sexual acts – or which otherwise treat lesbians, gays or bisexuals less favourably than heterosexuals – has therefore been an important objective for would-be reformers. At the same time, the law has come to be seen as a means of *protecting* lesbians, bisexuals and gays against hostile social treatment in day-to-day life – treatment which, it is sometimes argued, is further encouraged when the law itself appears openly hostile.[5]

There is considerable – and stark – evidence to illustrate the hostility often experienced by lesbians, bisexuals and gays in everyday life.[6] Three recent surveys are particularly instructive. First, out of 3166 lesbians, bisexuals and gays who provided information for a nationwide survey carried out in Britain in 1995, 35 per cent claimed to have fallen victim to violent attack because of their sexual orientation at least once during the previous five years; 16.5 per cent said they had been hit, punched or kicked; and 4.5 per cent said they had been attacked with a weapon. In the same survey, 52 per cent of lesbian and gay teenagers claimed to have been the victim of a violent attack.[7] Second, in an earlier British survey in which 1975 lesbians, bisexuals and gays participated, 16 per cent of respondents claimed to have suffered at least one definite experience of discrimination at work due to their sexual orientation, and a further 21 per cent suspected that they had been discriminated against; 8 per cent claimed to have been dismissed from a job because of their sexual orientation; and 48 per cent said they had been harassed at work, suffering treatment ranging from verbal abuse to violence and even death threats.[8] Finally, data from the USA suggest that between 16 per cent and 41 per cent of lesbians and gays are verbally harassed by their families; that between 4 per cent and 8 per cent are physically harassed, with 45 per cent of gay males and 20 per cent of lesbians experiencing physical or verbal harassment by the time they leave school; and that between 72 per cent and 82 per cent of victims of such attacks do not report them to the police because of perceptions that the police are homophobic.[9]

It might, of course, be suggested that these surveys tell us only that a sizeable percentage of respondents *believe* themselves to have been unfairly treated because they are lesbian, bisexual or gay – and that further, objective evidence is needed in order to verify their claims.[10] Two points can be made by way of reply to this objection. The first is that the UK employment survey in fact deliberately attempted to distinguish between respondents who merely suspected that they had been discriminated against because of their sexual orientation, and those who knew for sure.[11]

The second point, applicable to all three surveys, is that cast-iron, direct evidence of discrimination is always difficult to come by even where the type of discrimination is already prohibited by law.[12] This being so, the remarkable feature of these large-scale surveys is the consistently high percentage figures for those who believed or knew themselves to have been unfairly treated due to their sexual orientation.

Apart from failing to offer effective protection against the types of social hostility highlighted by these surveys, the law is itself actively hostile towards lesbians, bisexuals and gays in a number of contexts. As we will see in chapter 2, for example, sexual intercourse between persons of the same sex is still illegal in almost half the states of the USA, and day-to-day public expressions of affection of the types which are routine for heterosexual couples are prohibited between same-sex couples in the UK. Campaigning groups on both sides of the Atlantic have therefore pressed, with varying degrees of success, for the repeal of hostile laws and for the creation of new laws offering protection against social hostility.[13] It may seem puzzling that the law has been identified as a potential protection for lesbians, bisexuals and gays *as well as* an oppressive force which requires amendment. In fact, this is less a paradox than an example of the pervasive social power and prestige of law in western societies, which perhaps explains why political debates about whether to reform or maintain existing laws have generated the controversy they have among opponents as well as supporters of the lesbian and gay cause.[14] For, unless law was seen by both sides as a powerful and significant social force, it would seem unnecessary for either side to disagree with the vehemence they have characteristically employed about whether the law should penalize or protect lesbians, bisexuals and gays.

This was powerfully illustrated during the House of Commons debate in February 1994 on whether the UK's age of consent for male homosexual sex should be lowered and/or equalized with the age at which heterosexual sex is permissible. A strong belief in the social significance of law clearly underpinned arguments put forward by Members of Parliament on all sides of this debate. According to Chris Smith – at the time, Britain's only openly gay MP, and a supporter of an equal age of consent, set at 16, for homosexual and heterosexual sex –

> keeping the law in a discriminatory state *automatically means that* young gay men will be set apart from society. If we remove that

discrimination from the statute book, *it may go some way towards giving young gay men the self-respect and self-dignity to which they are entitled and should have.*[15]

And, as part of her argument for an equal age of consent, Edwina Currie MP asserted that

> The law is not only prejudicial and discriminatory; it is painfully effective . . . it is widely, if erratically, employed. Between 1988 and 1991 there were more than 2000 arrests for offences involving consensual sex with men under 21 years of age. Even in 1992 . . . men were still being committed to prison for consensual acts with other men. The fear of being arrested and questioned, and perhaps cautioned or charged, is real and ever present.[16]

Indeed, what was seen as the strong discriminatory effect of existing law was stressed repeatedly by reform-minded MPs.[17]

Defenders of an unequal age of consent – some of whom wanted the age at which gay sex was to be allowed to be left at 21 (as it was at the time of the debate), others of whom wanted it to be reduced to 18 (the age for which the House eventually voted) – tended to argue that it was the job of the criminal law to protect young men alleged to be confused about their sexual orientation.[18] There was, of course, a clear anti-gay assumption behind this argument, in that unless gay sex was considered to be somehow inferior to the heterosexual version, there would presumably be no need to 'protect' those who were allegedly tempted to try it. Leaving this assumption on one side, however, the interesting feature of the argument in favour of an unequal age is again its simple faith in the power of the criminal law – this time to 'protect' rather than to stigmatize. The Reverend Ian Paisley MP, one of the most strident opponents of change, almost seemed convinced of the criminal law's ability to work miracles on young men:

> We cannot say that 16 is the time [when males should be permitted to have sex with each other]. We cannot say that 14 is the time. We should be trying to save young men and young boys from going down the homosexual road. We should be bringing them to the joys of true marriage and raising a family.[19]

Concepts and questions

This book will examine some justifications of principle for reforming the law as it affects lesbians, bisexuals and gays, together with some of the limitations of law reform. Such justifications can also be used to support existing laws which are sympathetic towards lesbians and gays – by providing remedies against discrimination at work, for example. Examining these justifications is an important task since, under non-authoritarian systems of government – and it will be assumed, for present purposes, that such systems exist in the UK, the USA and Canada – decisions to introduce new law or alter existing law should depend upon how two central questions are answered. The first question, involving as it does the somewhat nebulous concepts of morality and justice, will require rather greater discussion than the second.

The first question is whether the new or revised law is justifiable *in principle*. Law is perhaps the strongest coercive tool which the state possesses: as an instrument of social regulation, it has the potential to impact upon people's lives in a wide-ranging fashion and to a serious extent (it is important to stress the word 'potential' here, for the degree to which law affects people's lives *in practice* is an uncertain issue, to be discussed in chapter 8).[20] Creating a new law may well restrict people's freedom (or a particular and valuable type of freedom) or be felt to impinge upon other types of important interest, such as those relating to fair and/or equal treatment.[21] To be regarded as morally legitimate, an individual law must therefore have the support of a sound normative justification.[22] Existing laws must be shown to have the support of such justifications in just the same way as proposals to alter the law, given that the law's potential for coercion is as great in both cases.[23]

A sound normative justification will show that the law in question is permissible according to a vision of how law ought to be used under a legitimate system of government. Such a vision will explain the interests which the law may properly protect and override, and the social ends which it may rightly be used to serve. Any such vision therefore entails both a theory of justice – that is, a theory about the proper distribution of entitlements between individuals or groups in society – and a theory of political morality.[24] Something may be classified as an issue of political morality, according to Neil MacCormick, if it raises a question about the right exercise of the public powers vested in agencies of state – legislators, governments, judges, police, and prosecutors. Whoever attempts to give a general answer to the question about the right exercise of such powers is necessarily committed to stating practical principles for the guidance of those who exercise them. And practical principles of right conduct are moral principles.[25]

It is these 'practical principles of right conduct' which will amount to a theory of political morality.

In fact, a theory of justice almost always implies a theory of political morality, given that its implementation will usually depend upon the use of state power. For whenever we argue that the law should support a particular distribution of entitlements among members of a society (whether these be property rights, employment rights or anything else), we are assuming both that the distribution of entitlements is legitimate – an assumption we defend by invoking a theory of justice – and that it is proper for the state to enforce that distribution through law – a judgement which must be defended using a theory of political morality. Even if we argue that a distribution of entitlements is legitimate but that state agencies and/or laws should have no role in enforcing it, we are still implying a theory of political morality – it is just that our theory now suggests that the proper role for the state is to remain on the sidelines. A theory of political morality may also presuppose a theory of justice, however. For, by formulating guidelines concerning how state power should be used, we are assuming that its use will affect people – the guidelines would otherwise be superfluous. So, by saying that the state must keep within a set of guidelines in exercising public power, we are adopting – if only by implication – a view about the entitlements of individuals or groups. If, for example, our 'practical principles of right conduct' dictate that the state must not regulate a particular area of life, it usually follows that individuals should be free to behave in that area as they like: that they have, in other words, some type of entitlement.

Given the close connections which exist between theories of justice and theories of political morality in the law reform context, it will therefore be most straightforward, when dealing with our first central question, simply to discuss each law reform justification in terms of its background vision of how law ought to be used in a legitimate system of government – avoiding attempts to subdivide each vision into components of justice and political morality. Our first central question is therefore concerned with what Raymond Plant describes as 'justifying the right way or ways and identifying the wrong ways in which political power [here, law] is to be exercised *and* the nature of the claims which citizens can make on the state and on each other'.[26]

In seeking a convincing justification for law reform (or for existing laws), we will be dealing with arguments which are usually seen as coming within the realms of political philosophy and jurisprudence – that is, the philosophy of law.[27] Legal and political philosophy can be viewed as indivisible in so far as they both deal with justifications for the use of state power through law,[28] especially given the overwhelmingly political role of law (at least in the modern state) as one of the primary instruments – perhaps *the* primary instrument – for implementing government policy. In consequence, the law reform justifications we will discuss can properly be described as 'philosophical justifications'. People who doubt that law exercises a political role need only reflect, for enlightenment, on the public order provisions of the Criminal Justice and Public Order Act 1994,[29] or on the fact that the UK government's policies on the overtly political topic of taxation are always contained in the annual Finance Act. The boundary between moral and legal/political philosophy is also rather blurred, at least in so far as our first question is concerned. For, as Robert Nozick suggests:

> moral philosophy sets the background for, and boundaries of, political philosophy. What persons may and may not do to one another limits what they may do through the apparatus of a state, or do to establish such an apparatus. The moral prohibitions it is legitimate to enforce are the source of whatever legitimacy the state's fundamental coercive power has.[30]

In talking of 'philosophical justifications', it would therefore be somewhat superfluous (at least for present purposes) to engage in extensive debate about the boundaries between moral, political and legal philosophy.

The concepts of morality and justice must now be defined more precisely. The preceding discussion has implied that morality is concerned with the distinction between right and wrong. In fact, the word 'morality' can be used in at least two senses. According to Ronald Dworkin, it may first be used simply to describe 'the attitudes [which a] group displays about the propriety of human conduct, qualities or goals' – that is, to describe the standards which are generally accepted within that group about what is right and what is wrong.[31] We are thus employing the descriptive sense of morality when talking of 'the morals of young people', or of any other group. The second sense of 'morality' is evaluative: if I say that I believe particular behaviour to be immoral, then I am making a *judgement* about its propriety according to my own standards of right and wrong. And, since people have sharply differing views about what is right and what is wrong, their moral evaluations of particular conduct will vary considerably. It is this second sense of morality – as a set of standards by which the rightness or wrongness of conduct can be judged – which is used here. This notion of morality can be employed in a number of contexts: we talk of political morality (as seen above) when evaluating exercises of state power, and of sexual morality when considering sexual conduct.[32]

Theories of justice are best seen as a specialist branch of the evaluative sense of morality. It was suggested above that each theory of justice is concerned with the proper distribution of entitlements between individuals or groups in society: the underlying concern of each theory is therefore with questions of right and wrong, i.e. with moral questions (for how else could any distribution of entitlements be described as proper or improper?), but their special concern is with the rightful and wrongful distributions of entitlements in society at large.[33] In consequence, something can count as a moral issue without also being an issue of justice: I may, for example, believe that it is immoral to hunt animals, but unless I also believe that animals either have or should have certain entitlements which society should protect, I cannot view hunting as raising an issue of justice. As we have already seen, however, theories of justice and theories of political morality are very closely interconnected in the law reform context.

Why, then, do the words morals *and* justice appear in the title of this book? The reason becomes apparent if we consider a common misconception about arguments concerning the legal position of lesbians and gays. It is sometimes said that such arguments tend to involve a clash between reformist theories of justice and conservative views about morality. Thus, law reformers will talk of 'achieving justice' for lesbians and gays or (less regularly nowadays) of not using the law to enforce morality, while conservatives may talk of the need for the law to defend 'traditional moral values'. If it is right to say that justice is a specialist branch of morality, however, then it cannot be accurate to categorize arguments about law reform in this way. For any theory of justice favoured by law reformers – which will presumably generate some sort of entitlement to sexual freedom – will clearly imply a broader theory of political morality, while conservative support for the legal enforcement of sexual morality must presuppose a theory of justice which restricts entitlements to sexual freedom (or, as some would have it, which maximizes *family* entitlements). Theories of *political* morality and justice therefore underpin the arguments on both sides of the debate, making it misleading to describe the debate as one between justice and morality *per se*. Any argument against the legal enforcement of sexual morality will still presuppose, ultimately, a theory of political morality. And, while the conservative's position may well be fuelled by views about sexual morality, it takes a further analytical step – involving the adoption of a theory of justice, implying a theory of *political* morality – before it can be claimed that the law can legitimately prohibit sexual acts between people of the same sex. A better description of law reform arguments is therefore to say that they involve clashes between different *theories* of justice and political morality.

It is important, however, to be aware of the motivations of the participants in law reform debates (as opposed to how the arguments in those debates should be categorized), for these can affect our interpretation of the arguments which are put forward. Conservative arguments against law reform are often, for example, fuelled by a view of *sexual* morality which holds that lesbian and gay sexual acts are immoral. And, as Robert Nozick suggested (see above), someone's moral view about what people can properly do with each other *is* likely strongly to influence their view of the proper role of the state. This is not always the case, of course: one mark of a committed pluralist is their belief that others should be entitled to engage in activities of which they personally morally disapprove. It is, nevertheless, foolish to lose sight of the fact that for many people, the more strongly they believe something to be immoral, the more tempting it is to argue that the state must do something to stop it. Perhaps the most extreme example of this type of thinking is the religious fundamentalist's desire to establish a theocratic state in which their own absolute moral order is imposed on society. While theories of justice and political morality are involved on both sides of law reform debates concerning lesbians and gays, therefore, it is often the case that the conservative position in any debate is fuelled by a view of sexual morality: hence the need to talk of morals *and* justice.

To summarize the discussion so far: our first question asks whether there are sound justifications for laws or law reform measures designed to improve the social or legal entitlements of lesbians and gays. The question of justification must also be applied to existing laws which appear to treat lesbians and gays in a hostile fashion, in order to ask whether such laws are themselves legitimate. Any justification will be based on a vision of how law should be used in a legitimate system of government – a vision which involves a theory of justice and a theory of political morality, both of which are interconnected. In addition, arguments may well (but do not have to) be influenced by views about personal or sexual morality. In evaluating the strength of each justification – the task which our first question is to perform – competing views about sexual morality, political morality and justice will therefore be brought into play.

The second question is whether the proposed law reform measures are likely to produce the desired results. Deliberate changes in the law are usually made with some social goal in mind, and there would be little point in campaigning for or creating new laws if they are unlikely to achieve their goal. We have already seen that law reform measures need to be justified given their potential for coercion; we are now asking whether that coercion actually works. This second question is clearly pragmatic in nature: it asks whether law reform is the best tactic for reaching a particular goal, usually in terms of the day-to-day treatment of those whom the law is intended to benefit.[34] The question also has implications of principle, however, for those who believe that, given law's coercive power, new laws should be created only where it is clear that they will work.[35] In terms of a theory of justice, the second question asks whether law reform measures are likely to guarantee that lesbians and gays will *in practice* be treated in ways which are just (according to the theory of justice concerned), rather than receiving formal but empty promises of rightful treatment.

We can now be more specific about how these two questions will be applied to the topic of law reform as it affects lesbians, bisexuals and gays. In examining the first question, we will ask whether there are principled justifications for laws which can penalize and therefore coerce lesbians and gays. If – as will be argued – there are not, then such laws are illegitimate and should be removed. We will also ask whether there are principled justifications for creating new laws intended to protect (or better protect) lesbians and gays against social hostility, including violence and employment discrimination. Such laws are likely, to some extent, to penalize and therefore coerce people who choose to discriminate, so a principled justification is needed before they can be seen as legitimate. This justification must explain why it is right in principle to use law to prohibit discrimination directed at lesbians and gays on account of their sexual orientation.

In examining the second, pragmatic question, we will ask whether (and if so, how far) law reform measures are likely to help in reducing or eliminating social hostility and discrimination directed against lesbians and gays — whether, in other words, the campaigners' faith in the importance of law is well founded. There has been concern in recent years about the apparent ineffectiveness of sex and race discrimination law in combating patterns of social and economic discrimination affecting women and ethnic minorities.[36] If it cannot be shown that existing, punitive laws clearly harm lesbians and gays in everyday life (for example, by reinforcing social prejudices), or if it cannot be shown that protective laws will encourage the growth of social tolerance towards lesbians and gays, then it may be the case that political campaigners would be better employed in outreach work rather than in campaigns for law reform.[37] If law reform is to be seen as a legitimate and relevant activity, our two questions must therefore receive affirmative answers based on coherent reasoning.

In subsequent chapters, it will be suggested that the law reform proposals which campaigners have advanced in recent years have rested on a series of divergent justifications: at different stages since the late 1950s, lesbians and gays (or, to be more precise, those people to whom these terms are now applied) have been told that they are fighting for privacy, for liberation and, most recently, for equality. Insufficient attention seems, however, to have been paid to the meanings of these concepts, to how they differ from each other, or to what concrete results each might yield in terms of justifiable and effective law reform measures. It is perhaps understandable that these issues have been overlooked: pressure groups are not usually equipped, after all, to address difficult philosophical and legal arguments. But the result, on both sides of the Atlantic, has been that campaigners have swapped their law reform justifications around with alarming regularity, giving insufficient thought to the relationship between each justification and the case for law reform. In fact, privacy, liberationism and equality all contain serious flaws when used as law reform justifications.[38] Furthermore, little attention has so far been paid to the question whether – and if so, why – it is *worthwhile* campaigning for anti-discrimination laws to protect lesbians and gays, given the many doubts which now exist about the effectiveness of laws prohibiting sexual and racial discrimination.[39]

The main tasks of this book will therefore be: first, after highlighting in greater detail the flaws which are present in justifications for laws which are hostile to lesbians and gays and in existing law reform justifications, to suggest a more robust, empowerment-based justification for lesbian and gay law reform; and second, to provide a realistic account of the limited social effects which are likely to result from legal change. Along the way, we will need to address a variety of historical, legal, philosophical and sociological issues. How, for example, does law affect lesbians and gays? What types of social discrimination and prejudice can and should law be used to rectify? When will the use of law be legitimate?[40] In seeking to answer these questions, the main focus of the book will be on criminal law and anti-discrimination law.[41]

Before going further, three preliminary points must be made. The first concerns terminology: throughout the book, the word 'law' will, unless otherwise indicated, be taken to include both statutes and case law, and 'law reform' will be taken to mean intentional alterations to existing law where these are designed to enhance the social or legal positions of lesbians and/or gays. This definition of 'law reform' covers the passing of new legislation as well as judicial reinterpretation of previous case law in what are known as test cases or 'hard cases'.[42] Furthermore, while the label 'lesbian and gay' is generally used throughout the book, this is not done in order to ignore bisexuals. 'Lesbian and gay' is used simply because it is commonly employed as a shorthand label in campaigning work and in law reform debates. No manageable set of words could, in any event, act as an entirely reliable label in this context. On a related note, hopefully it should be clear why the words 'morals' and 'justice' appear in the title of this book, given their significance for the argument which follows. The word 'sexuality' is used in the title – instead of the narrower phrase 'sexual orientation' – because some of the law reform justifications we shall consider (including the empowerment-based justification which will ultimately be supported in chapter 7) go beyond the topic of lesbian and gay sexual orientation, having implications for the permissibility of legal regulation of consenting sexual behaviour more generally.

It is important, second, to repeat that the book is an exploration of principled, philosophical justifications for, and practical limitations inherent in, the use of law. This means that the book is not intended as a comprehensive guide to the existing law, and should not be read as though it were.[43] Case law and statutes are instead used, where appropriate, to illustrate the main themes. It should be added that the reason for considering the UK, the USA and Canada is simply because campaigning groups have used analogous law reform arguments in all three countries; no deeper presumptions are made about possible affinities or differences between the three countries. Another, less obvious consequence of our focus is that it is vital to maintain the distinction between the *philosophical* arguments for law reform – with which we are concerned – and *precedent-based* constitutional or case law arguments used in test cases. The philosophical arguments, as suggested above, turn on an ultimately moral vision of how state power (in the form of law) *ought* to be employed, and are used to demonstrate that proposals to change statute law or case law are desirable (or undesirable) according to the theory of justice on which the relevant argument rests. Precedent-based arguments, by contrast, tell us whether the proposal fits in with the letter or spirit of existing case law or, where it exists, with an entrenched constitution or human rights code. Precedent-based arguments play a vital role in court, helping to establish how far, if at all, the court is *legally* empowered to reinterpret or develop existing law[44] – but for the purposes of this book, such arguments are useful only in so far as they highlight shortcomings in analogous philosophical arguments (a good example of this can be found in the area of privacy-based philosophical justifications, as we will see in chapter 6). Unless philosophical and precedent-based arguments are kept clearly separate, debate will become confused: we are concerned here with what states *should* be doing, as a matter of justice (however that is defined); constitutional or precedent-based arguments are concerned with what states *can* do as a matter of law.[45]

The third point is that just as political campaigners need to be concerned with broader issues of legal and political philosophy in order to advance coherent justifications for law reform, reconsideration of important philosophical issues can also be sparked off by political debate about the law's treatment of lesbians and gays. A classic example was the philosophical debate, in 1960s Britain, about law and the enforcement of morality, which was triggered by the Wolfenden Committee's proposal that male homosexual acts be at least partly decriminalized.[46] This suggests that the resolution of issues in legal and political philosophy is likely to be assisted by placing them in a practical context, just as much as our understanding of practical law reform arguments will be assisted by consideration of background philosophical issues.

A recent example of this interaction of theory and practice can be seen in the controversy surrounding the proposed Amendment 2 to the constitution of the US state of Colorado. Amendment 2 – passed in a state-wide referendum in 1992 after a vigorous lobbying campaign by the 'Christian' right – prohibited the state government and its agencies from enacting, adopting or enforcing

> any statute, regulation, ordinance or policy whereby homosexual, lesbian or bisexual orientation, conduct, practices or relationships shall constitute or otherwise be the basis of or entitle any person or class of persons to have or claim any minority status, quota preferences, protected status or claim of discrimination.

In short, Amendment 2 was seeking to prohibit the state government from ever giving any type of positive anti-discrimination protection to lesbians, bisexuals or gays. The constitutionality of the Amendment was later successfully challenged in the Colorado Supreme Court – where philosophers gave expert testimony in support of and against it – and in the US Supreme Court.[47] In the Colorado Supreme Court, legal philosopher John Finnis argued, in favour of the Amendment, that:

> A political community that judges that the stability and educative generosity of family life is of fundamental importance to the community's present and future can rightly judge that it has a compelling interest in denying that homosexual conduct – a 'gay lifestyle' – is a valid, humanly acceptable choice and form of life, *and in doing whatever it properly can . . . to discourage such conduct*.[48]

Finnis's views will be considered in detail in chapter 5. For the moment, his argument is significant because it highlights how a person's philosophical view of what it is appropriate for the law to do generally

– promoting 'the stability and educative generosity of family life', for Finnis – is likely to affect their view of how the law should, more specifically, treat lesbians and gays.

Structure

The two central questions of this book – concerning the philosophical justifications for law reform and the likely effectiveness or otherwise of such reform in combating social hostility and prejudice – appear throughout the following chapters. Earlier in this chapter, we considered some evidence relating to social hostility and discrimination directed against lesbians and gays. In chapter 2, we will examine the present state of the law in the UK, the USA and Canada. We will look at existing laws which might be said to penalize lesbians and gays, and at some statistically less common examples of laws designed to provide protection against social hostility. This will provide a necessary background to the discussion in later chapters.

We will next turn to discussion of law reform proper. In chapter 3, we will analyse the idea of 'lesbian and gay rights', the rallying cry which is habitually employed by law reform campaigners. Examination of what is meant by 'rights' in this context, as well as whom such 'rights' are intended to protect, will show that 'lesbian and gay rights' is best seen as a campaigning slogan of temporary value only, albeit one through which our two central questions can be considered. This offers an important but often forgotten lesson: that from the standpoint of justice for lesbians and gays, the crucial issue when formulating law reform demands is not sloganizing – whether about 'lesbian and gay rights' or anything else – but offering a suitable justification for the sought-after reform. Chapter 3 will also involve an analysis of the competing essentialist and constructionist theories of sexuality, as a result of which, a moderate constructionist theory will be proposed. As we will see in chapters 6 and 7, theories of sexuality can have important consequences in terms of whether particular law reform justifications can be regarded as plausible.

Chapters 4 to 7 consider in detail the issues raised by the various law reform justifications. In chapter 4, we will examine some general issues affecting the nature, operation and assessment of justifications. Perhaps the most significant of these issues is the role of the state in enforcing theories of morality and justice through the law. This is important for two reasons. First, because the creation of laws designed to protect lesbians and gays from social hostility cannot – regardless of the justification advanced to support them – be regarded as legitimate unless it can first be shown that the state can legitimately involve itself, through the law, in issues of justice. Second, because according to some theories of justice, the state is entitled to use law to enforce the personal morality of the majority of members of a community, regardless of the effects on sexual minorities such as lesbians and gays. If correct, this argument would clearly justify the prohibition of consenting sexual relations between people of the same sex. It will therefore be argued, in chapter 4, that although the state has a role, through law, in enforcing theories of justice (which generally involve issues of morality), this does not mean that the state may legitimately enforce a prohibitive or excessively restrictive morality. At the end of chapter 4, the criteria to be used in assessing the plausibility of the various law reform justifications (and of justifications for hostile legal regulation of lesbians and gays) will be outlined.

In chapter 5, we will consider the arguments advanced by conservative theorists such as Finnis to the effect that the state may not legitimately pass laws protecting lesbians and gays against social hostility, and must indeed discourage lesbian and gay sexuality. Building on the argument in chapter 4, it will be suggested that these theories involve unacceptable accounts of the state's role in social life, and of the types of morality which the law must enforce. It is important to consider these hostile, conservative justifications since one of the tasks of any sympathetic justification is to overcome them. We will then turn, in chapters 6 and 7, to justifications for legal rights to protect lesbians and gays. Deficiencies in the immutability, privacy, liberationist and equality justifications will be discussed, and a new, empowerment-based justification will be advanced (at the end of chapter 7) for reforming hostile criminal laws and for enacting anti-discrimination laws designed to protect lesbians and gays. This justification will be based on the moral value of consenting sexual activity as a fundamental aspect of autonomy, and on the dehumanizing nature of discriminatory social behaviour.

Finally, in chapter 8, we will consider how effective law reform is likely to be in diluting or overcoming social hostility directed at lesbians, bisexuals and gays. It will be suggested that while law is useful, it is not necessarily as valuable as some of our legislators or law reform campaigners have assumed, or valuable in the ways in which they have assumed it to be. While law reform may be justifiable and may sometimes be useful, it would therefore be foolish to assume that it is capable of working miracles.

Conclusion

Throughout this book, we will be concerned with the general arguments of principle which may be advanced in favour of more sympathetic legal treatment for lesbians and gays. While we will draw on many of the practical arguments which have been used by law reform campaigners, we will not be concerned with the detailed history, comparative merits or successes of particular law reform campaigns. Neither will any very detailed arguments be advanced for legal provisions to be drafted or structured in any particular way (we are not concerned with questions such as whether discrimination against lesbians and gays should be prohibited by legislation dealing specifically with sexual orientation, or whether it should be brought within the scope of existing sex discrimination law, for example).

Given law's coercive power, it is important to develop sound, lasting justifications for the creation of legal entitlements of any sort. To do so, we need to think carefully about what we consider the appropriate uses of law to be, how we understand notions of rights, and how – in this particular context – we perceive sexuality and particular sexual orientations. The message of this book is that existing ways of thinking about many of these topics are inadequate – as a consequence of which the new, empowerment-based justification is necessary. Even the strongest justification, however, has its limits. For law reform can only take us a certain distance in changing hostile social attitudes and behaviour. A much broader strategy of education and dialogue is necessary in order to accomplish genuine social change.

Notes

1. Richard Rorty, 'Human rights, rationality, and sentimentality', in Stephen Shute and Susan Hurley (eds), *On Human Rights* (New York: Basic Books, 1993), p. 125.
2. Jonathan N. Katz, *Gay American History: Lesbians and Gay Men in the U.S.A.* (New York: Meridian, rev. edn, 1992), p. 1.
3. There are several interesting accounts of the campaigning history. For the UK, see Stephen Jeffery-Poulter, *Peers, Queers and Commons – the Struggle for Gay Law Reform from 1950 to the Present* (London: Routledge, 1991); Jeffrey Weeks, *Coming Out – Homosexual Politics in Britain from the Nineteenth*

Century to the Present (London: Quartet, rev. edn, 1990); Antony Grey, *Quest for Justice – Towards Homosexual Emancipation* (London: Sinclair-Stevenson, 1992). For Canada, see Gary Kinsman, *The Regulation of Desire – Sexuality in Canada* (Montreal: Black Rose Books, 1987). For the USA, see Katz, *Gay American History*; John D'Emilio, *Making Trouble – Essays on Gay History, Politics and the University* (New York: Routledge, 1992), Part I. More generally, see the later sections of M. Duberman, M. Vicinus and G. Chauncey (eds), *Hidden from History: Reclaiming the Gay and Lesbian Past* (London: Penguin, 1991).

4. Precisely *how* law regulates is a question which will be considered in chapter 8.

5. It would be wrong to suggest that law reform campaigners always begin with demands for reform of the criminal law, before progressing to calls for the law to be used in a positive, protective fashion – in fact, the history of lesbian and gay campaigning suggests that the two sets of demands have often developed contemporaneously; see, generally, Jeffery-Poulter, *Peers, Queers and Commons*; a 'transition from criminal to human rights law reform' is, however, envisaged by Didi Herman, *Rights of Passage: Struggles for Lesbian and Gay Legal Equality* (Toronto: University of Toronto Press, 1994), pp. 29–31. Furthermore, the laws of the US state of Minnesota prohibit both discrimination on the ground of a person's sexual orientation and oral and anal sex – see further Robert Wintemute, *Sexual Orientation and Human Rights: The United States Constitution, the European Convention, and the Canadian Charter* (Oxford: Clarendon Press, 1995), pp. 267–9. The question how societies came to be concerned (one might say obsessively concerned) with the regulation of sexual behaviour lies somewhat outside the scope of this book; for an interesting argument, see Michel Foucault, *The History of Sexuality – Volume 1: An Introduction* (London: Penguin, 1981, English translation).

6. Plenty of examples can be found in the material in n. 1 above. The weekly issues of the *Pink Paper* (the UK's leading lesbian and gay newspaper) produced between April 1992 and January 1993 contain approximately thirty stories (i.e. more than one per week) detailing incidents of anti-lesbian or gay violence, employment discrimination or other unfavourable treatment. For more recent examples, see the *Pink Paper*, 7 July 1995, p. 16; *Gay Gazette*, 30 August 1995, p. 3. For useful US material, see Gregory Herek and Kevin Berrill (eds), *Hate Crimes: Confronting Violence Against Lesbians and Gay Men* (Newbury Park: Sage, 1992).

7. Survey carried out by the Stonewall Group, reported in the *Independent*, 9 November 1995, p. 5 ('One in three gays is victim of violence'); *Pink Paper*, 17 November 1995, p. 1 ('Violence study shows one in three attacked').

8. Anya Palmer, *Less Equal than Others: a survey of lesbians and gay men at work* (London: Stonewall, 1993). For two earlier surveys, based on much smaller data samples, see Phil Greasley, *Gay Men at Work: A report on discrimination against gay men in employment in London* (London: Lesbian and Gay Employment Rights, 1986); Nina Taylor (ed.), *All in A Day's Work: A report on anti-lesbian discrimination in employment and unemployment in London* (London: Lesbian Employment Rights, 1986).

9. *Gay and Lesbian Stats* figures, cited by Dale Peck in David Deitcher (ed.), *Over the Rainbow: Lesbian and Gay Politics in America Since Stonewall* (London: Boxtree/Channel Four, 1995), p. 200. Further data from the USA are discussed in chapter 3.

10. The research method used in Palmer's UK employment survey *Less Equal than Others* appears to have

been designed with the clear intention of avoiding obvious types of sample error – see pp. 3–4 of the survey.
11. Palmer, *Less Equal than Others*, p. 6.
12. For discussion of problems facing applicants in UK sex and race discrimination cases, see Laurence Lustgarten, 'Problems of proof in employment discrimination cases' (1977) 6 *Industrial Law Journal* 212; *West Midlands Passenger Transport Executive* v. *Singh* [1988] IRLR 186; *Carrington* v. *Helix* [1990] IRLR 6.
13. There are several examples. In 1995, the Stonewall Group (a UK Parliamentary lobbying organization) launched a Sexual Orientation Discrimination Bill covering employment – see *Pink Paper*, 21 July 1995, esp. pp. 2, 14; this would appear to follow in the footsteps of the Homosexual Equality Bill, presented by the same organization in conjunction with the pressure group Liberty during the run-up to the 1992 general election. Calls for a comprehensive Homosexual Law Reform Bill can be found as early as 1975, however – see Jeffery-Poulter, *Peers, Queers and Commons*, p. 112. For recent UK litigation concerning employment issues, compare: Nicholas Bamforth, 'Sexual orientation and dismissal from employment', (1994) 144 *New Law Journal* 1402; *R* v. *Secretary of State for Defence, ex parte Smith* [1995] 4 All ER 473 (Divisional Court), [1996] 1 All ER 257 (Court of Appeal).
14. For a useful discussion of this topic in the context of law reform debates in Canada, see Herman, *Rights of Passage*, chs 3, 4 and 6. For an analogous discussion of apparently contradictory perceptions of law, see Roger Cotterrell, *Law's Community: Legal Theory in Sociological Perspective* (Oxford: Clarendon Press, 1995), p. 253.
15. H.C. Deb., 21 February 1994, Column 111 (emphasis added). The new age of consent provisions are contained in the Criminal Justice and Public Order Act 1994, ss. 144–5.
16. H.C. Deb., 21 February 1994, Column 76.
17. See, e.g., H.C. Deb., 21 February 1994, Columns 97, 99 (Tony Blair MP), Column 105 (Mike Watson MP).
18. See, e.g., H.C. Deb., 21 February 1994, Columns 93, 97 (Michael Howard MP).
19. H.C. Deb., 21 February 1994, Column 115.
20. See, somewhat more broadly, Judith Jarvis Thomson, *The Realm of Rights* (Cambridge, MA: Harvard University Press, 1990), ch. 3.
21. Opinions will of course differ about which interests are seen as valuable, and about whether the law has violated a valuable interest (or has the potential to do so) in any given case. Among those who see the issue in terms of the need to defend freedom, there is controversy about whether it is general freedom or particular, valuable freedoms which require defence – see Joseph Raz, *The Morality of Freedom* (Oxford: Clarendon Press, 1986), pp. 13 *et seq.*
22. For discussion of the connections between models of democracy and legitimacy, see David Held, *Models of Democracy* (Oxford: Blackwell, 2nd edn, 1996); Anthony Birch, *The Concepts and Theories of Modern Democracy* (London: Routledge, 1993), chs 3, 4. A further development of the notion of legitimacy is attempted by T. R. S. Allan in 'Citizenship and obligation: Civil disobedience and civil dissent' [1996] 55 *Cambridge Law Journal* 89, esp. at 93–8.
23. The question of justification does not, therefore, collapse in this context into what Joseph Raz describes as the 'conservative presumption' – see *The Morality of Freedom*, p. 12.
24. For a slightly different account, see Thomas Nagel, *Equality and Partiality* (New York: Oxford University Press, 1991), pp. 8–9.
25. Neil MacCormick, *Legal Right and Social Democracy: Essays in Legal*

and Political Philosophy (Oxford: Clarendon Press, 1982), p. 18; cf. Raz, *The Morality of Freedom*, pp. 2–3. While Richard Posner seeks to present an economic account of the regulation of sexual behaviour – which he contrasts with overtly 'moral' theories – he nevertheless accepts that economic theories are themselves 'moral' in so far as they are used to guide social policy (including the enactment of laws) – *Sex and Reason* (Cambridge, MA: Harvard University Press, 1992), pp. 3, 181 (see also ch. 8).

26. Raymond Plant, *Modern Political Thought* (Oxford: Basil Blackwell, 1991) p. 2 (emphasis added).

27. For present purposes, the terms 'jurisprudence' (more accurately, 'Jurisprudence') and 'legal philosophy' are treated as synonymous.

28. From some perspectives, though, this approach is controversial – see further Roger Cotterrell, *The Politics of Jurisprudence: A Critical Introduction to Legal Philosophy* (London: Butterworths, 1989), ch. 1.

29. Criminal Justice and Public Order Act 1994, Part V.

30. Robert Nozick, *Anarchy, State, and Utopia* (New York: Basic Books, 1974), p. 6.

31. Ronald Dworkin, *Taking Rights Seriously* (London: Duckworth, 1977), p. 248. For other views, see H. L. A. Hart, *Law, Liberty, and Morality* (Oxford: Clarendon Press, 1963), pp. 17–24; *Essays in Jurisprudence and Philosophy* (Oxford: Clarendon Press, 1983), chs 2, 11, 16.

32. The notion of morality must, however, be fashioned a little more sharply in practice – for as H. L. A. Hart has pointed out, conduct may be described as 'right' or 'wrong' in a technical sense, in that it complies with or breaches the internal rules of a game or activity. Conduct in the game of chess is, for example, 'wrong' if it breaches the rules of chess, but we would not describe such conduct as morally wrong unless it also violated a moral standard of the community. The rules of the game of chess would seem designed to promote an efficient game and to distinguish chess from other games – not to regulate notions of morality. See Hart, *Essays in Jurisprudence and Philosophy*, essay 16, esp. pp. 349–51.

33. For a variety of views on the nature of justice, see e.g. H. L. A. Hart, *The Concept of Law* (Oxford: Clarendon Press, 2nd edn, 1994), ch. 8; Alan Ryan (ed.), *Justice* (Oxford: Oxford University Press, 1993); John Rawls, *A Theory of Justice* (Oxford: Clarendon Press, 1972); Dworkin, *Taking Rights Seriously*, esp. ch. 6.

34. See further chapter 8. The distinction between the two questions may be said to echo John Stuart Mill's distinction between the tyranny of the magistrate and the tyranny of prevailing opinion and feeling – *On Liberty*, ed. Stefan Collini (Cambridge: Cambridge University Press, 1989 edn), p. 8.

35. For an example of such an approach, see Paul Roberts, 'Consent and the criminal law: Philosophical foundations', Appendix C to Law Commission Consultation Paper No. 139, *Consent in the Criminal Law* (London: HMSO, 1995). I would not disagree with Roberts's choice of principles dealt with under his second, 'all things considered' heading. The principles he mentions are indeed important in evaluating the legitimacy of any law reform measure, and would clearly arise when debating any concrete law reform proposals. Given the generality of Roberts's 'all things considered' criteria, however, it does not seem appropriate to devote space to them when evaluating general justifications for law reform measures affecting lesbians and gays.

36. See further chapter 8.

37. It is possible to opt for a middle position by supporting some law reform measures to benefit lesbians and gays, but using a different protective regime (i.e. different types

of law) from that which currently applies to other groups. This position still assumes, however, that law reform is effective to some extent, and is concerned with the *type* of law reform to be implemented rather than with the more basic (and logically antecedent) question whether law reform will be effective *at all*.
38. See further chapters 4, 6 and 7.
39. See further chapter 8.
40. Such issues could, of course, generate several books in themselves, and each is touched on here only to the extent that it is relevant to our two central questions.
41. For a rights-based discussion of family law, see Helen Reece, 'The paramountcy principle: Consensus or construct?' (1996) 49 *Current Legal Problems*, Part 2, 267.
42. The term 'law reform' can, of course, be used in a wider sense in other contexts, where it might include any change in the law, whether deliberate or inadvertent, and which worked to hinder as well as benefit lesbians and gays.
43. See, for UK law, Paul Crane's slightly outdated *Gays and the Law* (London: Pluto Press, 1982); Mark Guthrie and Angus Hamilton, *The Lesbian and Gay Rights Handbook* (London: Cassell, forthcoming); Robert Wintemute, 'Sexual orientation discrimination', ch. 15 in Christopher McCrudden and Gerald Chambers (eds), *Individual Rights and the Law in Britain* (Oxford: Clarendon Press, 1994). For European Community law and the European Convention on Human Rights, see Kees Waaldijk and Andrew Clapham (eds), *Homosexuality: A European Community Issue – Essays on Lesbian and Gay Rights in European Law and Policy* (Dordrecht: Martinus Nijhoff, 1993), discussed in Nicholas Bamforth, 'Sexuality and law in the new Europe' (1995) 58 *Modern Law Review* 109. In international law, see Eric Heinze, *Sexual Orientation: a Human Right* (Dordrecht: Martinus Nijhoff, 1995).
44. For an excellent precedent-based analysis of lesbian and gay law reform issues, see Wintemute, *Sexual Orientation and Human Rights*.
45. Confusion of this nature is evident in Richard Mohr's book *Gays/Justice: A Study of Ethics, Society, and Law* (New York: Columbia University Press, 1988): at pp. 3–4, Mohr suggests that his arguments are philosophical, but the argument in subsequent chapters is clearly rooted in US constitutional law (see especially chs 2 to 4). While an American *philosophical* argument may be of considerable use to the British or Canadian reader, an American *constitutional law* argument is helpful only for information or by way of analogy.
46. *The Report of the Committee on Homosexual Offences and Prostitution* ('the Wolfenden Committee'), Command Paper No. 247 (1957). The political arguments surrounding the Committee's proposals are summarized in chs 1 to 4 of Jeffery-Poulter's *Peers, Queers and Commons*. The two main protagonists in the philosophical debate prompted by the proposals were H. L. A. Hart – see his *Law, Liberty, and Morality* – and Lord Devlin – see his *The Enforcement of Morals* (Oxford: Oxford University Press, 1965).
47. *Romer v. Evans* (1993) 854 P 2d 1270 (Colorado Supreme Court); (1996) 116 S Ct 1620 (US Supreme Court). For argument against the Amendment, see Martha Nussbaum, 'Platonic love and Colorado law: the relevance of ancient Greek norms to modern sexual controversies' (1994) 80 *Virginia Law Review* 1515.
48. John Finnis, 'Law, morality and "sexual orientation"' (1993–4) 69 *Notre Dame Law Review* 1049 at 1070 (emphasis added). This article is based on Finnis's evidence in the Colorado case.

2

Injustice under Law?

Introduction

During the Second World War, the Nazis imprisoned many tens of thousands of gay men in the concentration camps because of their sexual orientation: all were ill-treated – often hideously – and a large proportion died due to hunger, disease or physical violence.[1] Estimates vary as to the exact number imprisoned or killed – as Richard Plant suggests, 'However meticulous the Nazis were in their mania for keeping records, they were also eager to conceal the extent of their savagery.'[2] The stories of these men have been told in harrowing detail elsewhere, although official recognition of their suffering is still scandalously slight. What is of concern here is the fate of those who survived when they were finally released in 1945. For, as David Fernbach notes, the new West German government kept in force the anti-homosexual legislation – the infamous section 175 of the German Penal Code – under which the Nazis had originally incarcerated the men.[3]

Since the new West German government saw itself as the legal successor to the Nazi regime, it granted financial compensation to victims of Nazism who had been persecuted on grounds of race or conscience. It refused, however, to compensate any of the gay men who survived, arguing that they had been legitimately imprisoned under the still valid section 175. In consequence, the men's years of suffering quite literally counted for nothing. In the words of Heinz Heger, one of the survivors:

> My request for compensation for the years of concentration camp was rejected by our democratic authorities, for as a pink-triangle prisoner, a homosexual, I had been condemned for a criminal offence, even if I'd not harmed anyone. No restitution is granted to 'criminal' concentration-camp victims.[4]

The West German government's behaviour illustrates – in about as blunt a fashion as it is possible to imagine, given the horrors which the concentration camp victims had suffered – how the law can be used to legitimate even the most appalling treatment of sexual minorities. It would be foolish to claim that the application of the present-day laws of the UK, the USA and Canada can be seen in quite the same light, but the laws of all three countries (especially the first two) may still be said to single out lesbians and gays for many types of adverse treatment, or may be felt to reinforce or reflect the types of social hostility considered in chapter 1.[5]

In this chapter, we will consider some of the present-day laws which have aroused concern among political campaigners because they are felt to be hostile to lesbians and gays; we will also touch on some of the attempts which have been made to harness the law as a means of protection against social hostility. Consideration of these examples will give us a practical background against which to locate the discussion, in later chapters, of possible justifications for the use of law and for law reform. Opinions will inevitably differ about the degree to which existing laws can be described as 'unjust', and about the extent to which they need reforming. Each person's view will turn upon what they believe the justification to be (if any) for law reform, and upon how effective (if at all) they think law reform is likely to be in remedying existing social injustices. It must be stressed that only a selection of examples will be presented in this chapter, which is not intended as a complete guide to the laws applicable in any of the three countries.[6]

In trying to amend laws which are seen as hostile, and in campaigning for the introduction of laws intended to serve as a protection against social hostility, lesbian and gay campaigning groups have relied on two tactics: lobbying state and national parliaments for legislative reform, and bringing test cases to challenge the validity of existing government policies or, in the USA and Canada, to review the constitutionality of existing laws. The outcome of any test case should depend on the arguments of legal or constitutional principle which can be mounted by each side. The philosophical justifications for law reform – with which this book is concerned – can be used either as part of a moral and political case for legislative reform, or in order to assess the moral and political legitimacy both of the decisions in test cases and of the deliberations of legislatures.

Law reform debates in the UK, the USA and Canada have tended to focus on either or both of two connected issues. One issue – usually the first to be considered – has been whether the criminal law should permit sexual relations and sexual contact between persons of the same sex, and if so under what circumstances. This issue is particularly prominent in the USA, where acts of oral and anal sex are still wholly illegal in roughly half the states which make up the Union – a position which the US Supreme Court found to be constitutionally permissible (at least under the Due Process provisions of the US Constitution) in *Bowers* v. *Hardwick* in 1986.[7] While sexual acts between persons of the same sex are generally legal in the UK, a more restrictive regime applies to sexual acts between men than to heterosexual acts. Three aspects of current criminal law are particularly contentious: the existence of a higher age of consent for male homosexual acts than for heterosexual or lesbian sex; the existence of a special and restrictive 'privacy' rule covering male homosexual acts; and the apparent prohibition on public expressions of affection between persons of the same sex – whether gay or lesbian – under the public order provisions of the criminal law. In Canada, the criminal law's regulation of lesbian and gay sexual acts no longer seems to be a live concern.[8]

The second issue concerns the degree of tolerance which the state is prepared to accord lesbians and gays more generally. There are both positive and negative sides to this issue. Considered in a positive light, the issue focuses on whether lesbians and gays should be entitled to civil-rights-type protections – and if so, to which ones. Should lesbians and gays be protected by anti-discrimination laws in areas like employment, for example? Should effective legal protection be granted against violent attacks and harassment motivated by anti-lesbian and gay bias? Should lesbians and gays be granted partnership rights equivalent to those enjoyed by heterosexuals – a question which has important consequences for inheritance, property and social security rights?[9] Should lesbian and gay parents stand a fair chance of obtaining rights to custody over or parental access to their children? Questions of this sort are currently causing controversy in the UK, the USA and Canada. In this chapter, however, we will simply describe the position under existing law – it will be the task of future chapters to look at what should be the case.

Considered in negative terms, the tolerance issue focuses on the question whether the state should take an active role in censoring lesbians and gays, even if lesbian and gay sex is permitted. Censorship sometimes assumes a fairly precisely targeted form, such as preventing lesbians and gays from meeting together, from organizing social events or from publishing newspapers and magazines. On other occasions, censorship can take the form of rather more general and explicit legislative expressions of public policy, recent examples of which include section 28 of the 1988 Local Government Act in the UK, and the contentious Amendment 2 to the Colorado State Constitution in the USA.

When considering both issues, it will be important to think about how the law is applied as well as what it actually says. A provision which is drafted in explicitly anti-lesbian or gay language may, for example, turn out to cause less concern on a day-to-day basis if it is not enforced than would a neutrally-worded provision which is often exercised to the clear disadvantage of lesbian and gays and lesbian and gay organizations – for example, police raids under general public order law which are specially targeted at gay meeting places because of alleged 'complaints' from members of the public. We will now consider the various aspects of the two issues in turn.

Criminal regulation: intercourse and intimacy

In regulating lesbian and gay sexual behaviour, the criminal law generally uses either or both of two types of provision: first, provisions which regulate acts of full sexual intercourse (and the procuring of intercourse); and second, provisions which regulate acts of intimacy falling short of intercourse, such as holding hands or kissing in the street. In the UK, provisions of the first type have tended, historically, to be directed more at sexual activity between men rather than between women; in the USA, such provisions have been used to regulate both sexes. The reasons for the UK's gender-specific approach remain ambiguous, but are probably connected with the fact that when the relevant provisions were drafted, public acknowledgement of female sexuality would have been unthinkable in English society.[10] Sexual acts between men were unmentionable in polite company, but their existence was at least recognized at the level of public policy, although they were perceived as the product of sinfulness or mental illness rather than a stable sexual orientation; they were therefore legislated against and punished, albeit under oblique names such as 'gross indecency'.[11] Sexual acts between women were simply ignored.[12]

The criminal law issue of greatest contemporary concern in the USA is clearly the continuing illegality, in twenty-two US states, of private, consensual acts of oral and anal sex (each state in the USA has its own constitution, laws and courts; above these are the federal constitution, legal system and courts, whose rulings can invalidate state laws and constitutions for incompatibility with federal provisions).[13] Such acts are currently illegal between all adults, regardless of sexual orientation, in Alabama, Arizona, Florida, Georgia, Idaho, Louisiana, Maryland, Michigan, Minnesota, Mississippi, North Carolina, Oklahoma, Rhode Island, South Carolina, Utah and Virginia. Although these prohibitions are enforceable regardless of sexual orientation, they would appear to impact much more strongly on lesbians and gays than on heterosexuals, given the availability to the latter group of vaginal intercourse (as well as the fact that policing tactics are usually directed, if anywhere, at lesbians and gays). The general anti-lesbian and gay tenor of these laws would appear to be confirmed by the fact that oral and anal sex are currently illegal *only* between adults of the same sex in Arkansas, Kansas, Missouri, Montana, Tennessee and Texas – sometimes after such acts have been decriminalized between heterosexuals.[14] The very language of these state laws often appears hostile, with the offences under which acts of oral and anal intercourse are punishable tending to labour under emotive names like 'the detestable and abominable crime against nature' (a label which graces Mississippi state law).[15]

Lobbying campaigns continue on a state-by-state basis for the repeal of such laws, but were dealt a severe blow by the ruling of the United States Supreme Court in the *Bowers* v. *Hardwick* case in 1986.[16] Michael Hardwick, a gay man, was arrested by police in his bedroom while engaging in consenting oral sex with another man; he was held at a police station overnight, and charged with violating Georgia's anti-sodomy law. The prosecution was formally dropped a short while later, but Hardwick chose to challenge the constitutionality of the Georgia state law on the ground that his 'right to privacy', which he argued was protected by the Due Process Clauses of the US Constitution, had been violated.

The case raises a host of important constitutional issues, which lie beyond the scope of this chapter.[17] For present purposes, it is sufficient to note that the US Supreme Court found against Hardwick, ruling in favour of the constitutional validity of the Georgia law by a majority of one. Justice White, delivering the opinion of the majority, tried to stress that the court was concerned only with the correct interpretation of the federal constitution, rather than with overtly moral questions: 'This case does not require a judgment on whether laws against sodomy between consenting adults in general, or between homosexuals in particular, are wise or desirable.'[18] One might be forgiven, however, for thinking otherwise, given the language in which the majority judgments were cast. Both Justice White and Chief Justice Burger insisted on describing Hardwick's claim as being for a right to commit 'homosexual sodomy', rather than the more usual formulation that he was claiming the protection of a wider constitutional right to privacy. In addition, Chief Justice Burger insisted on discussing 'the history of Western civilization' and 'Judaeo-Christian moral and ethical standards' – hardly the types of reference one might expect in a morally neutral constitutional adjudication.[19]

Justice White declared for the majority that previous case law had not conferred 'a right of privacy that extends to homosexual sodomy'.[20] In previous 'privacy' cases, activities connected with the family, marriage or procreation had received constitutional protection, but 'homosexual sodomy' could show no connection with these, and it was 'unsupportable' to claim that the cases conferred any general right to protection from state regulation of private sexual activity.[21] Furthermore, the Supreme Court would not now declare 'a fundamental right to engage in homosexual sodomy' to exist – for it could not be said to be deeply rooted in the nation's history and tradition, nor implicit in the concept of ordered liberty.[22] Indeed, said Justice White – clearly revealing his distaste for Michael Hardwick's case – the claim that there could be such a right was 'at best, facetious'.[23] The fact that homosexual conduct occurred in the privacy of the home rather than in public was unimportant, and a belief, shared by the majority of people, that homosexuality was immoral could not be said to be an insufficient basis for supporting the constitutionality of an anti-sodomy law.[24]

Again invoking forces of 'tradition', Chief Justice Burger asserted in his concurring judgment that 'To hold that the act of homosexual sodomy is somehow protected as a fundamental [constitutional] right would be to cast aside millennia of moral teaching.'[25] For Justice Powell, who later acknowledged that he may have been mistaken to vote with the majority to uphold the Georgia law (which he had only decided to do after some hesitation), the fact that Hardwick had not actually been tried, convicted or sentenced of an offence made his challenge to the state law one of hypothetical interest only.[26]

William Rubenstein argues that the decision in *Bowers* v. *Hardwick* has had a number of consequences.[27] First, while anti-sodomy laws are rarely directly enforced, lesbians and gays must nevertheless run the risk, in roughly half the USA, of being arrested for expressing private sexual affection for one another – as Michael Hardwick's own treatment at the hands of the Georgia police demonstrates. Second, the decision has encouraged lesbian and gay litigants to switch their attentions away from the US federal courts – in which *Bowers* v. *Hardwick* was fought – and into the state courts, where some post-*Hardwick* challenges to anti-sodomy laws have still been successful.[28] Third, and perhaps most importantly, the decision has been used to undermine attempts by lesbians and gays to show that they fall within the scope of other constitutional protections – although this trend may now have been reversed, a point to which we shall return below. In addition, Kendall Thomas has argued that at a broader, social level, anti-sodomy laws of the type upheld in *Bowers* v. *Hardwick* can only serve to legitimate homophobic assaults and violence, already very common in the United States.[29]

In addition to the widespread existence of anti-sodomy statutes, the criminal laws of many US states also regulate public expressions of same-sex intimacy falling short of intercourse. Courts have, it seems, generally been willing to impose harsh penalties on lesbians and gays arrested for general expressions of affection towards each other in public, as well as penalizing sex in quasi-public places and conduct which amounts to 'loitering with a lewd purpose'.[30] As we will see below, US law is in this respect quite close to the criminal law applicable in the UK.

Provisions of the criminal law in the UK raise related but slightly different concerns (it should be remembered that it is technically inaccurate to talk of one 'UK legal system': for the UK in fact has three distinct legal systems – one each for Scotland, Northern Ireland, and England and Wales). In England and Wales, sexual relations between men were wholly illegal until the passage of the 1967 Sexual Offences Act, which decriminalized 'buggery' (anal intercourse) and 'gross indecency' (i.e. any other form of sexual contact, including oral sex and masturbation in the presence of another, whether or not the act is mutual) between men so long as both were aged 21 or over and the act took place 'in private'.[31] In *R* v. *Reakes*, the Court of Appeal found that whether an act took place in private would depend on the surrounding circumstances, including the time of day or night, the nature of the place including the lighting, and the likelihood of a third party coming upon the scene.[32] Scotland and Northern Ireland had to wait until 1980 and 1982, respectively, for partial decriminalization on similar terms.[33] The age at which 'buggery' and 'gross indecency' between men is legally permissible was reduced to 18 in the 1994 Criminal Justice and Public Order Act, but the 'privacy' constraints remain.[34] Sexual relations between women are not (and have never been) illegal in the UK, provided that the women concerned have reached the heterosexual age of consent – currently 16 – and have consented.[35]

Some striking contrasts can be drawn between the treatment of male homosexual and heterosexual or lesbian intercourse in the laws of the UK. First, heterosexual sex is presumed to be legal unless specifically declared otherwise, whereas sexual acts between men are declared to be *illegal* in the Sexual Offences Act 1956, and must be presumed to be so unless they fall within one of the categories permitted under the 1967 and 1994 Acts.[36] This reverse presumption – which also applies to common law offences associated with homosexual behaviour, which are presumed to remain offences unless specifically repealed by the Acts – results from the step-by-step method by which the law applicable to gay sexual activity has been relaxed. The reverse presumption can have illogical and restrictive consequences, however, as was vividly demonstrated in *R v. Knuller* – a case in which the House of Lords upheld the convictions of the publishers of a magazine containing a page of contact advertisements (that is, advertisements in which male readers asked for other men to contact them to arrange sexual encounters) for the common law offence of conspiring to corrupt public morals.[37]

In *Knuller*, the House of Lords flatly rejected the publishers' argument that since it had been legal for males over the age of consent (then 21) to commit homosexual acts in private since the 1967 Act, it could not be an offence at common law to put in touch with each other people who wanted to commit such acts. According to Lord Morris, the 1967 Sexual Offences Act

> provide[d] that certain acts which previously were criminal offences should no longer be criminal offences. But that does not mean that it is not open to a jury to say that to assist or to encourage persons to take part in such acts may be to corrupt them.[38]

In Lord Reid's words, 'there is a material difference between merely exempting certain conduct from criminal penalties and making it lawful in the full sense'. The 1967 Act merely exempted homosexual acts committed in private between two males; but there was

> nothing in the Act to indicate that Parliament thought or intended to lay down that indulgence in these practices is not corrupting. I read the Act as saying that, even though it may be corrupting, if people choose to corrupt themselves in this way that is their affair and the law will not interfere. But no licence is given to others to encourage the practice.[39]

It is therefore illegal at common law to facilitate a perfectly legal sexual act between two men, on the basis that this involves a conspiracy to corrupt public morals (it is also possible for steps leading to the commission of a legal homosexual act to fall foul of the statutory offences of 'procuring'[40] or 'importuning'[41]). *Knuller*'s case is thus a clear demonstration of the narrowness of the 1967 reforms, embodied in the criminal law's use of the reverse presumption as to legality in the case of homosexual activity.

A second striking contrast is that the criminal laws of the three UK legal systems retain unequal age of consent provisions – 18 for sex between men and 16 for heterosexual (or lesbian) intercourse.[42] As Andrew Ashworth has argued, it is difficult to find strong evidence to support the notion that males aged between 16 and 18 need 'protection' from homosexual but not heterosexual activity, especially when females of the same age are not felt to need the law's protection from the attentions of older males or females. The anomaly is increased, Ashworth suggests, by the fact that two males under 18 are liable to be imprisoned for up to two years if convicted of consensual 'gross indecency' with each other.[43]

The third important contrast lies in the restrictive 'privacy' requirement, which attaches to gay but not to heterosexual or lesbian sex. Quite apart from the rather loose criteria laid down in the *Reakes* case (discussed above) as to when a court is likely to find that an act was committed 'in private', the 1967 Act also specifically states that a homosexual act is not committed in private 'when more than two persons take part or are present'[44] – a rather different regime from that applicable to sexual acts between one man and two or more women, which are presumptively legal.

One slightly puzzling feature is that *heterosexual* buggery is still totally illegal in the UK.[45] In the late twentieth century, this difference might look like the product of an historical accident; but whatever its cause, it cannot be used to rebut the argument that the criminal law treats gays more harshly than heterosexuals. At a practical level, buggery and oral sex are common ingredients in sexual intercourse between men; by contrast, vaginal intercourse appears to be the social norm in sex between men and women. In logic, a prohibition on heterosexual buggery – while unjustifiable according to the arguments to be developed in later chapters – cannot be viewed in the same light as a complete prohibition on homosexual buggery, the equivalent of which would be a complete prohibition on *vaginal* intercourse between heterosexuals.

Turning to the law on public expressions of intimacy which fall short of intercourse, it seems fairly clear that two persons of the same sex – whether men or women – kissing or otherwise expressing physical affection in a public place might be convicted of the Public Order Act 1986 offence of using threatening, abusive or insulting words or behaviour within the sight or hearing of a person likely to be caused harassment, alarm or distress thereby.[46] The Public Order Act does not single out lesbian and gay expressions of affection – as opposed to their heterosexual equivalents – for censure, but it seems unlikely that two heterosexuals would be prosecuted for merely kissing or holding hands in public, and even if they were, it is almost impossible to imagine that a court would deem such behaviour to be likely to cause harassment, alarm or distress.

This mirrors the contrasting approaches, on the part of the police and the courts, to the enforcement of the criminal law. Full public sexual intercourse between a heterosexual couple would itself be illegal under the public order provisions of the criminal law, but on the rare occasions when such matters are brought to court, they appear to be treated lightly.[47] By contrast, many police forces seem to attach high priority to arresting men for engaging in public sexual acts with other men, especially where these occur in toilets (which are specifically exempted from the 'privacy' protections of the 1967 Act).[48] In general, courts have imposed heavy penalties for these and other displays of public affection, as well as for sexual activity in the home which nevertheless falls outside the 'privacy' provisions of the 1967 and 1994 Acts.[49] While the *Knuller*-type 'conspiracy' offence tends not to be enforced nowadays, lesbian and gay publications remain in a vulnerable position due to the ease with which such a prosecution *could* be brought should the authorities at any stage choose to do so.

UK criminal law thus seems to conform with the sentiments of Lord Arran, one of the main sponsors of the 1967 Act during its passage through Parliament. Speaking during the House of Lords' Third Reading debate, he warned that:

> Any form of ostentatious [gay] behaviour now, or in the future, any form of public flaunting, would be utterly distasteful and would, I believe, make the sponsors of the Bill regret that they have done what they have done. Homosexuals must remember that while there is nothing bad in being a homosexual, there is certainly nothing good.[50]

Robert Wintemute suggests, rather more succinctly, that in the eyes of English law 'any person who considers themselves gay, lesbian, or bisexual, or who ever engages in any aspect of same-sex emotional-sexual conduct [is] clearly a second-class citizen'.[51] Such a comment could be applied in magnified form to the criminal laws of the US, given the existence of anti-sodomy statutes in so many US states, especially statutes aimed specifically at sexual acts between persons of the same sex.

One other contentious criminal law issue in the UK is the status of sado-masochistic sexual activity. In *R v. Brown*, a majority of the House of Lords held that a group of men who engaged in consenting sado-masochistic sexual acts which involved the infliction of more than transient or trifling injury could be found guilty of wounding or causing actual bodily harm contrary to the Offences Against the Person Act 1861.[52] In consequence, most types of consenting sado-masochistic sex are now illegal. While the sado-masochists in the case were gay men, the decision also applies to heterosexuals, causing some to suggest that the decision should be seen as raising issues of general sexual liberty rather than issues of specific concern to lesbians and gays.[53] One's view on this question will ultimately depend upon which law reform justification one favours – a point to which we will return in later chapters.

Degrees of tolerance

Reform of the laws regulating sexual acts and expressions of affection between people of the same sex nowadays constitutes just one part of the lesbian and gay campaigning agenda; in recent years, lesbians and gays have also tried to encourage the law to adopt a more accepting approach to their sexual orientation in other, wider contexts. At the same time, a range of what may be described as aggressive 'New Christian Right' pressure groups have been trying, in the USA and Canada, to push back – with varying degrees of success – any advances made by lesbian and gay campaigners,[54] and to push for the introduction of laws – such as Amendment 2 in Colorado – which would block civil rights protections for lesbians and gays.[55] There has been a rather less vehement reaction to the efforts of lesbian and gay campaigners in the UK, although there was a clear anti-lesbian and gay backlash at the end of the 1980s, exemplified by the passage of section 28 of the Local Government Act 1988.[56] Expressions of intolerance also emerged more recently during the Parliamentary debates on the age of consent sections of the Criminal Justice and Public Order Act 1994.

There are many different ways in which the legal issues discussed in this section could be arranged. Here, they will be grouped together and analysed under three main headings – although there will be several overlaps between the material considered in each. The first heading concerns the availability – or, more frequently, the non-availability – of legal protection from discrimination, as exemplified by discrimination in employment (that is, dismissals of people from employment because they are lesbian or gay, or refusals to employ them for this reason), including military employment. The second heading deals with claims to legal rights of a partnership or family-related nature in the UK, the USA and Canada, including attempts to obtain legal recognition of lesbian or gay partnerships, and the case law concerning custody of children. The third heading deals with what was earlier described as the negative side to the tolerance issue, in that it concerns attempts to censor lesbian and gay participation in the political process, or to prevent lesbians and gays gaining civil rights protections. As a general point, it should also be noted that there is considerable concern among campaigners on both sides of the Atlantic about the general absence of effective legal redress against violence directed at lesbians and gays because of their sexual orientation, and about the use, in some US and UK cases, of the victim's lesbian or gay sexual orientation as the basis for allowing attackers to rely on the defence of provocation.[57]

General protections from discrimination

In this section, we will examine the few protections available to lesbians and gays against discrimination in employment, and some of the attempts which have been made to redress this position. In the three legal systems in question, anti-discrimination protections available in the employment context will often apply to other areas as well – existing UK sex discrimination laws, for example (which, on one view, may cover discrimination on the basis of sexual orientation), apply to the provision of goods, facilities and services in shops, pubs and restaurants, as well as to employment.[58]

It is important to realize that anti-discrimination provisions can operate at a variety of levels – and against different bodies, according to the level in question – in the three different legal systems. This has affected the types of protection which lesbian and gay litigants have sought. Canada and the USA are both federal states, with constitutional anti-discrimination provisions entrenched at federal level – in the Canadian Charter of Rights and Freedoms and the US Constitution respectively. The federal courts of each nation can review laws and regulations made at federal level, as well as those made by the constituent provinces and territories (in Canada) or states (in the USA), to ensure that they comply with the human rights protections entrenched in the Charter or Constitution, as appropriate. In theory, courts can only use the Charter or US Constitution to set aside exercises of *state* power – that is, laws, regulations and other types of government action, whether made at federal or at state/provincial level (although there is in fact a controversy surrounding the precise ambit of the Charter). When acting against a *private* employer, litigants are supposed to use the anti-discrimination provisions contained in ordinary laws made at federal or at state/provincial level. There is no entrenched human rights code in the UK, by contrast, and litigants can use statutory anti-discrimination provisions against government and private employer alike. The one relevant exception occurs in the case of allegedly discriminatory decisions or actions of a public law nature, which must be challenged via judicial review. European Community law does now provide a background and overarching framework of rules, many of which are applicable in ordinary employment and sex discrimination cases; it remains to be seen whether they will be of much assistance in cases of sexual orientation-related discrimination.[59]

In examining the current situation in the USA and Canada, we will see that attempts to bring lesbians and gays within the protection of the Constitution and the Charter anti-discrimination provisions have met respectively with limited and mixed success. If lesbians and gays were authoritatively included within the scope of the provisions at this level in either country, then laws or government-sponsored distinctions which were deemed to discriminate against them – whether at federal or at state/provincial level – could be set aside by the appropriate courts. At present, sexual orientation-related discrimination by private employers is occasionally forbidden by legislation passed at state or city level in the USA, and often forbidden by legislation passed at provincial level in Canada (as is discrimination by state/provincial governments, either by legislation or by constitutional provisions enacted at this level).[60] Where sexual orientation comes to be included as a prohibited ground for discrimination at state/provincial level, this is often as a result of lesbian and gay-influenced lobbying campaigns.[61]

In Canada, a large amount of federal-level litigation has focused on section 15(1) of the Canadian Charter. Section 15(1) states that:

> Every individual is equal before and under the law and has the right to the equal protection and equal benefit of the law without discrimination and, in particular, without discrimination based on race, national or ethnic origin, colour, religion, sex, age, or mental or physical disability.

It is well-established that section 15(1) prohibits discrimination not only on the grounds listed in it (the 'enumerated grounds'), but also on grounds which are deemed to be 'analogous' to them.[62] If an applicant can highlight an enumerated or analogous ground of discrimination, they must then show that the legislative distinction which the government is seeking to defend has had a discriminatory impact upon them.[63] If the applicant can successfully establish these points, then they are deemed to have shown that a *prima facie* violation of section 15(1) has occurred. The government can then escape liability only if it can be demonstrated that the violation is justifiable 'in a free and democratic society' according to section 1 of the Charter. In *Egan* v. *Canada* (decided in 1995[64]), the Supreme Court of Canada unanimously agreed that discrimination on the ground of sexual orientation is deemed to be an 'analogous ground' of discrimination for the purposes of section 15(1).[65] Among factors cited by different judges in support of this conclusion were the deeply personal nature of an individual's sexual orientation, as well as the deep-rooted patterns of social, economic and political disadvantage suffered by lesbians and gays.

The significance of this decision for anti-discrimination protection for lesbians and gays, however, remains to be demonstrated. This is because of two important points.[66] First, the Charter, as mentioned earlier, technically can only be used in cases involving discrimination caused by the application or operation of law; in theory, it does not apply to discrimination claims where purely private actors are involved.[67] If a lesbian or gay man taking action against a private sector employer cannot rely on the Charter directly, the significance of *Egan* is therefore confined to public sector cases. Use of the Charter might, however, be available indirectly via *Haig* v. *Canada*, a controversial decision in which the Ontario Court of Appeal ruled that, assuming that sexual orientation was an analogous ground under section 15(1) of the Charter (the point which *Egan* has now confirmed), it must be read into section 3(1) of the Canadian Human Rights Act – a federal law which *does* apply against private employers – as a prohibited ground of discrimination under that statute.[68] If *Haig* is correct, discrimination by private employers on the ground of sexual orientation is therefore prohibited across Canada, at least where benefits to individuals rather than couples are concerned. Given that it involves a dramatic extension of the application of the Charter, however, the validity of the reasoning used in the *Haig* decision is likely to be tested in the Canadian Supreme Court before too long.[69] This means that in cases involving only private actors, the usefulness of the *Egan* 'analogous ground' reasoning – and the potential protection available to lesbians and gays – remains uncertain for the time being, especially given the general failure of cases under the 'family status' head of section 3(1), to be discussed below.

Second, even in cases of a public sector nature – i.e. those which are clearly within the scope of section 15(1) – it is necessary for the applicant to show more than just an 'analogous ground'. They must also show that the distinction employed by the government has had a discriminatory impact on them, and that the violation of section 15(1) cannot be justified. It is by no means guaranteed that lesbians and gays will receive a favourable response from Canadian courts on these points. The decision in *Egan* provides a good example. On its facts, the case was concerned with the social security entitlements of an elderly gay couple, rather than with individual employment. Even though the case had what could be described as 'model' facts in the partnership context, the Supreme Court of Canada only found by a narrow margin that there had been a discriminatory impact, before going on to reject the applicants' claim on the justification point (we will consider these matters further when discussing partnership rights). It must therefore be uncertain how the Canadian courts will treat the discriminatory impact and justification points when an *Egan*-based 'analogous ground' claim is used in contexts such as employment.

The most reliable examples of protection for Canadian lesbians and gays against discriminatory treatment (at least at the hands of private sector employers) would thus seem, for the time being, to be found predominantly in province-level laws. It should be noted, however, that the employment of lesbians and gays in the military is no longer a contentious legal issue in Canada: there have been no restrictions on those seeking to serve since 1992 – a result partly achieved, it seems, by the threat of litigation under the Charter.[70]

However mixed the position of lesbians and gays under Canadian law may be, it is certainly more secure than is the case in the USA. For the implication of *Bowers* v. *Hardwick* was effectively to tar lesbians and gays, as a social group, as potential criminals – people whose very basis for being seen as a group was their shared propensity for engaging in sexual acts which the state could properly criminalize. Until mid-1996, this seemed to suggest that it would be very difficult for lesbians and gays to seek effective protection, under the US Constitution's Equal Protection provisions, from social discrimination in public sector employment (whether civilian or military). The implications of the Supreme Court's recent ruling in *Romer* v. *Evans*[71] – which Ronald Dworkin has suggested is difficult to reconcile with *Bowers* v. *Hardwick*, and may sound the death-knell for the latter decision[72] – seem to be a little more promising, however, although the precise effects of the decision have yet to be seen. This is because classic Equal Protection reasoning was not deployed in *Romer* (which, on its facts, was concerned with Colorado's Amendment 2 rather than with military employment), and the *Romer* reasoning may not in any event produce more positive results when applied to military employment cases. We will return to *Romer* after considering the post-*Bowers* military employment cases.

Under classic Equal Protection analysis, US courts may apply three standards when reviewing the legitimacy of laws or government regulations: the strongest standard is strict scrutiny, which applies only where a suspect classification is established; the intermediate standard is called heightened scrutiny; and the lowest standard is known as rational basis review.[73] In a number of post-*Hardwick* decisions, including *High Tech Gays* v. *Defense Industrial Security Clearance Office*, it has been ruled improper and illogical to find that lesbians and gays can constitute a suspect classification – thereby ruling out strict scrutiny of whatever regulations are being challenged – given that *Hardwick* had declared that there was no constitutional right to engage in same-sex oral or anal sex.[74]

US courts have not been entirely consistent on this point, however. A notable example of a court declaring that lesbians and gays *do* constitute a suspect classification, leading to strict scrutiny, was the initial decision of the US Court of Appeals in *Watkins* v. *U.S. Army*.[75] Circuit Judge Norris found that US Army Regulations then in force – which barred from military service any person who had 'committed homosexual acts or is an admitted homosexual but as to whom there is no evidence that they have engaged in homosexual acts' – violated the Constitution's Equal Protection guarantees. Sergeant Watkins, who had been described by his commanding officer as 'one of our most respected and trusted soldiers, both by his superiors and his subordinates',[76] was discharged under the Regulations because he admitted that he was gay and that he had engaged in sexual acts with other men. By accepting that lesbians and gays constituted a suspect classification, Circuit Judge Norris was saying that because they were, as a group, in an especially disadvantageous social position, the state needed to advance a legitimate and compelling interest in order to justify, to the standard required under strict scrutiny, any measures which discriminated against them.

The judge used the following factors in reaching this conclusion.[77] First, the group had a history of suffering purposeful discrimination.[78] Second, discrimination against lesbians and gays embodied a gross unfairness that was sufficiently inconsistent with the ideals of equal protection of the laws that it could be termed invidious – for the Regulations defined the group by a trait (their sexual orientation) which bore no relevance to their ability to work in the army.[79] The group had suffered grave social disadvantage because of prejudice or inaccurate stereotypes. Furthermore, the trait defining the members of the group was immutable, in that changing it would involve a major physical change or a traumatic change of identity for those concerned, or it was so central to the identity of those falling within the group that it would be abhorrent for the government to penalize them for refusing to change it. Circuit Judge Norris argued that,

> Although the causes of homosexuality are not fully understood, scientific research indicates that we have little control over our sexual orientation and that, once acquired, our sexual orientation is largely impervious to change. . . . Scientific proof aside, it seems appropriate to ask whether heterosexuals feel capable of changing their sexual orientation. Would heterosexuals living in a city that passed an ordinance banning those who engaged in or desired to engage in sex with persons of the opposite sex find it easy not only to abstain from heterosexual activity but also to shift the object of their sexual desires to persons of the same sex?[80]

Third, lesbians and gays were a 'discrete and insular minority' – that is, they lacked the political power necessary to obtain political redress from the government.[81] The Regulations were therefore set aside – Judge Norris finding that the Army could not prove that they were necessary to promote a compelling government interest – and the Army was ordered to consider Sergeant Watkins' re-enlistment without regard to his sexual orientation.[82]

The crucial point, however, is that the Court of Appeals was able to reach this conclusion only on the basis that the Regulations penalized lesbians and gays because of their sexual orientation *per se* – i.e. because of their *status* as lesbians and gays, rather than because of their sexual *conduct*. Circuit Judge Norris was able to argue that on the basis of their wording, the Regulations did not penalize soldiers for engaging in homosexual *acts* as such – rather, they only penalized soldiers who had engaged in homosexual acts if the Army decided that the soldiers were also gay as a matter of *orientation*.[83] In consequence, the Court of Appeals was able to dismiss the argument that it would be incongruous to protect lesbians and gays under Equal Protection analysis when *Bowers* v. *Hardwick* had found that there was no constitutional right to engage in homosexual *activity*. Circuit Judge Norris suggested that, 'while *Hardwick* does indeed hold that the Due Process clause provides no substantive privacy protection for *acts* of private homosexual sodomy, nothing in *Hardwick* suggests that the state may penalize gays for their sexual *orientation*';[84] and that, 'we see no principled way to transmogrify the Court's holding that the State may criminalize specific sexual *conduct* commonly engaged in by homosexuals into a state license to pass . . . laws imposing special restrictions on people because they are gay'.[85] Significantly, Judge Norris accepted that *Bowers* v. *Hardwick* foreclosed any Due Process or Equal Protection claim that the Army Regulations impinged on a fundamental right to engage in homosexual acts – but this was, he argued, wholly different from Sergeant Watkins' claim that he was discriminated against on the basis of his membership of a disfavoured group.[86]

Despite its often supportive tone, the *Watkins* judgment cannot be seen as any kind of breakthrough. First, while Judge Norris's reasoning remains perhaps the strongest example of status-based Equal Protection analysis in this area of US law, its precedent value was minimized because the Court of Appeals later reheard the case *en banc* and withdrew the judgment, finding instead that Sergeant Watkins should be re-enlisted on the technical ground of equitable estoppel. In their judgments at the rehearing stage, Judges Norris and Canby continued to rely on their earlier Equal Protection analysis, and concurred only in the result reached by the majority.[87] The result of the majority's withdrawal of the earlier judgment at rehearing stage was, however, to clear the path for the Court of Appeals (Ninth Circuit) to ignore the original Equal Protection analysis when it reached its decision in *High Tech Gays*.[88]

The second point is that Judge Norris's status-based analysis would, in any event, afford little or no protection to lesbians and gays who were clearly penalized for being sexually active. There is, as Patricia Cain has argued, 'a certain degree of absurdity' in making legal arguments to protect lesbians and gays when these arguments deliberately screen out lesbian and gay sexual activity – for such activity plays, after all, a definitional role as one of the unifying aspects of being lesbian or gay.[89] Protecting soldiers from discharge due to their sexual orientation, but giving them no protection for engaging in the types of activity which make that orientation socially meaningful or significant, provides a level of protection which is, as Judge Reinhardt pointed out in his dissenting judgment in *Watkins*, 'hollow indeed'. Judge Reinhardt disapproved of *Bowers* v. *Hardwick* in his dissenting judgment, but suggested that since the Supreme Court had drastically restricted the possibility of lawful physical intimacy for lesbians and gays (i.e. to types of intimacy which did not fall foul of the oral and anal sex prohibitions), it was 'hypocritical at best' to suggest that lesbians and gays simultaneously had special protection under the Equal Protection clause.[90]

In *High Tech Gays*, which followed close on the heels of the *Watkins* rehearing, the US Court of Appeals was therefore able to opt for a conduct-based interpretation (bringing the regulations under challenge within the conduct-oriented approach in *Hardwick*). The case involved an Equal Protection challenge to Department of Defense Security Clearance Regulations requiring lesbian and gay applicants for security clearance to be subjected to special vetting procedures. Circuit Judge Brunetti found that lesbians and gays had suffered a history of discrimination, but that homosexuality was an aspect of behaviour rather than an immutable characteristic, and was therefore fundamentally different from the types of characteristic which defined suspect classes. Since lesbians and gays could not constitute a suspect class, it was necessary to subject the Regulations only to the lowest level of scrutiny – rational basis review – to test whether they served a legitimate government interest or were rationally related to such an interest.[91] While not necessarily fatal to an applicant's claim,[92] the rational basis standard is relatively easy for the state to clear (as in *High Tech Gays*): for example, it has been found using this standard that the military has a legitimate interest in preventing sexual acts between people of the same sex, and that there is a sufficient connection between a person saying that they are lesbian or gay and engaging in prohibited sexual acts, so that a policy of not admitting openly lesbian or gay individuals to the military can survive rational basis scrutiny.[93]

In *Romer v. Evans*, the US Supreme Court sought to avoid many of the awkward issues raised by the possible definition of a lesbian and gay 'class'. The Court did this by ruling that a law which was inexplicable by anything but animus towards the group it affected would not survive rational basis scrutiny. Laws which merely disadvantage a class would survive if they serve a legitimate governmental interest, but the sheer breadth of Amendment 2 – its total denial of legal protections for lesbians and gays – meant that it could be motivated only by an illegitimate animus towards them. Issues of 'suspect classifications' and levels of scrutiny are thus effectively bypassed. Ronald Dworkin argues that this reasoning is significant in two respects. First, it cannot be reconciled with the Supreme Court's earlier assertion, in *Bowers v. Hardwick*, that the majority's moral disapproval of a particular group *was* sufficient to legitimate a law which penalized that group.[94] This suggests, Dworkin argues, that the Supreme Court 'may have begun the process of isolating and finally overriding

[*Bowers*] altogether'.[95] The results of the two cases certainly appear inconsistent: lesbians and gays may be imprisoned because of their sexual practices, but not put at an electoral disadvantage. Second, however, the new requirement of animus may leave the results in military employment cases unaffected. Dworkin points out that the animus test does not put lesbians and gays

> in as secure a position as they would enjoy if they were designated a suspect or quasi-suspect class. They have the burden of proof in showing that a particular rule or law that harms them serves no legitimate purpose, but only the illegitimate one of expressing 'animus,' and they might find that burden difficult to sustain in many cases – in challenging the military's opposition to retaining openly homosexual soldiers, for example.[96]

It seems possible, however, that criminal prohibitions on same-sex sexual acts might now be found unconstitutional on the basis that they served no purpose beyond an expression of animus.

On the whole, therefore, the position for lesbians and gays seeking constitutional protection from discrimination in public employment does not look particularly promising. Unless they can draw a clear distinction between sexual orientation and sexual conduct, arguing for protection only on the basis of the former, it seems unlikely that lesbians and gays will achieve suspect classification/strict scrutiny protection so long as *Bowers* v. *Hardwick* survives. The status/conduct distinction is anyway artificial, and adopting a purely status-based approach (as in the original *Watkins* decision) would seem unlikely to result in a meaningful level of protection, given that it would not prohibit discrimination due to sexual activity. Circuit Judge Norris's approach in *Watkins* has been described as 'a valiant attempt to make the best of a bad situation';[97] this is probably true, but it does not make the result any less hollow in terms of the practical protection which it would afford to lesbians and gays in public employment, whether civilian or military. Furthermore, the animus test does not seem strong enough to improve matters in the military context, given the military's typical use of 'national security' justifications to explain why its exclusions policy is not based on animus. It thus seems likely that the Supreme Court will have openly to overturn *Bowers* v. *Hardwick* before genuine constitutional anti-discrimination protection can be attained.

Two further points must be made: first, the US military regulations prohibiting lesbians and gays from serving were effectively put on a statutory basis in 1993, albeit under a slightly revised format colloquially known as 'don't ask, don't tell'. This seems to offer little or no additional protection for lesbian or gay service personnel, and is currently the subject of challenge in the US courts on the basis that the statute curtails First Amendment rights to freedom of expression.[98] Second, the above discussion has concentrated on litigation under the US Constitution – and therefore on public employment – given the current controversy surrounding this area. As noted earlier, lesbians and gays *have* attained some protection in a very few parts of the USA under state or city laws prohibiting discrimination by *private* employers.[99] As we will see below, however, this type of protection is vulnerable to the activities of the 'Christian' right, who have been actively promoting amendments to state constitutions – such as Amendment 2 in Colorado – which would prohibit such protections.

The position of lesbian and gay employees also appears vulnerable – although with potential for change – in the UK. Cases decided to date suggest that civilian employers are not liable for unfair dismissal if they sack a lesbian or gay employee, so long as the dismissal is motivated by fear that other members of the workforce or customers will react in a hostile fashion, thereby damaging the business, if the employee is kept on.[100] Perhaps the most notable example is *Saunders* v. *Scottish National Camps*,[101] where a groundsman at a children's holiday camp was dismissed when his employers became aware that he was gay and that he had been involved in what was described as a 'homosexual incident' in a nearby town. The employers feared that some of the children's parents might feel anxiety if they knew that the groundsman worked at the camp. The Employment Appeal Tribunal concluded that, if a considerable proportion of employers would take the view that the employment of a gay man should be restricted where the job involved closeness to and contact with children, then the dismissal could be justified.[102] This ruling was affirmed, on appeal, by the Scottish Court of Session, legitimating Mr Saunders' dismissal. Another noteworthy case is *Boychuk* v. *Symons Holdings*,[103] where the Employment Appeal Tribunal found that the dismissal of an employee for refusing to remove her badge at work – the badge said 'Lesbians Ignite' – was fair. Phillips

J. asserted that a reasonable employer was allowed to make judgements, on reflection and mature consideration, about what customers and fellow employees could be expected to find offensive.[104]

The judges in these cases were keen to stress that the dismissals did not stem from the employees' sexual orientation *per se*: in *Boychuk*, Phillips J. claimed that such a situation 'would be entirely different and [would] raise entirely different questions'.[105] On its facts, he argued, the case was solely concerned with the employee's conduct in refusing to remove her badge at work. In *Saunders*, the Court of Session stressed that the groundsman was not dismissed solely because he was gay: the important factor was the employer's fear of the parents' (i.e. their customers') reaction if he remained in employment at the camp.[106] This reasoning seems distinctly artificial, however: for even if the adverse reaction – whether from customers or other members of the workforce – which the employer claimed they wanted to avoid actually occurred (a hypothetical question, on the facts of *Saunders*), it could amount to little more than an expression of prejudice about the presence of a lesbian or gay employee: something like 'we don't want our children on the same camp site as one of those gays because they're all child molesters'. In logic, an employer is only reinforcing prejudices of this type by using their actual or possible existence to justify dismissing a lesbian or gay employee, making it impossible to separate the employer's action from the prejudice itself.

On one interpretation, it may be unlawful direct discrimination – under sex discrimination law applicable in the UK – to dismiss or to refuse to employ someone because of their sexual orientation.[107] If an essential aspect of a person's sexual orientation is the sex of those to whom they are sexually attracted or with whom they have relationships, then it could be claimed that it is direct sex discrimination to dismiss a female employee for having a sexual relationship with another woman, when a male employee would not be dismissed for doing so.[108] The current status of this argument is, however, unclear: it received some support in an Industrial Tribunal's advisory opinion in a Scottish case concerning direct discrimination under the Sex Discrimination Act 1975,[109] but received short shrift at the hands of the Divisional Court and the Court of Appeal in the military employment case *R v. Ministry of Defence, ex parte Smith*, in the context of direct discrimination under the European Community Equal Treatment Directive.[110] The correctness of the *Smith* reasoning has since been implicitly challenged, however: in a significant decision in the

P v. *S* case, the European Court of Justice has ruled that the dismissal of a transsexual *is* prohibited under the Directive. According to the Court:

> the scope of the [D]irective cannot be confined simply to discrimination based on the fact that a person is of one or other sex. In view of its purpose and the nature of the rights which it seeks to safeguard, the scope of the [D]irective is also such as to apply to discrimination arising, as in this case, from the gender reassignment of the person concerned.[111]

This expansive reasoning clearly implies that members of other groups may seek protection under the Directive where discrimination against them is based 'not simply on the fact' that they are male or female. If transsexualism is protected in this way, it is certainly difficult as a matter of logic to see why a person's sexual orientation – contrary to *Smith* – does not also count as a prohibited basis for discrimination under the Directive. The European Court of Justice will shortly be required to make a definite ruling one way or the other.[112]

The message from other jurisdictions about the use of sex discrimination arguments is mixed: such arguments have been rejected in Canadian courts, but have been accepted by the Hawaiian Supreme Court and in some international contexts.[113] Until we have a clear decision from the European Court of Justice, it cannot be said that there is any clearly effective means of protection from discrimination in civilian employment for lesbians and gays in the UK. It is for this reason that a number of draft anti-discrimination bills have been produced by campaigning groups, one aim of which would be to prohibit discrimination in employment due to a person's sexual orientation.[114] Prohibiting such discrimination by legislation would depend, however, on generating sufficient Parliamentary support.

The civilian employment position is paralleled in the controversy over whether lesbians and gays should be allowed to serve in the military – an issue which is distinct, as a matter of English law, from the civilian cases since it turns on whether the government policy (implemented via the prerogative) of discharging openly lesbian and gay service personnel is legally valid, a matter which must be challenged by judicial review.[115] While the Criminal Justice and Public Order Act 1994 ended the total criminalization of gay sex involving members of the armed forces or of the merchant navy aboard ship, it remained permissible to discharge people for such behaviour, and members of the armed forces (lesbians as well as gay men) continued to be punished under laws specifically applicable to the military.[116] In the *ex parte Smith* litigation, English courts have so far felt unable to strike down the policy of discharging known lesbians and gays – whether as sufficiently irrational that it cannot survive judicial review, or by relying on arguments derived from the European Convention on Human Rights.[117] The policy would clearly have to be reversed, however, should the European Court of Justice recognize the logical implication of the *P* v. *S* reasoning for lesbians and gays.

Partnership rights

Lesbian and gay partnerships or marriages are not legally recognized in the UK,[118] Canada[119] or – with one disputed exception – in the United States.[120] The sole US exception is the decision of the Hawaii Supreme Court, in *Baehr* v. *Lewin*, that it is *prima facie* sex discrimination under the Hawaii state constitution to exclude lesbian or gay couples from marriage.[121] The case is currently being appealed to the Supreme Court, and in the meantime the federal authorities have passed the Defense of Marriage Act 1996 in an attempt to confine the definition of marriage to heterosexual unions only. The prevalent exclusionary stance is sometimes seen as being a form of discrimination in itself against lesbians and gays, in that legal recognition of heterosexual relationships, via the civil marriage ceremony, is a basic element of social life in all three societies.[122] There are, however, mixed feelings among lesbians and gays about the notion that the law should simply recognize a same-sex equivalent of heterosexual marriage.[123] While this particular argument lies beyond the scope of this chapter, it is clear for present purposes that refusal to grant legal status to same-sex partnerships can have tangible and disadvantageous consequences for members of such partnerships in fields such as property rights, inheritance and social security.

Examples can be found in all three legal systems. In England, a lesbian whose partner had died was denied the right to succeed to the partner's tenancy of their home, for such a right was defined in legislation as applying only to unmarried heterosexual couples.[124] In the USA, the families of deceased lesbians and gays can effectively exclude their partners, should they so choose, from having access to the deathbed, the body or the funeral. If the deceased partner has not left a will, their property will be inherited by their family rather than passing to the surviving partner, sometimes resulting in the surviving partner losing their home if they were cohabiting with the partner who died. The 1996 Defense of Marriage Act – the constitutionality of which will be made clear once the Supreme Court has considered *Baehr* v. *Lewin* – explicitly denies federal social security benefits to partners in a same-sex marriage. The position would be reversed, it has been argued, by the legal recognition of lesbian and gay partnerships – whether on the same level as unmarried but cohabiting heterosexuals, or on the level of heterosexual marriage.[125]

The most obvious recent example in Canadian law is the *Egan* case, where the Supreme Court of Canada held that it is permissible under the Charter to confine the payment of a social security benefit to partners in heterosexual relationships.[126] The facts of the case were as follows. Canadian old age security legislation provides for a 'spousal allowance' to be paid to spouses of pensioners, when the spouse is aged between 60 and 65 and the combined income of the couple falls below a certain level.[127] The statutory definition of 'spouse' is confined to persons of the opposite sex, so that Egan's same-sex partner was refused the allowance when he applied for it, even though the two men had lived together since 1948 and their combined income was below the requisite level. The main argument advanced by the two men was therefore that the legislative definition of 'spouse' violated section 15(1) of the Charter, discriminating on the basis of sexual orientation.

Having accepted that sexual orientation could constitute an 'analogous ground' (see above), the Canadian Supreme Court decided by a majority of only one that there had been discriminatory impact, on the grounds that the opposite sex definition of 'spouse' in the legislation could only be based on sexual orientation, and that it reinforced the derogatory stereotype that homosexuals could not form caring and lasting relationships. By a majority, however, the Court dismissed the applicants' claim on the justifiability point, finding that given the limited funds available for assisting disadvantaged groups, it was legitimate for the government to decide to prioritize assisting poor elderly couples of a heterosexual variety before assisting their same-sex equivalents. Carl Stychin notes that the majority's treatment of the section 1 justifiability point shows a 'quite unprecedented' degree of deference to the government.[128]

A particularly controversial set of cases concerns parents who have 'come out' as lesbian or gay (although the more accurate label, in some circumstances, might be bisexual) and who seek custody over or rights of access to their children from a previous heterosexual relationship.[129] These cases raise two relevant issues. The first is whether lesbian and gay parents are being treated fairly by the courts. The second issue is how the courts react to parents who are in a new relationship with a partner of the same sex.

In English law, there is no automatic presumption that a lesbian or gay parent's wishes will be overridden in custody or access decisions. In *Re D*, a case where a gay man sought to prevent the adoption of his son by his ex-wife and her new husband, the House of Lords ruled that it was justifiable, on the facts, to dispense with his objections to the adoption order, but Lord Wilberforce took care to stress that:

> there is nothing in the present decision which would warrant or support a general principle of dispensing with a parent's consent on the ground of homosexual conduct alone. The courts in these cases are not concerned to condemn, or tolerate, the way in which adults choose, legally, to live.[130]

In other cases, courts have stressed that a parent's living in a relationship with someone of the same sex will not automatically act as a bar to their gaining custody, although it will *always* be a factor to be taken into account.[131]

Giving judgment in *Re D*, Lord Wilberforce went on to stress, however, that:

> Whatever new attitudes Parliament, or public tolerance, may have chosen to take as regards the behaviour of consenting adults ... *inter se*, these should not entitle the courts to relax, in any degree, the vigilance and severity with which they should regard the risk of children, at critical ages, being exposed or introduced to ways of life which ... may lead to severance from normal society, to psychological stresses and unhappiness and possibly even to physical experiences which may scar them for life.[132]

This highlights two particular anxieties which courts have been eager to take into account in custody disputes: what has been labelled the 'corruption' argument, and what is known as the 'reputation' or stigmatization argument.[133]

The corruption argument, crudely put, centres on the fear that children brought up in lesbian or gay households will be 'turned into homosexuals'.[134] Such a possibility has generally been discounted on the facts of most cases,[135] but courts remain disturbingly willing to accept the idea as a theoretical possibility. An interesting example is *B* v. *B*, a case concerning the custody of a 2-year-old boy whose mother was now cohabiting with another woman, and whose father was living in a heterosexual relationship.[136] Judge Callman appeared to accept medical evidence suggesting that the very idea of 'corruption' was a nonsense, yet still tested for the possibility on the facts – concluding that 'there is no need for any concern about [the boy] on that score' due to his 'unequivocal [*sic*] boyish appearance and conduct', to the fact that the father would retain an active role in his upbringing, and to the fact that the mother wished the boy to grow up heterosexual.[137]

The 'reputation' or stigmatization argument concerns the possibility that if a child is brought up in a lesbian or gay household, they will suffer teasing or ostracism from schoolmates, causing the child distress or embarrassment. Sir John Arnold P. observed in *Re P* that 'One does not have to be a psychiatrist to appreciate that a lesbian household would quite likely be the subject of embarrassing conduct and comment, particularly among the child's friends', and that this 'disadvantage' had to be weighed in the balance in making the custody decision.[138] 'Stigmatization' has been treated as an important factor in a number of cases: in *B* v. *B*, for example, Judge Callman described the stigmatization and 'reputation' issue as 'the most worrying aspect of this case, and I have borne this very much in mind'.[139]

In consequence, the approaches taken in these cases have at least two disturbing aspects from the perspective of lesbian and gay parents. An obvious and practical worry is that while there is no official presumption against lesbian or gay parents obtaining custody or access, they do face the extra hurdles – which a heterosexual parent would not – of having to fend off the stigmatization argument and its less powerful 'corruption' counterpart. Their personal relationship is automatically a factor to be weighed in the balance, whereas that of the heterosexual parent is not.

The second worry is that although courts have been prepared to grant custody to the lesbian or gay parent in a number of cases,[140] a very negative picture of lesbians and gays appears to inform all the decisions. It may seem unlikely that a court would nowadays echo the opinion of the trial judge in *Re D* (decided in 1976) to the effect that a reasonable father, knowing that he was gay, would want to protect his son by severing contact with him forever so as to free the son from the danger of coming to know about his father's lifestyle (an opinion which the House of Lords endorsed).[141] A very negative picture still seems to emerge from later cases, however: in *Re P*, Watkins LJ began his judgment by talking of his unease at having to leave the child in the custody of her (lesbian) mother:

> This is neither the time nor the place to moralize about sexual deviance and its consequences by those who practise it . . . [but] the possible effect on a young child living in proximity to that practice is of crucial importance to that child and to the public interest.[142]

A child, the judge believed, should be left in the custody of a mother who was carrying on a lesbian relationship only when there was 'no other acceptable alternative form of custody'.[143]

A regular concern of English family courts in these cases is to ensure that lesbian or gay parents do not 'flaunt' their sexual orientation. In *Whitfield* v. *Whitfield*, where the mother and (heterosexual) father were awarded joint custody of their daughters, Ormrod LJ said that he would:

> leave it . . . to the good sense of the mother to conduct her own personal life in such a way that it does not impinge too much on her children because I cannot really believe that she wants her twins to grow up as homosexual girls rather than normal girls . . .[144]

In *C v. C*, Glidewell LJ observed that despite the changes in sexual morality which had taken place over the previous thirty years, it was 'axiomatic that the ideal environment for the upbringing of a child is the home of loving, caring and sensible parents, her father and her mother'. Other alternatives might have to be considered when that ideal could not be attained, but a lesbian relationship remained an unusual background against which to bring up a child. Doubtless the mother realized this, the judge suggested, since she chose not to 'flaunt' her relationship.[145]

Perhaps the most graphic expression of concerns about 'flaunting' can be found in Judge Callman's judgment in *B v. B*:

> Let me say categorically, and I want to state this as [a] matter of principle: what is so important in cases is to distinguish between militant lesbians who try to convert others to their way of life, where there may well be risks that counterbalance other aspects of welfare and are detrimental to the long-term interests of children either in relation to

their sexual identity or corruption, and lesbians in private. In this case, I am dealing with two lesbians who are private persons who both do not believe in advertising their lesbianism and acting in the public field in favour of promoting lesbianism. It is their personal relationship . . . so it is a wholly different kind of case from that of the militant lesbianism, where the risks which a judge has to assess in the balancing exercise on the question of sexual identity may be so much greater.[146]

Judge Callman fails to explain how, *as a matter of principle*, one is to distinguish between a militant lesbian and a private lesbian. Nevertheless, the judge's statement encapsulates what could be described as the crux of the second worry for lesbian and gay parents: for the 'corruption' argument and concerns about 'flaunting' only carry weight if one first assumes that it is a morally inferior or second-class situation to start off or end up with a lesbian or gay sexual orientation. The not very well concealed message emerging from the cases is that lesbian and gay parents will be tolerated only if they keep their sexual orientation hidden from others – especially children – who may be 'tarnished' if they come into contact with it.

This raises another interesting aspect of the cases, namely the fragile picture of heterosexuality which many of the judges appear to possess (in the language of chapter 3, some of them might even be said to veer towards a radical constructionist approach). For the 'corruption' argument again makes sense only if it is assumed that a heterosexual orientation can easily be snatched away from children unless proper care is taken.

Similar types of concern seem to be evident in the US case law, which exhibits a wide variety of approaches in child custody cases – some of which are distinctly harsher to lesbian and gay parents than the stance adopted by English courts. The paramount consideration in US child custody cases is the interests of the child.[147] In consequence, lesbian or gay parents have been denied custody on the basis (as in English law) of fears about stigmatization, fears about the child's moral well-being, or fears about the child's sexual orientation if left with the non-heterosexual parent.[148] Each of these arguments can be seen, as in the English cases, to rest on a hostile attitude towards the validity of lesbian and gay relationships.[149] It has been suggested that the crucial factor in custody decisions, even if they are couched only in terms of the parents' sexual orientation in the abstract, is whether they are in a relationship with a partner of the same sex.[150] In *M.J.P.* v. *J.G.P.*, the existence of an openly acknowledged same-sex relationship was found to be sufficient to merit a change in the custody decision,[151] and in other cases courts have suggested that the parent's participation or continued participation in a lesbian or gay relationship was crucial in the final decision concerning custody or access rights.[152]

Given the variation in the law applicable from state to state, it has been suggested that three distinct approaches can be discerned in the custody cases.[153] In US states such as Missouri and Virginia, a parent's participation in a lesbian or gay relationship gives rise to an irrebuttable presumption that they should not be granted custody of the child – clearly a harsher approach than that adopted by English courts.[154] In other cases, lesbian or gay parents have been required to disprove a rebuttable presumption that it would harm the child if they were granted custody.[155] In yet another group of US states, including Alaska and Massachusetts, it appears to be the case that courts cannot deny custody solely on the basis of a parent's sexual orientation, although a decision may sometimes be taken against the lesbian or gay parent on the basis that a 'nexus' of harm to the child's welfare can be established.[156] The approach of the English courts would appear to fall somewhere between these latter two groups of cases.

A factor which has been influential in some US cases is the widespread illegality of lesbian and gay sexual acts in the USA (a factor which is not, of course, important in the recent English custody decisions). Thus, state anti-sodomy statutes have been cited as embodying a state interest against homosexuality or as giving rise to an assumption that a lesbian or gay parent is a criminal and therefore not a fit parent.[157] More recently, the ever-present *Bowers* v. *Hardwick* has been cited in support of a New Hampshire law prohibiting lesbians and gays from fostering and adopting children.[158] These types of assumption would not come into play in custody, adoption or fostering cases involving heterosexual parents.

State intolerance: lesbians and gays in the political process

The issues which are discussed in this section are connected with the ability of lesbians and gays to express their political concerns (including law reform demands), and with recent attempts to censor discussion of lesbian and gay issues and to prevent lesbians and gays from successfully pressing for law reform measures.

The most obvious example in the UK of officially encouraged censorship of lesbian and gay issues – not to say censure of lesbians and gays[159] – is section 28 of the 1988 Local Government Act. The section's *raison d'être* is instantly revealed in its wording:

A local authority shall not –

(a) intentionally promote homosexuality or publish material with the intention of promoting homosexuality;

(b) promote the teaching in any maintained school of the acceptability of homosexuality as a pretended family relationship.[160]

Kenneth Norrie suggests that the wording of the section involves 'a logical impossibility', in that 'people already are homosexual. People do not choose to be converted to homosexuality, just as they do not choose to be converted to heterosexuality.'[161] As we will see in chapter 3, Norrie's argument in fact may not be seen as sound if one adopts a radical constructionist perspective, but it does highlight the section's perception of homosexuality as a morally inferior way of life from which people can be discouraged. In this sense, the section appears to embody the type of belief common among those on the 'Christian' right in the USA, to the effect that 'becoming' lesbian or gay is a matter of choice. The words 'acceptability . . . as a pretended family relationship' also reveal a degree of animus usually absent from legislative drafting in the UK.

The practical effect of section 28 has been rather hard to measure. It has never been the subject of authoritative judicial interpretation, and the word 'promote' is altogether too vague to offer any clear guidance to local authorities.[162] According to Madeleine Colvin and Jane Hawksley, some local authorities imposed 'censorship and discrimination' shortly after the section became law,[163] but the legislation seems to have receded into general obscurity since then. A recent – and rare – example of section 28 being invoked occurred in 1995, when one local authority used the section to justify its refusal to stock a lesbian and gay newspaper in its public libraries. The authority rapidly backed down when threatened with legal action, however.[164] Given that courts may seek guidance from ministerial statements recorded in *Hansard*, the record of Parliamentary debates, when interpreting obscure legislation,[165] it may be the case that local authorities would simply have difficulty relying on section 28 in court in light of the long list of things expressly declared by ministers to be *excluded* from the scope of the section.[166] Section 28 is, therefore, a classic example of a law which is too vague to be enforced on a widespread basis. While the section may not have had the drastic impact on local authority services feared at the time of its passage, however, it still remains an ugly and very public symbol of officially sanctioned prejudice against lesbians and gays, which may be felt by some to confer legitimacy on their personal prejudices.[167]

More precisely tailored laws are sometimes used in the UK to censor lesbian and gay materials, including magazines and books. Apart from the 'conspiracy to corrupt public morals' offence used against the contact advertisements in *Knuller*,[168] the common law offence of blasphemous libel has been used against the then-prominent lesbian and gay publication *Gay News*, in a case brought by the 'family values' campaigner Mary Whitehouse in connection with a poem describing a homosexual fantasy involving Christ.[169] The range of statutory offences contained in the Obscene Publications Acts 1959 and 1964 might also be used to censor lesbian and gay publications, and lesbian and gay bookshops have often found themselves on the receiving end of raids or prosecutions relating to the importation or sending of prohibited materials.[170]

In the US, 'Christian' right-inspired campaigns against lesbians and gays have developed such momentum that they have evolved from attempts to repeal state-level anti-discrimination protections through to attempts to prohibit – via amendments to state constitutions – the possible adoption of such measures.[171] A common campaigning tactic is to claim that anti-discrimination protections amount to 'special rights' for lesbians and gays. Amendment 2 to the Colorado State Constitution (the text of which was set out in chapter 1) was perhaps the best-known product of a campaign of this sort. We have already discussed the animus-based Equal Protection analysis used by the US Supreme Court to rule the Amendment unconstitutional in *Romer* v. *Evans*. In the Colorado Supreme Court, the Amendment had been set aside on the ground that the Equal Protection provisions of the US Constitution uphold a fundamental right to participate equally in the political process, that a state constitutional amendment which infringed this by excluding an independently identifiable class of people – including lesbians and gays – would be subjected to strict scrutiny, and that no compelling state interest in favour of Amendment 2 could be shown.[172] Despite its limitations, the US Supreme Court's ruling has at least granted lesbians and gays the minimal protection of not having existing legal safeguards repealed at state level as a result of expressly hostile campaigns.

Given the First Amendment guarantee of freedom of expression, one area where lesbians and gays are granted some constitutional protection is in the organization of public demonstrations, discussions and statements about their sexual orientation.[173] People who choose to take advantage of this freedom may, however, still find themselves legally penalized if they work for a public employer – like the military – which prohibits its employees from engaging in same-sex oral and anal intercourse: as the *Ben-Shalom* case demonstrates, a statement of one's sexual orientation may be interpreted as implying a desire to commit sexual acts with people of the same sex, thereby permitting one's discharge from the military.[174] In *Shahar* v. *Bowers*, an analogous case – albeit one which did not directly concern expression – a law student who had accepted an offer of employment in the Georgia Attorney General's office (i.e. the office which had been involved in *Bowers* v. *Hardwick*) found the offer withdrawn when it emerged that she and her female partner were about to undergo a commitment ceremony.[175] Her challenge to the withdrawal of the offer failed on the ground that, while her relationship may have been a constitutionally protected intimate association, her openness about it showed a lack of discretion and her employment would have hampered the Attorney General's efforts to enforce Georgia's anti-sodomy law.

Conclusion

At an intuitive level, one may well react with concern to many or all of the legal issues outlined in this chapter. What is crucial, however – at least if a coherent law reform strategy is to be devised – is to consider the issues presented here in terms of our two central questions. Why, in other words, are some or all of the laws presented here to be seen as sufficiently objectionable that amending or repealing them is justifiable in principle? And will such amendment or repeal produce results which are worthwhile in practice? It is only in terms of a workable justification for law reform that we can properly claim that the present law involves *injustice*; and it is only if law reform will help remedy that injustice in practice that it is really worth pressing for.

These central questions give rise, in turn, to a whole host of subsidiary issues. Can the same justification be used for reforming all of the laws set out here? If not, is this a reason for searching for an alternative justification, or is it a reason for saying that some of the issues which have been presented should not really be of concern to lesbians and gays? How, furthermore, does our second central question impact on the first in practice? The military employment cases provide a useful example here, in that it is sometimes argued that while lesbian and gay service personnel are treated unjustifiably under UK and US law, little or no priority should not be given to campaigning on this issue since to do so would merely serve to validate the military as an institution in which it is *desirable* to serve.[176] This leads to the broader question of the order of priority which should be attached to reforming the different laws set out here which are hostile to lesbians and gays, if one believes that reform is justifiable in principle.

A connected question is whether (and which of) the legal issues discussed here should be described as raising matters of lesbian and gay rights. Chapter 3 is intended to provide the apparatus by which this question can be answered. For the moment, it is sufficient to observe that supporters of different law reform justifications will undoubtedly have different views about the matter. It is also important to consider how far the interests of lesbians and gays in reforming any of the laws discussed in this chapter should be counterbalanced by the interests of others. Is it possible, for example, that society may sometimes legitimately declare, under a just system of family law, that children have interests which are in opposition to those of lesbian and gay parents and which should outweigh them? In practice, many questions of law reform will involve a balancing exercise between countervailing justifications, as well as consideration of competing rights and responsibilities.

The material presented in this chapter is, then, designed to serve as a practical backdrop against which the broader questions of later chapters can be considered. It is to these which we now turn.

Notes

1. See further Richard Plant, *The Pink Triangle: The Nazi War Against Homosexuals* (Edinburgh: Mainstream Publishing, 1987), esp. pp. 148–9, 153–4, 230–2; Heinz Heger, *The Men With The Pink Triangle* (London: GMP, 1972, intro. by David Fernbach), pp. 13–15;

Gunter Grau (ed.), *Hidden Holocaust?: Gay and Lesbian Persecution in Germany 1933–45* (London: Cassell, 1995). These materials suggest that while many lesbians were persecuted in Nazi Germany, this did not occur on such a scale as – or with the ideological fervour devoted to – the persecution of gay men: see Plant, pp. 114–16; Grau (ed.), pp. xxv, 8–15.
2. Plant, *The Pink Triangle*, p. 148.
3. In Heger, *The Men With The Pink Triangle*, pp. 8–9. The relevant law was contained in section 175 of the German Penal Code, set out in Grau (ed.), *Hidden Holocaust?*, pp. 64–6.
4. Heger, *The Men With The Pink Triangle*, p. 114.
5. Disturbing evidence as to the extent of homophobia and violent homophobic attacks in the USA is to be found in David Deitcher (ed.), *Over the Rainbow: Lesbian and Gay Politics in America Since Stonewall* (London: Boxtree/Channel Four, 1995).
6. For a more comprehensive account of English law (albeit written before the passage of the Criminal Justice and Public Order Act 1994), see Robert Wintemute, 'Sexual orientation discrimination', ch. 15 in Christopher McCrudden and Gerald Chambers (eds), *Individual Rights and the Law in Britain* (Oxford: Clarendon Press, 1994), esp. pp. 498–515. A somewhat outdated, but nevertheless useful book is Paul Crane's *Gays and the Law* (London: Pluto Press, 1982). See also Mark Guthrie and Angus Hamilton, *The Lesbian and Gay Rights Handbook* (London: Cassell, forthcoming).
7. (1986) 106 S Crt 2841.
8. Cf. Robert Wintemute, *Sexual Orientation and Human Rights: The United States Constitution, the European Convention, and the Canadian Charter* (Oxford: Clarendon Press, 1995), p. 150.
9. Another important issue here is insurance – on which, see Peter Roth and Wesley Gryk, 'AIDS and insurance', ch. 6 in Richard Haigh and Dai Harris (eds), *AIDS: A Guide to the Law* (London: Routledge, 2nd edn, 1995).
10. See Jeffrey Weeks, *Coming Out: Homosexual Politics in Britain from the Nineteenth Century to the Present* (London: Quartet, 1977), chs 7–9 (see especially pp. 106–7 for discussion of the rejection, in 1921, of an attempt to extend the provisions of the 1885 Criminal Law Amendment Act governing male homosexual acts to women).
11. In England and Wales, 'buggery with another person or with an animal' and 'gross indecency' were categorized as 'unnatural offences' in the Sexual Offences Act 1956, ss. 12, 13.
12. See Stephen Jeffery-Poulter, *Peers, Queers and Commons: the Struggle for Gay Law Reform from 1950 to the Present* (London: Routledge, 1991), pp. 8–10.
13. For general discussion of US law, see Note, 'Developments in the law – Sexual orientation' (1989) 102 *Harvard Law Review* 1508.
14. It is unclear whether the state law in a twenty-third state, Massachusetts, is still constitutionally enforceable.
15. Mississippi Code Ann. s. 97–29–59 (1972).
16. (1986) 106 S Crt 2841.
17. For a useful discussion, see Wintemute, *Sexual Orientation and Human Rights*, ch. 2.
18. (1986) 106 S Crt at 2843.
19. *Ibid.* at 2847.
20. *Ibid.* at 2843.
21. *Ibid.* at 2844.
22. *Ibid.* at 2844.
23. *Ibid.* at 2846.
24. *Ibid.* at 2846–7.
25. *Ibid.* at 2847.
26. *Ibid.* at 2848. Justice Powell's views of the case are discussed in William Rubenstein (ed.), *Lesbians, Gay Men and the Law* (New York: New Press, 1993), pp. 148–9.
27. *Ibid.*, pp. 152–4.
28. See *Commonwealth v. Wasson* (1992) 842 SW 2d 487 (Kentucky Supreme Court); *State v. Morales*

(1992) 826 SW 2d 201 (Texas Court of Appeal), reversed at (1994) 869 SW 2d 941 (Texas Supreme Court).
29. 'Beyond the privacy principle' (1992) 92 *Columbia Law Review* 1431; see also David Deitcher, 'Law and desire', ch. 3 in Deitcher (ed.), *Over the Rainbow*.
30. See, e.g., *Carter v. State* (1973) 500 SW 2d 368 (Arkansas); *Canfield v. State* (1973) 506 F 2d 987 (Oklahoma); *People v. Superior Court* (1988) 758 P 2d 1046 (California).
31. Sexual Offences Act 1967, s. 1 (amending Sexual Offences Act 1956, ss. 12 and 13). Homosexual acts in public lavatories and 'where more than two people take part or are present' are specifically deemed to be illegal in s. 1(2) of the 1967 Act. For judicial interpretation of 'gross indecency', see *R. v. Preece* [1970] Crim LR 296.
32. [1974] Crim LR 615.
33. Criminal Justice (Scotland) Act 1980, s. 80; Homosexual Offences (Northern Ireland) Order 1982, s. 3. Decriminalization in Northern Ireland followed the ruling of the European Court of Human Rights in *Dudgeon v. United Kingdom* (1981) 4 EHRR 149 (for related decisions, see *Norris v. Ireland* (1989) 13 EHRR 187; *Modinos v. Cyprus* (1993) 16 EHRR 485).
34. Criminal Justice and Public Order Act 1994, ss. 143, 145(1) (respectively amending Sexual Offences Act 1956, s. 12 and Sexual Offences Act 1967, s. 1). The law applicable in Scotland and Northern Ireland was similarly amended by s. 145 of the 1994 Act.
35. Cf. Sexual Offences Act 1956, s. 14.
36. Sections 12 and 13 of the Sexual Offences Act 1956 (codifying the earlier criminal law) declared 'buggery' and 'gross indecency' to be wholly illegal; as a matter of drafting, these sections were merely watered down rather than repealed in the 1967 and 1994 Acts.
37. [1973] AC 435.
38. *Ibid*. at 460.
39. *Ibid*. at 457. For an analogous reading of the 1967 Act, see *Re D* [1977] AC 603 at 629 (Lord Wilberforce), 637 (Lord Simon).
40. Sexual Offences Act 1956, s. 13; Sexual Offences Act 1967, s. 4.
41. Sexual Offences Act 1956, s. 32; *R. v. Kirkup* (1993) 96 Cr App Rep 352.
42. For the position in other EC member states, see Kees Waaldijk, 'The legal situation in the member states', ch. 3 in Kees Waaldijk and Andrew Clapham (eds), *Homosexuality: A European Community Issue* (Dordrecht: Martinus Nijhoff, 1993), pp. 85–6. An application concerning the UK's age of consent provisions is currently before the European Commission on Human Rights for adjudication under the provisions of the European Convention on Human Rights, binding on the UK in international law.
43. Andrew Ashworth, *Principles of Criminal Law* (Oxford: Clarendon Press, 2nd edn, 1995) p. 352; see also J. Clifford Hindley, 'The age of consent for male homosexuals' [1986] *Criminal Law Review* 595.
44. 1967 Sexual Offences Act, s. 1(2)(a).
45. Sexual Offences Act 1956, s. 12.
46. Public Order Act 1986, s. 5(1). This replaces the old statutory offence of using 'insulting behaviour' whereby a breach of the peace may be occasioned – an offence for which two men who had been kissing at a public bus stop at 2 a.m. were convicted in *Masterson v. Holden* [1986] 3 All ER 39. For recent authority on the s. 5(1) offence, see *DPP v. Orum* [1989] 1 WLR 88. See generally Frances Russell, 'Soliciting discrimination' (1996) 146 *New Law Journal* 187 and 223.
47. See Wintemute, 'Sexual orientation discrimination', p. 501.
48. Sexual Offences Act 1967, s. 1(2)(b). See also *R. v. Preece*, n. 31 above;

Parkin v. Norman [1983] QB 92; Chief Constable of Hampshire v. Mace (1987) 84 Cr App Rep 40; R. v. Kirkup, n. 41 above. For recent examples, see H.C. Deb., 13 July 1990, columns 649–50, 653; Pink Paper, 21 July 1995, p. 1.

49. See, e.g., R. v. Kirkup, n. 41 above; Crane, Gays and the Law, pp. 20, 22, 25, 34–5.

50. Cited in Antony Grey, Quest for Justice: Towards Homosexual Emancipation (London: Sinclair-Stevenson, 1992), pp. 125–6.

51. Wintemute, 'Sexual orientation discrimination', p. 498. The same argument can be made about the laws of Scotland and Northern Ireland.

52. [1994] 1 AC 212. The decision of the House of Lords was later upheld by the European Court of Human Rights: Laskey, Jaggard and Brown v. United Kingdom (109/1995/615/703–705), 19 February 1997.

53. See, e.g., Wintemute, Sexual Orientation and Human Rights, pp. 11–12. However, R. v. Wilson, The Times 5 March 1996, suggests that a more lenient attitude may be taken towards physically injurious activity between a married heterosexual couple.

54. For a recent example, see the Guardian, 2 January 1996, p. 12 – 'Christians are boycotting Disney for giving benefits to gays'.

55. By far the best account of the workings of 'New Christian Right' groups in Canada can be found in Didi Herman's Rights of Passage: Struggles for Lesbian and Gay Legal Equality (Toronto: University of Toronto Press, 1994), esp. chs 5 and 6.

56. For discussion of the 1980s backlash, see Jeffery-Poulter, Peers, Queers and Commons, chs 10 and 11; Davina Cooper, Sexing the City: Lesbian and Gay Politics Within the Activist State (London: Rivers Oram, 1994).

57. Cf. the Independent, 9 November 1995, p.5; the Guardian Weekend, 25 November 1995, p. 14; Mab Segrest, 'Visibility and backlash', in Deitcher (ed.), Over the Rainbow, ch. 2; Richard Mohr, Gays/Justice: A Study of Ethics, Society, and Law (New York: Columbia University Press, 1988), pp. 164–8. An analogous issue is the possibility of blackmail of gay men caught engaging in technically illegal sexual acts – cf. the reported comments of Judge Crabtree when sentencing a defendant found guilty of blackmailing rich gays (whom the defendant had presumably caught 'cottaging' in a public lavatory): 'I don't have a lot of time for homosexuals who clutter up lavatories, but they don't deserve what you have done to them' (The Times, 27 January 1996, p. 4).

58. Cf. Sex Discrimination Act 1975, Part III; Race Relations Act 1987, Part III. For an example of discrimination in the provision of 'goods, facilities and services', see Gill & Coote v. El Vino Co [1983] QB 425.

59. The European Convention on Human Rights (often mistakenly confused with EC law by non-lawyers) is a largely separate body of rules which binds the UK only as a matter of international law – see R v. Home Secretary, ex parte Brind [1991] 1 AC 696.

60. In the USA, discrimination on the ground of a person's sexual orientation is prohibited in California, Connecticut, District of Columbia, Hawaii, Massachusetts, Minnesota, New Jersey, Vermont and Wisconsin; in Canada, it is prohibited in British Columbia, Manitoba, New Brunswick, Nova Scotia, Ontario, Quebec, Saskatchewan and Yukon Territory.

61. See, e.g., Herman, Rights of Passage, ch. 3.

62. Andrews v. Law Society of British Columbia [1989] 1 SCR 143. For further discussion, see Marc Gold, 'Comment: Andrews v. Law Society of British Columbia' (1989) 34 McGill Law Journal 1063, esp. at 1069; Wintemute, Sexual Orientation and Human Rights, pp. 154–62.

63. Andrews v. Law Society of British Columbia, n. 62 above.

64. At Federal Court of Appeal level, Robertson JA argued that the lesbian and gay cases could be divided into two categories. First, cases in which an *individual* had been denied access to or was disentitled from receiving a benefit. Issues of discrimination in employment and the provision of housing and services fell within this category, to which province or territory-level anti-discrimination laws often applied. Second, cases where the issue was of criteria governing entitlement to a benefit being based on *spousal* status (including *Egan* itself) – (1993) 103 DLR (4th) 336 at 383–9.
65. [1995] 2 SCR 513. Previous decisions of lower courts where this point was accepted (or conceded) include *Veysey* v. *Canada (Correctional Services)* [1990] 1 FC 321 at 364 (Trial Division); (1990) 109 NR 300 at 304 (FCA); *Knodel* v. *British Columbia (Medical Services Commission)* (1991) 58 BCLR (2d) 356 at 371; *Haig* v. *Canada* (1992) 9 OR (3d) 495 at 501.
66. For comment on *Egan*, see Wintemute, *Sexual Orientation and Human Rights*, pp. 254–60; 'Discrimination against same-sex couples: Sections 15(1) and 1 of the *Charter*' (1995) 74 *Canadian Bar Review* 682; Carl Stychin, 'Novel concepts: A comment on *Egan and Nesbit* v. *The Queen*' (1995) 6 *Constitutional Forum Constitutionnel* 101; Leon Trakman, 'Section 15: Equality? Where?' (1995) 6 *Constitutional Forum Constitutionnel* 112.
67. Canadian Charter of Rights and Freedoms, s. 32; *Retail, Wholesale & Department Store Union* v. *Dolphin Delivery* [1986] 2 SCR 573; *Andrews* v. *Law Society of British Columbia*, n. 62 above; *Canada (Attorney-General)* v. *Mossop* (1990) 71 DLR (4th) 661 at 677 (Marceau JA).
68. See n. 65 above.
69. See Wintemute, *Sexual Orientation and Human Rights*, pp. 223–4.
70. *Ibid.*, p. 222.
71. (1996) 116 S Ct 1620.
72. Ronald Dworkin, 'Sex, death, and the courts', *New York Review of Books*, 8 August 1996, p. 44.
73. See, e.g., *High Tech Gays* v. *Defense Industrial Security Clearance Office* (1990) 895 F 2d 563 at 571.
74. See n. 7 above at 571. See also *Ben-Shalom* v. *Marsh* (1989) 871 F 2d 454 at 464–5; *Woodward* v. *U.S.* (1989) 871 F 2d 1068 at 1076.
75. *Watkins* v. *U.S. Army* (1988) 837 F 2d 1428.
76. *Ibid.* at 1331.
77. For alternative Equal Protection formulations, see Wintemute, *Sexual Orientation and Human Rights*, pp. 61–78.
78. See n. 75 above at 1345.
79. *Ibid.* at 1345–7.
80. *Ibid.* at 1347–8. See also *Equality Foundation of Greater Cincinnati* v. *City of Cincinnati* (1994) 860 F Supp 417 at 437 (reversed by Court of Appeals, 1995, unreported).
81. See n. 75 above at 1348. The 'discrete and insular minority' formulation derives from *U.S.* v. *Carolene Products* (1938) 304 US 144 at 152–3 n. 4.
82. See n. 75 above at 1349–52.
83. *Ibid.* at 1336–9.
84. *Ibid.* at 1340 (emphasis added).
85. *Ibid.* at 1345.
86. *Ibid.* at 1345. The possible impact of *Bowers* v. *Hardwick* on Equal Protection claims is discussed by Richard Posner, *Sex and Reason* (Cambridge, MA: Harvard University Press, 1992), pp. 341–50.
87. (1989) 875 F 2d 699 at 711 (Circuit Judge Norris), 731 (Judge Canby).
88. See n. 73 above.
89. 'Litigating for lesbian and gay rights: A legal history' (1993) 79 *Virginia Law Review* 1551 at 1641.
90. See n. 75 above at 1358.
91. See n. 73 above at 571, 574–7. See also *Steffan* v. *Perry* (1991) 780 F Supp 1.
92. See, e.g., *Opinion of the Justices* (1987) 530 A 2d 21; *Doe* v. *Sparkes* (1990) 733 F Supp 227.
93. *Steffan* v. *Perry* (1994) 41 F 3d 677; see also *Ben-Shalom*, n. 74 above. For further discussion, see Wintemute, *Sexual Orientation and Human Rights*, pp. 78–83, 86–90;

Carl Stychin, *Law's Desire: Sexuality and the Limits of Justice* (London: Routledge, 1995), ch. 5. For an intermediate constitutional position, see *National Gay Task Force v. City of Oklahoma* (1984) 729 F 2d 1270.
94. See n. 7 above at 2846–7.
95. Dworkin, 'Sex, death, and the courts', p. 50.
96. *Ibid.*
97. Wintemute, *Sexual Orientation and Human Rights*, p. 72.
98. *Able v. U.S.* (1995, unreported).
99. The states are California, Connecticut, District of Columbia, Hawaii, Massachusetts, Minnesota, New Jersey, Vermont and Wisconsin. Under common law, see *Collins v. Shell Oil* (1991) 56 Fair Employment Prac. Cas. 440.
100. See Nicholas Bamforth, 'Sexual orientation and dismissal from employment' (1994) 144 *New Law Journal* 1402; R. A. Watt, 'HIV, discrimination, unfair dismissal and pressure to dismiss' (1992) 21 *Industrial Law Journal* 280, esp. pp. 281–4, 289–92; J. M. Thomson, 'Crime, morality and unfair dismissal' (1982) 98 *Law Quarterly Review* 423, pp. 449, 459–61.
101. [1980] IRLR 174 (EAT); [1981] IRLR 277 (Court of Session).
102. Compare *Wiseman v. Salford C.C.* [1981] IRLR 202.
103. [1977] IRLR 395.
104. Cases dealing with fellow employees include *Bell v. Devon & Cornwall Police Authority* [1978] IRLR 283; *Buck v. The Letchworth Palace* (1987, unreported).
105. See n. 103 above at 396.
106. See n. 101 above at 277 (Court of Session); see also *Buck*, discussed in Watt, 'HIV, discrimination, unfair dismissal and pressure to dismiss' at 283.
107. See further Bamforth, 'Sexual orientation and dismissal from employment'.
108. This argument depends upon the 'but for' test for direct discrimination adopted by the House of Lords in *R v. Birmingham City Council, ex parte E.O.C.* [1989] 1 AC 1155 and *James v. Eastleigh B.C.* [1990] 2 AC 751.
109. *Wallace & O'Rourke v. B.G. Turnkey Services (Scotland) Ltd* (unreported, 9 July 1993); for discussion, see Bamforth, 'Sexual orientation and dismissal from employment'.
110. *R v. Ministry of Defence, ex parte Smith* [1995] 4 All ER 427 at 449–51; (Divisional Court); [1996] 1 All ER 257 (Court of Appeal).
111. [1996] All ER (EC) 397 at 410 (para. 20).
112. The question whether lesbians and gays fall within the scope of the Directive after *P v. S* (which, if true, would mean that *Smith* was wrongly decided) will form the central issue in the *Grant* case, which was recently referred to the Court – see 'Europe court to rule in test case on gay rights at work', *Guardian*, 23 July 1996, p. 7.
113. For discussion of the Canadian context, see Wintemute, *Sexual Orientation and Human Rights*, ch. 8. The Hawaiian Supreme Court decision, *Baehr v. Lewin* (1993) 852 P 2d 44, was made only on the basis of the Hawaii state constitution. *Toonen v. Australia Communication* (1994) 1–3 IHRR 97 concerned the International Covenant on Civil and Political Rights; *S v. U.K.* (1986) 4 D&R 274 concerned the European Convention on Human Rights.
114. Examples include the Liberty/Stonewall Homosexual Equality Bill (published in 1992), and a distant offspring, the Sexual Orientation Discrimination Bill, introduced in the House of Lords in 1995.
115. On the general public law issues, see *Council of Civil Service Unions v. Minister for the Civil Service* [1985] 1 AC 374.
116. Criminal Justice and Public Order Act 1994, ss. 146–7.
117. See n. 110 above.
118. Matrimonial Causes Act 1773, s. 11(c). See *Corbett v. Corbett* [1970] 2 All ER 33.
119. *Layland v. Ontario (Minister of Consumer and Commercial*

Relations) (1993) 14 OR (3d) 658.
120. See, e.g., *Singer v. Hara* (1974) 522 P 2d 1187; *Dean v. District of Columbia* (1995) 653 A 2d 307 at 361.
121. See n. 113 above.
122. See, e.g., Andrew Sullivan, *Virtually Normal: An Argument About Homosexuality* (London: Picador, 1995), pp. 178–87.
123. Compare Didi Herman, 'Are we family? Lesbian rights and women's liberation' (1990) 28 *Osgoode Hall Law Journal* 789 and Herman, *Rights of Passage*, ch. 8; Suzanne Sherman (ed.), *Lesbian and Gay Marriages: Private Commitments, Public Ceremonies* (Philadelphia: Temple University Press, 1992); Nancy Polikoff 'We will not get what we ask for: Why legalizing gay and lesbian marriage will not "dismantle the legal structure of gender in every marriage"' (1993) 79 *Virginia Law Review* 1535.
124. *Harrogate B.C. v. Simpson* [1986] 2 Family LR 91.
125. For some harrowing examples of the current position in the USA, see Deitcher (ed.), *Over the Rainbow*, pp. 147–56. Note also that it would appear to be legitimate, in the USA, for employers to dismiss employees who declare that they are (or wish to be) in a same-sex marriage: *Singer v. U.S. Civil Service Commission* (1976) 530 F 2d 247; *Shahar v. Bowers* (1993) 836 F Supp 859.
126. See n. 65 above. An analogous issue, in Canadian law, is whether 'family status' protection under s. 3(1) of the Canadian Human Rights Act can apply to same-sex couples – see *Mossop v. Canada*, n. 67 above (Court of Appeal), [1993] 1 SCR 554 (Supreme Court).
127. Old Age Security Act, s. 2(1).
128. Stychin, 'Novel concepts', at 104.
129. See, generally, David Bradley, 'Homosexuality and child custody in English law' (1987) 1 *International Journal of Law and the Family* 155.
130. See n. 39 above at 629.
131. *Re P* (1983) 4 FLR 401; *B v. B* [1991] 1 FLR 402; *C v. C* [1991] 1 FLR 223 at 229, 231–2. In Scottish law, however, see now the more liberal decision in *T, Petitioner, The Times*, 20 August 1996.
132. See n. 39 above at 629.
133. *Re P*, n. 131 above at 404–5.
134. *S v. S* (1980) 1 FLR 143 at 146, per Orr LJ.
135. *Ibid.*; *Re P*, n. 131 above; *B v. B*, n. 131 above. The argument seems, however, to have played some role in *Re D*, n. 39 above.
136. See n. 131 above.
137. *Ibid.* at 405.
138. *Ibid.*
139. *Ibid.* at 406. See also *S v. S*, n. 134 above; *C v. C*, n. 131 above at 229, per Glidewell LJ. For an attempt to rebut such reasoning, see Helen Reece, 'The paramountcy principle: concensus or construct?' (1996) 49 *Current Legal Problems* Part 2, 267; 'Subverting the stigmatization argument' (1996) 23 *Journal of Law and Society* 484.
140. *S v. S*, n. 134 above; *Re P*, n. 131 above; *B v. B*, n. 131 above. See further Bradley, 'Homosexuality and child custody in English law', pp. 173–201.
141. See n. 39 above at 624, 632, 640, 641, 650.
142. See n. 131 above at 405.
143. *Ibid.*
144. Unreported, 4 November 1976.
145. See n. 131 above at 228.
146. See n. 131 above at 410.
147. See, e.g., *Pikula v. Pikula* (1985) 374 NW 2d 705 at 711 (Minnesota).
148. For further analysis, see Note, 'Custody denials to parents in same-sex relationships: an Equal Protection analysis' (1989) 102 *Harvard Law Review* 617 at 620.
149. For specific argument in the US constitutional context, see *ibid.* at 630–6.
150. *Ibid.* at 618.
151. (1982) 640 P 2d 966 (Oklahoma).
152. See, e.g., *A v. A* (1973) 514 P 2d 358; *N.K.M. v. L.E.M.* (1980) 606 SW 2d 179; *Conkel v. Conkel* (1987) 509 NE 2d 983.
153. Note, 'Custody denials to parents', at 619.
154. See *N.K.M. v. L.E.M.*, n. 152 above at 186; *Roe v. Roe* (1985) 324

SE 2d 691; *G.A. v. D.A.* (1987) 745 SW 2d 726 at 728.
155. Contrast *Hall v. Hall* (1980) 291 NW 2d 143; *Jacobson v. Jacobson* (1981) 314 NW 2d 79 at 80; *M.J.P. v. J.G.P.*, n. 151 above; *Constant A. v. Paul C.A.* (1985) 496 A 2d 1 at 5.
156. Contrast *Doe v. Doe* (1983) 452 NE 2d 293; *S.N.E. v. R.L.B.* (1985) 699 P 2d 875 at 879; with *D.H. v. J.H.* (1981) 418 NE 2d 286 at 293.
157. See, e.g., *Chaffin v. Fyre* (1975) 119 Cal Rptr 22 at 26; *L. v. D.* (1982) 630 SW 2d 240 at 243; *Roe v. Roe*, n. 154 above at 694; *Constant A. v. Paul C.A.*, n. 155 above at 5.
158. *Opinion of the Justices*, n. 92 above.
159. John Gardner describes Section 28 as a form of 'lifestyle censorship' – 'Freedom of expression' in McCrudden and Chambers (eds), *Individual Rights and the Law in Britain*, p. 211.
160. Local Government Act 1988, s. 28, inserting new s. 2A(1) into Local Government Act 1986. For discussion, see Madeleine Colvin and Jane Hawksley, *Section 28: A Practical Guide to the Law and its Implementation* (London: National Council for Civil Liberties, 1989).
161. Kenneth McK. Norrie, 'Symbolic and meaningless legislation' (September 1988) *Journal of the Law Society of Scotland* 310 at 312.
162. *Ibid.*; Wintemute, 'Sexual orientation discrimination', at 508–9.
163. Colvin and Hawksley, *Section 28*, pp. 5–6.
164. See the *Pink Paper*, 3 February 1995, p. 1.
165. *Pepper v. Hart* [1992] 3 WLR 1032.
166. See Colvin and Hawksley, *Section 28*, pp. 67–72.
167. See Wintemute, 'Sexual orientation discrimination', p. 509. On the effects of section 28 in schools, see Neville Harris, *The Law Relating to Schools* (London: Tolley, 2nd edn 1995), pp. 204–5.
168. See n. 37 above.
169. *Whitehouse v. Lemon* [1979] AC 617.
170. See, e.g., *R v. Bow Street Magistrates, ex parte Noncyp* [1988] 3 WLR 827.
171. See Wintemute, *Sexual Orientation and Human Rights*, pp. 57–8, for examples.
172. (1993) 854 P 2d 1270. Other cases where the validity of such amendments have been questioned include *Citizens for Responsible Behavior v. Superior Court* (1991) 2 Cal Rptr 2d 648 (California); *Mabon v. Keisling* (1993) 856 P 2d 1023 (Oregon); *American Civil Liberties Union v. Echohawk* (1993) 857 P 2d 626 (Idaho); *Equality Foundation of Greater Cincinnati v. City of Cincinnati*, n. 80 above (reversed by Court of Appeals, 1995, unreported).
173. See, e.g., *Gay Students Organization v. Bonner* (1974) 509 F 2d 652; *Gay Student Services v. Texas A.&M. University* (1984) 737 F 2d 1317; *National Gay Task Force v. Board of Education*, n. 93 above; *Irish-American Gay, Lesbian and Bisexual Group of Boston v. City of Boston* (1994) 636 NE 2d 1293.
174. See n. 74 above.
175. See n. 125 above. For Robin and Fran Shahar's own account of the case, see Deitcher (ed.), *Over the Rainbow*, pp. 174–80.
176. Contrast Peter Tatchell, *We Don't Want To March Straight: Masculinity, Queers and the Military* (London: Cassell, 1995); Andrew Sullivan, *Virtually Normal*; Edmund Hall, *We Can't Even March Straight: Homosexuality and the British Armed Forces* (London: Vintage, 1995).

3

Understanding Lesbian and Gay Rights

Introduction

The phrase 'lesbian and gay rights' first crept into political discourse, in the more gender-specific form 'gay rights', in the 1970s. Its precise origins are a little uncertain. The word 'gay' became popularly associated with non-heterosexual men and women with the rise of the Gay Liberation Front after the 1969 Stonewall Riot in New York, although the word had been widely used as a self-description for some years prior to this.[1] While the liberationists may have popularized the word 'gay', however, according to Barry Adam, '[g]ay liberation never thought of itself as a civil rights movement for a particular minority'.[2] Instead, the Gay Liberation Front presented itself, on both sides of the Atlantic, as a revolutionary force dedicated to overthrowing, in conjunction with other groups, the existing system of government and society, as well as fixed sexual categories of any sort.[3]

John D'Emilio has therefore suggested that the idea of 'gay rights' – that is, civil rights *under the existing system of government*, a reformist rather than a revolutionary demand – came into its own only after the more moderate Gay Activists Alliance split away from the New York Gay Liberation Front in November 1969.[4] Gay liberationist philosophy was never wholly clear-cut, however. Keith Birch points out that members of the Front were influenced by a combination of libertarian, counter-cultural and socialist ideals,[5] and Jeffrey Weeks has argued that the London Gay Liberation Front's 'revolutionary rhetoric masked a unity that was located around reformist aims, ones which could be attained within the framework of liberal bourgeois society'.[6] It is not wholly surprising, therefore, that some of the Front's demands, on both sides of the Atlantic, were expressed in the *language* of 'rights', even though these were conceived of as a different sort of rights from those subsequently claimed as 'gay rights' by reformist groups.

Whatever its precise origins, the idea of 'lesbian and gay rights' is widely used today – mainly by less radical campaigning groups – in the context of, among other issues, civil rights and law reform.[7] Inheritors of the liberationist tradition tend, nowadays, to use the language of 'queer', although talk of 'rights' can still be associated with such an approach.[8] Given the widespread perception and discussion of law reform as a 'lesbian and gay rights' issue, it is therefore helpful to analyse this phrase in greater depth before conducting a detailed analysis, in later chapters, of philosophical justifications for law reform. Getting to grips with 'lesbian and gay rights' is in fact a surprisingly difficult task: for it is, like many political catch-phrases, a rather loose umbrella term concealing a variety of connected ideas which, once identified, will reveal rather more than the original phrase itself.

The argument in this chapter will proceed in four stages. First, the word 'rights' will be analysed, in order to demonstrate that calls for 'lesbian and gay rights' may in fact be invoking one or more of three senses of 'rights'. Second, the debate between essentialist and constructionist theorists of sexuality will be examined, highlighting some difficult definitional problems concerning the 'lesbian and gay' half of the phrase 'lesbian and gay rights'. Third, an attempt will be made to explain why particular rights count as 'lesbian and gay rights' rather than rights of any other sort. This will involve a preliminary discussion of some of the philosophical justifications advanced in favour of law reform exercises to benefit lesbians and gays. It will be argued that while 'lesbian and gay rights' are always directly linked with lesbian or gay sexual orientation (however this is defined), the range of substantive protections which are categorized as 'lesbian and gay rights' will vary according to the philosophical justification for law reform in play. Finally, some of the difficulties presented by rights-based strategies will be discussed. The chapter will conclude by suggesting that while 'lesbian and gay rights' has value as a campaigning slogan, complacency about its meaning and scope – assuming, for example, that there is only one possible view of what can count as a 'lesbian and gay rights' issue, or that the ambit of the slogan is sufficiently self-evident that deeper exploration is unnecessary – is likely to distort political debate and conceal some difficult issues which must be addressed if lesbian and gay law reform is to be tackled coherently.[9] It is as a sign of the uncertain ambit and meaning of 'lesbian and gay rights' – and not because of disrespect for the moral claims which may underpin the phrase – that inverted commas have been placed around it in the discussion which follows.[10]

Rights as entitlements

In 1970, the Male Representatives of National Gay Liberation made the following claim in the United States:

> We Demand: . . . The right to be gay anytime, anyplace . . . The right of free dress and movement . . . That all modes of human sexual self-expression deserve protection of the law, and social sanction . . . That gays be represented in all governmental and community institutions . . . That gays determine the destiny of their own community . . . Finally, the end of domination of one person by another.[11]

In similar vein, the London arm of the Gay Liberation Front argued, in the winter of 1970/71, that: 'We believe . . . every person has the right to develop and extend their character and explore their sexuality through relationships with any other human being, without moral, social or political pressure.' In consequence, the Front called for:

> The same right to public expressions of love and affection as society grants to expressions of hate and scorn. The right to behave, without harm to others, in public and private, in any way we choose, in any manner or style, with any words or gestures, to wear whatever clothes we like or to go naked, to draw or write or read or publish any material or information we wish, at any time and in any place.[12]

Given what has been said about the origins of 'gay rights', neither of these liberationist sets of demands should be seen as calls for 'lesbian and gay rights' in the contemporary, purely civil rights sense of the phrase. But the two liberationist claims do illustrate, just as well as any current demand for 'lesbian and gay rights', the different senses in which 'rights' can operate. For, despite their stirring language, the substance of both liberationist rights claims is rather ambiguous. Although the first claim demands legal *and* social protection for all modes of sexual self-expression, neither claim makes clear what type of protection is being sought for any of the *other* rights which they demand. If we assume, very generally, that a 'right' means a protected entitlement of some variety,[13] it is obvious that things which we commonly call 'rights' can be protected in at least two ways: by the law, in the sense that the holder of the entitlement can (for example) obtain a legal remedy if the entitlement is damaged in a way which the law prohibits; and, in society at large, by people's attitudes – someone could, for example, be viewed as having a social entitlement to behave in a particular way if it were socially unthinkable ('not the done thing') to try to stop them from behaving in that fashion, and if people who did try to stop them were socially censured.[14] A social *entitlement* to do something is therefore much stronger than the mere *ability* to get away with doing it unhindered.[15] So, in demanding the right to freedom of dress and movement, the right publicly to express love and affection and the right to go naked, the US and UK gay liberationists were asking not only to be legally entitled to do these things, but – as the London Gay Liberation Front Manifesto, issued in 1971, made clear – also to be socially entitled as part of a broader upheaval in society at large.[16]

The London Gay Liberation Front's 1970/71 claim also contains a third sense of the word 'right'. The Front began by asserting its belief that 'every person has the right to develop and extend their character and explore their sexuality', and used this belief to justify its demand for the list of rights discussed in the previous paragraph. The rights in this list appear to be legal and/or social; in stating its belief that lesbians and gays had 'a right' to these things, however, the Front can only have been staking a moral claim to them. The Front was, in short, saying that lesbians and gays were morally entitled – i.e. had a moral right – to the legal and/or social entitlements it was apparently demanding. As we saw in chapter 1, such a claim would be rooted in a (probably implicit) theory of justice, which would in turn presuppose an underlying theory of political morality. And, while the US statement did not refer explicitly to moral rights, it is likely that its authors must have believed lesbians and gays to be morally entitled to the freedoms they were claiming – for on what other basis could they have made such demands?

Contemporary 'lesbian and gay rights' claims invoke the varying legal, moral and social senses of 'rights' in much the same way as did the liberationist claims. In 1984, for example, lesbian and gay groups in the United States lobbied the Democratic Party convention with a series of reformist 'lesbian and gay rights' demands. These included calls for social entitlements – such as social services for lesbian and gay youth and the ending of violent attacks on lesbians and gay men – as well as demands for legal entitlements, in the form of a national lesbian and gay rights law, the prohibition of discrimination in the workplace, and the enforcement of civil rights legislation to protect lesbians and gays.[17]

In 1989, the *Report of the Secretary's Task Force on Youth Suicide* – an official report commissioned by the United States Department of Health and Human Services – concluded that young lesbians and gays were two to three times more likely to attempt suicide than other young people in the USA; that lesbian and gay youth suicides may comprise up to 30 per cent of youth suicides in the United States each year; that young lesbians and gays often face extreme physical and verbal abuse, rejection and isolation from family and peers; and that American society was 'the greatest risk factor in gay youth suicide'.[18] In making this last suggestion, the report observed that:

> [g]ay and lesbian youth are strongly affected by the negative attitudes and hostile responses of society to homosexuality. The resulting poor self-esteem, depression and fear can be a fatal blow to a fragile identity. Two ways that society influences suicidal behavior by gay and lesbian youth are: (1) the ongoing discrimination against and oppression of homosexuals, and (2) the portrayal of homosexuals as being self-destructive.[19]

The report cited evidence (collected by the National Gay and Lesbian Task Force) suggesting that 45 per cent of young gay males and nearly 20 per cent of lesbians had been verbally or physically assaulted at school.[20] 'Youth who have a growing awareness of a gay or lesbian orientation', the report observed, 'become painfully aware that they do not fit the "social script". They see the hostility directed toward homosexuals by others and hear taunts of "dyke" and "faggot" used indiscriminately by peers. They become alarmed and realize that they must make some social adaptation to the situation.'[21] The report cited a further survey conducted by the National Gay and Lesbian Task Force which had found that, out of 2100 lesbians and gay men surveyed, more than 90 per cent had experienced verbal or physical assault because of their sexual orientation.[22]

The findings on lesbian and gay youth suicide formed only one chapter of the report, but caused the Bush Administration, then in power in the United States, to attempt to suppress the entire document because of its incompatibility with the Republican Party's 'Christian' agenda.[23] Four years later, a Commission on Gay and Lesbian Youth, appointed by Massachusetts Governor William Weld (also a Republican, but on the socially liberal wing of the party) found that, of 398 students surveyed in one school, 97 per cent reported hearing anti-gay comments at school, and 60 per cent admitted that they would be afraid if people thought they were lesbian, gay or bisexual.[24] This climate of fear extended to teachers: the Commission heard testimony from many former teachers who had been dismissed because they were lesbian or gay, and cited an academic survey which suggested that a majority of school administrators in the USA would want to dismiss lesbian and gay teachers.[25]

Both the Secretary's Report and the Governor's Commission identified law reform as one of a series of measures needed to tackle the misery and social discrimination which they uncovered. The Secretary's report argued that the hostile laws of many US States – which we have discussed in chapter 2 – played an important role:

> Half of the States still prohibit homosexual relationships between consenting adults. Homosexuals are not allowed to legally marry and form 'legitimate' long-term relationships. The vast majority of States and municipalities still discriminate against lesbians and gay men in housing, employment, and other areas. *Gay and lesbian youth see this and take it to heart.*[26]

In consequence, the report called both for the repeal of laws which prohibited lesbian and gay sex, and for the introduction of protective laws which would prohibit discrimination in housing and employment and would penalize violence against lesbians and gays.[27] 'Laws', the report argued, 'can help to establish the principle of equality for lesbians and gay men and define the conduct of others in their interactions with them.'[28] In similar fashion, the Governor's Commission in Massachusetts called for the introduction of outreach and anti-discrimination awareness programmes in schools, and for the passage of a state law to prohibit discrimination against school students on the basis of their sexual orientation.[29]

Implicit in the proposals made in the report and by the Commission is the notion that the *legal* entitlements of lesbians and gays have some effect on their *social* well-being and entitlements. Both bodies suggested that removing legal prohibitions on consenting same-sex relationships[30] and introducing protective laws to prohibit discrimination in specified contexts – that is, improving the *legal* entitlements of lesbians and gays – would help in tackling some of the social discrimination faced by young lesbians and gays – in other words, would help improve their *social* entitlements. And, as with the gay liberationist claims of the early 1970s, it is clear that these calls for greater legal and social protection could not have been made unless it were believed that gay and lesbian youth had certain *moral* entitlements to respect for their sexual orientation.[31]

Not all legal or social rights possessed by or given to people who happen to be lesbian or gay will count as 'lesbian and gay rights', of course, and from some perspectives, the entitlements proposed by the Secretary's Report and the Governor's Commission would be categorized not as 'lesbian and gay rights' but as general *human* rights to respect for physical integrity and to a violence-free educational environment. It will be argued later in this chapter that, for a right to be categorized as a 'lesbian and gay right', there must be a specific linkage between the right and the lesbian or gay sexual orientation of the person to whom it is given, and that the range of entitlements falling within the scope of 'lesbian and gay rights' will vary according to the philosophical justification invoked in support of such rights. People will, in consequence, have different views as to when a legal or social entitlement should be categorized as a 'lesbian and gay right' rather than, for example, an environmental right or a property right.

However the entitlements proposed in the Secretary's Report and the Governor's Commission are categorized, they provide another useful example of the notion that 'rights' can refer to entitlements of a moral, legal *or* social character. In consequence, when campaigning groups refer to 'lesbian and gay rights', it is necessary to ask which sense of the word 'rights' they have in mind. The call for 'equal rights for lesbians and gays' can mean equal legal entitlements or equal social entitlements. And, if campaigners are more precise and call for an improvement in lesbian and gay *legal* rights, it is likely that one of their objectives is to improve lesbian and gay *social* entitlements, and that their law reform demands presuppose some notion of lesbian and gay *moral* rights. Acknowledging these three senses of 'lesbian and gay rights' allows us to adopt a broad view of debates about lesbian and gay law reform, by focusing attention on issues such as which social entitlements are considered desirable and why law reform is seen as a useful way of attaining them. Jonathan Katz highlights the possibilities for debate in his assertion that:

> Most Gay people now see the ending of homosexual oppression . . . as a matter of law reform, of obtaining civil rights, and of fitting into

this society as it is constituted. Others, myself among them, see the movement for Gay law reform and civil rights as only the present form of a much larger struggle by Gay people and others for power and control over those civil institutions which most affect our lives.[32]

Some refinements must now be built into the argument. For we have ignored, so far, some important philosophical questions about how to understand the notion of a right.[33] When and why, for example, does a right come into existence? How does it guarantee the interest it is supposed to protect? Can a right be defeated by another interest? Do rights vest in individuals or in groups? It is unnecessary to answer all of these questions here, but the analytical distinction between moral, legal and social entitlements will become clearer if we consider a few of these points in further detail.[34] For our understanding of the strength and nature of any right – the way in which it works, the effect which it has, and the criteria which must be satisfied for it to be classified as a right – will vary to some extent depending upon whether we are thinking of it in legal, moral, or social terms.

One long-standing philosophical disagreement about the nature of rights is whether legal and moral rights are to be understood according to the 'will theory' or the 'interest theory'. Neil MacCormick suggests that when each theory is put forward in its strongest form,

> the 'will theory', asserts that an individual's having a right of some kind depends upon the legal (or, *mutatis mutandis*, moral) recognition of his will, his choice, as being preeminent over that of others in relation to a given subject matter and within a given relationship. The 'interest theory', by contrast, contends that what is essential to . . . a right is the legal (or moral) protection or promotion of one person's interests as against some other person or the world at large, by the imposition on the latter of duties, disabilities or liabilities in respect of the party favoured.[35]

In other words, according to the 'will theory', 'X having a right to something' means that X has the power to decide whether or not to enforce an obligation against Y in relation to that thing; the right is classified as legal if the law recognizes X's power to decide, and moral if X's power is protected by considerations of morality. In either case, the essence of the right lies in *X's power to trigger Y's obligation*. According to the 'interest theory', X has a right to a thing if protecting X's interest is viewed as a sufficient reason for triggering Y's obligation; the right is classified as legal where the law identifies the protection of X's interest as sufficient reason, and moral where considerations of morality do so. Under the 'interest theory', the essence of a right therefore lies in *the protection of X's interest*.

There has been extensive argument about the merits and flaws of each theory and on balance, the 'interest theory' appears to be the more convincing: for, as MacCormick points out, the 'will theory' cannot explain the existence of paternalistic laws, such as those concerned with protecting health and safety at work, which protect people's interests by granting them rights which they *cannot* waive.[36] The notion of rights as entitlements, advanced earlier, is best understood as underpinned by the 'interest theory', which can be further integrated into our analysis of legal, moral and social rights. In relation to legal rights, MacCormick observes that, 'The first point to be made ... must seem ... to be of breath-taking banality. The point is that legal rights are conferred by legal rules, or (if you will) by laws.'[37] As such, legal rights are intended to protect their holder's possession or enjoyment of a particular asset or thing, or their freedom to behave in a particular way – their 'interest', in other words – and the right-holder can in consequence obtain a legal remedy if the relevant possession, enjoyment or freedom is violated.[38] While all three senses of 'rights' are concerned with entitlements, only legal rights are enforceable in court.

If it is based on proper criteria,[39] the view that 'X *should be* entitled to something' clearly concerns the protection of X's rights or entitlements in the *moral* sense.[40] As Michael Freeden observes, 'People *do* assume that moral rights exist'.[41] How, though, do moral rights work?[42] John Gardner has suggested that the effect of possessing a moral right – for example, to do or to have something – is that it creates a special moral weapon with which to repel arguments for restricting that activity or thing. A moral right, Gardner argues,

> fires two different calibres of normative ammunition at hostile arguments. Some arguments for restricting the pursuit of [the activity or thing covered by the right] ... simply fall to be outweighed by the right, whereas others are excluded from consideration altogether.[43]

Jan Narveson suggests, to similar effect, that if someone possesses a moral right, there must be certain features or properties of those who 'have' [the right] . . . such that we have *good reason to acknowledge* the obligation to refrain from interfering with, or possibly to sometimes help their bearers to do the things they are said to have the right to do, or have those things they are said to have a right to have.[44]

As Gardner observes, however, moral rights are not absolute:

> it does not follow that [the right] . . . can force every argument for restricting [the activity or thing which it covers] . . . into retreat. Both outweighing and excluding have their limitations, and some hostile arguments survive them both. After all, a [moral] right is only as powerful as its justification can make it.[45]

In fact, the philosophical justification for a moral right performs two tasks: it justifies the existence of the right (which other people are, in consequence, morally obliged to respect), by explaining why we should view the activity or thing covered by the right as deserving moral respect; and it explains the amount of respect which the activity or thing deserves, determining how strong we think the particular moral right is and how many opposing arguments it can outweigh.[46] Reformulated in the language of the 'interest theory', the activity or thing covered by the right is the 'interest' which the right protects, and the justification provides the reason why it is protected.

It is here that our first central question – whether there are principled justifications for laws designed to protect lesbians and gays (and a lack of justification for punitive laws) – comes into play. For the philosophical justifications for some perceived moral rights should also be capable of legitimating the use of law to protect those moral rights. With a sound justification, a perceived moral right can therefore be protected by the creation of a parallel legal right – or, in terms of the 'interest theory', if the reason for protecting a particular interest is strong enough, that reason may justify the existence of a legal as well as a moral right. Reformulated in terms of *lesbian and gay* moral rights, our first central question asks whether, if we believe that such moral rights exist, there is a principled justification for creating parallel legal rights to protect them. Our second, pragmatic question – whether law reform is likely to have positive results – can be reformulated in terms of the social sense of rights. For, if campaigns for 'lesbian and gay rights' are seeking not just legal rights, but also, as a consequence, the entitlement to live free from social sanctions,[47] then the second, pragmatic question in fact asks whether the creation or alteration of legal rights will help to improve the social entitlements of lesbians and gays.

A further connection between legal, moral and social entitlements can also be highlighted. For many people, the fact that something is protected as a legal right means that it also carries moral weight. This connection is epitomized in popular sentiments such as 'the law deserves respect' and 'the law should be obeyed', neither of which would make sense unless it is assumed that the fact that a right or rule is contained within the law – i.e. is a legal right or rule – means that there is a moral (as well as a legal) obligation to respect or obey it.[48] Supporters of this view are likely to believe that legal rights, because of their inherent moral weight, should receive social respect and protection, i.e. be treated as social entitlements. This view is, however, controversial.

Conceptions of sexuality

Whether they are seen in moral, legal or social terms, who are 'lesbian and gay rights' intended to protect? This question forces us to consider an important and long-standing debate between constructionist and essentialist theorists about how sexual categories such as 'lesbian and gay' (or 'lesbian' and 'gay') should be understood.[49] The significance of this debate, for present purposes, is captured in Diana Fuss's observation that:

> Few . . . issues have been as divisive . . . in gay and lesbian theory as the question of whether a 'gay identity' is empirical fact or political fiction. Amongst political organizers in the gay movement, the notion of a gay essence is relied upon to mobilize and to legitimate gay activism; 'gay pride', 'gay culture', 'gay sensibility' are all summoned as cornerstones of the gay community, indices of the emergence of a long-repressed collective identity. Recent [constructionist] gay theory, on the other hand, has . . . rejected any such adherence to a natural, essential or universal gay identity.[50]

If it is possible meaningfully to rely on the idea of a 'gay essence', then it appears relatively simple to define the 'lesbian and gay' part of the phrase 'lesbian and gay rights', thereby singling out and delimiting the group of people whom such rights are intended to protect – for such an exercise would involve the use of a fixed, easily-identifiable definition. But if a constructionist approach is adopted, then establishing who or what 'lesbian and gay rights' are supposed to protect becomes a rather more convoluted exercise. For if there is no such thing as a universal gay identity, how can it be possible to talk in general terms of 'lesbian and gay rights'?

The essentialist versus constructionist debate has generated a wealth of literature, which has focused not just on social understandings of sexual categories, but also on the social categorization of attributes such as sex and race. It will be impossible here to do more than evaluate a few of the many arguments which are potentially relevant to the question of 'lesbian and gay rights' and law reform, and to suggest which arguments appear the more plausible.[51] It is important to remember that there is no one composite essentialist or constructionist view: there are in fact many subtle differences between the views of theorists within each camp, and inevitably only a selection of views can be highlighted.[52] After the essentialist versus constructionist debate has been examined in greater detail, some of its implications for the meaning of 'lesbian and gay rights' and arguments about law reform will be discussed.

Essentialism, according to Diana Fuss, is '*most commonly* understood as a belief in the real, true essence of things, the invariable and fixed properties [of] which define the "whatness" of a given entity'.[53] An essentialist theory of gender, therefore, might maintain that it has always been possible to categorize humans as 'male' or as 'female' because each category can be distinguished according to certain eternal, transhistorical and immutable characteristics. In other words, an essentialist theorist would believe that the categories 'male' and 'female' possess a fixed essence, explaining why a given individual can always be identified as belonging to one category or the other.[54]

Constructionists argue, by contrast, that social categories are, to varying degrees, culture-specific – that is, they are the product of social dialogues and assumptions which vary from society to society and age to age.[55] In Fuss's words, 'Constructionism . . . insists that essence is itself a[n] historical construction'.[56] So for constructionists, 'male' and 'female' are not fixed and unchanging categories – instead, they are social constructs through which a person's biological sex is understood in western societies in the current era; in other societies and at other times, one's biological sex may have been understood differently, or have assumed a different social significance.[57]

Essentialist and constructionist analyses are capable of producing radically divergent conclusions when applied to sexual orientation. Steven Epstein suggests that:

> Where essentialism took for granted that all societies consist of people who are either heterosexuals or homosexuals (with perhaps some bisexuals), constructionists demonstrated that the notion of 'the homosexual' is a sociohistorical product, not universally applicable . . . and where essentialism would treat the self-attribution of a 'homosexual identity' as unproblematic – as simply the conscious recognition of a true, underlying 'orientation' – constructionism focused attention on identity as a complex developmental outcome, the consequence of an interactive process of social labelling and self-identification.[58]

Epstein's analysis suggests that there are two connected aspects to the essentialist versus constructionist debate. The first aspect relates to the stability and universality of social categories such as 'heterosexual' or 'straight', 'homosexual' or 'gay', 'lesbian' and 'bisexual'. For the essentialist, it is possible to divide members of any society into such categories, since each category retains a fixed, timeless meaning: homosexuals and lesbians are exclusively attracted to and/or have sex with people of the same sex; heterosexuals are solely attracted to and/or have sex with people of the opposite sex; and bisexuals are, to varying degrees, inclined in both directions. For the constructionist, by contrast, such categories are unstable, contingent devices. People may always have engaged in *sexual relations* with others of the same sex, but the *social significance* of these activities, and the ways in which people who engage in them are labelled and categorized, vary from one society or time period to another. According to constructionist historian John D'Emilio:

> Sexuality consists of acts with meanings. Although the acts may have a universal existence, the meanings may vary considerably. And it is through meaning, through an understanding of behavior which culture provides, that patterns of behavior take on social significance.[59]

In similar vein, Jeffrey Weeks suggests that:

In different cultures (and at different historical moments ... within the same culture) very different meanings are given to ... same-sex activity both by society at large and by the individual participants. The physical acts might be similar, but the social construction of meanings around them are profoundly different.[60]

Constructionist historians have pointed to societies where sexual relations have been permitted, or even encouraged, between partners of the same sex, but where such acts, and the people who engaged in them, would not be categorized as they are today. A prime example is ancient Greece, where sexual acts between people of the same sex appeared to be common. Constructionist historians have suggested that it would be artificial to perceive the ancient Greeks in terms of modern sexual categories.[61] According to David Halperin, 'it never occurred to premodern cultures to ascribe a person's sexual tastes to some positive, structural, or constitutive feature of his or her personality'.[62] Rather:

> In classical Athens ... sexual partners came in two different kinds – not male and female but active and passive, dominant and submissive. The relevant features of a sexual object were not so much determined by a physical typology of genders as by the social articulation of power ... the currently fashionable distinction between homosexuality and heterosexuality had no meaning for classical Athenians. There were not, so far as they knew, two different kinds of 'sexuality', two differently structured psychosexual states or modes of affective orientation, but a single form of sexual experience, which all free adult males shared.[63]

A rather different example can be found in English history. Although English criminal law has long been concerned to penalize sexual activity between men, the idea of 'homosexuals' as a distinct, despised social category had only clearly become part of political discourse by the time of the Wolfenden Committee Report in 1957. In the Victorian era and earlier, sexual relations between men and sodomy between married couples had both tended, if publicly acknowledged, to be viewed as forms of 'improper behaviour' by which *most* males could be tempted if their morals were not properly guarded.[64] What was originally understood as a general problem of *behaviour* only later came to be viewed as an issue going to the social *status* of a particular, identifiable group.

The second aspect of the essentialist versus constructionist debate could be said to relate to the self-identity or self-perception of members of the social categories associated with particular sexual orientations. John Boswell, author of the ground-breaking study *Christianity, Social Tolerance and Homosexuality*, is generally portrayed as an essentialist historian.[65] Boswell argued that religious intolerance of homosexual behaviour was a relatively modern phenomenon, and that in the medieval period and earlier, homosexual behaviour and Christianity were treated as entirely compatible. One controversial aspect of Boswell's study was his assertion that throughout history, it has been possible to identify a group of people who *self-identified as gay*, where:

> 'Gay' . . . refers to persons who are conscious of erotic inclination toward their own gender as a distinguishing characteristic or, loosely, to things associated with such people, as 'gay poetry'. 'Gay sexuality' refers only to eroticism associated with a conscious preference.[66]

Since constructionists do not believe that social categories possess fixed essences, it follows that they also refute any assertion that people who are sexually attracted to members of the same sex would *necessarily* perceive themselves as 'gay' within Boswell's definition, or that they would view the direction of their sexual attraction as one of their distinguishing characteristics. If people who are attracted to members of the same sex have only been categorized, or categorized themselves, as 'lesbian' and 'gay' in western societies in the present era, it follows that people who lived in societies like ancient Greece, where the labels 'lesbian' and 'gay' were socially meaningless, would have defined themselves and their sexual behaviour differently. As Carl Stychin observes, social constructionists 'argue that the relationship of sexual act to sexual identity and the construction of identities themselves are not historically fixed, but rather are contingent and thus capable of cultural redefinition'.[67] More succinctly, Jeffrey Weeks draws a sharp distinction between 'homosexual behaviour, which is universal, and a homosexual identity, which is historically specific'.[68]

At the heart of the essentialist versus constructionist debate lies an argument about how humans relate to and are influenced by their social surroundings, and about the ways in which they understand themselves and others. Robert Padgug argues, in strongly constructionist fashion, that:

within certain limits, human beings have no fixed, inherited nature. We *become* human only in human society. . . . Social reality cannot simply be 'peeled off' to reveal 'natural man' lurking beneath. . . . The forms, content and context of sexuality always differ. There is no abstract and universal category of 'the erotic' or 'the sexual' applicable without change to all societies . . . the general distinguishing mark of human sexuality, as of all social reality, is the unique role played in its construction by language, consciousness, symbolism, and labor.[69]

At this point, it will be useful to draw a distinction between radical and moderate constructionism. A radical constructionist is one who believes that human beings lack an innate sexuality of *any* particular variety, and that people's *individual* sexual desires are socially determined, as is their understanding of what counts as sexual desire. A moderate constructionist, by contrast, would suggest that while a person's *direction* of sexual attraction may effectively be fixed and beyond their control, whether as a result of biological or psychological factors ('nature' or 'nurture'), a person's *perception* of sexuality and sexual categories – both their own and other people's – is determined by their social surroundings.[70] People who would nowadays categorize themselves as gay could not have done so in ancient Greece since the Athenians did not have a social categorization corresponding with today's notion that those who enjoy sexual relations with others of the same sex are 'gay'.

On balance, the moderate constructionist argument appears to be the most appealing. For it would be odd, if not arrogant, to refuse to acknowledge that different societies and their members have, throughout history, organized and understood themselves in different ways, and that we must make allowance for this if we are to understand such societies properly. It also seems implausible to refuse to acknowledge that the ways in which people come to understand their social significance and role are, like the language in which they first learn to communicate, at least initially dependent on their social surroundings. To this extent, the strongly essentialist argument that sexual categories and perceptions are fixed and unchanging, is unconvincing.[71] Even if it were ever conclusively proven that human sexual orientation is biologically determined – an idea popularly known as the 'gay gene' theory[72] – it would remain analytically untidy to categorize as 'gay' people who lived in societies which lacked an equivalent of the modern idea of what being gay means. For 'gay' is best seen as a *social* label, not a *biological* one: it is a shorthand description of how people who are attracted to members of the same sex are generally understood, and understand themselves, in western societies in the current era. Subscribers to the 'gay gene' theory may well argue that in all societies and at all times, there have been people who were sexually attracted, because of their biological make-up, to persons of their own sex – but this is not the same as claiming that those people understood themselves, or were understood by other members of the societies in which they lived, as 'gay' in the modern sense of the term. That would require the further argument that patterns of social understanding remain constant across time and cultures.

By the same token, however, the radical constructionist argument – that people's *actual* sexual desires are socially constructed, as opposed merely to their *perceptions* of sexuality and sexual orientation – appears to downplay the sentiment of many lesbians, gays *and heterosexuals* that they have been aware of the direction of their sexual attraction from a young age; to borrow Steven Epstein's words, radical constructionism is '"out of sync" with the self-understandings of many gay people'.[73] Given that radical constructionism entails a rejection of the 'gay gene' theory – for it would otherwise be impossible to say that the direction of individual sexual desire is socially constructed – it is also vulnerable to scientific disproof should conclusive evidence in support of the existence of a 'gay gene' come to light.[74] Moderate constructionism is, by contrast, neutral as between 'nature' and 'nurture'-driven accounts of the origins of individual sexual orientation, and can survive the discovery of firm scientific proof either way.[75] An added political danger in radical constructionism is that it could, if interpreted carelessly, be seen as lending support to the argument that it is possible and desirable to *alter* an individual's direction of sexual attraction by social conditioning – a view sometimes advocated by so-called 'ex-gay' groups on the 'Christian' right. This is not, of course, to say that lesbian and gay radical constructionists would condemn any less strongly than other lesbians and gays the idea of 'converting' people into heterosexuals; the worry is that radical constructionism could easily be misinterpreted as appearing to lend intellectual support to such a process.

Aspects of the moderate constructionist approach also dovetail neatly with the currently popular argument that essentialist and constructionist theories are not, in fact, as far removed from each other as has sometimes been suggested.[76] Diana Fuss, for example, argues that there are 'many instances which suggest that essentialism is more entrenched in constructionism than we previously thought . . . it is difficult to see how constructionism can *be* constructionism without a fundamental dependency upon essentialism.'[77] An obvious example is that most constructionists (whether radicals or moderates) appear content to assume that there have always been biologically distinct male and female sexes, and that there have always been human beings who have had sexual relations with people of the same biological sex – for the whole thrust of constructionism rests upon the possibility of comparing what are said to be basic human characteristics with the contrasting ways in which such characteristics are perceived and categorized in different societies and time-periods. For such an analysis to work, it is clear that it must first be assumed that the biological or sexual differences in question *are* universal, transhistorical and basic human characteristics – an assumption which, however reasonable, appears to be essentialist in approach. As Edward Stein has suggested, 'social constructionism is an interesting position *about sexual orientation* only if the relativism involved in it is limited'.[78]

John Boswell's work also demonstrates that it is possible for an apparently essentialist theory to possess constructionist features. Boswell never appeared entirely happy with the description of his work as essentialist, and later clarified and moved away from the position he had adopted in *Christianity, Social Tolerance and Homosexuality*. In later writings, Boswell accepted that his earlier work had presupposed that 'gay persons' were widely and identifiably present in Western society since at least Greco-Roman times, but suggested that he would 'now define "gay persons" more simply as those whose erotic interest is predominantly directed toward their own gender (i.e. regardless of how conscious they are of this as a distinguishing characteristic)'.[79] Boswell's removal of the self-identity element from his definition of 'gay' suggests a considerable softening of hostility towards the constructionist position. It should also be noted that Boswell's early work was not as strongly essentialist as may be supposed. For Boswell accepted that perceptions of homosexual behaviour in the ancient world were very different from those of 1980s America, and that different categorizations of sexual behaviour meant that while homosexual behaviour featured strongly in classical literature, the modern terms 'homosexual' and 'heterosexual' did not. The explanation, Boswell argued – in apparently constructionist fashion – was that:

> Majorities . . . create minorities, in one very real sense, by deciding to categorize them. Left-handed people may be statistically less numerous in all human societies, but they are really a minority only where manual preference takes on social significance and people make it their business to categorize their countrymen on that basis. In the ancient world so few people cared to categorize their contemporaries on the basis of the gender to which they were erotically attracted that no [homosexual/heterosexual] dichotomy to express the distinction was in common use. People were thought of as 'chaste' or 'unchaste', 'romantic' or 'unromantic', 'married' or 'single', even 'active' or 'passive', but no one thought it useful or important to distinguish on the basis of genders alone, and the categories 'homosexual' and 'heterosexual' simply did not intrude on the consciousness of most Greeks or . . . Romans.[80]

Supporting a moderate constructionist rather than an essentialist theory will impact upon our understanding of 'lesbian and gay rights' and law reform demands in three connected ways. First, it will affect the way in which we define and evaluate 'lesbian and gay rights' – both in terms of the range of people we regard as falling within their protection, and in terms of the nature of the phrase itself. Second, it will narrow down the range of philosophical justifications for 'lesbian and gay legal rights' which can potentially be viewed as sound. Third, it will suggest that 'lesbian and gay rights' claims must be seen as demands for individual rather than group rights. We will now examine each of these points in turn.

The first of the three effects goes, at root, to whether 'lesbian and gay rights' should be seen as a currently popular campaigning slogan or as a deeper and more permanent philosophical concept. If Boswell's early theory of sexuality is followed, then an essentialist account of 'lesbian and gay rights' might maintain that such rights – whether moral, legal or social – are intended to protect people whom societies categorize, and who themselves self-identify, as lesbian or gay. The law reform issues of concern to such people would presumably vary from society to society according to contemporary political circumstances, but the transhistorical nature of the essentialist definitions of 'lesbian' and 'gay' would make it possible for essentialists – so long as they agreed about which philosophical justification for 'lesbian and gay legal rights' was in play – to formulate a fixed definition of 'lesbian and gay rights' issues, applicable in all societies. A strongly essentialist theorist or campaigner could therefore see 'lesbian and gay rights' as something deeper than just today's political slogan – such rights would, instead, constitute a list of identifiable, definable and basically invariable moral entitlements possessed by an unchanging sexual minority.[81] It should be noted that this position could survive most disputes about where the boundary of the category 'lesbian and gay' should be seen as falling – witness Boswell's subtle alteration of view on this issue – instead, it would just be necessary for the category *itself* to be permanent.

By contrast, neither radical nor moderate constructionists would see the phrase 'lesbian and gay rights' as anything more than a contemporary campaigning slogan. If one does not believe in the possibility of a universal, transhistorical lesbian and gay identity, it follows logically that one would only see the phrase 'lesbian and gay rights' as possessing significance in societies where the idea of a distinct lesbian and gay sexual minority, with customs and mores of its own, has current social meaning. Law reform debates which we at present categorize, in our own society, as involving issues of 'lesbian and gay rights' may have taken place in societies where the terms 'lesbian' and 'gay' lacked social meaning – but if so, such debates could not sensibly be described in terms of our contemporary social understandings. For both radical and moderate constructionists, therefore, 'lesbian and gay rights' is at most a political label for particular entitlements claimed by or for those who fall within the *current* social categories of lesbian and gay, social categories and political labels being subject to change. Adopting a constructionist view of sexuality does not mean that talk of 'lesbian and gay rights' must be abandoned – instead, the moderate constructionist can acknowledge the phrase as a political slogan which, while potentially useful in current campaigning work, may easily be superseded in the face of changes in the social understanding of sexual orientation.

The second, connected consequence of opting for a constructionist rather than an essentialist theory is that it will narrow down the range of philosophical justifications for law reform which can be viewed as plausible. For it must follow from the constructionist rejection of the idea of a general, transhistorical lesbian and gay identity that any justification for law reform which depends upon such a notion must also be seen as untenable, given that it would rest on the use of something which constructionists regard as a fiction. It was suggested above that it is not implausible for constructionists to use the phrase 'lesbian and gay rights' as a temporary, localized campaigning slogan, so long as it is made clear that this does not imply support for the idea of a universal and transhistorical lesbian and gay identity. There is, however, a considerable difference between a political slogan and a philosophical justification for legal rights or law reform. While different societies may recognize different philosophical justifications as valid, we will see in chapters 4, 6 and 7 that to legitimate the use of state power in the form of law, a philosophical justification must ideally be long-lasting in nature, and will usually aspire towards generality. In consequence, social categorizations such as 'lesbian' and 'gay', or concepts such as a 'lesbian and gay identity', cannot form an integral part of justifications of this sort – for such categorizations and concepts are too temporary and too localized in character. So, if constructionists are to be consistent, they cannot support – as a philosophical justification (or part of a justification) for legal protections for lesbians and gays – any theory which relies on the notion of a 'lesbian and gay identity'; a justification of this sort could only plausibly be supported by essentialists.

The third consequence of supporting a moderate constructionist account of sexual orientation is that 'lesbian and gay rights' claims must be seen as claims for individual rights. Considerable philosophical controversy surrounds the question whether (and if so, when) rights – whether moral, legal or social – can be claimed or held by groups as well as by individuals.[82] Post-war liberal political philosophy has tended to regard rights as the property of individuals, and theorists who seek – whether from a liberal perspective or from any other – to claim that rights can be held by groups face the uphill task of establishing when and why this view is justifiable, what effect such rights will have on individuals, and how such rights can be slotted into western legal systems which are generally individualistic in nature.[83] Quite apart from these questions, it is also necessary for supporters of collective entitlements to define, as a practical matter, who exactly comprise the social groups which they desire to protect by group rights. To be described as a social group, a set of individuals must share a significant attribute or attributes, and must probably possess some type of common experience and/or outlook – and, unless it can be said that a set of people constitute a defined social group, it is impossible to talk of them possessing *group* rights (as opposed, for example, to the assorted rights of a random collections of individuals). While essentialists in the early Boswell mode could, if they believed in the notion of lesbian and gay group rights, provide a timeless and universally valid definition of the group they wished to protect, constructionists would be unable to do so. Given their belief that 'lesbian' and 'gay' are merely transient social labels and that the notion of a lesbian and gay group identity is meaningless, it would indeed be somewhat artificial for constructionists, whether radical or moderate, to think in terms of lesbian and gay group rights. Unless it was felt to be desirable for the law to attempt to *arrest* further developments in the social understanding of sexuality by embodying fixed definitions of 'lesbian' and 'gay' (which could anyway be interpreted in terms of individual rights),[84] the only consistent approach for constructionists is to argue for *individual* legal rights which are not tied to the notion of a lesbian and gay identity, and which are drafted in sufficiently general terms as to be capable of withstanding a change in the social categorization of the lesbians and gays who hold them.

The varying scope of 'lesbian and gay rights'

Lesbians and gays, like heterosexuals, possess legal entitlements covering areas of life which appear – in day-to-day, practical terms – to be largely unrelated to their sexual orientation. Like many heterosexuals, some lesbians and gays also favour the creation of new legal rights to engage in activities which the law currently prohibits, whatever a person's sexual orientation – driving at eighty miles per hour on a motorway, for example, or possessing soft drugs. Since it would seem bizarre to categorize legal entitlements or sought-after legal entitlements of this sort as 'lesbian and gay rights', it is necessary to explore why some law reform questions count as 'lesbian and gay rights' issues rather than issues of any other sort, and how boundary lines are drawn between existing 'lesbian and gay legal rights' and other legal entitlements which happen to be possessed by people who are lesbian or gay.

Talk of the substantive entitlements which fall within the scope of 'lesbian and gay rights' – or which it is felt should do so – can assume at least two different forms. On the one hand, the term 'lesbian and gay rights' is sometimes used as a collective label for currently existing legal rights which either offer some protection for the sexual and affectional conduct of lesbians and gays, or which appear to offer protection against social hostility in contexts such as employment and housing.[85] On the other hand, claims for new legal or social entitlements tend to be categorized as 'lesbian and gay rights' issues, given that they involve the assertion of a perceived moral right to the sought-after entitlements.[86] Unless the ambit of such categorizations or rights claims is properly laid down using a clear set of criteria, however, claims that something is or is not a 'lesbian and gay legal right' or a 'lesbian and gay rights' issue will degenerate into semantic squabbles.

The question as to which legal rights and rights issues warrant the prefix 'lesbian and gay' can best be resolved by employing the various philosophical justifications on which such rights or rights claims are based. The philosophical justifications explain why the law can properly be used to penalize some social practices – discrimination against sexual minorities, for example – and why it must seek to protect other things, such as the ability freely to engage in consenting sexual acts. As these two examples suggest, each justification, when performing its task, should be capable of marking out at least broadly the types of social practice or thing which it believes, because they share a particular attribute, should be penalized or protected by the law. An equality-based justification would support the law's intervention in social situations which are categorized as involving the type of social inequality against which the justification is directed. Similarly, a privacy-based justification would support the law's intervention in social situations where there would otherwise be unjustified invasions of privacy, and an empowerment-based justification would seek to counter restrictions on fundamental freedoms. The distinction between each possible justification (the comparative advantages and disadvantages of which will be considered in later chapters) turns on the type of moral wrong which it regards as inherent in the hostile treatment of or failure to protect lesbians and gays. As well as explaining why the perceived moral entitlements of lesbians and gays deserve the protection of parallel legal rights, each philosophical justification can therefore draw at least a broad distinction between legal entitlements and sought-after legal entitlements which do, and those which do not, fall within its scope.

A practical demonstration can be provided by considering the equality-based justification for law reform, relied upon for some years now by lesbian and gay civil rights campaigners on both sides of the Atlantic.[87] Broadly speaking, this justification could be said to identify, as the moral wrong which it seeks to counter, any unequal treatment, assessment or categorization of lesbians and gays by comparison with heterosexuals. The notion of 'equality' poses many definitional questions and rests upon a range of controversial social and philosophical assumptions which will be considered in chapter 7, but it should for now be clear that it is, as a justification, only capable of explaining and supporting law reform measures designed to remedy inequality between persons of different sexual orientations. In consequence, it is only where social situations can be categorized as involving inequalities of this type that they can be seen by supporters of an equality-based justification as raising 'lesbian and gay rights' issues, and a legal right will only be identified as a 'lesbian and gay legal right' if it serves to combat inequality between lesbians or gays and heterosexuals. Supporters of equality-based justifications have therefore argued that if the law prohibits, to an equal degree, lesbians, gays and heterosexuals from engaging in particular sexual practices – consenting sado-masochistic acts, for example – then the matter cannot be seen as raising any 'lesbian and gay rights' issue.[88]

If the scope of 'lesbian and gay rights' can be determined by reference to an equality-based justification, it must logically follow that other justifications are capable of yielding their own interpretations of the term. Supporters of alternative justifications may not have employed the language of 'lesbian and gay rights' in practice – such language is clearly associated with the civil rights-based equality justification, with which it fits conceptually – but this is a matter of historical rather than logical significance. For if it is possible to describe a group of people as lesbian or gay, it is logically possible to talk of 'lesbian and gay rights' so long as one can supply a philosophical justification, whether or not that justification is equality-based. If an empowerment- or privacy-based justification were employed, giving rise to empowerment- or privacy-driven conceptions of 'lesbian and gay rights', then the legal regulation of consenting sado-masochistic acts *could* be seen as raising a 'lesbian and gay rights' issue, since it would involve restricting the sexual freedom or privacy of the participants. Indeed, the regulation of any consenting sexual act between two people of the same sex would in logic raise the same moral issue, whether or not sado-masochism were involved.[89] That such a perception of 'lesbian and gay rights' *does* still exist is perhaps reflected in the outpouring of concern on the part of non-S&M lesbians and gays in the United Kingdom at the *Brown* decision, in which the House of Lords declared that all consenting sado-masochistic acts were illegal.[90]

Empowerment- and privacy-based justifications are in this respect more expansive than an equality-based justification, but the privacy-based justification is, overall, perhaps the narrowest of the three – for it would be difficult to justify, on the ground of respect for privacy, the creation of legal rights against dismissal from employment or against discrimination in the provision of goods and services – two areas where an equality-based justification would work comfortably. In addition, empowerment- and privacy-based justifications cannot, on their own, provide as precise an account of the scope of 'lesbian and gay rights' as can an equality-based justification. At first sight, for example, an empowerment justification may appear to entail identifying the traffic speed limit on motorways as a 'lesbian and gay rights' issue, given that the present (or indeed any) speed limit restricts the liberty of lesbian and gay drivers who wish to travel more quickly; similarly, prohibitions on using soft drugs in private would become a 'lesbian and gay rights' issue for supporters of both empowerment- and privacy-based justifications. If either justification is to be used, therefore, the boundaries of its application must be qualified in order to keep the scope of 'lesbian and gay rights' within sensible confines. This can be done – although not unproblematically – by suggesting that the range of rights which the empowerment- or privacy-based justifications are capable of yielding are confined to those situations where there is a clear link with the right-holder's lesbian or gay sexual orientation – as opposed, for example, to situations where we are concerned with the right-holder's status as a voter in an election, as an employee, or as a property-owner. Such an assertion could be supported by essentialists and constructionists alike – subject, of course, to their differing views as to the nature and operation of sexual categories such as 'lesbian' and 'gay'.

This approach poses two problems, however. The first problem concerns the way in which we regard it as appropriate to describe particular social situations. It is unlikely that many people would disagree with the suggestion that it is appropriate to describe consenting sexual relations between adults of the same sex as an activity which is directly connected with the lesbian or gay sexual orientation of the participants and, as we will see in chapters 6 and 7, it is comparatively easy to construct an empowerment- or privacy-based justification for keeping the law out of consenting sexual relations. Beyond this core area, however, the appropriateness of describing something as being 'clearly linked' with a person's sexual orientation becomes more questionable. A problematical example for the privacy-based justification would be dismissal from employment: in some UK cases, employees have been dismissed when their employer discovered that they were, or had been, having sexual relations with a person or persons of the same sex.[91] In framing a legal claim – usually for unfair dismissal – employees have tended to characterize the dismissal as being because of their sexual orientation; employers, by contrast, have argued – often as part of a successful defence – that the employee was dismissed because of the adverse reaction (actual or anticipated) of customers or other workers if they had been allowed to remain in their job. The legitimacy of this type of employer response is questionable both legally and morally,[92] but it highlights the scope for disagreement about whether dismissals can be categorized as clearly linked to the employee's sexual orientation, for the employee's case will be based on the argument that there is such a connection, and the employer's response will implicitly be based on the assumption that there was not.

The second problematical issue is whether it is *possible* for people neatly to distinguish between various areas of their social existence. It is often assumed that a person's behaviour as a voter or as a property-owner may be affected by their sexual orientation, and vice versa.[93] People have any number of social roles in a lifetime, often possessing several simultaneously – but this does not mean that each role can be neatly cut off from its counterparts, none of which exerts influence upon any other.[94] To make such a suggestion would be to deny that human personalities can ever be seen as integrated (or at least partially integrated) wholes. In consequence, it may be artificial to demarcate particular areas of life as being clearly linked with a person's sexual orientation, and to talk of 'lesbian and gay rights' as being concerned only with those areas, for many people would claim that it is impossible to isolate their sexual orientation from the rest of their social existence.

Three points can be made about these objections. First, while the equality-based justification does not need, unlike the other justifications, explicitly to stake out a clear link with the right-holder's sexual orientation in its definition of 'lesbian and gay rights', this is because such a linkage is already implicit in its understanding of 'lesbian and gay rights' as concerned with areas where there is inequality between lesbians or gays by comparison with heterosexuals. To categorize a social situation as involving inequality between persons of different sexual orientations presupposes, after all, that the relevant sexual orientations have some bearing on the situation: in other words, that there is something equivalent to the 'clear link' which we have been discussing in the case of the empowerment- and privacy-based justifications. It would therefore be fair to say that, using *any* of these three justifications, a clear link between an entitlement (or sought-after entitlement) and the lesbian or gay sexual orientation of its holder (or would-be holder) must in practice be shown before the entitlement can be categorized as a 'lesbian and gay right' (or the situation as raising 'lesbian and gay rights' issues). Within this limit, however, the range of legal rights or rights claims which can be categorized as involving 'lesbian and gay rights' will vary according to the philosophical justification in play. And, while the imprecision associated with needing to show a clear link with the right-holder's sexual orientation may be present *whichever* justification is used, each justification – by identifying a fairly precise moral connection between the fact-situations which fall within its scope – at least limits any imprecision. If our criterion for determining whether something counted as a 'lesbian and gay rights' issue was, by contrast, based *solely* upon proving a link between the legal entitlement in issue and the right-holder's lesbian or gay sexual orientation (i.e. if the role of the justifications were removed), then the door would truly have been opened to semantic disputes.

The second point, which reinforces the first, is that some ambiguities of meaning always exist when we reach the boundaries of words or concepts associated with the law. Joseph Raz has observed that 'It seems to be a common philosophical mistake to think that the core justification of a right or any other normative institution is sufficient for fixing its boundaries. The boundaries of a right are greatly affected by existing local conventions and practices'.[95] And H. L. A. Hart has suggested that however smoothly concepts work 'over the great mass of ordinary cases, [they] will, at some point where their application is in question, prove indeterminate; they will have what has been termed an *open texture* . . . uncertainty at the borderline is the price to be paid for the use of general classifying terms in any form of communication covering matters of fact.'[96]

When discussing 'lesbian and gay rights', it is of course important to remember that so long as we adhere to the moderate constructionist account of sexual orientation, we are merely referring to a political slogan rather than a deeper philosophical concept. Even so, if the boundaries of deeper philosophical concepts, as Hart and Raz argue, are indeterminate or shaped by local conventions and practices, it must follow that the boundaries of a political slogan are bound to be somewhat blurred.

The third point is that the truly important issue, in determining which conception of 'lesbian and gay rights' we should favour, is the validity or otherwise of the philosophical justification which underpins it. In deciding whether to opt for an equality-driven notion, an empowerment-driven notion or a privacy-driven notion of 'lesbian and gay rights', it is the comparative merits of equality, empowerment and privacy as philosophical justifications for legal rights and law reform which should carry weight – rather than concern over the neatness of their differing interpretations of a mere political slogan such as 'lesbian and gay rights'. We will return to the comparative merits of each justification in chapters 6 and 7.

Rights problems

So far in this chapter, we have identified and discussed three sets of issues affecting the meaning of 'lesbian and gay rights'. We must now consider some concerns about the effectiveness and legitimacy of rights-based approaches in campaigning for legal and social change. Concerns about rights-based approaches have been raised by theorists from a variety of perspectives.

Recent feminist writers have tended to be particularly critical of the effectiveness of rights-based approaches as a means of improving women's legal, social and economic positions. As we will see, many of these feminist criticisms can easily be transposed to the lesbian and gay context (it is more accurate to talk of 'feminist criticisms' instead of 'a feminist critique' of rights, given the differences of view between the writers concerned). Carol Smart questions the effectiveness of rights-based approaches on four grounds. First, a rights-based approach may oversimplify complex power relations: the creation of legal rights to cover a given area may wrongly give the appearance of having solved deep-rooted problems of social and economic disadvantage. Smart suggests, for example, that women may be deterred from exercising legal rights to protection from domestic violence because they are economically dependent on the violent male, or because concern for the welfare of their children may cause them to feel that on balance, it is better to keep the father in the family. As Smart observes, this argument should alert us to the fact that legal rights do not necessarily resolve social problems – the creation or use of rights is not an instant, utopian solution.[97] We will see in chapter 8 that very similar arguments about the limits of legal rights can be made in the lesbian and gay context, where an obvious parallel to Smart's domestic violence example can be found in 'queerbashing' attacks on lesbians and gays, which often go unreported due to fear on the part of victims that reporting will lead to public exposure of their sexual orientation, which may lead to problems at work or from their families.[98] A legal right to freedom from violent assault is clearly of little value to people whose social circumstances prevent them from enjoying its protection or challenging its violation.

Smart's second argument is that rights formulated to protect the individual against the state, or the weak against the strong, may be appropriated by the strong to defend their own interests.[99] Some good examples can be found in the area of freedom of expression. An Australian law designed to promote balanced access to the media for both rich and poor election candidates by regulating the purchasing of political advertising during election campaigns was recently struck down by the Australian High Court as an undue restriction on the freedom of expression of candidates who could *afford* to purchase advertising.[100] And in the USA, the First Amendment guarantee of freedom of expression – arguably designed to safeguard citizens' political speech – has been widely used by companies in challenging restrictions on commercial advertising.[101] As the English High Court judge Sir Stephen Sedley has observed, freedom of expression cases of this sort involve

> a very particular and partisan view of what free speech is: because democracy demands a free flow of ideas, the court holds that to accord a hearing to ideas in proportion to the wealth of those who hold them is not only a democratic course but the only democratic course; and in so doing it assumes a symmetry which simply does not exist between freedom of speech and freedom of information . . . human rights can be treated as commodities and, like commodities, appropriated by those who have the means to do so.[102]

In the lesbian and gay context, an analogous example can be found in the 1967 Sexual Offences Act in the UK. The Act decriminalized sex between males, but only where both parties were over 21 and the sexual act occurred 'in private' – that is, where no more than two people were present and no one could stumble upon the scene. One consequence of this restrictive notion of 'privacy' was that criminal conviction rates for 'indecency' offences between males remained almost the same twenty years after the Act as ten years before it, while convictions for some homosexual offences actually *increased* after the passage of the Act.[103] Campaigners for new legal rights for lesbians and gays (indeed, for new legal rights of any sort) clearly need to be very careful when drafting their reform proposals, in order to minimize the danger of new legal rights either being used by groups which were not intended to benefit from them, or from being distorted in their application.

Smart's third argument is that while legal rights may be formulated to deal with social wrongs, they are nearly always focused (at least in the UK) on the individual who has to prove that her rights have been violated. Smart argues that legislation 'like the Sex Discrimination Act 1975 provides certain rights, yet for these to have any impact for women in general requires that vast numbers of individual women can prove that they have been denied their rights through a form of unlawful discrimination'.[104] In consequence, any benefits from the existence of this law have been confined to women who have successfully taken action under it. If Smart's argument is sound, it suggests that caution is necessary in relation to 'lesbian and gay rights' legislation – for, as was argued earlier in the chapter, such legislation can only coherently rest on notions of individual rights (such caution may not be necessary in relation to legislation designed to protect more readily definable groups). Smart's argument may, however, be undermined by her failure to take proper account of the effect of judicial decisions. For, given the system of precedent, a court's ruling on the workings or interpretation of legislation will bind courts of similar or inferior rank in their application of the law in future cases (unless the court is the House of Lords, which may depart from its own decisions). Employers who have received legal advice on the workings of the relevant legislation are more likely to be aware of cases where individual litigants have been successful, and to be cautious about flying in the face of the rulings in those cases. In consequence, while the effectiveness of UK anti-discrimination law may be undermined by the absence of any type of 'class action' provision, it may still be possible for an individual litigant's success to filter down and affect others. The fact that it may not do so on a wide scale is due to the general limits of the law, to be discussed in chapter 8.

A final argument, highlighted both by Smart and by Elizabeth Kingdom, is that the invocation of a right may prompt the invocation by one's opponents of an irreconcilable counter-right, provoking interminable and futile squabbling.[105] It is certainly clear at the level of political debate that couching an argument solely in terms of competing rights, as opposed to the values which lie behind them, may well cause the dispute to degenerate into a series of competing semantic assertions: 'lesbian and gay rights' versus 'the right to uphold family values', for example. This has been highlighted by Kingdom in her observation that the polemical nature of appeals to rights, while perhaps irresistible in adversarial situations, may frustrate the development of substantive and detailed policies.[106] Difficult policy and tactical issues can, in short, get lost amidst strident rights rhetoric. Kingdom warns us that:

> Feminists have long been alert to the way that an appeal to a [specific] right can be transformed into a general right, and its significance for women lost in the process. If feminists claim that a woman has the right to reproduce, there is no obvious reason why that right should not be claimed for men too, and on traditional liberal grounds of equality it would be difficult to oppose that claim . . . [and] there is every reason to suppose that the medical profession and the courts will continue, however subtly, to give priority to a man's right.[107]

An analogous point has been made by Gary Kinsman, in connection with the use of general 'right to privacy' arguments in the 1960s by supporters of the partial decriminalization, in Canada, of sexual acts between persons of the same sex. Kinsman observes that during the course of the Canadian debate, 'No one defended the civil and human rights of lesbians and gay men, let alone our sexuality. The reform camp managed to tie the sickness model [of homosexual behaviour] to their distinction between the public and private spheres. Privacy was narrowly defined, public broadly.'[108] Privacy rhetoric, in other words, operated so as to conceal the underlying concerns of lesbians and gays – the people actually affected by the law reform measure being debated – allowing a false picture of the policy arguments to be painted.

The four objections considered so far are essentially tactical in nature, and opinions as to how powerful they are will inevitably differ. Despite her caution about the use of rights-based arguments in feminist campaigning, Elizabeth Kingdom believes that such arguments may be of some limited use; she therefore suggests that 'the decision whether or not to invoke rights . . . is one that must be based on calculations of likely success or failure of the campaigns so presented . . . it is not always possible to choose the terrain of feminist politics, and it is not always possible to choose the terms in which those politics are conducted.'[109] Carol Smart concludes, by contrast, that 'we are . . . entering into a new era in which rights claims may be becoming less and less valuable. Indeed, it may be that rights claims are becoming counter-productive'.[110]

It is difficult to adopt a firm view on the effectiveness or otherwise of legal rights campaigns without first forming a view about the effectiveness of law more generally as a means of challenging hostility directed at members of socially disfavoured groups. This is an issue which we will consider in chapter 8. For the moment, it will suffice to observe that the arguments considered so far suggest that 'lesbian and gay rights' campaigns may be less likely to achieve dramatic social change than some of their more dogmatic supporters might believe. This need not be a reason for abandoning such campaigns altogether, for, as we will see in chapter 8, it can still plausibly be argued that beneficial effects may sometimes result from 'lesbian and gay rights' campaigning and from law reform more generally. Tactical arguments about rights-based campaigns should, however, encourage us to be cautious about their long-term usefulness or effects, and to be careful about how rights-based arguments for law reform are presented.

Rights-based approaches have also been attacked on the deeper, principled basis that they entail a mistaken conception of the relationship between the individual and society, and that they are individualistic and selfish in nature, thereby downplaying or eclipsing the importance of social responsibility. Charles Taylor suggests, from a communitarian perspective, that 'the free individual of the West is only what he is by virtue of the whole society and civilization which brought him to be and which nourishes him'. There is, in consequence, 'a significant obligation to belong', to commit oneself to such a society or civilization 'whatever are the conditions of its survival'.[111] Conceiving the relationship between the individual and society in terms of the primacy of the individual's rights without a corresponding notion of social obligation is, according to Taylor, incoherent. An analogous argument has been advanced by conservative communitarian Mary Ann Glendon, who suggests that:

> In its silence concerning responsibilities, [the rights-based approach] seems to condone the acceptance of the benefits of living in a democratic social welfare state, without accepting the corresponding personal and civic obligations. In its relentless individualism, it fosters a climate that is inhospitable to society's losers. . . . In its neglect of civil society, it undermines the principal seedbeds of civic and personal virtue.[112]

A feminist perspective on the distinction between rights-based and responsibility-based approaches is developed in Carol Gilligan's controversial book *In a Different Voice*. Gilligan suggests that men tend to see morality in terms of conflicting rights and rules, which are formal and absolute entities, while women tend to view morality in terms of responsibilities and relationships involving others. Gilligan argues that 'the morality of rights differs from the morality of responsibility in its emphasis on [social] separation rather than connection, in its consideration of the individual rather than the relationship as primary'.[113] The morality of rights involves a balancing of claims of self and other, while the morality of responsibility turns on understanding others, giving rise to compassion and care. A rights-based morality (which, one could argue, is what underpins the law) rests on assumptions about justice and equal treatment, while a responsibility-based morality rests on a premise of non-violence, in other words on the idea that no one should be hurt.[114] Gilligan's argument has been attacked on a number of fronts,[115] but for present purposes its importance lies in her conclusion that a proper understanding of social relations will only be provided by a dialogue between the moralities of right and responsibility. If this conclusion is correct, it must cast doubt on approaches to social and legal reform which lay emphasis solely on rights.

These criticisms of rights-based approaches cannot, however, be sustained – for, as Will Kymlicka observes, they involve a misreading of the nature of rights. Gilligan's theory in fact holds good only if one adopts a libertarian theory of absolute rights; other political theories, by contrast, see rights as balanced against responsibilities, thereby presupposing the existence of duties to care for the welfare of others – a point Gilligan ignores.[116] Gilligan's justice framework may emphasize the role of rights but, Kymlicka argues, 'it is quite appropriate to say that these rights impose responsibilities on others'.[117] Responsibility is therefore central to notions of justice – for the question of who people are supposed to care for is itself an issue of justice. And, while Kymlicka attacks Taylor's 'social thesis', it is clear that Taylor's idea of a balance between individual rights and social obligation is compatible with non-communitarian political theories.[118] Rights-based approaches need not, therefore, be incompatible with responsibility; rather, the important issue is the *balance* between rights and responsibility struck by each theory of justice. This argument does not claim, of course, that there is necessarily any relationship between rights and responsibilities owed to society at large rather than to individual right-holders; wider social responsibilities are the concern of each separate theory of justice. This argument is perhaps ironically reinforced by Mary Ann Glendon, who makes clear that it is only notions of *absolute* rights which she is attacking, and that rights talk may be acceptable if reformulated as a dialogue with responsibility.[119] The passage from Glendon's work cited above in fact begins, 'Our rights talk, *in its absoluteness*, promotes unrealistic expectations, heightens social conflict, and inhibits dialogue that might lead towards consensus, accommodation, or at least the discovery of common ground.'[120]

The strength of Kymlicka's argument becomes apparent if we recall the rival interest and duty-based theories of rights discussed earlier in this chapter.[121] For, under a duty-based theory, rights impose responsibilities on other individuals or on the state since the essence of having a right to do something lies in one's ability to enforce other peoples' or the state's duties (responsibilities) to respect one's ability to do that thing. Under the rather more coherent interest-based account, the essence of a right lies in the protection of an interest, but the protection of that interest must still involve the imposition of duties (responsibilities) on others. By definition, therefore, rights and responsibilities go hand in hand: my right is your responsibility, and vice versa. It follows from this that while rights may be individualistic, they are not asocial or anti-social: for the notion of a right entails the existence of some type of relationship between the right-holder and those subject to the right; and this, in turn, presupposes the existence of an organized collection of people who understand and respect the concept of entitlement.[122] It is most unlikely that rights would have any meaning for a solitary human being who had never encountered other members of the species and who had never had access to human literature and learning.

We can thus see that rights-based approaches are compatible with responsibility so long as one does not support a libertarian theory of absolute, unqualifiable rights (as we will see in chapter 6, libertarianism is, in any event, deficient as a political theory). In consequence, the crucial question for any theory of justice is how strong it believes the rights it seeks to promote to be (whether those rights are to be enforceable between individuals or by individuals against the state). It is certainly mistaken, as Kymlicka argues, to attack non-libertarian rights-based approaches for ignoring responsibility; but this does not mean that particular non-libertarian approaches necessarily place the right amount of *emphasis* on responsibility. In fact, the strength of the duties which rights impose on others will depend to a large extent on the theory of justice – that is, the justification for legal rights – which is in play. We saw earlier that moral and legal rights are only as strong as their justification can make them. It must follow that a weak right is capable of imposing only a weak obligation on others, and that a strong obligation can only be imposed by a strong legal right, which must in turn have a strong philosophical justification.

Conclusion: the value of lesbian and gay rights

In this chapter, we have seen that the slogan 'lesbian and gay rights' has no single or blindingly obvious meaning. Subject to the caveat that for something to be a 'lesbian and gay rights' issue it must have a clear link with the right-holder's lesbian or gay sexual orientation, what we count as a 'lesbian and gay rights' issue will depend upon what we see as the justification for law reform. The phrase is also, depending on the context in which it is used, capable of referring to entitlements of a social, legal or moral variety. When political campaigners talk of 'lesbian and gay rights', we therefore need to extract further information before being certain of the exact meaning they attach to the term. In addition, we must not expect that relying on the language of rights will leave us free from problems – queries have been raised over the efficacy of rights rhetoric, and it is also important to remember that rights are intimately related to responsibilities. Furthermore, the adoption of a moderate constructionist account of sexuality and social categories means that we must constantly be prepared to revise our perceptions, including our understanding of contemporary social categories such as 'lesbian' and 'gay'.

What, then, is the remaining value of 'lesbian and gay rights' rhetoric? Campaigning language of this sort is not timeless, any value it possesses being limited and temporary. And, in discussing the slogan, it is important to remember Kingdom's warning about preventing arguments for law reform from becoming obscured by the rhetoric of 'rights'. Nevertheless, it is as a short-hand label for changes explained or envisaged by the law reform justifications that the language of 'lesbian and gay rights' can play a part. We saw earlier how in Canada, excessive reliance on the rhetoric of privacy froze lesbians and gays out of the political picture when it came to law reform in the 1960s. If the language of 'lesbian and gay rights' has one virtue, by contrast, it is that when the phrase is applied to law reform exercises, its beneficiaries are identifiable and obvious.

Strong justifications will be needed for future law reform exercises, but the language of 'lesbian and gay rights' is now so well-established in the campaigning lexicon that so long as we understand its true, limited nature, it may continue to play some role as a slogan. The purpose of this chapter has simply been to clarify, before discussing the topic of law and law reform more fully, some of the uncertainties which might otherwise have surrounded this favoured slogan of law reform campaigners. If we think back to chapter 2, it should now be clear that which of the legal entitlements currently possessed by lesbians and gays *we ourselves* regard as lesbian and gay legal rights, and which law reform demands *we* regard as raising 'lesbian and gay rights' issues, will depend upon which philosophical justification we favour.

Notes
1. Jeffrey Weeks, *Coming Out: Homosexual Politics in Britain from the Nineteenth Century to the Present* (London: Quartet, 1977), p. 190.
2. Barry Adam, *The Rise of a Gay and Lesbian Movement* (Boston: Twayne, 1987), p. 78.
3. See further Weeks, *Coming Out*, ch. 16; Chris Woods, *State of the Queer Nation: A Critique of Gay and Lesbian Politics in 1990s Britain* (London: Cassell, 1995), pp. 6–9; Stephen Jeffery-Poulter, *Peers, Queers and Commons: The Struggle for Gay Law Reform from 1950 to the Present* (London: Routledge, 1991), chs 4 and 5; John D'Emilio, *Making Trouble: Essays on Gay History, Politics, and the University* (New York: Routledge, 1992), esp. ch. 20; and 'Gay politics and community in San Francisco since World War II', in M. B. Duberman, M. Vicinus and G. Chauncey (eds), *Hidden from History: Reclaiming the Gay and Lesbian Past* (London: Penguin, 1989); J. Gomez, 'Out of the past', in D. Deitcher (ed.), *Over the Rainbow: Lesbian and Gay Politics in America Since Stonewall* (London: Boxtree/

Channel Four, 1995); Simon Watney, 'The ideology of the GLF', in Gay Left Collective (eds), *Homosexuality: Power and Politics* (London: Allison & Busby, 1980); the most detailed history of the London GLF is Lisa Power's *No Bath But Plenty of Bubbles: An Oral History of the Gay Liberation Front 1970–73* (London: Cassell, 1995).

4. D'Emilio, *Making Trouble*, pp. 246–7; Adam, *The Rise of a Gay and Lesbian Movement*, chs 5 and 7.

5. Keith Birch, 'A community of interests', in Bob Cant and Susan Hemmings (eds), *Radical Records: Thirty Years of Lesbian and Gay History* (London: Routledge, 1988), pp. 51, 57.

6. Weeks, *Coming Out*, p. 205.

7. Cf. Adam, *The Rise of a Gay and Lesbian Movement*, ch. 7. For practical examples, see, e.g., the *Independent*, 18 August 1995, p. 8; Anya Palmer, 'Lesbian and gay rights campaigning: A report from the coalface', in Angelia R. Wilson (ed.), *A Simple Matter of Justice?* (London: Cassell, 1995) – note, however, that Palmer's account of the history of 'lesbian and gay rights' campaigning may not be universally accepted.

8. See, e.g., Peter Tatchell, *We Don't Want to March Straight: Masculinity, Queers and the Military* (London: Cassell, 1995). For general discussion of queer legal theory and approaches to rights, see chapter 6 below.

9. Examples of complacency are reported by Wilson (ed.), *A Simple Matter of Justice?*, pp. 146–7.

10. The title of John Finnis's article, 'Law, morality, and "sexual orientation"' (1993–4) 69 *Notre Dame Law Review* 1049 would, by contrast, appear to be disrespectful (indeed, Finnis seems generally to use inverted commas for concepts of which he disapproves – see, e.g., 'On "The critical legal studies movement"' (1985) 30 *American Journal of Jurisprudence* 21).

11. Statement of Demands to the Revolutionary Peoples Constitutional Convention from the Male Representatives of National Gay Liberation; reprinted in Deitcher (ed.), *Over the Rainbow*, p. 30.

12. *The Gay Liberation Front Demands*, cited in Jeffery-Poulter, *Peers, Queers and Commons*, pp. 100–1.

13. For further discussion, see Michael Freeden, *Rights* (Milton Keynes: Open University Press, 1991), pp. 6–7. The word 'right' is often used in the context of socially important entitlements such as the right to freedom of expression, but more mundane entitlements are also protected as rights where the relevant criteria have been met. We can therefore conceive of a right to park a car in a particular place, or a right to blow one's nose while walking in the street.

14. Cf. H. L. A. Hart, *The Concept of Law* (Oxford: Clarendon Press, 2nd edn, 1994), pp. 86–7.

15. Richard Mohr's definition of a right (whether social or legal is unclear) as 'at . . . minimum, . . . a *permission* to act in accordance with one's own desires' is therefore inaccurate: Richard Mohr, *Gay Ideas: Outing and Other Controversies* (Boston: Beacon Press, 1992), p. 25.

16. See further the 1971 London GLF Manifesto, reproduced in Power, *No Bath But Plenty of Bubbles*, Appendix 2, esp. pp. 321–30. Legal/social overlaps are also apparent in the demands put forward in the UK in the 1970s by the moderate Campaign for Homosexual Equality – see John Marshall, 'The politics of tea and sympathy', in Gay Left Collective (eds), *Homosexuality: Power and Politics*, pp. 82–3.

17. Adam, *The Rise of a Gay and Lesbian Movement*, pp. 128–9. For an analogous example in the UK, see Wilson (ed.), *A Simple Matter of Justice?*, pp. 146–7.

18. *Report of the Secretary's Task Force on Youth Suicide: Volume 3. Prevention and Interventions in Youth Suicide* (U.S. Department of Health and Human Services, 1989), p. 41; page references here are to the reproduced version of the report

contained in Gary Remafedi (ed.), *Death By Denial: Studies of suicide in gay and lesbian teenagers* (Boston: Alyson Publications, 1994). For analysis of the UK position, see *Gay Times*, April 1996, p. 16 (Terry Sanderson).
19. *Report of the Secretary's Task Force*, pp. 41–2.
20. *Ibid.*, p. 20; also discussed at p. 161.
21. *Ibid.*, p. 28.
22. *Ibid.*, p. 42. See further the discussion in Dale Peck's 'Making history', ch. 4 in Deitcher (ed.), *Over the Rainbow*, pp. 199–202.
23. *Report of the Secretary's Task Force*, pp. 8, 156.
24. *Ibid.*, p. 170.
25. *Ibid.*, pp. 174–7.
26. *Ibid.*, p. 42 (emphasis added).
27. *Ibid.*, pp. 54–5.
28. *Ibid.*, p. 55.
29. *Ibid.*, pp. 154, 193–4.
30. In fact, the report's use of the word 'relationship' is slightly inaccurate, in that it is sexual acts (usually oral and anal sex) which are prohibited.
31. This is implicit in the Commission's discussion, cited above, of the 'principle of equality' – *ibid.*, p. 55.
32. Jonathan N. Katz, *Gay American History: Lesbians and Gay Men in the U.S.A.* (New York: Meridian, rev. edn 1992), p. 9.
33. Useful (and contrasting) analyses include: Joseph Raz, *The Morality of Freedom* (Oxford: Clarendon Press, 1986), chs 7, 8 and 10; Ronald Dworkin, *Taking Rights Seriously* (London: Duckworth, 1977), esp. chs 4 and 7; *A Matter of Principle* (Oxford: Clarendon Press, 1986), ch. 17; Neil MacCormick, 'Rights in legislation', ch. 11 in P. M. S. Hacker and J. Raz (eds), *Law, Morality and Society: Essays in Honour of H. L. A. Hart* (Oxford: Clarendon Press, 1977); H. L. A. Hart, *Essays on Bentham* (Oxford: Clarendon Press, 1982), ch. 7; John Finnis, *Natural Law and Natural Rights* (Oxford: Clarendon Press, 1980), esp. ch. 8; Judith Jarvis Thomson, *The Realm of Rights* (Cambridge, MA: Harvard University Press, 1990), esp. chs 1–7.
34. For a recent analysis, see Thomson, *The Realm of Rights*, pp. 73–6. Thomson is clearly correct to highlight the existence of overlaps between the legal and moral 'realms' of rights, but it seems possible, at least from a lawyer's perspective, to draw a stronger distinction than the author attempts; this position is reflected in the text here. The inclusion of 'social' entitlements here may clarify some of the concerns in David Friedman's 'A positive account of property rights', ch. 1 in Ellen Frankel Paul, Fred Miller and Jeffrey Paul (eds), *Property Rights* (Cambridge: Cambridge University Press, 1994).
35. MacCormick, 'Rights in legislation', p. 192; see also Raz, *The Morality of Freedom*, ch. 7, *Ethics in the Public Domain: Essays in the Morality of Law and Politics* (Oxford: Clarendon Press, 1994), ch. 11. For a defence of the 'will theory', see Hart, *Essays on Bentham*, chs 7 and 8.
36. MacCormick, 'Rights in legislation', pp. 207–8. For useful general discussion of each theory, see Michael Freeman, *Lloyd's Introduction to Jurisprudence* (London: Sweet & Maxwell, 6th edn, 1994), pp. 387–90; Paul Craig, *Public Law and Democracy in the United Kingdom and the United States of America* (Oxford: Clarendon Press, 1990), pp. 193–207.
37. MacCormick, 'Rights in legislation', p. 189.
38. This is, of course, an extremely simplistic definition. For more detailed analysis, compare W. N. Hohfeld, 'Fundamental legal conceptions as applied in judicial reasoning', ch. 1 in W. W. Cook (ed.), *Fundamental Legal Conceptions* (New Haven, CT: Yale University Press, 1923); P. J. Fitzgerald, *Salmond on Jurisprudence* (London: Sweet & Maxwell, 12th edn, 1966), pp. 221–2; Thomson, *The Realm of Rights*, chs 1 and 2; MacCormick, 'Rights in legislation'.
39. For argument concerning the need to distinguish between 'moral positions'

and opinions or positions based on prejudice, see Dworkin, *Taking Rights Seriously*, pp. 248–53.
40. For further discussion, see Joel Feinberg, 'In defence of moral rights' (1992) 12 *Oxford Journal of Legal Studies* 149; H. J. McCloskey, 'Respect for human moral rights versus maximising good', in R. G. Frey (ed.), *Utility and Rights* (Oxford: Basil Blackwell, 1984). It is assumed, in the discussion which follows, that views will differ as to which moral rights people have.
41. Freeden, *Rights*, p. 5. See also Charles Taylor's discussion in 'Atomism', *Philosophy and the Human Sciences: Philosophical Papers, Volume 2* (Cambridge: Cambridge University Press, 1985), p. 195.
42. While there are many practical distinctions between the moral and legal senses, Judith Jarvis Thomson is surely correct to argue that they overlap in that law itself is widely seen as possessing a moral weight (as, in consequence, must legal rights) – *The Realm of Rights*, pp. 73–6.
43. John Gardner, 'Freedom of expression', in Christopher McCrudden and Gerald Chambers (eds), *Individual Rights and the Law in Britain* (Oxford: Clarendon Press, 1994), p. 209.
44. Jan Narveson, 'Contractarian rights', in Frey (ed.), *Utility and Rights*, p. 164.
45. Gardner, 'Freedom of expression', pp. 209–10; see further Feinberg, 'In defence of moral rights', pp. 165–9.
46. See further Raz, *The Morality of Freedom*, pp. 166, 186; Thomson, *The Realm of Rights*, chs 3 and 5. Some philosophers believe such justifications to be based on fixed, objective criteria, so that there is an objective notion of 'right' and 'wrong', while others believe that they turn on subjective, personal choice, so that morality is inherently relative. See further Feinberg, 'In defence of moral rights', pp. 166–9; Attracta Ingram, *A Political Theory of Rights* (Oxford: Clarendon Press, 1994), Part II.
47. For an example of such a sanction, see the *Guardian*, 15 August 1995, p. 1, for the story of a gay man who was denied the right to be a godparent in a church due to the local clergy's feelings about his sexuality – a social entitlement which the church would not have denied to an unmarried heterosexual.
48. For general discussion, see Kent Greenawalt, *Conflicts of Law and Morality* (Oxford: Clarendon Press, 1987), esp. ch. 3.
49. Jeffrey Weeks characterizes the debate as concerning the 'question of the nature of our sexual natures' (*Against Nature: Essays on History, Sexuality and Identity* (London: Rivers Oram, 1991), p. 86).
50. Diana Fuss, *Essentially Speaking: Feminism, Nature & Difference* (New York: Routledge, 1990), p. 97; for a controversial argument concerning the uses of 'community' in lesbian and gay politics, see, however, Woods, *State of the Queer Nation*. Jeffrey Weeks suggests that the political popularity of the idea of a 'gay identity' has increased with the advent of the AIDS epidemic, perhaps as a perceived means of building group solidarity in the face of prejudice – *Against Nature*, pp. 68, 103–4.
51. Useful and rather fuller treatments of the arguments are to be found in Edward Stein (ed.), *Forms of Desire: Sexual Orientation and the Social Constructionist Controversy* (New York: Garland, 1990); Michael Warner (ed.), *Fear of a Queer Planet: Queer Politics and Social Theory* (Minneapolis: University of Minnesota Press, 1993); Fuss, *Essentially Speaking*; Elizabeth Frazer and Nicola Lacey, *The Politics of Community: A Feminist Critique of the Liberal-Communitarian Debate* (Hemel Hempstead: Harvester Wheatsheaf, 1993); Weeks, *Against Nature*.
52. An instructive comparison can be drawn here between the views expressed by Steven Epstein and Edward Stein in chs 10 and 12,

respectively, of *Forms of Desire*.
53. Fuss, *Essentially Speaking*, pp. xi (emphasis added), 2. See also Weeks, *Against Nature*, p. 95; Edward Stein, 'The Essentials of Constructionism and the construction of essentialism' in *Forms of Desire*, pp. 325–6.
54. This is not to say, however, that it is impossible to conceive of an essentialist theory of transsexualism.
55. Edward Stein suggests that different constructionist theorists pursue this argument to varying extents – see his ch. 12 in *Forms of Desire*.
56. Fuss, *Essentially Speaking*, p. 2.
57. For an example of such an approach, see S. B. Ortner and H. Whitehead (eds), *Sexual Meanings: The Cultural Construction of Gender and Sexuality* (Cambridge: Cambridge University Press, 1981), esp. ch. 1.
58. Steven Epstein, 'Gay politics, ethnic identity: The limits of social constructionism', in Stein (ed.), *Forms of Desire*, pp. 250–1; see, however, Stein's critique of Epstein's own interpretation of sexuality, at pp. 327–30.
59. D'Emilio, *Making Trouble*, p. 183.
60. Weeks, *Against Nature*, p. 15.
61. It is instructive to read David Halperin's essay 'Sex before sexuality: Pederasty, politics, and power in Classical Athens', and Robert Padgug's 'Sexual matters: Rethinking sexuality in history' – both in Duberman *et al.*, *Hidden from History*.
62. Halperin, 'Sex before sexuality', p. 42.
63. *Ibid.*, pp. 50–1.
64. Jeffery-Poulter, *Peers, Queers and Commons*, chs 1 and 2. Peter Bartlett's currently unpublished paper 'Another sodomitical erection', presented at the Lancaster University Lesbian and Gay Legal Studies Conference in September 1995, highlights the criminal law's early focus on commission of the *act* of sodomy – as opposed to commission of *heterosexual* or *homosexual* sodomy – as the factor on which punishment turned.
65. For Boswell's own view, see his 'Categories, experience and sexuality', in Stein (ed.), *Forms of Desire*; Jeffrey Weeks conducts a survey of early essentialist work in 'Discourse, desire and sexual deviance: Some problems in a history of homosexuality', in Kenneth Plummer (ed.), *The Making of the Modern Homosexual* (London: Hutchinson, 1981).
66. John Boswell, *Christianity, Social Tolerance, and Homosexuality: Gay People in Western Europe from the Beginning of the Christian Era to the Fourteenth Century* (Chicago: University of Chicago Press, 1980), p. 44.
67. 'Essential rights and contested identities: Sexual orientation and equality rights jurisprudence in Canada' (1995) 8 *Canadian Journal of Law and Jurisprudence* 49 at 54.
68. Weeks, *Coming Out*, p. 3 (cf. pp. x–xi). See also Robert Padgug, 'Sexual matters', pp. 59–60; Gary Kinsman, *The Regulation of Desire: Sexuality in Canada* (Montreal: Black Rose Books, 1987), p. 15; Katz, *Gay American History*, pp. 6–7.
69. Padgug, 'Sexual matters', p. 57; see also Edward Stein's comments in *Forms of Desire*, pp. 340–4.
70. For discussion of a variety of constructionist views, see Stein, 'The essentials of constructionism and the construction of essentialism', pp. 340 *et seq*.
71. For a feminist critique of pure essentialism, see Frazer and Lacey, *The Politics of Community*, esp. pp. 131–4.
72. See, e.g., Dean Hamer and Peter Copeland, *The Science of Desire: The Search for the Gay Gene and the Biology of Behavior* (New York: Simon & Schuster, 1994); for a critique, see Walter Bodmer and Robin McKie, *The Book of Man: The Quest to Discover Our Genetic Heritage* (London: Abacus, 1995), pp. 203–4.
73. See further Epstein's argument in 'Gay politics, ethnic identity', p. 258.
74. Edward Stein's assertion that 'if

one's sexual orientation is caused by having a certain gene, then social constructionism is wrong' (in *Forms of Desire*, p. 352) must therefore be rebutted. What I have categorized as radical constructionism could not survive such a proof; moderate constructionism could.

75. Richard Mohr's rather strident attack on all constructionist theories, in his *Gays/Justice: A Study of Ethics, Society, and Law* (New York: Columbia University Press, 1988), pp. 39–42, can therefore be rejected; while radical constructionism may be problematic, moderate constructionism is a viable theory. In any event, Mohr's later discussion of constructionism, in his *Gay Ideas*, chs 7 and 8, suggests a retreat from his earlier, blanket condemnation of constructionism.

76. See, e.g., Fuss, *Essentially Speaking*, ch. 1; Frazer and Lacey, *The Politics of Community*, esp. ch. 6. Michael Warner suggests that the debate between the two camps has largely run its course – *Fear of a Queer Planet*, p. x; see also Janet Halley's arguments, *ibid*., pp. 97–9 (developed in her useful article 'Sexual orientation and the politics of biology: A critique of the argument from immutability' (1994) 46 *Stanford Law Review* 503, esp. at 546–66).

77. Fuss, *Essentially Speaking*, p. 4.

78. Stein (ed.), *Forms of Desire*, p. 350 (note also Stein's discussion of the background to this comment, at pp. 349–50).

79. Boswell, 'Revolutions, universals, and sexual categories', in Duberman *et al.*, *Hidden from History*, p. 35.

80. Boswell, *Christianity, Social Tolerance, and Homosexuality*, p. 59; see also the distinction between 'gay' and 'homosexual', p. 44.

81. This is not to say that essentialists such as Boswell would necessarily subscribe to this view – it is simply a logical consequence of the general essentialist position.

82. It is important to be clear, in any discussion of 'group', 'collective' or 'minority' rights, about exactly which social minority groups are viewed as being entitled to the rights concerned – see Will Kymlicka, *Liberalism, Community, and Culture* (Oxford: Clarendon Press, 1989), pp. 138–9; see also, however, Kymlicka's *Multicultural Citizenship* (Oxford: Clarendon Press, 1995), p. 19.

83. For discussion, see, e.g., Nathan Glazer, 'Individual rights against group rights', in his *Ethnic Dilemmas: 1964–1982* (Cambridge, MA: Harvard University Press, 1982); Raz, *The Morality of Freedom*, pp. 207–9; Michael Hartney, 'Some confusions concerning collective rights' (1991) 4 *Canadian Journal of Law and Jurisprudence* 293; Leslie Green, 'Two views of collective rights', (1991) 4 *Canadian Journal of Law and Jurisprudence* 315; Nicola Lacey, 'From individual to group?', in Bob Hepple and Erica Szyszczak (eds), *Discrimination: the Limits of Law* (London: Mansell, 1992); J. Angelo Corlett, 'The problem of collective moral rights', (1994) 7 *Canadian Journal of Law and Jurisprudence* 237; Kymlicka, *Multicultural Citizenship*; Maleiha Malik, 'Communal goods as human rights', ch. 7 in Conor Gearty and Adam Tomkins (eds), *Understanding Human Rights* (London: Mansell, 1996). See also Charles Taylor's discussion of 'collective ends' in his essay 'The politics of recognition', in Amy Gutmann (ed.), *Multiculturalism: Examining the Politics of Recognition* (Princeton, NJ: Princeton University Press, 1994).

84. See Glazer's discussion of analogous issues, 'Individual rights against group rights'.

85. See, e.g., Mark Guthrie and Angus Hamilton, *The Lesbian and Gay Rights Handbook* (London: Cassell, forthcoming).

86. See, e.g., Palmer, 'Lesbian and gay rights campaigning'. Martha Nussbaum's discussion – in 'Lesbian and gay rights: Pro', ch. 7 in Michael Leahy and Dan Cohn-Sherbok (eds),

The Liberation Debate: Rights at Issue (London: Routledge, 1996) – lacks any general explanation, based on a philosophical justification, of what counts as a 'lesbian and gay rights' issue; in consequence, Nussbaum veers uneasily between describing existing 'rights' and recommending new ones.

87. In the UK, the law reform oriented Stonewall Group employs the campaigning slogan 'fighting for lesbian and gay equality'. For analysis and critique of the current position in the US see, e.g., Steven Seidman, 'Identity and politics in a "postmodern" gay culture', in Warner (ed.), *Fear of a Queer Planet*; Adam, *The Rise of a Gay and Lesbian Movement*; D'Emilio, *Making Trouble*, esp. ch. 13.

88. Such a prohibition currently applies in English law as a result of *R v. Brown* [1994] 1 AC 212. The decision of the House of Lords was upheld by the European Court of Human Rights in *Laskey, Jaggard and Brown v. United Kingdom* (109/1995/615/703–705), 19 February 1997. An equality-based approach clearly underpins Robert Wintemute's argument that *Brown* does not raise issues of 'sexual orientation discrimination' – *Sexual Orientation and Human Rights: The United States Constitution, the European Convention, and the Canadian Charter* (Oxford: Clarendon Press, 1995), pp. 11–12.

89. See Nicholas Bamforth, 'Sadomasochism and consent' [1994] *Criminal Law Review* 661.

90. [1994] 1 AC 212. See, e.g., the *Pink Paper*, 10 March 1995, p. 1; 27 January 1995, pp. 1, 2, 16–17; 21 March 1993, pp. 1, 3, 6, 10.

91. An obvious example is *Saunders v. Scottish National Camps Association* [1980] IRLR 174 (Employment Appeal Tribunal), [1981] IRLR 277 (Court of Session).

92. For legal arguments, see R. A. Watt, 'HIV, discrimination, unfair dismissal and pressure to dismiss' (1992) 21 *Industrial Law Journal* 280.

93. Although see Stephen Jeffery-Poulter's account of lesbian and gay voting behaviour during the 1987 British general election – *Peers, Queers and Commons*, ch. 10.

94. Cf., however, Frazer and Lacey, *The Politics of Community*, pp. 201–2.

95. Raz, *Ethics in the Public Domain*, p. 133.

96. H. L. A. Hart, *The Concept of Law* (Oxford: Clarendon Press, 2nd edn, 1994), pp. 127–8 (see also p. 12 for discussion of ambiguities in legal rules); see also 'Definition and theory in jurisprudence', reprinted in H. L. A. Hart, *Essays in Jurisprudence and Philosophy* (Oxford: Clarendon Press, 1983).

97. Carol Smart, *Feminism and the Power of Law* (London: Routledge, 1989), pp. 144–5. See also Smart's 'Feminism and law: Some problems of analysis and strategy' (1986) 14 *International Journal of the Sociology of Law* 109; Elizabeth Kingdom, *What's Wrong With Rights? Problems for Feminist Politics of Law* (Edinburgh: Edinburgh University Press, 1991), esp. pp. 47, 63.

98. For a practical example, see the *Independent*, 9 November 1995, p. 5 ('Stigma creates fear of reporting attacks'). For discussion of the US context, see Mohr, *Gays/Justice*, ch. 6. Note, however, Mohr's somewhat over-optimistic view as to the effectiveness of civil rights legislation.

99. Smart, *Feminism and the Power of Law*, pp. 145–6.

100. *Australian Capital Television v. Commonwealth of Australia* (1992) 177 C.L.R. 106.

101. See Eric Barendt, *Freedom of Speech* (Oxford: Clarendon Press, 1985), pp. 54–63.

102. Sir Stephen Sedley, 'Human rights: a twenty-first century agenda' [1995] *Public Law* 386 at 394.

103. Jeffery-Poulter, *Peers, Queers and Commons*, pp. 257–8.

104. Smart, *Feminism and the Power of Law*, p. 145. See also Lacey, 'From individual to group?', esp. pp. 101–6.

105. Kingdom, *What's Wrong With Rights?*, esp. pp. 2–6; Smart,

Feminism and the Power of Law, p. 145. See also Didi Herman, *Rights of Passage: Struggles for Lesbian and Gay Legal Equality* (Toronto: University of Toronto Press, 1994), esp. pp. 148–9.
106. Kingdom, *What's Wrong With Rights?*, p. 63.
107. *Ibid.*, p. 79. For further discussion of the 'male' nature of law, see Catharine MacKinnon, 'Feminism, Marxism, method, and the state: An agenda for theory' (1982) 7 *Signs: Journal of Women in Culture and Society* 515, and 'Feminism, Marxism, method, and the state: Toward feminist jurisprudence' (1983) 8 *Signs: Journal of Women in Culture and Society* 635.
108. Kinsman, *The Regulation of Desire*, p. 170.
109. Kingdom, *What's Wrong With Rights?*, p. 130; see also pp. 4, 141–2, 148.
110. Smart, *Feminism and the Power of Law*, p. 146.
111. Taylor, 'Atomism', pp. 206–7; for criticism, see Will Kymlicka, *Contemporary Political Philosophy: An Introduction* (Oxford: Clarendon Press, 1990), pp. 216–30.
112. Mary Anne Glendon, *Rights Talk: The Impoverishment of Political Discourse* (New York: Free Press, 1991), p. 14.
113. Carol Gilligan, *In a Different Voice: Psychological Theory and Women's Development* (Cambridge, MA: Harvard University Press, rev. edn, 1993), p. 19.
114. *Ibid.*, pp. 164–5, 174.
115. For feminist critique, see Catharine MacKinnon, *Feminism Unmodified: Discourses on Life and Law* (Cambridge, MA: Harvard University Press, 1987), pp. 38–9; Smart, *Feminism and the Power of Law*, pp. 73–6; Frazer and Lacey, *The Politics of Community*, pp. 63–4, 131.
116. Kymlicka, *Contemporary Political Philosophy*, pp. 275–86. For discussion of the notion of socialist rights, see Tom Campbell, *The Left and Rights: A Conceptual Analysis of the Idea of Socialist Rights* (London: Routledge, 1983), esp. ch. 10.
117. Kymlicka, *Contemporary Political Philosophy*, p. 275.
118. *Ibid.*
119. Glendon, *Rights Talk*, p. 15 and ch. 7. See also Didi Herman's argument in *Rights of Passage*, pp. 148–9.
120. Glendon, *Rights Talk*, p. 14 (emphasis added).
121. As chapter 4 will make clear, however, I do not agree with Kymlicka's support for the concept of a neutral state.
122. For an analogous point, see Campbell, *The Left and Rights*, p. 107.

4

Justifications: Their Nature and Operation

> *Interference with individual liberty may be thought an evil requiring justification ... for it is itself the infliction of a special form of suffering. ... This is of particular importance in the case of laws enforcing a sexual morality. They may create misery of a quite special degree. For both the difficulties involved in the repression of sexual impulses and the consequences of repression are quite different from those involved in the abstention from 'ordinary' crime.*
>
> — H. L. A. Hart[1]

> *The standard modern position involves a number of explicit or implicit judgments about the proper role of law and the compelling interests of political communities, and about the evil of homosexual conduct. Can these be defended by reflective, critical, publicly intelligible and rational arguments? I believe they can ...*
>
> — John Finnis[2]

Introduction

Each of the above remarks forms part of a philosophical argument about the law's treatment of lesbians and gays. Professor Hart, lecturing in 1962, was seeking to defend, on a principled basis, the Wolfenden Committee's recommendation that private, consenting sexual acts between men should be decriminalized in England and Wales. Professor Finnis – who, as we saw in chapter 1, gave testimony in *Romer* v. *Evans* in support of Colorado's failed Amendment 2 – was arguing in 1993 from principles of his own that while the 'modern' European state did not and generally should not use law to prohibit private, consenting sexual acts between adults of the same sex, such acts remained morally unacceptable and the state *could* legitimately try to discourage them by enacting laws like Amendment 2. Viewed against the political background of the early 1960s, Hart's argument could be described as sympathetic to the position of gay and bisexual men; by contrast, lesbian and gay campaigners would doubtless describe Finnis's attitude, when viewed against the contemporary US political background, as overtly hostile.

We will consider the substantive merits of each argument (and of others) in the following three chapters. What is of interest, for the time being, is the assumption shared by *both* theorists – despite their very different standpoints – that the legitimacy of the laws (or proposed laws) they were considering turned on broader philosophical arguments. The main theme of Hart's 1962 lecture was the legal enforcement of morality, in connection with which he posed the following question: 'Is the fact that certain conduct is by common standards immoral sufficient to justify making that conduct punishable by law? Is it morally permissible to enforce morality as such? Ought immorality as such to be a crime?'[3] A central feature of this question, Hart noted, was 'that it is a question of *justification*. In asking it we are committed to the general critical principle that the use of legal coercion by any society calls for justification as something *prima facie* objectionable to be tolerated only for the sake of some countervailing good.'[4]

Hart was, in short, asking whether there was a justification for laws which enforced particular (or any) views of morality. As we saw in chapter 1, any justification for law or law reform invokes a vision of how law should be used in a legitimate system of government. Such a vision will rest on a theory of justice – that is, a theory concerning rightful and wrongful distributions of entitlements among members of society – which is closely connected with a theory of political morality, concerning the principles which should guide the exercise of public power by state institutions. In this case, Hart's background theories clearly valued individual liberty sufficiently highly that *unless* a 'countervailing good' could be shown justifying the law's (i.e., the state's) interference with liberty, the interference would be illegitimate. Starting from this basis, Hart went on to develop his argument that private consenting sexual acts between men should not be prohibited by the criminal law.

In his argument – based in part on his testimony in *Romer v. Evans*[5] – Finnis stressed the need for 'reflective, critical, publicly intelligible and rational' criteria to demonstrate the legitimacy of what he described as the law's 'standard modern position' (although given the differing legal and political positions on each side of the Atlantic, it is in fact disingenuous for Finnis to use what he presents – with questionable accuracy – as the prevailing *European* legal standard as the backdrop against which an element of the often harsher US regime is to be assessed[6]). After focusing in detail on what he described as 'the underlying issue which receives far too little public discussion: What is wrong with homosexual conduct?',[7] Finnis argued that the permissible actions of the government of a political community are limited by its general justifying aim, purpose or rationale, which is to promote the common good of that community.[8] The legitimacy of a law such as Amendment 2 thus depended on its complying with this general justifying aim, rationale or purpose.[9] It is in this light that we have to understand Finnis's emphasis on the word 'properly' in his remark (originally cited in chapter 1) that a political community which judges that family life is of fundamental importance to the common good 'can rightly judge that it has a compelling interest in denying that homosexual conduct – a "gay lifestyle" – is a valid, humanly acceptable choice and form of life, and in doing whatever it *properly* can . . . to discourage such conduct'.[10] The word 'properly' in fact underlines Finnis's belief that the community's power to enact law is subject to moral limits, stemming from its general justifying aim, purpose or rationale.[11] In consequence, it can be seen that the 'question of justification' – to borrow Hart's phrase – for any law under Finnis's background theories must concern whether it falls within these moral limits. As we will see in chapter 5, Finnis's current view is that a state can 'properly' enact a law such as Amendment 2, but in general cannot legitimately criminalize private lesbian or gay sexual acts.[12]

In chapters 5 to 7, we will examine the main philosophical justifications which have been advanced to demonstrate the legitimacy either of laws which could be said to treat lesbians and gays in a hostile fashion, or of law reform measures of a sympathetic nature. In this chapter, we must carry out some necessary preparation by considering four issues concerning the nature of philosophical justifications in general – an exercise which is necessary if we are to make sense of the justifications to be considered in subsequent chapters. The first issue raises the point that the need to find a justification for law or law reform will in itself exclude certain theories of justice and political morality from consideration. The second issue concerns the evolution and reach of any justification, in the sense of asking whether the applicability of a justification varies from society to society according to local conditions, or whether the theories of justice and political morality underpinning a justification can legitimately be used to assess the propriety of conduct in whatever society and time period it occurs. The third issue concerns the theme of Professor Hart's lecture, namely whether it is permissible for the law to enforce views about morality – and if so, what type of morality. In chapter 1 we argued that questions of justice, political morality and frequently sexual morality arise in law reform debates concerning the entitlements of lesbians and gays. Before considering (in chapters 5 to 7) the arguments which can actually be used in such debates, it is therefore necessary to analyse how considerations of morality may *legitimately* be used, if at all. The fourth issue is to identify the criteria which should be used in assessing the strengths and weaknesses of each individual justification – for without such criteria, we will be unable properly to assess any of the justifications to be discussed in chapters 5, 6 and 7.

The first issue: rejecting totalitarianism and the conservative presumption

This issue can be dealt with relatively quickly. We have seen that each justification invokes a particular vision of how law should be used in a legitimate system of government – a vision which involves theories of justice and political morality. It is important to realize, however, that merely by identifying a need to find justifications for law *and* law reform, we are by definition ruling out from consideration certain background theories of justice and political morality – those which support totalitarian systems of government – as well as rejecting the conservative presumption which maintains that attempts to reform the law must be justified more strenuously than the continued existence of current laws.

Taking totalitarianism first, it was argued in chapter 1 that the perceived need to find a justification for laws and law reform stems from the coercive potential of law – a perception which rests on the assumption that individuals are entitled not to be coerced without justification. By committing ourselves to the proposition that is necessary to find a justification for law or law reform (whatever justification we ultimately favour), we are therefore suggesting that we support a theory of political morality which places moral limits of some sort on the power of the state.[13] A totalitarian theorist would, by contrast, believe that as a matter of political morality, there are no such limits: instead, states could legitimately implement whatever laws they chose, regardless of the consequences or merits of those laws. As a matter of totalitarian justice, there would be no protected entitlements for individuals, given that the state could legitimately revoke them at any given moment. For a totalitarian, therefore, there is no need to find a justification before any new law is introduced: for to insist on a justification would be to deny that the state's power is limitless. Someone who is a totalitarian could therefore deny the need to find a philosophical justification for the use of law while remaining true to their own theories of political morality and justice.

In consequence, the suggestion that a justification is necessary in order to legitimate any use of law or any law reform measure must, to a limited extent, be politically loaded. This is not to say, of course, that totalitarianism is an acceptable political position – such an idea would surely be repugnant to right-thinking people. The example of totalitarianism is simply useful in highlighting the fact that arguments about law reform justifications are already value-loaded, given that they exclude totalitarian political theories, even before we consider which substantive justification (and background theories of justice and political morality) we prefer.

A related type of value-loading can be found in the claim that justifications for existing laws are just as necessary as justifications for law reform measures. This claim may appear to make sense analytically, given that in the absence of any complicating factors, existing law has just as great a coercive potential as new laws. It is possible to imagine the type of simple conservative theorist who would maintain, however, that change requires a stronger justification than sticking with what we already have[14] – perhaps because of the greater complication or disruption which it may be felt to entail, for example. This type of theorist may well maintain that the fact that something is already law gives it special weight – as a consequence of which, it does not need to be justified in the same way, or to the same extent, as law reform proposals. By arguing that justifications must be found both for existing and new laws, we are by contrast rejecting this simple conservative presumption.

The second issue: when and where do justifications apply?

In August 1995, the Zimbabwean President, Robert Mugabe, launched a campaign against what he categorized as the threat of moral corruption posed to his country by male homosexuality. When challenged by protests from human rights groups in Western Europe, North America and South Africa, the Zimbabwean government responded by suggesting that it was inappropriate for people from other countries to use *their* moral standards instead of those which, it was claimed, prevailed in Zimbabwean society, to evaluate the legitimacy of this campaign. The Zimbabwean government claimed that their campaign was merely reinforcing traditional African values, and that it was tantamount to moral imperialism for nations with different moral standards to judge Zimbabwe by those standards.[15]

There is considerable dispute about the accuracy of the Zimbabwean government's implicit characterization of male homosexuality as a 'white man's disease' alien to 'natural' Zimbabwean society, and about its interpretation of traditional African moral standards.[16] Doubt has also been cast on the government's motives in launching the campaign: a common western reaction was to assume that the issue had been seized upon to provide the Zimbabwean electorate with a convenient distraction from the country's poor economic performance. What is of interest for present purposes, however, is the moral relativism employed by the Zimbabwean government in order to defend its campaign. For the government's 'traditional African values' argument clearly presumes that it is wrong to suggest that there are universally applicable, transcultural and transhistorical standards by which a state's conduct can be judged, and that instead, the proper criteria for assessing the legitimacy of state action are local standards which form part of the culture of the society concerned. It seems likely, by contrast, that the protests of the non-Zimbabwean human rights groups did presume – for there is no evidence that these groups attempted to base their arguments on any alternative interpretation of 'African values' – that there *are* general, transcultural standards relating to individual liberty, according to which the Zimbabwean government's conduct could properly be condemned.

The dispute between the Zimbabwean government and the human rights groups neatly parallels the topic to be examined in this section – namely the *range of circumstances* in which each law reform justification is applicable. The basic question is whether the same philosophical justification can be employed with equal validity across time and across cultures. In other words, is it appropriate to condemn *all* societies whose laws fail to match up to the standards demanded by the theories of justice and political morality underpinning the justification, or can each justification only validly be used in assessing the laws of the particular society or societies in which it evolved? The importance of this issue can be seen if we hypothetically assume that the Zimbabwean government decided to use its 'traditional African values' argument to justify the introduction of new legislation which overtly discriminated against gay men. Could non-Zimbabweans legitimately condemn this, using their own theories of justice, as an unjustifiable use of state power? Equally, if non-Zimbabweans were to campaign for the removal of existing anti-lesbian and gay laws in Zimbabwe, and for the introduction of non-discrimination legislation there, could such law reform measures be properly justified using arguments which could be shown to be alien to Zimbabwean culture? These questions, which go to the legitimacy of law reform justifications, are concerned at root with whether law reform justifications and background theories of justice and political morality can reach from one society and time period to another.

Inquiry into the question of the legitimate reach of law reform justifications brings into play aspects of what is loosely described as the liberal–communitarian debate concerning the comparative moral significance of the individual and the community in any theory of justice or political morality, and the practical and moral role of the cultural and political values which are shared in a community.[17] The phrase 'loosely described' is used since the precise boundary between liberal and communitarian thought is difficult to define; indeed, it must be doubted whether there is any such thing as a general 'liberal' or 'communitarian' position.[18] At the risk of oversimplification, however, it may be ventured that communitarians have tended to see a person's identity as the product of their social surroundings, and to accord a community's shared social and moral understandings some weight in theories of justice and political morality. Liberals, by contrast, have tended to stress the moral pre-eminence of the individual and have, to varying extents, downplayed or denied the existence of a role for shared community values in a liberal theory of justice or political morality.[19] In consequence, many liberals defend the possibility of theories of justice (leading to law reform justifications) which are valid across cultures and across time, while communitarians tend to reject, in postmodernist fashion, any such 'grand theorizing' – instead employing notions of moral relativism of the type advanced by the Zimbabwean government.[20] Which approach, on balance, is preferable? It will be argued in this section that the proper answer is 'neither': both approaches contain serious pitfalls, and a coherent and acceptable account of the reach of justifications for laws and law reform (and of their underlying theories of justice and political morality) will only be provided if a third approach is adopted. In order to reach this third approach, we will first need to consider some communitarian and liberal theories in greater detail.

Turning first to what has been labelled a communitarian theory (for the label 'communitarian' tends to be applied to theorists rather more often than it is claimed by them), Michael Walzer argues that ideas about human rights do not emerge from any conception of a common, universal humanity: rather, conceptions of rights and rights-claims are 'local and particular in character'.[21] It is therefore a mistake to search for a single underlying sense of (distributive) justice which all societies can rightfully embrace – rather, different societies will have their own varying notions.[22] 'History', Walzer suggests, 'reveals no single good and no naturally dominant good' in the context of theories of justice;[23] and, since social meanings are historical in character, what counts as a just or unjust distribution of goods will change over time.[24] Theorists should not, according to this view, seek to devise ideal and universally applicable notions of justice (and hence justifications for law reform) – rather, they should search for theories which are appropriate to the society from which they are drawn, and whose common life they reflect.[25] For in matters of morality, argument is no more than an appeal to the common meanings which prevail in a given political community and which vary according to the community in question.[26] Indeed, Walzer claims, 'Justice is rooted in [a community's own] distinct understandings of places, honours, jobs, things of all sorts that constitute a shared way of life. To override these understandings is (always) to act unjustly.'[27]

As Raymond Plant observes, the consequence of Walzer's reasoning must be that any struggle against the existing social (or legal) order of a given society must take place from within that society, and cannot – if it is to be counted as just – be based upon some claim that the society fails to meet an externally determined (i.e. transhistorical or transcultural) standard of justice.[28] And, as part of a more general attack on communitarianism – which he mistakenly equates with postmodernism – the convinced liberal Richard Mohr argues that:

> In the postmodern [sic] view, politics permeates all our ideas, and the values that inform that politics are always, like everything else, culturally determined. Since the meaning of a thing is derived from its social context, there can be no values outside of a society from which one can evaluate the society itself. Postmodernism [sic] is committed to ethical relativism . . . at the level of the society.[29]

According to a communitarian view such as Walzer's, there can, in short, be no universal, transcultural justification by which the laws of a society can properly be judged or challenged, *whether from outside that society or from the inside*. Lesbians and gays in Zimbabwe, in order to defend themselves, would have to find their own interpretation of 'traditional African values' on which to base their argument (as would the non-Zimbabwean human rights groups), rather than seeking to rely on privacy or equality-based arguments from outside traditional Zimbabwean culture. For such arguments could be met, for a moral relativist, with the rebuttal that 'this is the way we've always done things here, so it's none of your business'.

The danger inherent in moral relativism is clearly seen in the Zimbabwean example. For relativism, as Ernest Gellner has noted, must 'allow illiberal values their place in the sun' and 'deprives us of the means – indeed of the right – to express deep revulsion' at such values.[30] By what means, Gellner asks rhetorically, could a relativist condemn a society which condoned, as part of its *own* deep-rooted moral code, slavery, gulags, female circumcision or gas chambers? This difficulty paves the way for a related complaint which is often made against communitarian theories, namely that however progressive they may appear to be at first sight, their emphasis on the moral power of shared cultural values, whether in shaping individual identities or in the decision-making process more generally, opens the door to the enforcement of deep-seated restrictive or discriminatory values which are prevalent in any society.[31] As Will Kymlicka notes, 'the problem of the exclusion of historically marginalized groups is endemic to the communitarian project'.[32] If, as the moral relativist seems to suggest, marginalized groups can appeal only to the values internal to their culture in order to build justifications for law reform –

that is, to the values of the culture which is *already* oppressing them – they would appear to be in an almost hopeless position.[33] As well as hampering the prospects of groups who consider *themselves* oppressed within a culture, moral relativism would also seem to make it difficult to assess whether a group can even properly be described as unfairly oppressed. To quote Richard Mohr once again:

> We can tell from within a culture (say, from its jokes and slang) that some group is humiliated, held in contempt, but without culturally-neutral values, one cannot tell whether that group does or does not indeed deserve the contempt. Without culturally-neutral values, we cannot know that certain groups aren't simply being put in their proper place . . . we are unable to tell when ill-treatment and ill-will is warranted and when they constitute oppression.[34]

This call for transcultural standards of justice has been echoed by Gellner. The unattractive aspects of a communitarian approach to law reform justifications – namely the general difficulty it would appear to face in resisting oppressive values which form part of the traditional culture of a society, together with the deficiencies of its inherently relativist treatment of concepts of justice – encourage Gellner to argue that:

> The possibility of criticism of a social and political order is an essential ingredient of liberty, but it doesn't make sense unless it is accepted that independent criteria are at least thinkable. A society which is merely a 'plural' congeries of styles and values cannot criticise part of itself. . . . Modern liberty differs from its ancient predecessor not merely because it stresses individual freedom over collective self-rule: it also includes the notion of trans-ethnic or trans-political truth, which is not simply engendered by a culture and its practices.[35]

A related argument has been developed by Ronald Dworkin, who suggests that if anything can be seen as a traditional community social practice, it is that of worrying about what justice really is – of presuming that justice is a critic of the community's practices rather than their mirror. Justice could thus be seen as a matter of general, transcultural standards by which a society can be evaluated and criticized. Ultimately, Dworkin claims,

> political theory can make no contribution to how we govern ourselves except by struggling, against all the impulses that drag us back into

our own culture, toward generality and some reflective basis for deciding which of our traditional distinctions and discriminations are genuine and which spurious, which contribute to the flourishing of the ideals we want, after reflection, to embrace, and which serve only to protect us from the personal costs of that demanding process. We cannot leave justice to convention and anecdote.[36]

Belief in universally applicable standards of justice and political morality is not confined to liberals such as Dworkin and Gellner: from a more conservative standpoint, John Finnis believes in the existence of universal principles which indicate the basic forms of human flourishing as goods to be pursued, together with a set of basic methodological requirements of 'practical reasonableness' which distinguish morally right and wrong ways of acting. In consequence, Finnis claims, one can formulate a set of general moral standards and identify a set of goods which are self-evidently important to human well-being.[37] As we will see in chapter 5, Finnis uses this set of universal standards to support his claim that sexual acts between people of the same sex are always immoral.

Given the deficiencies of communitarianism, the idea of universally valid theories of justice and political morality – from which transcultural and transhistorical justifications for particular laws or law reform measures could be deduced – may initially appear to be attractive, provided the theory adopted is liberal in nature. It would allow us to develop clear criteria for assessing the propriety of laws anywhere, and the underlying theories could be said to yield a truly universal set of human rights. It would also, as Dworkin suggests, fit in with many of our intuitions about justice as something which stands above localized, day-to-day life. The dangers of moral relativism would be avoided, and it would be possible – at least if a universalist liberal theory of justice is adopted – to provide lesbians and gays in Zimbabwe-type situations with clear lines of defence.

Unfortunately, theories which lay claim to universal validity are open to the same types of criticism as those made of essentialist theories of sexuality in chapter 3. The roles of the two types of theory are of course very different, but both could be said to fail to take account, in their respective spheres of operation, of the sheer variety of ways in which it is possible to understand and to theorize about human behaviour across time and across cultures. For it is surely facile not to acknowledge that moral assessments *do* vary, to an extent, from society to society and age to age, and it can only be presumptive and arrogant (not to say presumptively illiberal for universalist theories of a liberal variety) simply to assert that one's theory of justice and political morality applies regardless of circumstances. If particular concepts of justice are entirely alien to a society, it is both artificial and undesirable to claim that they still apply to that society (at least unless a fuller justification is offered), for such a claim amounts to little more than talking of 'civilizing the natives'. Like essentialist assessments of sexuality and sexual categories, such an exercise could be said to amount to the assertion that 'we know best and your own experiences count for nothing'. Claims of moral imperialism do, in short, carry weight if a theory is simply presumed, without more, to be an automatically valid standard by which the laws of all societies can be judged.

Richard Rorty suggests that a universalist approach may also be unhelpful if we are concerned to guarantee effective protection in day-to-day life from discrimination or ill-treatment. For Rorty argues that declarations of universally valid human rights are at best empty if they mean nothing to the people whose behaviour they are supposed to constrain. Many people, Rorty suggests, live in a world in which their sense of moral community extends no further than their family, clan or tribe. If they have never conceived that they might owe moral commitments to members of other groups (or of certain specified groups, such as ethnic minorities in their locality), or that members of those groups deserve moral respect, then abstract demands to respect the moral status and entitlements of members of those groups are likely to seem nonsensical. According to Rorty:

> To get whites to be nicer to Blacks, males to females, Serbs to Muslims, or straights to gays, to help our species link up into . . . a 'planetary community' dominated by a culture of human rights, it is of no use whatever to say, with Kant: Notice that what you have in common, your humanity, is more important than these trivial differences. For the people we are trying to convince will rejoin that they notice nothing of the sort.[38]

Hence, a theory of justice and political morality which claimed to be universal would, in many societies, lack meaning for large groups of people, who would in consequence fail to understand or to respect the rules of behaviour which the theory sought to justify. The consequence of Rorty's view is that law reform justifications can only hope to provide an *effective* underpinning for better legal or social treatment for lesbians and gays in societies where the justifications make sense according to local understandings: abstract, universal theories which say nothing about people's day-to-day lives will have little resonance and little ability to afford effective protection.

Rorty suggests that a preferable means of securing better treatment for members of minority groups would be via a process of 'sentimental education' – that is, by portraying accounts of their lives, and of how and why they feel ill treated, in terms which *are* comprehensible to members of majority social groupings because they rely on the type of shallow, sentimental story-telling employed by all social groups. Members of minority groups should thus be portrayed in terms of simple social relationships – as someone's friend, daughter, partner, etc. – relationships which are so basic that they may 'humanize' members of the groups concerned in ways which abstract appeals to universal rights or common moral entitlements could not.[39] If Rorty's approach is correct, then attempts to develop universal justifications for law reform will be unhelpful, and should give way to portrayals of the lives of lesbians and gays as members of human relationships and as part of the broader social canvas – an approach which would be more likely to generate intuitive understanding among heterosexuals.

This theory is, of course, controversial, for many would argue that appeals to rights can accord a 'human' status to members of social minorities in ways which Rorty would appear to deny. What is useful about Rorty's theory, for present purposes, is its apparent implication that law reform justifications which claim to rest on universal values are unlikely to yield effective law reform measures in societies where those values are in fact incomprehensible given local traditions and understandings. For this argument *can* be supported by practical examples, perhaps the key contemporary illustration being the apparent failure of western liberal political values to take root, despite the many attempts to encourage them to do so, in many of the former communist countries of Eastern Europe – a frequently suggested explanation for which is the incompatibility between liberal values and the deep-rooted political traditions of the countries concerned.[40] We will see below that this aspect of Rorty's argument can play a useful role in the third approach to the reach of law reform justifications.

The discussion so far has suggested that both the moral relativist and universalist approaches contain many deep-seated problems. It is therefore desirable to develop a third, intermediate view. This can be done by building on strands of argument contained in the moral relativist and universalist approaches, for, despite the apparent divergences highlighted so far, aspects of these approaches may in practice be impossible fully to separate.[41] Many of the theories which we have so far described as relativist in fact contain some notion of universally applicable values (and it has also been argued that liberal universalist theories in fact incorporate concessions to local community standards[42]). Despite the moral relativism of much of his work, for example, Michael Walzer has acknowledged the existence of 'a kind of minimal and universal moral code' which operates on a transcultural basis in the sense that nearly all societies have prohibitions on murder, cruelty, deception and betrayal.[43] Richard Rorty's theory is also only relativist to a degree. For while Rorty doubts the efficacy of appeals to abstract, universal theories of rights which may mean nothing in alien political cultures, his appeal to 'sentimental stories' *does* clearly presume the existence of some shared, transcultural sense of values, if only at an emotional level, to which the stories will appeal. A 'sentimental story' about the suffering of a Bosnian Muslim would, for instance, mean nothing to a Bosnian Serb (one of the examples Rorty uses) unless both story-teller and listener shared some common feelings about sadness and happiness – and implicitly about good and bad – despite their different cultural backgrounds.[44]

Charles Taylor, another leading communitarian, offers a slightly different account of a possible role for transcultural values. He suggests, as a general rule-of-thumb, that while there is a 'real possibility' that 'we might be forced to recognize that certain goods are only such granted the existence of humans within a certain cultural form', this is unlikely to be true in practice.[45] The values of some societies may turn out to be incommensurable (in this context, incapable of proper evaluation by the standards of another society), but there is no reason to *assume* that this will be so, the question whether values are incommensurable being a question of fact to be determined from case to case. Until we reach a clear situation of incommensurability, Taylor suggests,

> there is no reason not to think of the goods we are trying to define and criticize as universal, provided we afford the same status to those

of other societies we are trying to understand. This does *not* mean of course that all our, or all their, supposed goods will turn out at the end of the day to be defensible as such; just that we don't start with a preshrunk moral universe in which we take as given that their goods have nothing to say to us or perhaps ours to them.[46]

The liberal philosopher Bernard Williams also draws attention, as part of his critique of moral relativism, to a universalist feature of relativist argument. Williams suggests that, as a general matter:

> In its vulgar and unregenerate form . . . [relativism] consists of three propositions: that 'right' means (can only be coherently understood as meaning) 'right for a given society'; that 'right for a given society' is to be understood in a functionalist sense; and that (therefore) it is wrong for people in one society to condemn, interfere with, etc., the values of another society.[47]

As Williams points out, the third proposition is clearly *nonrelative*: for moral relativists appear to be claiming that it is *always* wrong to condemn from the outside the moral values of another society – a claim which is itself of a universal, transcultural nature.

In constructing a third approach to the reach of law reform justifications, some of these connections between the universalist and moral relativist approaches can be developed. A useful starting-point is Sir Stephen Sedley's discussion of human rights. For Sedley argues that we can accept that statements of human rights are always rooted in a particular time and culture without consigning them 'to the bin of relativism'.[48] In fact, 'It is perfectly possible to recognise the localisation of ideas in time and place and to assert that they are none the worse for it: indeed, that ideas which pretend to universality are historical delusions.'[49] A society's premises and assumptions about the content of fundamental human rights will vary with the times, Sedley suggests, and any list of currently accepted human rights will itself be a product of a particular time and place.[50] Claims of 'universal' human rights can only properly be understood when set against their particular historical backdrop.

Sedley's theory so far is relativist. The non-relativist element begins to appear in two further arguments. The first is that while there are no universal truths (a claim which Sedley recognizes is itself universalist) and while a society's perceptions of its fundamental needs and concerns will vary over time,

> there are moral and practical continuities – of which the democratic principle is one – which can be powerfully represented as fundamental values, at least within the temporal and social horizons of each society. This relatively modest foundation for the legitimacy of human rights has perhaps the virtue that, without reducing all discourse to incoherent subjectivity, it recognises that a single 'right' outcome to every issue is attainable, if at all, only locally and temporarily.[51]

This argument is still largely relativist, especially given Sedley's later suggestion that the basis for each society's notion of human rights lies in its internal consensus about its 'ground rules'. Nevertheless, the idea of 'continuities' would seem to imply that each society has a *bedrock* of fundamental values which can be interpreted and developed to provide a satisfactory answer at any given time. The interpretation and the answer may vary, but the outline values to which they pay lip-service are nevertheless more permanent.

It is Sedley's second argument which clearly distinguishes his theory from pure moral relativism. For Sedley claims that:

> If . . . without abandoning principle, we are to escape the cold wind of history which blows sooner or later on [universal] higher-order laws and self-evident truths, it is to our present epoch's consensus about society's ground rules that we should turn. To admit this is to admit, as perhaps we should, that different societies will agree on different ground rules, *and to accept accordingly that we have both a right to review and recast our standards and an obligation to make the case for the adoption of them by others rather than continue to assert loftily that ours, being self-evident, are the only acceptable ones.*[52]

This passage suggests that while Sedley denies that there are universally valid notions of human rights, he also rejects the relativist view that it is impermissible to use our own standards to measure or criticize those of other societies. Sedley is, in other words, jettisoning what Williams describes as moral relativism's third proposition, namely that it is wrong for people in one society to condemn the values of another society. For Sedley is claiming that while it may be wrong to work from the unrealistic universalist assumption that ours are the only valid standards – in other words, to prejudge situations on the basis that our standards *automatically* apply – it is permissible to press others to adopt our standards on their merits if, at the same time, we are ourselves willing to listen to other people's arguments. This approach must imply that we *can* properly rank certain values as superior on their merits, if only for our own benefit, for on what other basis could we seek properly to persuade others of them? We can make an assumption about the superiority of our own values only if we have some sort of intuitive notion of justice according to which we can compare our values with those of other societies, and, given that it is used to compare values, such an intuitive notion would have to be (at least to an extent) general and transcultural in nature.

Sedley's theory therefore leaves room for, without specifically endorsing, Dworkin's idea (discussed earlier) that people tend intuitively to measure the standards of their own society against visions of justice which stand above localized, day-to-day life – the idea that notions of justice act as a critic, rather than as a mirror of society. For Sedley's argument allows us to reject what could be described as the moral imperialism of universalist theories – that is, their assumption that a theory of justice can automatically apply to all societies at all times – while preserving the ability to criticize, according to our own theory of justice, the values of our own society and those of others. We can believe that our own theory is better than any alternative, but acknowledge that it is necessary to convince members of other societies of this point rather than just to assert that our theory applies to them.

It is this position which forms the basis of the third approach to the reach of philosophical justifications for laws or law reform. This approach, while endorsing Rorty's view that presumptively universal theories are likely to be ineffective, would nevertheless refuse to opt for moral relativism. The third approach may in fact go beyond Sedley's first argument in acknowledging that people can properly believe that their theory or justification *should* be regarded as universally applicable. It seems unlikely, after all, that anyone who believed strongly in a theory of justice would think otherwise; as we saw with Bernard Williams' argument, even relativists assume that their overall position is universally valid. And, as Rorty's argument for 'sentimental stories' illustrates, it is nearly impossible in practice to engage in a dialogue which involves correspondence or comparison between one's own values and those of other societies without at least intuitively employing some transcultural standards. But the third approach departs from the universalist outlook in its scepticism about the ability of presumptively universal standards to enhance the position of unpopular social minorities in societies whose values are radically different from our own. The third approach therefore refuses to talk of automatically applicable standards, and in this respect seeks to avoid moral imperialism in practice.

Applying the third approach, we can say that we believe other societies to be at fault according to our own standards, but we cannot plausibly maintain that we are offering effective protection to minority groups within those societies by simply declaring that our standards are universally applicable. It may be that some societies are so much at fault that we would be justified, according to our own standards, in taking political, economic or even military action against them, but short of this point, meaningful protection for persecuted groups is – as Rorty suggests and Sedley implies – more likely to result from dialogue, which takes account of the differing values of *both* sides, rather than from empty declarations of 'universal' rights.[53] We need not surrender to the supine non-intervention of moral relativism by saying that we have no right to condemn other societies; but at the same time, we can avoid the arrogance of universalism by accepting the practical reality of the need to engage in dialogue with others, a process which will involve give as well as take.

In opting for the third position, it is also possible for us to accept the plausible communitarian claim that any justification, theory of justice and theory of political morality is likely to be shaped (or at least influenced) by the cultural background or perspective of its author.[54] The roots of this claim lie in the communitarian argument that individuals and their ends and interests cannot be understood independently of their social background and culture, from which it follows that political theories created by individuals must themselves be heavily influenced by their author's circumstances. As Elizabeth Frazer and Nicola Lacey suggest:

> On the interpretivist view which seems to be shared in some form by all communitarians, a political theory's analysis of society ... [is] informed by the historical, social and political position which the theorist occupies. Our ideas of what should and could be are rooted in our experience of what is. ... Similarly, the theorist's utopias are grounded in her interpretation of the culture within which she lives and works.[55]

The third issue: justifications and morality

We noted in chapter 1 that the Wolfenden Committee concluded, in its 1957 Report, that the functions of the criminal law should be confined to

> preserv[ing] public order and decency, to protect[ing] the citizen from what is offensive or injurious, and to provid[ing] sufficient safeguards against exploitation and corruption of others, particularly those who are specially vulnerable because they are young, weak in body or mind, inexperienced, or in a state of special physical, official or economic dependence.[56]

The Committee argued that the law should not seek 'to intervene in the private lives of citizens, or to . . . enforce any particular pattern of behaviour, further than is necessary to carry out the purposes we have outlined',[57] so that

> Unless a deliberate attempt is made by society, acting through the agency of the law, to equate the sphere of crime with that of sin, there must remain a realm of private morality and immorality which is, in brief and crude terms, not the law's business.[58]

The Committee thus believed that law should not be used to enforce considerations of sexual morality where the behaviour to which those considerations related occurred in the private arena between persons who were capable of consenting and who had actually done so. The justification for the Committee's law reform proposals was therefore that law should respect individual privacy, however defined, and that consenting sexual behaviour falls within the realm of the private – a view which would only be regarded as valid by those who support theories of justice and political morality which stress the importance of respecting individual privacy. We will evaluate the strength of respect for privacy as a law reform justification in chapter 6. For the moment, the Wolfenden Committee's conclusions are important because they illustrate rather neatly the main theme of this section – namely that justifications for existing laws and for law reform will contain or imply a view about how far (if at all) law should take account of or enforce considerations of morality.

A qualification must immediately be entered, for the word 'morality' is, on its own, far too vague. We are in fact dealing with morality in two distinct contexts – the political and the sexual. First, as we saw in chapter 1, each justification is underpinned by a theory of political morality, that is, a theory which specifies the ways in which it is legitimate for institutions of the state, including those institutions empowered to make law, to exercise their powers. Given that the enactment, alteration and repeal of law are all forms of political action, it follows that an argument literally cannot be a justification for existing law or for law reform *unless* it entails a theory of political morality. And, given that each justification is concerned with practical law reform measures, it must follow – at least if it is to serve any useful role in practice – that it is prepared to see its underpinning theory of political morality put into play, i.e. enforced, through the laws or law reform measures concerned. It can thus properly be claimed that each justification is inevitably concerned with the enforcement of a theory of political morality, for it could not otherwise be a justification for law or for law reform.

Second, each justification may, as a consequence of its background theories of justice and political morality, imply a view about what type of sexual morality, if any, the law should enforce. Imagine a theory of justice which maintained that people should be free to engage in whatever sexual acts they chose with each other, so long as they had fully consented. Such a theory would, in consequence, clearly maintain that it is illegitimate for the state to enforce, through law, views of sexual morality which maintained that the sexual practices in which some adults willingly engaged were in fact immoral. People could argue as a matter of conscience that such acts were immoral, but that would not be a reason for the law to enforce their beliefs by prohibiting the acts concerned. But the theory *could* be used to legitimize the use of law to punish sexual assaults carried out on a person without their consent. Such a conclusion logically follows from the importance attached by the theory to notions of choice and full consent, and could be said to amount to an enforcement of the popular view that it is immoral to exploit a person for sexual purposes when they have not consented. The example clearly shows, in other words, that the theories of justice and political morality underpinning a justification *can* cause that justification to adopt a particular stance about which considerations of sexual morality the law should enforce. This implication will, of course, be found only in justifications for laws which touch in some way upon sexuality, and does not amount to the suggestion that such laws will *always* lead to the enforcement of a theory of sexual morality.

In consequence, choices between justifications (whether for existing law or for law reform measures) should not be seen as involving a simple decision between support for or opposition to the legal enforcement of morality. For *all* relevant justifications entail a theory of political morality which is to be enforced by the laws which they justify (they could not otherwise be meaningfully described as justifications) and will, as a matter of logic, imply their own views – derived from their theories of justice and political morality – as to whether any type of sexual morality can legitimately be enforced by the law, and if so, which type and to what extent. In choosing between justifications, we are therefore deciding which theory of political morality we wish to see enforced, and whether we wish in addition to see legal support for any notion of sexual morality. Any choice between justifications is in any event itself a question of morality in the sense in which the word is used in chapter 1.[59]

At first sight, these claims may seem to fall foul of the objection, raised by some theorists, that one cannot properly justify the legal enforcement of morality simply by pointing out that we already have a wide range of laws, such as those prohibiting sexual assault, which could be said to do so.[60] After all, deriving an 'ought' statement ('law should enforce morality') from an 'is' statement ('law already enforces morality') is surely the type of logical jump which falls foul of the analytical rule known as 'Hume's Fork' – the idea that one cannot derive a normative 'ought' claim from a description of what 'is'.[61] According to this objection, we should not assume that our only concern is with choosing the type of morality which the law may permissibly enforce; instead, we should first ask whether it is permissible for the law to enforce morality at all.

In fact, while 'Hume's Fork' is a perfectly logical and defensible analytical proposition, the objection advanced in the preceding paragraph misunderstands the argument which has so far been advanced concerning law and morality. For, as Raymond Plant points out, 'Hume's Fork' articulates

> the principle that there can be nothing in the conclusion of a valid argument which is not already present in the premises. If we draw an evaluative conclusion then either the premises contain evaluative elements . . . or the inference cannot go through if the premises do not contain normative elements.[62]

This point about premises is crucial: for, as the preceding discussion (together with the discussion in chapter 1) may have suggested, there *is* a 'normative element' in the assumptions underpinning our analysis. This element takes the form of the claim that because of some background factor – the coercive potential of law, according to Hart, or the community's general justifying aim, rationale or purpose, according to Finnis – any new or existing law must be supported by a sound philosophical justification if it is to be regarded as legitimate. It is the task of each justification to demonstrate the law's legitimacy according to a vision of justice and political morality, and the very nature of this task makes it inevitable that we, together with Hart, Finnis and other theorists who have examined the question of justifications for laws and law reform, will be concerned with the legal enforcement of theories of political morality. To abandon this concern would be to discard our present understanding of the very nature of law as something which, in a non-totalitarian regime, requires normative justification when it is used. As a consequence of this concern, we have to accept that law is inseparable from considerations of political morality.

The objection also fails adequately to distinguish between political and sexual morality. A consequence of the argument in the previous paragraph is that it is misconceived to ask whether law should enforce any theory of political morality, for it is clear that if the law did not do so, it would not be law as we understand it. This is not to say, however, that law should always enforce a view about *sexual* morality, and that it is up to us merely to choose which view. Justifications for existing law or law reform may *imply* a view about sexual morality, but only some justifications will wish to enforce that view, and then only in certain contexts, as in the sexual assault example considered above. While we may not have a choice about whether law should enforce political morality, therefore, we do have a choice about whether to support justifications which would seek to enforce a view about sexual morality. The stance adopted by an individual justification, and in particular the type of sexual morality, if any, which it seeks to enforce, is therefore likely to be relevant in assessing its desirability.[63]

One practical aspect of the argument should, however, be emphasized. This is that while in principle we possess a choice as to whether considerations of sexual morality should be enforced, it can realistically be claimed that in practice, most justifications for enacting laws to protect lesbians and gays from social discrimination and for placing same-sex sexual acts and relationships on the same legal footing as their heterosexual counterparts do to some extent entail the enforcement of considerations of sexual morality. Such enforcement occurs at two levels. First, proponents of just about every relevant law reform justification regard it as legitimate for the law to prohibit sexual acts involving young children or animals. Such a position can consistently be maintained since a justification which stressed that the law must respect each individual's freedom to engage in consenting sexual acts with others must presuppose that the 'others' concerned have the capacity to make proper decisions about sexual conduct for themselves, something which children and animals are commonly assumed to lack. Such a justification would therefore contain a notion of sexual morality in the form of the idea that legitimate, rightful sexual acts are those which take place between persons who are capable of giving – and have actually given – their consent. Any law based upon this justification could be said to be enforcing such a view of sexual morality. Second, as we will see in chapters 6 and 7, some law reform justifications positively assert that sexual acts and relationships between persons of the same sex are morally acceptable and should be permitted, while others maintain that they are insufficiently unacceptable that their prohibition can be justified, even if this is only on an all-things-considered basis once the costs of prohibition have been taken into account. These views of sexual morality would clearly be enforced through any law enacted on the basis of the justifications concerned.

This point can be further illustrated by considering the heated debate which took place in the late 1950s and early 1960s between Professor Hart and Lord Devlin (at the time a judge in the English Court of Appeal) concerning the validity of the Wolfenden Committee's views.[64] The central question in the Hart–Devlin debate was whether criminal law should be used to enforce sexual morality, and if so whether the morality to be enforced should be that of the majority of members of (or its near-equivalent, the average and reasonable person within) society. Devlin was originally a supporter of the Wolfenden Committee's position, but changed his mind while researching the topic.[65] His considered view – that a society was held together by its common morality, which the law could legitimately enforce – was first presented in his Maccabean Lecture in Jurisprudence, delivered to the British Academy in March 1959. We will consider Devlin's arguments in detail in chapter 5. Hart's defence of the Wolfenden position and rebuttal of Devlin's assertions first appeared in an article published in the *Listener* in the same year, and was developed in a series of lectures in the US, including the 1962 lecture mentioned at the start of the chapter.[66]

For the time being, it is sufficient to note that even if Devlin's conclusions are rejected, his critique of the Wolfenden approach demonstrates the practical difficulty involved in conceiving of a law reform justification which does not to some extent support the legal enforcement of a conception of sexual morality. For, as Devlin pointed out, the Wolfenden recommendations would be internally inconsistent if the Report is read as suggesting that law has *no* role to play in the enforcement of sexual morality.[67] This is because the Committee argued that while certain areas of social life should be seen as realms of private morality into which the law should not as a matter of principle intrude – the commission of sexual acts between consenting adults in private being one such area – the criminal law could nevertheless be used to prevent people from exploiting and corrupting others, especially the young – a use of law which, as suggested above, clearly would involve the enforcement of considerations of sexual morality. It cannot, therefore, be maintained that the Wolfenden Committee opposed the enforcement of sexual morality as a blanket principle. This enabled Devlin to argue that, if the exploitation of human weakness justified the intervention of the law in some areas, as for example to protect the young, then it would be inconsistent, without more, to argue against the enforcement of morality in other areas. There was, Devlin suggested, 'virtually no field of morality which can be defined in such a way as to exclude the law'.[68] If attempts are made to set pre-ordained theoretical limits to the state's power to legislate on questions of morality, or to delimit fixed areas of life into which the law can never intrude, these are likely in practice to come to nothing.[69]

It does seem logical to argue, with Devlin, that a blanket prohibition on the enforcement of sexual morality through law is unlikely to be attainable in practice. Ironically, the strength of this aspect of Devlin's argument becomes clearer if we consider Hart's views. In defending the Wolfenden position, Hart seemed more concerned to rebut Devlin's contentions than to present a detailed picture of his own concerning law and the enforcement of morality.[70] In his first lecture, however, Hart indicated his qualified support for what is known as John Stuart Mill's harm principle, a central liberal criterion for distinguishing between legitimate and illegitimate uses of law.[71] According to Mill:

the only purpose for which power can rightfully be exercised over any member of a civilised community, against his will, is to prevent harm to others. His own good, either physical or moral, is not a sufficient warrant. He cannot rightfully be compelled to do or forbear because it will be better for him to do so, because it will make him happier, because, in the opinions of others, to do so would be wise, or even right. . . . The only part of the conduct of any one, for which he is amenable to society, is that which concerns others. In the part which merely concerns himself, his independence is, of right, absolute.[72]

Two points can be made here. The first is that the harm principle can itself be seen as a recipe for the enforcement of morality, sexual or otherwise. According to Neil MacCormick:

the harm principle . . . seems to legitimize the legal enforcement of a central moral value, that of securing individuals from harms wilfully inflicted by others. The criminal law, in prohibiting wilfully harmful behaviour and subjecting harm-doers to punishment seems directly to enforce requirements which are also moral requirements.[73]

This point can be reinforced by the fact that, in order to function properly, the harm principle requires us to decide which activities should be categorized as 'harms' justifying the intervention of the law, and which interests are to be protected by the law from 'harm' – deliberations which may themselves turn on considerations of morality. As Joseph Raz has suggested:

Since 'causing harm' entails by its very meaning that the action is prima facie wrong, it is a normative concept acquiring its specific meaning from the moral theory within which it is embedded. Without such a connection to a moral theory the harm principle is a formal principle lacking specific concrete content and leading to no policy conclusions.[74]

That different moral theories specify their own definitions of 'harm' is highlighted by Paul Roberts' suggestion that Lord Devlin's views might *themselves* be seen as a variation on the harm principle, albeit a variation which contains a much broader definition of harm than most liberal theorists would be prepared to countenance.[75] Analytically speaking, the harm principle can itself be said to rest on moral considerations, and any theorist's definition of the types of 'harm' which the principle seeks to counter may well be fed by the theorist's conception of justice, political morality and – if 'harm' is defined broadly enough that it encompasses harm to the moral fabric of a society – sexual morality.

The second point is that Hart went beyond Mill in claiming that law *could* properly be used to regulate conduct even in situations where people had willingly consented to the 'harm' inflicted on them. For example, Hart claimed that the supply of certain 'soft' and 'hard' drugs to willing users, and activities such as euthanasia or mercy killings where the victim had consented, could legitimately be prohibited – despite the participants' willing consent – on the basis of paternalism. The law could thus, Hart maintained, be concerned to prevent individuals from suffering, and could do so *without* seeking to enforce morality.[76] Hart therefore suggested that:

> It is too often assumed that if a law is not designed to protect one man from another its only rationale can be that it is designed to punish moral wickedness or, in Lord Devlin's words, 'to enforce a moral principle'. Thus it is often urged that statutes punishing cruelty to animals can only be explained in that way. But it is certainly intelligible, both as an account of the original motives inspiring such legislation and as the specification of an aim widely held to be worth pursuing, to say that the law is here concerned with the *suffering*, albeit only of animals, rather than with the immorality of torturing them.[77]

In addition, Hart argued, bigamists (people who contracted more than one marriage simultaneously) were punished not because their behaviour was immoral, but because it was a nuisance.[78]

Hart's argument that 'nuisance' and 'paternalism' are separable from the imposition of morality is in fact weak, but it is relevant for present purposes because it underlines yet again how difficult it is to separate law from morality, however defined. The argument is weak because Hart fails to produce evidence to back up his explanations of the rationales for the various laws he cites as examples, and does not explain at a conceptual level how any separation could work.[79] In fact, it quickly becomes clear that a separation could not work, given that paternalism must itself rest on certain assumptions about what is good for people or animals, and notions of nuisance must entail assumptions about what is bad for them. After all, we only want to protect people from something, that is, to act in a paternalistic fashion towards them, where the 'something' from which they are to be protected appears to us to be harmful; and, as noted above, notions of harm are often, if not usually, fed by moral beliefs.[80] Equally, something is likely to appear as a nuisance only where it contravenes our standards of what is socially acceptable, and such standards are very frequently, at least in the sexual arena, fed by considerations of morality. Hart is undoubtedly correct to say that *some* standards by which the acceptability of conduct is measured relate to procedure, not morals[81] – the rules of a game such as chess are an obvious example. But rules of law, including those relating to procedure, almost inevitably affect people's substantive entitlements, in turn affecting our moral perception of and justifications for those entitlements. It must also be clear that a bigamous 'marriage' is only ever likely to amount to a nuisance because it offends people due to its contravention of accepted moral standards. Hart simply goes too far in attempting to separate what are, in reality, integrally connected issues. As Devlin suggests, Hart's paternalism and nuisance exceptions are potentially so wide that they fatally undermine the rest of his argument against the legal enforcement of morality.[82]

The discussion so far has suggested that all justifications seek to enforce notions of political morality, and many seek to enforce considerations of sexual morality as well; that even the apparently 'neutral' liberal harm principle rests on notions of political morality, and may, depending upon the definition of 'harm' in play (something which itself depends upon moral considerations), be used to enforce considerations of sexual morality; that the Wolfenden Committee's conclusions entailed the enforcement of some moral views about sexual morality; and that Hart's arguments about 'paternalism' and 'nuisance' are a somewhat spurious cover for the enforcement of morality (sexual morality in the bigamy example), even if Hart himself did not acknowledge this. We remain in theory free to decide whether considerations of sexual morality should be enforced by the law, but the argument surrounding the Wolfenden Committee's conclusions suggests that most law reform justifications will find it difficult in practice to maintain an abstentionist stance. In fact, as chapters 6 and 7 will demonstrate, most justifications for an improved legal regime for lesbians and gays do entail the enforcement of some notion of sexual morality, so that our practical choice, in selecting a justification, is indeed one between these different notions.

This conclusion may at first sight seem alarming. After all, the idea that the state has a role to play in enforcing morality is usually associated with reactionaries, most recently with fundamentalist 'Christians' in the USA and Canada. Such alarm is misplaced, however. For the conclusions reached here are of a largely analytical nature: they claim that as a matter of logic, law is concerned with theories of political and frequently sexual morality in the sense of notions of right and wrong conduct in certain areas of life. It is not being suggested that the particular theories of morality favoured by the 'Christian' right should be enforced through law. The purpose of the argument so far has been to make a logical point, often overlooked, about the nature of justifications for law and law reform. The precise type of morality which we want to see enforced will be considered in chapters 5 to 7. Hart's difficulties with 'paternalism' and 'nuisance' ought to show us, however, that the best way of fighting justifications for the enforcement of unacceptable moralities is not by pretending that law should have nothing to do with the enforcement of morality – as we have seen, such a claim cannot be sustained; instead, it is necessary to find a counter-justification based on a preferable theory of morality.

The difficulties involved in claiming that law should have nothing to do with the enforcement of morality, political or sexual, can be further highlighted if we briefly consider the broader, background debate about whether the law should remain neutral between competing conceptions of what counts as a good life – conceptions which stem from rival theories of justice and political morality. Arguments surrounding the law's proper position in relation to conceptions of sexual morality may in fact be classed as a subsidiary part of this debate, given that freedom to engage in sexual relations and relationships would count as part of many people's conceptions of a good life. Roughly summarized, the classic liberal position on neutrality is that although the law may be analysed as resting on theories of political morality, it may only legitimately enforce theories which respect people's freedom, within limits, to arrive at and to live out their own conception of what counts as a good life. The state should not enforce its own view of the good life, and should therefore allow individuals the freedom to engage in sexual activity with any consenting adult partner, as well as freedom to choose how they spend their leisure time, which political party (if any) to support, and so on. This view of the law's role can be described as anti-perfectionist.[83]

If this liberal position is followed, the law is not, analytically speaking, adopting a strictly neutral role: for we are required to accept that pro-neutrality theories of political morality should be enforced through law. We are therefore concerned with neutrality within limits, a position defended by pro-neutrality liberals such as Will Kymlicka[84] and attacked by perfectionist theorists such as Joseph Raz, who maintain that choice is not valuable for its own sake, and that the state has some role in directing people towards meaningful and valuable forms of life.[85] The debate about the substantive merits of neutrality within limits cannot be analysed in great detail here,[86] but one aspect of the debate can be used to highlight – in a way which parallels the arguments concerning sexual morality – the difficulties facing those who wish to claim that the law can and should maintain a policy of neutrality between considerations of morality.

This aspect is found in Ronald Dworkin's defence of neutrality within limits.[87] Dworkin formulates a central distinction between the state treating people equally in the distribution of some resource or opportunity, and the state treating people as equals in the sense that they are entitled to its equal concern and respect. Treating people as equals, Dworkin maintains, requires the government to remain neutral on questions of the good life, preferring no one view to any other. Political decisions must be, so far as possible, independent of any conception of the good life, for people's conceptions of such a life will differ, and a state would not be treating them as equals if it preferred one conception to another.[88] A person's right to equality of concern and respect would thus entitle them to live an unpopular lifestyle free from state interference. The argument so far may seem to be a standard form of neutrality theory, but Dworkin proceeds to explain neutrality in terms of a theory of liberalism based on equality, in which state neutrality is necessary *only to the extent that treating people as equals requires it*. Wealthier members of a community can therefore, Dworkin argues, sometimes be required by law to make larger than average financial sacrifices for the sake of the community, without being regarded as having been treated unequally.[89]

The compulsory redistribution envisaged in Dworkin's example is, however, one of the most obvious (and, to many, most obviously coercive) types of legal enforcement of morality which it is possible to imagine. Dworkin certainly accepts that his conception of neutrality is qualified under liberalism as equality, but if this is so then it becomes difficult to accept that anything which can meaningfully be described as state 'neutrality' remains. For, as Neil MacCormick has argued:

> No less moral issues, nor less controversial ones, are those concerning such matters of public law as taxation on the one hand and welfare rights on the other: how much ought people to contribute in tax to the common revenues of the state; how much ought they to receive in cash or kind for the relief of what needs?[90]

Any tax and welfare benefits system is based on conceptions of morality and justice: on notions of one's obligations to the community and of the community's obligations to its members, on notions of how low a person's income must be before it is impermissible to leave them to fend for themselves, and how high it must be before they are forced to make some financial contribution to the well-being of others. Any system of law which obliges people to pay tax and entitles them to welfare benefits is clearly enforcing notions of morality and justice; and – a sobering thought for 'neutrality' enthusiasts – life in any modern state would be virtually unthinkable without such a system.[91] Dworkin's arguments certainly show how slippery ideas of 'neutrality' can be, in whatever context they are used. Given the centrality of tax and welfare benefit systems in the contemporary state, however, MacCormick's point underlines quite how far law is nowadays synonymous with the enforcement of theories of morality, and quite how difficult it would be for *any* theorist to draw a line between the two.

The legal enforcement of morality is not, therefore, something which we should seek to avoid. The real question, at least in western states at the present time, is to find acceptable theories of justice, political morality and, more often than not, sexual morality. Such considerations are not confined to the criminal law: while the main focus of the Hart–Devlin debate was on the criminal law, it should be noted that Devlin saw his arguments as applying to other branches of the law as well.[92] Contemporary arguments about theories of justice and political morality are, furthermore, clearly relevant in relation to the creation of anti-discrimination laws to protect lesbians and gays, and considerations of sexual morality would be involved in any decision to legalize same-sex marriages or to allow lesbian and gay parents a legal right to bring up children. In short, an anti-perfectionist position would be incoherent.

The fourth issue: criteria for assessing justifications

Before the merits of the various justifications for existing laws or for law reform can be analysed in the next three chapters, we need to set out the criteria which will be used in this exercise. Failure to establish clear criteria would leave us with no valid basis for comparing and evaluating the various justifications, causing any analysis to degenerate into a set of disconnected, *ad hoc* expressions of taste. If the legitimacy of existing laws and law reform exercises depends upon showing that they are supported by clear philosophical justifications, it follows that we must employ regular criteria for assessing the merits of each possible justification. Any choice of assessment criteria will inevitably be influenced by one's view of the function and nature of philosophical justifications, and the criteria to be employed here are no exception. For they are intended to reflect three issues considered so far in this chapter: first, the interconnection between law reform justifications and their underlying theories of justice and political morality; second, the need for justifications and their underlying theories to take proper account of the cultures to which they are said to apply, if they aim to be effective; and third, the continuing role in moral assessments of intuitive notions of justice as something external to society, to which appeal may be made. The two families of assessment criteria – which go to the consistency and substantive attractiveness of a justification – will be treated as alternative rather than cumulative grounds on which any justification may be rejected. Some more specific points about their application to particular justifications will be made at the start of chapter 6.

The criteria which go to consistency ask whether a purported justification works on its own terms. These criteria require us to consider whether the justification is properly consistent with the theories of justice and political morality underpinning it, whether such theories are consistent with each other, and whether all elements within the justification are internally consistent. These criteria effectively constitute a threshold test which can be used to assess the validity of any philosophical argument – for they are concerned, at heart, with an argument's analytical validity. Substantive attractiveness criteria are, by contrast, concerned with the merits of a justification. Three criteria – relevance, plausibility and acceptability – come within this family. Any assessment of an argument's merits will, of course, depend to an extent on the definition of 'merit' which is favoured, subjectively, by the person conducting the assessment. It is fair to say, however, that the first two criteria, while depending to an extent on the theorist's personal, subjective assessments, do so to a much lesser extent than the third. We will now consider each criterion in turn.

The relevance criterion asks whether the purported justification makes sense given the circumstances of the society or societies in which it is supposed to apply. This criterion can assume two, and possibly three, forms. First, as we noted earlier when discussing Richard Rorty's views, any justification that is couched in terms which are incomprehensible in a given society is unlikely to offer effective protection to disadvantaged groups within that society. It would in consequence make little sense to employ that justification in the society concerned. A justification must be rejected as irrelevant if it fails to employ concepts which are meaningful, given the background against which it has to operate.

The second and slightly more subtle version of the relevance criterion can be applied to the introduction of new laws. Laws, after their introduction, can remain in existence for decades and sometimes centuries (this is as true for rules of common law as it is for statutes). In consequence, a justification which is comprehensible when the law to which it relates is introduced may become meaningless with time. If a law is to remain legitimate over a long time period, its justification must therefore be capable of adapting to changing perceptions of justice. Once a justification ceases to have a discernible basis in contemporary understandings of justice and political morality, the law which it supports will no longer appear to be (or indeed be) legitimate unless a new justification can be found – a process which is in itself rather artificial. Equally, if a justification rests upon social understandings or categorizations which have since become redundant, it will cease to be a relevant justification for the law concerned – again calling that law's legitimacy into question.[93] All justifications for laws should expect to undergo revision and reinterpretation over time, as should the laws themselves. The point of the present argument is to suggest that justifications which are too clearly located in one time period or set of circumstances run a much greater risk of becoming irrelevant with time than do more broadly structured justifications (the relevance of a justification, it should be added, has nothing to do with its current popularity – a separate issue which, it will be argued in chapter 5, should not affect a justification's validity). It is therefore crucial to frame justifications so as to enable them to adapt to or to withstand changes in social perceptions, any justification which is unable to do this being likely to fail, within a relatively short period of time, for irrelevance.

A good example of this second argument can be seen in criticisms of the current prohibition, under the criminal law of England and Wales, on blasphemy against the Christian religion. An effective justification for the offence of blasphemy might have been possible at a time when the population was predominantly and actively Christian in religious affiliation. Nowadays, the blasphemy law is widely felt to be illegitimate, either on the ground that society values freedom of expression sufficiently strongly that special protection for the Christian faith is illegitimate, or on the basis (as was argued unsuccessfully in the *Choudhury* case) that as England and Wales are now multi-racial, multi-faith nations, a law which protects one religion alone can no longer be justified.[94] The first of these grounds may be said to rest on changing perceptions of justice – the idea that the moral right to freedom of expression now assumes a higher priority in contemporary theories of justice than does the defence of the state religion – while the second clearly rests on changing social perceptions of what constitutes religion. Supporters of each ground would, of course, opt for opposite law reform solutions – complete repeal of the blasphemy law in the first case, and its extension to protect non-Christian religions in the second.

A possible third version of the relevance criterion concerns the purpose(s) of the law concerned when considered against the social background in which it will operate. For it can be argued that laws, given their coercive potential, should only be introduced where it is clear that they will further some meaningful purpose in the society in which they apply. This purpose may just be symbolic – it is sometimes felt, for example, that anti-discrimination laws serve as a sign of a society's disapproval of the practices which they prohibit rather more effectively than as a means of redress for the victims of prohibited discrimination – but, as will be argued in chapter 8, a symbolic purpose may still be useful in the society concerned. Concrete examples of this possible third version in operation can be seen in anti-discrimination law on both sides of the Atlantic: for it seems to be assumed, in both the UK and the USA, that law should not be used to prohibit types of discrimination unless they have clearly been shown to constitute a social problem. In the UK, religious but not racial discrimination is prohibited under the law of

Northern Ireland, but the reverse is true under the law of England and Wales, a difference which can only be explained in the light of the very different social environments in which both sets of laws operate, and of the contrasting social problems thrown up by each. In the USA, as we saw in chapter 2, courts will consider – in determining whether a social group should be brought within the Equal Protection limb of the Fourteenth Amendment – whether that group has suffered a history of purposeful discrimination and whether it constitutes a 'discrete and insular minority'.[95] Again, reasoning of this sort seems to assume that a clear social problem must exist before constitutional anti-discrimination protections can intervene.

These considerations will only constitute a third version of the relevance criterion, however, if it is clear that they go to the *legitimacy* of the laws under consideration – that is, if we are claiming, in relation to the examples considered in the previous paragraph, that there can be no *justification* for laws which do not exist to counter identifiable social problems.[96] For it is also possible to argue that these examples instead illustrate our second central question, that is, whether the introduction of a (presumptively legitimate) law will, in a given set of circumstances, be *effective* in attaining its social goal. The legitimacy and effectiveness questions are, as we saw in chapter 1, logically separable: it is quite possible to think of a wish-list of laws whose introduction one could justify, but which would be pointless because ineffective (a practical example is the thin-end-of-the-wedge argument against capital punishment or harsher sentencing policies in the criminal law – an argument which maintains that these types of penalty might be justifiable in principle but that their introduction would be pointless because they cannot be shown to work). The difficulty is that the two questions are sometimes hard to distinguish in practice: supporters of the libertarian ideal of a minimum state *would*, for example, clearly treat the examples we are dealing with here as part of our first central question, that is, as going to the legitimacy of the laws concerned. It is thus fair to conclude that while anti-discrimination legislation should address itself to clearly existing social problems in the society in which it operates, it is only our background theory of justice which will determine whether this raises issues of legitimacy or effectiveness. Our background theory of justice is also likely to influence our reasoning when determining what counts as a social problem of sufficient seriousness that the law's intervention is justified, and which *actual* social issues match up to this standard. Assessments of 'relevance' will therefore vary according to our personal, background theories.[97]

The same is true of the plausibility criterion, which asks whether the reasoning within or the conclusions reached by a justification appear sensible, given the circumstances of the society to which they apply. A theory might be described as implausible, for example, if it contained a highly exaggerated account of the effectiveness of a law reform measure in altering the social climate of a particular society, or if it rested on the assumption (that is, if it lacked coherent reasoning which established, in the face of mathematical orthodoxy) that two plus two equalled five. While 'plausibility' assessments tend to rest on almost universally accepted, 'common sense' understandings of the workings of the world, the mathematics example should, however, show that such understandings are ultimately a matter of opinion: after all, people only agree that two plus two equals four because they accept a particular set of mathematical precepts.

The most clearly subjective assessment criterion relates to the overall acceptability of a justification. This criterion asks openly whether a justification's implications or ramifications are acceptable in terms of our background theories of justice and political morality, as well as our assessments of sexual morality. This criterion explicitly appeals to the theorist's own position, and it must be accepted that different people will ultimately give different, subjective answers to the question posed by the justification, according to their perspective. The criterion thus reflects the point, discussed in chapter 1, that any evaluation of law reform justifications will be influenced by one's existing background theories of justice and political morality. This is, however, an inevitable feature of debate about questions of this sort. Thus, believers in a morally pluralist society will reject justifications for laws which aim excessively to regulate permissible sexual behaviour among lesbians and gays, for otherwise, they could not be true to their background theories of justice and political morality; by contrast, those who believe that the state must enforce religious or restrictive theories of sexual morality will support justifications for hostile laws. It may be, though, that debate about appropriate roles for the law will persuade supporters of one side to alter their background theories of justice and political morality. In any event, one example of this assessment criterion in operation is the argument that a particular law reform justification should be rejected because it can support an inadequate range of legal changes (or, conversely, too many), for such an argument can only carry weight if background theories of justice and political morality, which envisage a desirable range of reforms, are first envisaged.

An important aspect of this rather selective process of evaluation concerns how we ultimately come to favour a particular justification on its merits. It is probably fair to say that people usually favour something because it looks good *and* any alternative they can think of (even if no alternative is explicitly presented to them) appears worse. Decisions are often dressed up only in positive terms: the idea that A is desirable just because it is morally good. Usually implicit in such a statement, however, is the thought that any alternative to A seems morally dubious. In practice, these things usually work on a scale: some decisions are sufficiently knife-edged that people will acknowledge that in reaching them, they have engaged in a process of weighing up the pros and cons. Other choices seem obvious from the start, and no open weighing process is necessary. There is likely still to have been an implicit weighing process here, however: it is simply that the choice between alternatives is so stark, or so heavily loaded in one direction, that no real reflection is necessary. Weighing processes of both sorts are catered for in the acceptability assessment criterion. It may be that for some people, the claim made at the end of chapter 7 – that it is always wrong to regulate consenting sexual behaviour and to discriminate against lesbians and gays – will seem so obviously acceptable, on its merits, that no open weighing process is necessary. The merits of that conclusion are likely to be more strongly appreciated, however, if justifications which favour legal hostility towards sexual minorities are first considered. This is the task of chapter 5.

Conclusion

We can conclude by reiterating two propositions concerning the proper working of justifications for law and law reform. First, justifications may lay claim to universal applicability, but should not be assumed automatically to apply on a universal basis. Justifications can be used to judge the laws of societies other than the theorist's own, but it is unlikely that they will yield law reform measures which stand any chance of improving the position of lesbians and gays in those societies if they are addressed in terms which have no resonance in the societies concerned. Progress, where there is social difference, can best be achieved through dialogue rather than by making moral assumptions. Debate in the following chapters has therefore deliberately been confined to the UK, the USA and Canada. Second, each justification is underpinned by a theory of justice and political morality – often associated, given the context, with a theory of sexual morality – which the justification will seek to enforce through law. Notions of the law's 'neutrality' between notions of morality are artificial and should be discarded. The essential question in the next three chapters will instead be to find a justification which is acceptable, given the underpinning theories of justice and political morality which accompany each one. We are engaged, then, in a clearly political exercise, and it is in this light that our assessment of the different justifications, using the consistency and substantive attractiveness criteria, must be carried out.

Notes

1. Reprinted in H. L. A. Hart, *Law, Liberty, and Morality* (Oxford: Oxford University Press, 1963), p. 22.
2. John Finnis, 'Law, morality and "sexual orientation"' (1993–4) 69 *Notre Dame Law Review* 1049 at 1055.
3. Hart, *Law, Liberty, and Morality*, p. 4.
4. *Ibid.*, p. 20. Distinctions between critical and positive morality are discussed at pp. 17–20.
5. (1993) 854 P 2d 1270 (Finnis gave testimony in the Colorado Supreme Court only).
6. See further the discussion in chapter 2. That Finnis's presentation of the 'European' position involves considerable over-simplification is clear from Kees Waaldijk and Andrew Clapham (eds), *Homosexuality: A European Community Issue – Essays on Lesbian and Gay Rights in European Law and Policy* (Dordrecht: Martinus Nijhoff, 1993), and Robert Wintemute, *Sexual Orientation and Human Rights: The United States Constitution, the European Convention, and the Canadian Charter* (Oxford: Clarendon Press, 1995), chs 4 and 5.
7. Finnis, 'Law, morality and "sexual orientation"', p. 1055.
8. *Ibid.*, pp. 1070 *et seq.*
9. See further Finnis's discussion in *Natural Law and Natural Rights* (Oxford: Clarendon Press, 1980), pp. 260, 351–68.
10. Finnis, 'Law, morality and "sexual orientation"', p. 1070.
11. *Ibid.*
12. Finnis appears to argue, *ibid.* p. 1076, that it would be illegitimate for the US Supreme Court to strike down an anti-sodomy statute if to do so would entail the adoption of any positive protections for lesbians and gays.
13. See further Hart, *Law, Liberty, and Morality*, ch. 1. Note that the argument does not rely on any notion of a presumption of liberty, criticized by Joseph Raz – see *The Morality of Freedom* (Oxford: Clarendon Press, 1986), pp. 8–16; see, more generally, chapters 3 and 4 of the same work.
14. This type of position is envisaged by Paul Roberts in his analysis 'Consent and the criminal law: Philosophical foundations', Appendix C to Law Commission Consultation Paper No.

15. See, e.g., news reports in the *Pink Paper* on 11 August, 18 August and 1 September 1995; the *Guardian*, 3 August 1996, p. 15 ('Zimbabwe mob defies gay ruling').
16. Useful analysis is contained in Oliver Phillips's unpublished paper 'Zimbabwean law and the production of a white man's disease', delivered at the Lancaster University 'Legal Queeries' conference in September 1995. See also Peter Drucker, '"In the Tropics there is no sin": Sexuality and gay–lesbian movements in the Third World' (1996) 218 *New Left Review* 75.
17. Some of the more interesting non-liberal arguments can be found in Michael Sandel, *Liberalism and the Limits of Justice* (Cambridge: Cambridge University Press, 1982); Alasdair MacIntyre, *After Virtue: A Study in Moral Theory* (London: Duckworth, 2nd edn, 1985); *Whose Justice? Which Rationality?* (London: Duckworth, 1988); Michael Walzer, *Spheres of Justice: A Defence of Pluralism and Equality* (Oxford: Basil Blackwell, 1983); Charles Taylor, *Sources of the Self: The Making of the Modern Identity* (Cambridge: Cambridge University Press, 1989); and, arguably (given Rorty's liberal self-description) in Richard Rorty, *Contingency, Irony and Solidarity* (Cambridge: Cambridge University Press, 1989), *Objectivity, Relativism and Truth* (Cambridge: Cambridge University Press, 1991). See also Daniel Bell, *Communitarianism and its Critics* (Oxford: Clarendon Press, 1993).
18. Cf. Stephen Mulhall and Adam Swift, *Liberals and Communitarians* (Oxford: Basil Blackwell, 1992), pp. viii–xii; Elizabeth Frazer and Nicola Lacey, *The Politics of Community: A Feminist Critique of the Liberal-Communitarian Debate* (Hemel Hempstead: Harvester Wheatsheaf, 1993), p. 167; Joel Feinberg, *Harmless Wrongdoing*, vol. 4 of *The Moral Limits of the Criminal Law* (New York: Oxford University Press, 1990), p. 82.
19. Cf. however, Raz, *The Morality of Freedom*; John Rawls's position has developed significantly in response to critique of a communitarian nature – see his *Political Liberalism* (New York: Columbia University Press, 1993).
20. Cf. Frazer and Lacey, *The Politics of Community*, pp. 165–7.
21. Walzer, *Spheres of Justice*, p. xv.
22. *Ibid.*, pp. 4–5.
23. *Ibid.*, p. 11.
24. *Ibid.*, p. 9.
25. *Ibid.*, p. 26.
26. *Ibid.*, pp. 28–9.
27. *Ibid.*, p. 314.
28. Raymond Plant, *Modern Political Thought* (Oxford: Basil Blackwell, 1991), pp. 346–7.
29. Richard Mohr, 'The perils of postmodernity for gay rights' (1995) 8 *Canadian Journal of Law and Jurisprudence* 5 at 7. As Frazer and Lacey rightly argue (*The Politics of Community*), a postmodernist approach is but one strand of any communitarian theory of justice or political morality; Mohr, by contrast, mistakenly treats the strand as synonymous with the whole theory, against which his argument is in fact directed. A further inaccuracy in Mohr's use of theory lies in his assumption that there is simply one 'postmodern' view.
30. Ernest Gellner, 'Sauce for the liberal goose' *Prospect*, November 1995, 56 at 59.
31. For useful discussion, see Frazer and Lacey, *The Politics of Community*, ch. 5.
32. Will Kymlicka, *Contemporary Political Philosophy: An Introduction* (Oxford: Clarendon Press, 1990), p. 227.
33. Will Kymlicka, *Liberalism, Community and Culture* (Oxford: Clarendon Press, 1989), pp. 65–6.
34. Mohr, 'The perils of postmodernity', 12–13.
35. Gellner, 'Sauce for the liberal goose', 61.

36. Ronald Dworkin, *A Matter of Principle* (Oxford: Clarendon Press, 1986), pp. 219–20; see also Dworkin's distinction between morality as description and morality as justification in *Taking Rights Seriously* (London: Duckworth, 1977), p. 248. Another universalist liberal perspective is to be found in the earlier work of John Rawls – see *A Theory of Justice* (Oxford: Oxford University Press, 1972), esp. pp. 577–87. Rawls's later position has shifted strongly, however – see his *Political Liberalism*, and more specifically, his 'Kantian constructivism in moral theory' (1980) *Journal of Philosophy* 77.
37. Finnis, *Natural Law and Natural Rights*, chs 3 and 4.
38. Richard Rorty, 'Human rights, rationality, and sentimentality', in Stephen Shute and Susan Hurley (eds), *On Human Rights* (New York: Basic Books, 1993), p. 125.
39. *Ibid.*, pp. 128–34.
40. The simplistic assumption that liberal values *would* easily take hold is exemplified in Francis Fukuyama's now famous essay 'The end of history?' (Summer 1989) 16 *The National Interest* 3; see also his *The End of History and the Last Man* (New York: Free Press, 1992).
41. Cf. also David Lyons, *Ethics and the Rule of Law* (Cambridge: Cambridge University Press, 1984), ch. 1; Plant, *Modern Political Thought*, p. 375.
42. Cf. Stephen Guest, *Ronald Dworkin* (Edinburgh: Edinburgh University Press, 1992), pp. 156–8. John Rawls has argued, in his later work, that his original universalist theory of justice must in fact be understood in the context of North America and Europe, although this would appear to be a change, rather than a simple adaptation, of his earlier view: see n. 19 above and, more broadly, Rawls's 'Kantian constructivism in moral theory'. For discussion of the place of community standards in liberalism more generally, see Raz, *The Morality of Freedom*, pp. 307–13; Feinberg, *Harmless Wrongdoing*, ch. 29A.
43. Michael Walzer, *Interpretation and Social Criticism* (Cambridge, MA: Harvard University Press, 1987), p. 24.
44. For an analogous argument, albeit from a clearly universalist background, see Mary Midgley, *Can't We Make Moral Judgements?* (Bristol: The Bristol Press, 1991), chs 11 and 12, esp. pp. 81–6.
45. Taylor, *Sources of the Self*, p. 61.
46. *Ibid.*, p.62.
47. Bernard Williams, *Morality: An Introduction to Ethics* (Cambridge: Cambridge University Press, 1993, Canto edn), p. 20. See also Lyons, *Ethics and the Rule of Law*, p. 12.
48. Stephen Sedley, 'Human rights: A twenty-first century agenda' [1995] *Public Law* 386 at 386–7.
49. *Ibid.* at 387.
50. *Ibid.*
51. *Ibid.* at 390.
52. *Ibid.* at 396, emphasis added.
53. Determining where the point between intervention and dialogue falls is a matter which must be treated on a case-by-case basis.
54. The question about author perspective also raises the deeper question of how far, if at all, it is *possible* to have notions of 'objective morality', 'objective right' or 'objective truth' – a contentious matter which goes far beyond the liberal–communitarian debate. This matter will not be pursued in detail here; for debate, compare: J. L. Mackie, *Ethics: Inventing Right and Wrong* (London: Penguin, 1977), ch. 1; A. J. Ayer, *Freedom and Morality and Other Essays* (Oxford: Clarendon Press, 1984), pp. 17–34; Williams, *Morality*, esp. pp. 14–37; John Finnis, *Fundamentals of Ethics* (Oxford: Clarendon Press, 1983), ch. III and pp. 144–50; Thomas Nagel, *The View From Nowhere* (Oxford: Oxford University Press, 1986), esp. chs 9–11.
55. Frazer and Lacey, *The Politics of Community*, p. 117. See also Plant, *Modern Political Thought*, pp. 325–7; Walzer, *Spheres of Justice*, p. xiv.

56. (1957) Cmnd. 247, para. 13.
57. Ibid., para. 14.
58. Ibid., para. 61.
59. Hart, *Law, Liberty and Morality*, p. 17; Neil MacCormick, *Legal Right and Social Democracy: Essays in Legal and Political Philosophy* (Oxford: Clarendon Press, 1982), p. 18. See also Eric Heinze, *Sexual Orientation: A Human Right* (Dordrecht: Martinus Nijhoff, 1995), pp. 191–3.
60. Hart, *Law, Liberty, and Morality*, p. 17; MacCormick, *Legal Right and Social Democracy*, pp. 18–19.
61. For discussion of David Hume's position, see Plant, *Modern Political Thought*, pp. 11–12.
62. Ibid., p. 11.
63. Cf. also Stephen Macedo, *Liberal Virtues: Citizenship, Virtue and Community in Liberal Constitutionalism* (Oxford: Clarendon Press, 1990), ch. 7.
64. Hart, *Law, Liberty and Morality*; 'Social solidarity and the enforcement of morality' (first published in 1967), ch. 11 in Hart's *Essays in Jurisprudence and Philosophy* (Oxford: Clarendon Press, 1983); Patrick Devlin, *The Enforcement of Morals* (Oxford: Oxford University Press, 1965); 'Judges and law-makers' (1976) 39 *Modern Law Review* 1. For a recent analysis of this debate, see Robert George, *Making Men Moral: Civil Liberties and Public Morality* (Oxford: Clarendon Press, 1993), esp. chs 2 and 7.
65. Devlin, *The Enforcement of Morals*, pp. v–vii.
66. Hart, *Law, Liberty and Morality*, p. vi.
67. Devlin, *The Enforcement of Morals*, p. 12 (emphasis added).
68. Ibid.
69. Ibid., pp. 12–14.
70. Cf. Devlin's observations on Hart's debating style in *The Enforcement of Morals*, p. 125.
71. Hart, *Law, Liberty and Morality*, p. 5.
72. J. S. Mill, *On Liberty*, ed. Stefan Collini (Cambridge: Cambridge University Press, 1989 edn), p. 13.
73. MacCormick, *Legal Right and Social Democracy*, p. 28; for more detailed discussion of MacCormick's views, see his article 'A moralistic case for amoralistic law?' (1985) 20 *Valparaiso University Law Review* 1, esp. at 30–41. See also Raz, *The Morality of Freedom*, pp. 412–20; Roberts, 'Consent and the criminal law', para. C.72. For discussion of the definition of 'harm', see Joel Feinberg, *Harm to Others*, vol. 1 of *The Moral Limits of the Criminal Law* (New York: Oxford University Press, 1984), ch. 1.
74. Raz, *The Morality of Freedom*, p. 414. See also MacCormick, *Legal Right and Social Democracy*, p. 28; *H.L.A. Hart* (London: Edward Arnold, 1981), pp. 153–4; David Richards, *Sex, Drugs, Death, and the Law: An Essay on Human Rights and Overcriminalization* (Totowa: Rowman & Littlefield, 1982), p. 272 (although note that Richards would probably not agree with the more general analysis of law and the enforcement of morality developed here). For discussion of ranking harms, see Feinberg, *Harm to Others*, ch. 5.
75. Cf. Roberts, 'Consent and the criminal law', para. C.74.
76. Hart, *Law, Liberty, and Morality*, pp. 30–4. This section suggests that Hart saw the 'paternalism' cases as falling within the harm principle, broadly defined.
77. Ibid., p. 34.
78. Ibid., pp. 38–44.
79. See further Feinberg, *Harmless Wrongdoing*, pp. 16–17, 165–73; Devlin, *The Enforcement of Morals*, pp. 132–9 (for Hart's response, see *Law, Liberty, and Morality*, pp. viii–ix).
80. It is, however, open to argument how far a paternalist approach would entail the legal enforcement of morality, sexual or otherwise, in practice: for one view, see Feinberg, *Harm to Others*, p. 70, *Harmless Wrongdoing*, pp. 16–17.

81. Hart, *Essays in Jurisprudence and Philosophy*, essay 16.
82. Devlin, *The Enforcement of Morals*, p. 138.
83. For useful general definitions of the perfectionist and anti-perfectionist positions, see George, *Making Men Moral*, p. 20.
84. Cf. Kymlicka, *Liberalism, Community and Culture*, ch. 5; *Contemporary Political Thought*, ch. 6; 'Liberal individualism and liberal neutrality' (1989) 99 *Ethics* 883.
85. Cf. Raz, *The Morality of Freedom*, chs 5, 6, 14, 15; *Ethics in the Public Domain: Essays in the Morality of Law and Politics* (Oxford: Clarendon Press, 1994), ch. 3.
86. See, e.g., Lawrence Locke, 'Personhood and moral responsibility' (1990) 9 *Law and Philosophy* 39; Peter De Marneffe, 'Liberalism, liberty and neutrality' (1990) 19 *Philosophy and Public Affairs* 253; Nagel, *The View from Nowhere*, ch. 9; 'Moral conflict and political legitimacy' (1987) 16 *Philosophy and Public Affairs* 215; Robert Nozick, *Anarchy, State, and Utopia* (New York: Basic Books, 1974), pp. 30–3; Rawls, *A Theory of Justice*, ch. 3; *Political Liberalism*, Lectures I, IV, V; Chantal Mouffe, *The Return of the Political* (London: Verso, 1993), esp. ch. 9. For a general defence of perfectionism (which takes Joseph Raz to task for allegedly not going far enough), see George, *Making Men Moral*.
87. See, generally, Dworkin, *A Matter of Principle*, chs 8, 9, 17.
88. *Ibid.*, pp. 190–1.
89. *Ibid.*, pp. 205, 208–15.
90. MacCormick, *Legal Right and Social Democracy*, p. 30.
91. The mid-nineteenth-century UK position in relation to income tax and government expenditure seems difficult, nowadays, to comprehend – for useful discussion, see Roy Jenkins, *Gladstone* (London: Macmillan, 1995), pp. 148–57.
92. Devlin, *The Enforcement of Morals*, chs 2–4; cf., however, Hart's *Law, Liberty, and Morality*, pp. 17–18.
93. A superficially related argument has been developed by Richard Posner, who asserts that since theories of justice and political morality tend to be heavily based on factual assertions, they are often – with a little analysis – open to challenge on the ground of factual inaccuracy – *Sex and Reason* (Cambridge, MA: Harvard University Press, 1992), pp. 221–4. Posner's argument presumes too readily, however, that 'facts' are capable of a 'neutral' interpretation. As suggested earlier in this chapter, it seems far more likely that a theorist's interpretations of the world, including any 'factual' assertions they make, are already shaped, to an extent, by their background experiences and circumstances; this being so, clear-cut and 'neutral' interpretation of the 'facts' on which any theory relies is unlikely to be possible.
94. *R v. Chief Metropolitan Stipendiary Magistrate, ex parte Choudhury* [1991] 1 All ER 306.
95. Cf. *Watkins v. U.S. Army* (1988) 837 F 2d 1428 (and (1989) 875 F 2d 699).
96. For an approach where such criteria could be said to go to legitimacy, see Paul Roberts, 'Consent and the criminal law'.
97. I have developed this argument at greater length elsewhere: see my 'Setting the limits of anti-discrimination law: Some legal and social concepts', in Janet Dine and Bob Watt (eds), *Discrimination Law: Concepts, Limitations and Justifications* (Harlow: Longman, 1996), pp. 57–62. One consequence of the connection between assessments of relevance and background theories of justice is that relevance assessments may sometimes be felt to blur into the question of substantive attractiveness.

5

Justifications for Prohibition or Restriction

> *In England we believe in the Christian idea of marriage and therefore adopt monogamy as a moral principle . . . [marriage] remains there because it is built into the house in which we live and could not be removed without bringing it down . . . a non-Christian is bound by it, not because it is Christian but because, rightly or wrongly, it has been adopted by the society in which he lives . . . if he wants to live in the house, he must accept it as built in the way in which it is.*
>
> — Lord Devlin[1]

Introduction

In this chapter, we will analyse some of the main justifications which have been advanced either for totally prohibiting sexual acts between consenting adults of the same sex, or for placing greater legal controls on such acts (or other expressions of affection) than are applied to their heterosexual equivalents. Not all justifications favour the same degree of regulation by the criminal law, but all could be used to oppose the creation or existence of laws prohibiting sexual orientation-based discrimination against lesbians and gays, as well as the legal recognition of same-sex partnerships. More specifically, such justifications have been used in support of laws such as section 28 of the Local Government Act 1988 in the United Kingdom, and the now-defunct Colorado constitutional amendment in the United States.

As well as differing over the degree of regulation which it is appropriate for the criminal law to impose on sexual behaviour between consenting adults of the same sex, the justifications to be considered vary in the ways in which they use assessments of the moral status of such acts. One set of justifications treats them as *inherently wrongful* (usually, but not necessarily, in moral terms), meriting prohibition or substantial restriction by the law for this reason. Other justifications, by contrast, do not themselves adopt a particular opinion concerning the inherent moral status of such acts, but claim instead that the criminal law may justifiably be used to prohibit or restrict them because — and for so long as — either a majority of members of society believe them to be immoral, or the average member does so. John Finnis's arguments, introduced in chapter 4, are perhaps the strongest example of the first, 'inherent wrongfulness' approach. Lord Devlin's theory, epitomized by the quotation at the head of this chapter, is a classic example of the second 'populist morality' perspective.

There is no automatic link between the category into which a justification falls and the degree of regulation by or hostility in the law which it supports — theorists who believe that lesbian and gay sexual acts are inherently wrongful do not necessarily favour a harsher legal regime than theorists whose justifications come from the second category. Professor Finnis believes, for example, that it is only justifiable for the law to seek to discourage — rather than totally to prohibit — sexual acts between people of the same sex; Lord Devlin, by contrast, argued that a complete prohibition of homosexual acts was justifiable, at least at the time he was writing. Such contrasts tend to turn on differences between the theories of justice and political morality underpinning each justification.

As we will see, each category of justification rests on clearly articulated theories of justice and political morality. The justifications within each category also support the idea that it is legitimate for the law to enforce some view about sexual morality; indeed, the fundamental difference between each category is between whose view of sexual morality should be enforced. It would, however, be simplistic and wrong — following our discussion in chapter 4 — to criticize any of these justifications merely because they seek to enforce a view about sexual morality. Instead, a key question will be whether the view which they seek to enforce is an *acceptable* one. It should be added that while the justifications within each group contain speculation about the reasons for and extent of sexual attraction and behaviour between people of the same sex, they tend not to depend, for their force, on moral assessments of lesbian and gay sexual orientations alone.

The two categories of justification will now be considered in turn; criticism of each will be conducted using the criteria discussed in chapter

4. Suggestions that justifications in either category are unattractive – under the overall acceptability criterion – since they involve undesirably intrusive regulation of human sexuality or consenting sexual behaviour must be seen, at this stage, as slightly preliminary in character. For such suggestions assume that there is something good about freedom of sexuality or sexual behaviour – an assumption which can only be explained by invoking one of the justifications which we will consider in chapters 6 and 7.

'Inherent wrongfulness' justifications

Any justification falling within the 'inherent wrongfulness' category will, in logic, involve two main stages of argument. The first stage will turn on the claim that sexual acts between persons of the same sex entail some substantive wrong of a definable nature. The justification must show why the alleged wrong counts as a *moral* wrong – something which can be done by one of three methods, which depend to differing degrees on theories of sexual morality. Under the first method, the alleged wrongfulness is explained exclusively in terms of a theory of sexual morality. Finnis's justification, for example, relies entirely on a background theory of sexual morality to classify same-sex sexual acts as moral wrongs. Finnis claims that sexual intercourse can only properly occur where there is sufficient openness to the possibility of conception, and in any event within heterosexual marriage. He makes passing reference to the idea that same-sex sexual acts are 'unnatural', but this is explained in moral – rather than crude biological – terms. Under the second method, moral grounds are again used for distinguishing rightful from wrongful sexual behaviour – but stronger use is made of the labels 'unnatural' and 'perverse' to describe the sexual acts which are classified as wrongful. Under the third method, by contrast, an overtly *biological* claim about what is 'natural' is relied upon – although such a claim must, in reality, be coupled with a moral account of why the 'unnatural' must be condemned.[2] The second stage of argument in any 'inherent wrongfulness' justification will rest on assertions about justice and political morality – the task of such assertions being to show why the law may legitimately be used to penalize the 'wrong' concerned. An argument which claims that sexual relations between persons of the same sex are 'wrong' because they are biologically 'unnatural' would, for example, need to show at its second stage why it was legitimate for the state to use law to prohibit or restrict 'unnatural' acts – something which would entail the use of arguments about the appropriate role of state institutions and the entitlements of individuals.

An argument cannot amount to an 'inherent wrongfulness' justification for the use or alteration of law unless it can be broken down into these two stages. If an argument contained only the first stage, for example, it would amount to no more than an *assertion* that same-sex sexual relations are wrong. Without the second stage, it could support no programme of action involving the use of law. The *content* of each stage of argument is important too, for it is this which distinguishes 'inherent wrongfulness' justifications from those falling within the second, 'populist morality' category. While 'populist morality' justifications also contain two stages of argument, the content of each is rather different. As a first stage, a 'populist morality' justification must prove either that a majority of members of the society concerned view same-sex sexual acts as immoral, for whatever reason, or that the average member of such a society does so. Either claim – and in practice, both add up to much the same thing – is an *empirical* report of people's views about sexual morality, rather than an argument of sexual morality in itself. And, at the second stage, the theories of justice and political morality invoked by 'populist morality' justifications must seek to explain why it is legitimate for laws to override the wishes or interests of members of social minority groups because the majority of members of (or the average person within) a society believe this to be right.

Sometimes, justifications are advanced for restricting the legal entitlements of gays and/or lesbians – by refusing to enact anti-discrimination laws or by maintaining unequal ages of consent, for example – on the basis that the creation of such laws would have undesirable *consequences*. Analysis of such justifications will usually show, however, that they do not really form an additional, third category beyond 'inherent wrongfulness' and 'populist morality'. Instead, they typically depend on the same type of claim which is made at the first stage of one or other of these two categories – indeed, typical justifications in both categories may well themselves entail claims about the consequences of law reform, such claims being tied to assessments of 'inherent wrongfulness' or of when to enforce 'populist morality'.

The link between concern for consequences and views about 'inherent wrongfulness' can be highlighted if we consider the argument that the state is justified in not enacting laws prohibiting discrimination against lesbians and gays because such laws would prevent religious believers and churches from acting on their moral beliefs that same-sex sexual acts are wrongful (by refusing to employ a lesbian priest, for example).[3] Factually, this argument is easy to rebut since it is not customary for anti-discrimination laws to regulate religious institutions or to prevent discrimination in private arenas like the home. As a practical matter, however, it should be clear that no one is likely to be concerned with any allegedly undesirable consequences of law reform unless they first believed that same-sex sexual acts are wrongful. The same is true of the argument that passing anti-discrimination laws would immediately and adversely affect the moral climate of a society. Such a claim is, as we will see in chapter 8, unlikely on its own to prove realistic (it would in any event need proper empirical support). Again, though, it must turn for its force on the assumption that lesbian and gay sexuality is morally objectionable – for any alleged effect of new legal protections could not otherwise be seen as adverse. The roots of both arguments can logically be traced back to claims about 'inherent wrongfulness'. In similar vein, a 'populist morality' argument must lie at the root of the claim that a higher age of consent is necessary for same-sex than for heterosexual intercourse so that young lesbians and gays can be protected from social hostility. Supporters of this claim are effectively saying that it is preferable to restrict the legal entitlements of young lesbians and gays, rather than to use state power to curtail prevailing social intolerance – in other words, that it is right for the law to respect the majority's views about the wrongfulness of lesbian and gay sexuality or sexual intercourse.

Breaking each category of justification down into its two component stages is useful for exposition and criticism, as well as for comparison. John Finnis's theory is one of the few 'inherent wrongfulness' justifications in which the two stages of reasoning are properly differentiated. Finnis claims that his objective is to present 'reflective, critical, publicly intelligible and rational' arguments – of justice and political morality – which will show why the law may justifiably be used to discourage people, especially the young, from engaging in sexual acts with persons of the same sex.[4] Finnis acknowledges, however, that this objective first requires him to address an underlying question, namely '[w]hat is wrong with homosexual conduct?'.[5] Since Finnis therefore recognizes – correctly, in analytical terms – the need to separate the two stages of reasoning, his theory can be seen – and will be treated here – as a paradigm example of 'inherent wrongfulness' justifications. After analysing Finnis's justification and exploring its possible flaws, we will consider – by way of comparison – justifications which use one of the two alternative methods of categorizing same-sex sexual acts as 'wrongful'.

An outline of Finnis's justification

John Finnis is one of a number of contemporary thinkers who are known as 'new natural lawyers', and his arguments about sexuality are typical of this school.[6] The most complete presentation of his justification can be found in an article published in 1994,[7] based partly on his testimony to the Colorado Supreme Court in *Romer* v. *Evans*.[8] The 1994 article draws on a series of arguments developed by Finnis during the preceding twenty-five years,[9] and ambiguous sections of it have been clarified in a piece published in 1996.[10] It will be necessary to refer to these writings in order properly to understand and to criticize Finnis's justification. Finnis argues that in determining the proper scope of legal regulation, crucial distinctions can be drawn between public and private manifestations of non-heterosexual conduct.

Broadly-speaking, the first stage of Finnis's justification involves the claim that same-sex sexual acts – together with all forms of heterosexual intercourse outside marriage, non-vaginal sexual intercourse between partners who are married, and masturbation – violate a basic good or goods inherent in marital sexual acts of a potentially procreative variety, and that they are in consequence wrongful.[11] The justification's second stage turns on the argument that it is a legitimate function of the state – which exists to promote the common good – to seek to discourage such acts, but not totally to prohibit them. For the common good of society would, Finnis claims, be overlooked if

> laws criminalizing private acts of sodomy between adults were to be struck down . . . on any ground which would also constitutionally require the law to tolerate the advertising or marketing of homosexual services, the maintenance of places of resort for homosexual activity, or the promotion of homosexualist 'lifestyles' via education and public media of communication, or to recognize homosexual 'marriages' or promote the adoption of children by homosexually active people, and so forth.[12]

Finnis thus believed the failed Colorado constitutional amendment to be philosophically justifiable, as well as approving of section 28 of the Local Government Act 1988 in the United Kingdom.

To understand how Finnis arrives at these conclusions, it may be useful first to examine aspects of his broader 'new natural law' theory – something which will explain the meaning which he accords to terms like 'basic human good' and 'common good', and the *method* by which he argues that assessments (moral or otherwise) of right and wrong conduct can be made. This broader theory is set out in Finnis's book *Natural Law and Natural Rights*, in which he claims that natural law principles ultimately derive, not from assessments of 'human nature', but from indemonstrable, pre-moral propositions of practical reasonableness.[13] Finnis develops his overall theory using two sets of variables.[14] First, he argues that there is a set of basic forms of human flourishing – basic human goods – which everyone uses in one way or another in determining what they should do, regardless of their actual conclusions.[15] These goods – life, knowledge, play, aesthetic experience, friendship, practical reasonableness (being able to bring one's own intelligence to bear effectively in decisions relating to one's lifestyle and actions), and religion (broadly defined as meaning the capacity to speculate about the order of things, whatever one's thoughts about the existence or non-existence of a god)[16] – are described as self-evident, intrinsic values which need no demonstration and which are desirable for their own sake. They are presupposed in any demonstration, and do not depend upon further principles for their intelligibility or force. Regardless of perspective, Finnis claims, one can realize that these things are good and desirable for human beings, and this understanding requires no further justification.[17] The basic goods are thus categorized as pre-moral and objective.

Morality is brought into play via a second set of variables. To be free and responsible, a person must be able to make rational choices about which basic goods to pursue and when. This, according to Finnis, is done using the requirements of practical reasonableness, which provide criteria for distinguishing between ways of acting which are morally right and morally wrong.[18] Finnis claims that a decision acquires moral force by being practically reasonable (and is consequently immoral if it fails to be);[19] a moral judgement about something will thus sum up the bearing of some or all of the requirements of practical reasonableness, directing how the issue is to be resolved.[20] The nine requirements of practical reasonableness include adopting a coherent plan of life, not having arbitrary preferences for some of the basic human goods rather than others, not being selfish, respecting the basic human goods in each of your actions (that is, avoiding actions which of themselves damage or go against a basic good), following your conscience, and fostering the common good of your community.[21]

How, then, does Finnis fit sexual acts and sexual morality into this scheme? The first part of his justification – relating to the reasons why same-sex sexual acts are to be considered 'wrongful' – has varied over the years, something which becomes apparent if we compare Finnis's 1994 and 1996 arguments with those contained in an earlier piece published in 1970. In the 1970 article, Finnis asserted that 'a choice to exclude the possibility of procreation while engaging in [sexual] intercourse is always, and in an obvious and unambiguous way . . . a choice directly and immediately against a basic value'[22] and that:

> some sexual acts are . . . *always* wrong because [they are] an inadequate response, or direct closure, to the basic procreative value that they put in question. By a trick of certain European languages, we call the more visibly non-procreative of these acts 'unnatural'.[23]

In other words, Finnis was claiming that procreation is a basic human good (he later claimed that it fell within the basic good of life[24]) – and, using the terminology developed in *Natural Law and Natural Rights*, that a sexual act which is insufficiently open to the value of procreation violates the requirement of practical reasonableness that people should respect the basic goods in all their actions. Such a sexual act could thus be categorized as immoral.[25]

Heterosexual intercourse using contraception can also be condemned using this argument. Finnis asserted more broadly, however, that *any* sexual intercourse – involving partners of the opposite or the same sex – can be condemned if it occurs outside marriage. Finnis reached this position by arguing that within marriage, '*granted* an ideal of a profound, life-long, exclusive, loving union between man and woman . . . intercourse between these spouses is to be regarded as a very apt expression of their union, their common and exclusive project.'[26] That expression would, however, become less apt (or even impossible) if spoiled by pre- or extra-marital intercourse, which lacks true unitive significance for the participants.[27] Why, though, is marriage important? Crucially, for Finnis:

what, in the last analysis, makes sense of the conditions of the marital enterprise, its stability and exclusiveness, is not the worthy and delightful sentiments of love and affection which invite one to marry, but the desire for and demands of a *procreative* community, a family.[28]

So it is the importance of the basic value of procreation which demands – as a matter of practical reasonableness, using Finnis's later terminology – that people be sufficiently open to it, as a value, when engaging in an activity (sexual intercourse) which brings it into play. The good involved in procreation encompasses not just the production of children, according to Finnis, but also their birth into and development in a stable and loving environment where they will be able to appreciate the full range of human values[29] – in other words, their birth and development within a heterosexual marriage.

Why, though, should sexual activity be frowned upon outside marriage if it is calculated not to lead to pregnancy? Finnis argued that participation in *any* form of sexual activity demands openness to the value involved in procreation:

> all sexual activity involves an incohate version, or perhaps a kind of reminder, of the procreative causal potency of 'full' sexual intercourse [i.e. sex within marriage from which children may be produced] . . . this reminder or incohate version brings a sensitive man sufficiently within the range of the procreative value for that value to make its ordinary imperious claim (like the other basic values) to a sufficient openness and respect towards it.[30]

The first stage of Finnis's justification, as formulated in the 1970 article, thus claimed that sexual acts can only properly take place within marriage, and that they must always be open to the possibility of procreation (making marital intercourse illegitimate where contraception is used). By participating in any other sexual act (e.g., with a person of the same sex – an act which is incapable of inducing pregnancy), a person fails to pay proper respect to the value of procreation – part of a basic human good – making their action immoral.

The 'wrongfulness' part of the justification advanced in Finnis's 1994 article is clearly developed from his 1970 argument, although it is formulated in a slightly different – and more ambiguous – fashion. As a general matter, Finnis continues to claim that sexual acts between people of the same sex involve insufficient respect for a basic human good, and are therefore immoral when evaluated from the standpoint of practical reasonableness. Exactly which basic good is imperilled is, however, now less certain. For, while Finnis appears to talk of heterosexual marriage as involving *two* basic goods – the production of children, as part of the basic human good of life, *and* the good of friendship, via the amalgamation of the lives of the marriage partners (something which involves their communion, companionship, and mutual and exclusive commitment) – he also talks of these as *aspects* of the marriage partners' shared common good of *marriage*.[31] In his 1996 piece, Finnis confirms that the common good of marriage is *itself* a basic good (for the purposes of the 'wrongfulness' stage), extending the list of basic human goods set out in *Natural Law and Natural Rights*.[32] Robert George and Gerard Bradley – who are closely associated with Finnis as 'new natural lawyers' – expand on this by suggesting that:

> Marriage, considered . . . as a two-in-one flesh communion of persons that is consummated and actualized by sexual acts of the reproductive type, is an intrinsic (or . . . 'basic') human good; as such, marriage provides a noninstrumental reason for spouses . . . to perform such acts.[33]

The 'new natural lawyers' appear to be arguing that sexual intercourse within marriage serves no end *other than marriage itself* – a good which is actualized by sexual acts of the reproductive type. Procreation is not, therefore, itself the point of marital sex; rather, children conceived during marital intercourse participate in the good of their parents' marriage.[34]

George and Bradley also offer a revised account of the moral wrong involved in same-sex sexual acts. This account builds on Finnis's discussion in the 1994 article, although it appears to go beyond the argument as explicitly presented there. For George and Bradley claim that:

> In choosing to perform nonmarital orgasmic acts, including sodomitical acts . . . persons necessarily treat their bodies and those of their sexual partners (if any) as *means* or *instruments* in ways that damage their personal (and interpersonal) integrity; thus, regard for the basic human good of integrity provides a conclusive moral reason not to engage in sodomitical and other nonmarital sex acts.[35]

This introduces a new basic good – integrity – into the picture, giving rise to the claim that sexual acts between people of the same sex are wrong because they disregard this good – rather than procreation or friendship as such. According to this argument, the body may not be treated as a mere instrument without damaging a person's integrity as a unity of body, mind and spirit – and non-marital sexual acts involve using the body in this way.[36]

However we identify the exact goods involved in heterosexual marriage (even Robert George accepts that 'new natural law' theorizing can appear obscure[37]) – Finnis paints a strong picture in his 1994 article of marriage as an institution. He claims, first, that sterile marriages are in no way inferior to those which result in children, since marriage 'can exist and fulfill [sic] the spouses even if procreation happens to be impossible for them'.[38] Second, attempts to promote the goods involved in marriage by any type of orgasmic non-marital sex are 'simply an illusion'.[39] This argument contains positive and negative sides. The positive side focuses on marriage itself, via the claim that:

> The union of the reproductive organs of husband and wife really unites them biologically [so that] their sexual union . . . can *actualize* and allow them to *experience* their *real common good* – *their marriage* with the two goods, parenthood and friendship, which . . . are the parts of its wholeness as an intelligible common good.[40]

Biological union must involve, Finnis argues, at least the possibility of procreation, and therefore entails:

> the inseminatory union of male genital organ with female genital organ; in most circumstances it does not result in generation, but it is the behavior [sic] that unites biologically because it is the behavior which, as behavior, is suitable for generation.[41]

This argument means, of course, that even within marriage, acts of oral and anal sex go against Finnis's basic good(s). Finnis simply *assumes* that a marriage must involve partners of the opposite sex – something which shows through in his claim that:

> Sexual acts cannot *in reality* be self-giving unless they are acts by which a man and a woman actualize and experience sexually the real giving of themselves to each other – in biological, affective and volitional union in mutual commitment, both open-ended and exclusive – which . . . we call marriage.[42]

George and Bradley reinforce this by suggesting that the notions of marriage, reproductive acts and spouses are so interdefined that marriage is simply inherently heterosexual in nature.[43]

The negative side of Finnis's 'illusion' argument consists in the claim that people engaging in sexual acts with partners of the same sex are deluded if they believe that this involves or can achieve the human goods of marital sex. Any sexual relationship between people who are not and cannot (in Finnis's view) be married – those of the same sex, for example – has no connection with their having children by each other, and the union of their reproductive organs cannot make them a biological or personal unit:

> Reality is known in judgment, not in emotion, and *in reality*, whatever the generous hopes and dreams and thoughts of *giving* with which some same-sex partners may surround their sexual acts, those acts cannot express or do more than is expressed or done if two strangers engage in such activity to give each other pleasure, or a prostitute pleasures a client to give him pleasure in return for money, or (say) a man masturbates to give himself pleasure . . . there is no important distinction in essential moral worthlessness between solitary masturbation, being sodomized as a prostitute, and being sodomized for the pleasure of it.[44]

Regardless of any commitment which partners of the same sex may feel towards each other, their union does no more than give each partner *individual* gratification. Echoing George and Bradley's comment about disintegration, Finnis suggests that same-sex partners are merely using their bodies as unworthy means of pleasure.[45]

In short, Finnis claims, properly unitive sexual acts can only occur between partners in a heterosexual marriage, and must be of procreative significance. In other words, they must be the *type of act* which is, in general, capable of generating children – even if procreation is actually impossible for the couple concerned because they are sterile (thus enabling Finnis to avoid the charge that he contradicts his 1970 arguments). The activation of the sexual organs of unmarried partners – of whatever sex – cannot be an experiencing of the marital good in the way that marital intercourse can, even between sterile spouses. Under this formulation, vaginal intercourse is permissible within a heterosexual marriage. Other forms of marital intercourse – oral or anal sex, and any intercourse where contraception is used – are hostile to Finnis's conception of basic goods, as is any sexual act between partners (whether of the same sex or opposite sexes) who are unmarried.[46] Indeed, Finnis claims, even an open willingness to engage in sexual acts with people of the same sex – via, for example, an acknowledgement of one's gay or lesbian sexual orientation – is to treat human sexual capacities in a way which is 'deeply hostile to the self-understanding of those members of the community who are willing to commit themselves to real marriage'.[47] Sexual intercourse is an intrinsically apt way of expressing the exclusiveness and commitment of heterosexual marriage as something good in itself – something which is denied by sexual expression of a lesbian or gay orientation.

The second stage of Finnis's justification – set out in the 1994 article – focuses on how law should be used in the face of this perceived threat to heterosexual marriage. This stage of the justification begins with the claim that:

> A political community which judges that the stability and protective and educative generosity of family life is of fundamental importance to that community's present and future can rightly judge that it has a compelling interest in denying that homosexual conduct – a 'gay lifestyle' – is a valid, humanly acceptable choice and form of life, and in doing whatever it *properly* can, as a community with uniquely wide but still subsidiary functions, to discourage such conduct.[48]

In chapter 4, it was suggested that the crucial word in this passage is 'properly', given that it highlights Finnis's belief that there are limits to the range of goals which the state may legitimately pursue through law.[49] This idea is further developed in the 1994 article through the idea of 'subsidiary functions'.

Finnis claims that the ends which the state may pursue are inherently limited by its general justifying aim, rationale, or purpose, which is the pursuit of the common good of the political community. Finnis suggests that as a general matter, to say that a community has a common good is to say that the co-operation between its members – which is inherent in the notion of a community – has a particular point, with which the members roughly concur in their understanding and pursuits.[50] Some communities – marriages, for example – have basic human goods as their point, but the common good of the political community is, instead, instrumental – 'the securing of a whole ensemble of material and other conditions that tend to favour the realization, by each individual in the community, of his or her personal development'.[51] Put more directly, this type of common good is instrumental because the political community is one of the forms of collaboration needed to facilitate the availability of basic goods to its members.[52]

In furthering the basic goods, however, the political community should exercise a subsidiary function: that is, its proper role, as a matter of justice, is to help its members help themselves.[53] It can do so by helping them to co-ordinate their activities in pursuit of the objectives and commitments which they themselves have chosen (from among the basic goods, if they are following the requirements of practical reasonableness).[54] Although the state can monopolize the legitimate use of force, through law, its general justifying aim or rationale does not allow it to coerce people in matters of belief,[55] or in relation to private acts of virtue and vice (in this case, consenting sexual acts).[56] Finnis suggests that there are two interlinked reasons for this. First, proper, integral human fulfilment can only occur in a community beyond the ordinary political community – in 'the heavenly kingdom', a community which can be envisaged not by unaided reason (natural law theory) but only by divine revelation.[57] There is a common good beyond the reach of the political community: by implication, therefore, certain human choices (whether or not to engage in a sexual act, for example) should not be directed by the law. This ties in with Finnis's second reason – that it is only people *as individuals* who can make themselves good or evil through their own choices, even if they have moral responsibilities to encourage each other towards good.[58] The theories of justice and political morality underlying Finnis's justification therefore inhibit the lengths to which the state can go in enforcing sexual morality.

A critique of Finnis's justification

Finnis's justification can be assessed and criticized using the internal consistency, relevance, plausibility and acceptability criteria. We will begin with internal consistency. An unsettled controversy affecting the work of Finnis and the other 'new natural lawyers' concerns the extent to which their arguments are underpinned by – or make sense unless one shares – their conservative religious views (which, in Finnis's case, are made explicit in his writings on moral philosophy and theology[59]). This issue comes to the fore in the 1994 article since Finnis asks rhetorically if the judgment that [homosexual conduct] is morally wrong [is] inevitably a manifestation either of mere hostility to a hated minority, or of purely religious, theological, and sectarian belief which can ground no constitutionally valid determination disadvantaging those who do not conform to it?[60]

Finnis clearly presupposes that his justification will supply the analytical underpinning for a negative answer to this question. He is thus trying to produce a rationally defensible justification – which need not depend for its force upon hatred or purely religious convictions – for laws like the Colorado constitutional amendment. This certainly fits with Finnis's earlier efforts, in *Natural Law and Natural Rights*, to argue that his *general* natural law theory need not depend upon the 'question of God's existence or nature or will' – although he did suggest there that the existence of a god might provide a more complete understanding of the requirements of practical reasonableness.[61]

The internal consistency problem facing the 1994 article (the 1970 article is of a more openly theological character, so cannot be attacked for the same inconsistency) is that while Finnis makes a weak attempt to present his arguments in secular terms, they clearly do depend for their analytical force on his brand of Roman Catholic theology. Finnis uses Catholic teachings as authority for much of his argument – which would in any event make little analytical sense in the absence of such authority. Finnis uses Catholic teachings to support his views concerning the place of sexual intercourse within marriage, and for his discussion of the common good which the state is empowered – and required – to foster.[62] Finnis openly acknowledges that his arguments about the 'wrongfulness' of many sexual practices are 'an application of the theory of morality and natural law' developed by Germain Grisez, another 'new natural lawyer', in his work on moral theology;[63] and, in discussing the common good and the legitimate functions of the state, Finnis bases his argument on the stipulations of the Second Vatican Council.[64]

One might try to argue that Finnis is merely using the Church's teachings as incidental or additional – rather than direct – authority for his assertions. In *Natural Law and Natural Rights*, Finnis hinted that a more limited role of this sort might be helpful for explanatory purposes since the Catholic Church 'is perhaps unique in the modern world in claiming to be an authoritative exponent of natural law'.[65] And in the

1994 article, Finnis's rhetorical question seems to presume that he is trying to avoid religious doctrine; one section of the article is used to argue that Socrates, Plato and Aristotle would broadly support Finnis's justification; and it is claimed that the justification would have been reflected in the laws 'adopted in many nations and states both before and after the period when Christian beliefs as such were politically and socially dominant'.[66]

There are, however, two reasons why this rebuttal cannot work. First, the validity of Finnis's interpretation of the Greek philosophers has been challenged by the classical scholar Martha Nussbaum.[67] Detailed consideration of this dispute lies beyond the scope of this book, but it is clear that Finnis's account of the views of Socrates, Plato and Aristotle is controversial and cannot necessarily be taken at face value as authority for his justification – leaving the religious teachings as the only clear authority for his arguments. Second, the idea that Finnis uses the Catholic authority in a purely secondary capacity just does not fit the wording of the 1994 article.[68] Finnis uses his interpretation of the Greek philosophers as an introduction to and as secondary authority for his justification. The justification *itself* is only really developed in later sections of the article, by which stage the argument rests *directly* on the religious authority.

If we are properly to claim that Finnis's arguments depend for their analytical force on his religious beliefs, however, we need to do more than just discuss his uses of authority. We need to show that the arguments only *logically* carry weight – or carry weight in the way that Finnis assumes they do – if one first takes account of his understanding of Catholic teachings on sexual morality. The most obvious way to do this is by comparing Finnis's 1994 arguments with some of his more openly religious work. David Richards has suggested that there are 'two distinct strands' in Finnis's writing, namely 'the exoteric strand that writes [sic] for a broad secular academic audience and the esoteric strand that writes for a narrower [conservative Catholic] audience'.[69] *Natural Law and Natural Rights* exemplifies the 'exoteric' strand, while the 1970 article and works like Finnis's *Moral Absolutes* – a book concerning moral theology – fall within the 'esoteric'.[70] Examining how far Finnis's 'exoteric' writings resemble the 'esoteric' in their logical structure should help determine how far the former depend, for their analytical force, on the religious beliefs which openly underpin the latter. Significantly, Finnis himself acknowledges the interplay between arguments used in the two 'strands' –

thereby weakening any defence against an internal consistency critique of the 1994 justification.[71]

When considered together, Finnis's 1970 and 1994 articles provide a good example of the overlap between 'exoteric' and 'esoteric' arguments. Finnis's 1994 interpretation of the basic good(s) allegedly disregarded by same-sex sexual acts may differ slightly from his 1970 explanation, but both accounts are very similar in their analytical structure. The notion of basic goods plays the same role in the 'wrongfulness' claims in each article; and, even if the exact description of the relevant basic goods varies from one article to the other, both articles employ identical assumptions about the procreative marital context of sexual intercourse. While the 1994 article apparently claims to be non-sectarian, however, Finnis talked openly in the 1970 piece about the 'Christian grasp of natural law', and suggested that:

> The Christian knows the wise man when he sees him because he knows the word of God when he hears it in the scripture and tradition of the Church, whose saints and doctors and authentic teachers are warranted to be precisely the men most fully open (if only by grace of office) to the transcendent and . . . participated goods, and thus sound guides to the derivative moral goods, right and wrong, virtue and vice.[72]

In the 1970 article, Finnis presented his arguments about intercourse and basic goods as an application of Catholic theology.[73] And, if the 'wrongfulness' of same-sex sexual acts is based, according to the 1970 article, on the idea that they involve insufficient openness to the basic good(s) involved in marriage and procreation – basic goods which are clearly conceived of in religious terms – it is difficult to see how, in the absence of further qualification, the related assessment of 'wrongfulness' in the 1994 justification can be interpreted in broader, secular terms – especially since Finnis offers no guidance about how it might be separated from his 1970 arguments.

Finnis might claim, by way of defence, that while he personally interprets and applies his general natural law theory according to his religious beliefs, it is still possible to understand his arguments in secular terms. On this basis, Finnis's interpretation in *Moral Absolutes* of the precepts of natural law as god-given *and therefore* rational, as protecting some fundamental aspect of people's individual reality and as promoting human fulfilment (which Finnis describes as 'participation in the perfected community of the Kingdom which Christ will hand over to the Father')[74] – could be distinguished from his broader discussion of natural law in *Natural Law and Natural Rights*, as could his suggestion that '[m]oral action . . . is cooperation with the carrying out of God's plan'.[75] Even if we assume that such a distinction is plausible in relation to Finnis's broader natural law theory, however – itself a debatable assumption – it is still difficult to claim that the 1994 justification makes analytical sense *as a philosophical argument* unless we recognize its theological basis. For many of Finnis's claims about sexual intercourse do not inevitably follow, as a matter of logic, from his apparently 'neutral' conceptions of basic goods and practical reasonableness; in fact, they only follow if certain additional – theological – precepts are built into the argument.

Finnis's claims about sex and marriage provide a useful example. We have seen that in the 1994 article, Finnis suggests that marriage entails the companionship and mutual and exclusive commitment of the marriage partners. But this loose definition – which is consistent with the argument in *Natural Law and Natural Rights* – need not at face value be challenged by the idea of monogamous same-sex relationships or marriages. The participants in such relationships would, indeed, probably claim that their union – including sexual intercourse – does actualize, for them, the good of friendship (especially if they follow Finnis's claim that friendship is not instrumental to procreation); they might also want to undergo a civil marriage ceremony – if it were available to same-sex couples – for the same reason. Turning to Finnis's justification (and George and Bradley's supporting arguments), we find that these things are only forbidden them because of the claims about the inherently marital nature of sex – and Catholic teachings come into play as soon as we examine the analytical basis of such claims. Finnis's assertions that marital sexual acts 'really unite' the participants and are 'self-giving', that the partners in a monogamous lesbian or gay relationship are pursuing 'an illusion' and are engaged in selfish, individual gratification when they have sex, and that 'reality' is known in objective judgement, all mirror very closely long-standing Catholic teachings about marriage and sexual morality.[76] Indeed, the resemblance is so strong that it is inconceivable to think that Finnis's arguments could not have been dependent on them. As Finnis himself states in *Moral Absolutes*:

The same absoluteness of the properly . . . specified norm excluding adultery is found in the constant Christian tradition, from the beginning, against abortion, suicide, fornication, homosexual sex, and blasphemy and disclaimer of the faith. The tradition is massively solid.[77]

The underpinning role of Catholic sexual morality in Finnis's justification can be underlined by considering the arguments of another Catholic writer, Elizabeth Anscombe. Anscombe's interpretation of what is 'natural' is considerably less subtle than Finnis's, and her writings on sexual morality lack his sophisticated account of the basic goods (in this respect, she might be described as an 'old' natural lawyer).[78] Like Finnis, however, she argues that sexual intercourse is 'intrinsically apt' for marriage and the generation of children. Hence:

> This [factor] – that the good and the point of a sexual act is marriage – is why only what is capable of being a marriage act is natural sex. It's this that makes the division between straightforward fornication or adultery and the wickedness of the sins against nature and of contraceptive intercourse.[79]

Anscombe claims that sexual acts are *in their nature* the type of act that is capable of giving rise to procreation, even if not every sexual act in fact does so – in the same way, she argues, that acorns are intrinsically capable of maturing into oaks, although not every acorn will do so.[80] From this starting point, she suggests that people should be sufficiently open, in their sexual behaviour, to the intrinsic character of sexual acts – and therefore that sexual acts which are deemed to be closed to procreation should be condemned. The close resemblance (in vocabulary if nothing else) to many of Finnis's arguments could perhaps be dismissed as a coincidence were it not for the fact that Anscombe – like Finnis in 1970 – presents her argument as a defence of Catholic teachings.[81]

The theological basis of Finnis's claims can be demonstrated most clearly if we ask whether they actually make sense in the absence of the various Catholic assumptions about sexual morality. When Finnis's justification was presented in the previous section of this chapter, his citations from Catholic teachings were not mentioned. This was a deliberate omission, designed to show just how little substantive argument Finnis offers in support of his justification, leaving the reader of his articles with the uncomfortable impression that many of his claims – about 'intrinsic aptness' for example, or about 'reality', or about the rightful purpose of sex – make little sense as reasoned arguments. In the absence of supporting theological arguments, they simply look like bald assertions – fine for uninformed barrack room debate, but hardly the stuff on which a justification for the use of law or law reform can be built. The point is echoed (albeit unintentionally) by George and Bradley, who accept that '[i]ntrinsic value cannot . . . be demonstrated' – so that their arguments about sexuality may not make sense to non-Catholics[82] – and that, given the indemonstrability of their claims, there is a chance that they might 'simply [be] wrong in believing that marriage, as a one-flesh communion of persons, is possible'.[83]

Supporters of Finnis's justification are therefore left in a quandary. Without the religious authority, his arguments lack any real analytical foundation. If the religious authority is included, however, the overall justification must fail for internal inconsistency: for it is palpably false to claim, as Finnis appears to in answer to his rhetorical question, that the justification is of secular application and appeal. Finnis's claims make little or no analytical sense unless the Catholic teachings are first taken into account; his claims are, on their own, little more than unsupported assertions – statements of opinion, with little or nothing to back them up. As a matter of logic, therefore, Finnis's arguments can really serve only one of two purposes. First, they might still be used as a justification for the use of law – but only on the basis that such a justification is openly sectarian in nature. Such a justification would not, of course, share the aim which Finnis appears to present for his 1994 justification, and may perhaps be open to challenge on relevance grounds. Second, the arguments could, consistently with Finnis's existing aims, be used as a mere *statement* of religious belief – but a statement about why certain sexual acts should be considered 'wrongful' is only the first stage of an 'inherent wrongfulness' theory; on its own, it would fall far short of being a *justification* for the use of law. As mere statements of religious belief, Finnis's arguments are also open to direct challenge from more liberal Christian views of sexual morality; detailed consideration of these theological disputes lies beyond the scope of this book, however.[84]

If the internal consistency critique is correct, then it may also be possible, depending on how one interprets the notion of 'relevance', to criticize Finnis's justification on this ground as well. Some people (perhaps including Finnis, if his rhetorical question was genuinely intended) would argue that a justification for law or law reform cannot carry weight in a pluralist democracy – as opposed to a theocratic state – if it depends for its force on a set of theological assertions.[85] If a modern, constitutional state cannot – by definition – claim divine authority for its general capacity to create and enforce laws,[86] then it is difficult to see how it can legitimately use a theological justification to introduce or to enforce laws which specifically target lesbians and gays. More broadly, if the bulk of the population of a society is no longer actively religious – and does not subscribe to Finnis's conservative theological views about moral absolutes and the wrongfulness of masturbation and oral and anal sex even within marriage – it is hard to see how a justification could be relevant in that society when it depends on these types of theological assumption. Relevance-based criticism seems to be implicit in David Richards' argument that:

> [Finnis's] moral terrain is a pre-Reformation world of self-evident moral truths that takes seriously neither the injustice *and irreparable breakdown of that world* nor our corresponding moral and political needs to construct a basis for community founded not on unbelievable moral certainties but on the common threads of reasonable belief and action on which free persons can base civility and the toleration of equal respect.[87]

This relevance criticism may, though, fall foul of a practical objection when applied to Finnis's justification. This objection – which turns on a slightly different understanding of 'relevance' – runs as follows. We all need to obtain reasoned authority for our arguments from somewhere – especially if our argument is about how the law should be used.[88] If relevance turns only on current social attitudes and understandings, however, then the relevance of an argument or justification may well be reduced to a popularity contest in terms of current social understandings, and it may become difficult for radical new theories to survive scrutiny using this criterion. It could therefore be suggested that before the authority for an argument or justification can be dismissed as irrelevant, it must be positively disproved as an analytical matter. If this definition of relevance is adopted, then an argument, the logical basis of which lies in the claim that a particular deity definitely exists, could only be rejected for irrelevance by positively disproving that claim. The argument could, of course, still be challenged using other substantive attractiveness criteria

– it could be attacked for resting on highly implausible authority, for example, or for requiring us to believe in what seems to be a fairy tale. Since all justifications for the use of law rest at some point on intuitions about justice, however, it is difficult to see why religious assumptions should automatically be less relevant than other types of intuition.[89]

Opinions will differ sharply about which understanding of 'relevance' is preferable when applied to religious arguments. The first interpretation is somewhat empirical, in that something is deemed to be irrelevant if it makes no sense to people in a particular society at a given time. The second interpretation, by contrast, is analytical – it focuses on a theory's logical structure in testing whether it is relevant. It is likely to be more obvious whether a theory is irrelevant using the first interpretation – although supporters of this interpretation may well have greater trouble than supporters of the second in rebutting 'populist morality' justifications for restrictive legal regimes. It may make most sense to suggest that each test for relevance can appropriately be used in different circumstances. A justification for creating anti-discrimination laws to protect lesbians and gays needs to be relevant in the first, empirical sense – for otherwise, using the argument developed in chapter 4, the new law is unlikely to be effective since people will not understand its aims. The empirical sense of relevance, in this context, fits the goal of the justification that is being assessed. It would, by contrast, be more appropriate to use the second, analytical sense of relevance when assessing religious justifications – otherwise, we are always likely to end up dismissing the religious believer's arguments just because they are religious, drawing us into much deeper philosophical dispute about the place of theological arguments in modern, secular societies. It would seem safer and fairer to attack essentially theological justifications on their merits using the acceptability and plausibility grounds – in which case, the relevance criticism of Finnis's justification need be taken no further.

The other substantive attractiveness-based assessment criteria can, however, be deployed with some force whatever one's view of the relevance issue. This possibility is clearly implicit in David Richards' suggestion that 'even on their own sectarian terms', the writings coloured by the 'esoteric strand' are 'remarkably free of any close attention to history, to facts, or to ethically sensitive concern for persons as individuals'.[90] The most controversial feature of Finnis's justification is undoubtedly his theory of sexual morality. Finnis claims, as we have seen, that the only sexual acts which show sufficient respect for his basic good(s) – that are not immoral, within his broader natural law theory – are those which occur within a heterosexual marriage and are, in their nature, the type of act which can lead to the conception and birth of children. If this is correct, then all other sexual experiences, acts, feelings and desires count for nothing – are morally 'worthless', in Finnis's words, things which involve the participants in pursuing an 'illusion'. Given these claims, two types of criticism of Finnis's theory of sexual morality, and of his arguments about the role of law more generally, are possible within the substantive attractiveness family: the first concerns the plausibility of his views, the second their acceptability.

Perhaps the most implausible of Finnis's claims is his suggestion that the stability of 'real marriages' would be threatened by public tolerance of lesbian and gay sexuality. This claim is not confined to Catholic theology. The Rev Ian Paisley, MP, who opposed any reduction in the age of consent for male homosexual acts during the 1994 House of Commons debate, argued that:

> This country must realise that the unit of society, and the cement that holds it together, is the family. As goes the family, so will go the nation. If we do not have the cement of the family, society will disintegrate and be destroyed.[91]

Finnis – and Paisley – fail to support their claims with empirical or other evidence, or to explain how any 'threat' to marriages or to the family would work. It will be argued in chapter 8 that alterations in the law simply do not result in instant, dramatic social changes – a point which is especially evident when the institution allegedly under challenge has social roots as deep and long-lasting as those of heterosexual marriage and the family. Prior to the partial decriminalization of male homosexual acts in England and Wales in 1967, for example, the Catholic writer Michael Buckley argued – in terms rather similar, given their looseness, to Finnis's rhetoric about the so-called 'effects' of law reform – that the common good of society would undoubtedly be injured far more dramatically if the Wolfenden Committee's decriminalization proposals were implemented than if the law remained unchanged. Criminal prohibitions helped greatly to prevent homosexual behaviour, Buckley argued, and the individual should simply learn self-discipline.[92] Quite apart from Buckley's dubious (and unsupported) assertion about the deterrent effect of law, it is plain that partial decriminalization has not brought about a great diminution in the social hostility directed at gay men in the United Kingdom[93] – and it certainly did not lead to the sort of fundamental change in social attitudes concerning sexual behaviour (including the role of marriage) which Buckley seemed to assume it would. Given that basic decriminalization failed to have the dramatic effects which its opponents predicted, it becomes hard to see why further law reform measures should – at least in the absence of hard evidence to the contrary – be assumed to entail more radical consequences.

It is, of course, sometimes argued that the institution of marriage is nowadays under threat. The evidence usually cited for such an argument seems, however, to relate to the idea that *heterosexual* marriage partners are not taking the institution, and their responsibilities within it, seriously enough.[94] Legal regulation of lesbian and gay sexuality has nothing to do with this. Indeed, it might plausibly be claimed that marriage would be strengthened, as an institution, by affording greater social and legal tolerance to lesbians and gays. For a start, there would no longer be social pressure to enter into so-called 'marriages of convenience' with partners of the opposite sex. These can occur either by arrangement – for purposes of immigration, for example – or sometimes where one partner has deceived the other by claiming that they are heterosexual, in the hope that a marriage will help 'cure' latent lesbian or gay sexual tendencies which they are afraid, due to the potential for social hostility, to acknowledge. Clearly, both types of 'marriage' could be described as a mockery of the institution, and greater social and legal tolerance might reduce the possibility of people feeling compelled to enter into them. More positively, we might speculate that same-sex marriage could reinforce the institution both numerically and socially.[95] After all, banning same-sex marriages denies fairly large numbers of people who may want to marry the chance both to do so *and* to show that they can make a success of it.

Finnis might try to claim that he fears a longer-term and more insidious sort of 'threat', in that greater toleration of lesbian and gay sexuality might encourage people who would otherwise engage only in heterosexual practices to 'experiment' – thereby (perhaps) excluding themselves from the possibility of heterosexual marriage.[96] This claim – which sounds a little more plausible, and is perhaps closest to what Finnis meant in his 1994 article – nevertheless rests on questionable assumptions. The first such assumption – made explicit in Finnis's argument – is that same-sex sexual acts (and orientations) are morally less worthy than heterosexual intercourse: for there would otherwise be no reason to worry about a greater number of people engaging in them. We have already seen that this assumption is, in Finnis's theory, inseparable from his theology – leading to internal consistency problems; it is also open to challenge on substantive moral grounds, as we will see in chapters 6 and 7.

Finnis's second questionable assumption concerns the nature of sexuality more generally. His argument focuses solely on male homosexuality – something which is not atypical of those writing from a conservative Christian perspective.[97] It is unclear whether Finnis believes in the possibility of lesbianism, or how he would interpret it if he does (this omission must undermine Finnis's implicit claim to support equality between the sexes in the face of the 'devaluation of women' which, he argues, accompanies male homosexuality[98]). Finnis clearly views male homosexual conduct, however, as something 'alluring but bad' into which a large proportion of men can be tempted.[99] He accepts that a smaller number may be 'unfortunate enough to have innate or quasi-innate homosexual inclinations' – although he claims that 'a life involving homosexual conduct is bad' even for such people.[100] Nevertheless, his general view is 'temptation'-driven: Finnis thus suggests that male homosexual conduct involves an 'abdication of responsibility for the future of humankind' ('abdication' suggesting choice), and talks of the '*state of mind, will and character* whose self-interpretation came to be expressed in the deplorable but helpfully revealing name "gay"'.[101] By classifying gay sex as an immoral form of bad behaviour, in which a sizeable proportion of men could engage if tempted – as opposed to something which a definable group of people are *predisposed* to commit – Finnis is therefore able to claim that law *can* exercise a guiding or restraining function for most males, stopping them from 'being lured by temptation into falling away from their own aspirations to be people of integrated good character, and to be autonomous, self-controlled persons rather than slaves to impulse and sexual gratification'.[102]

Finnis's picture of male homosexuality is questionable, to say the least. It would certainly be shattered if a biological explanation was found for male homosexuality, and could also be rejected if the explanation were found to lie in a person's upbringing – for in neither case (although the argument is stronger in relation to the first explanation than the second) would participation in male homosexual acts be *mainly* a matter of being 'lured by temptation' into a particular act. People who engaged in such acts would instead be recognized as doing so because they were already predisposed to – from birth, if a biological explanation is preferred, and from a period of life before they could take full responsibility for their actions, according to 'upbringing' accounts. If Finnis's picture of sexuality is disproved, it follows that his belief that law can serve as a meaningful deterrent against 'luring' will be worthless – for it is difficult, if not impossible (save at a very great cost in terms of human misery and frustration), for the law to deter someone from being 'lured' into something which they are fundamentally inclined, or driven, to do. It should be stressed that this argument is not designed to make a case for either explanation for lesbian and gay sexuality – in fact, as chapter 6 will show, neither explanation is of real moral relevance when constructing a sound justification for the use of law in this field. Since Finnis's justification is dependent on *his* particular explanation, however, it will fail as soon as an alternative account of sexuality is proven.

The question of acceptability goes to Finnis's dismissal of the most personal and intimate feelings of countless numbers of people as 'worthless' – all because of their failure to match up to a set of pre-ordained, absolute moral rules which make little sense unless one subscribes to his particular brand of conservative theology, which he does not even attempt to defend in the 1994 article. Finnis's fairly obvious distaste for gay males shows through from the very start of the article – apart from his insistence on using the word gay only within inverted commas,[103] he also seems to regard it as necessary to draw attention to the sexual orientation of any scholar who is openly gay, as though this somehow disqualifies them from making an argument. Nowhere in the article do we find references to 'openly heterosexual' or 'openly Catholic' scholars – designations which are arguably more relevant.[104] Finnis is of course entitled to his feelings of private distaste, but it is quite another matter to dismiss – without any real authority for doing so – the sexual feelings and actions of all lesbians and gays, all heterosexuals who are unmarried but in sexual relationships, and all heterosexuals who are married but who do not confine their sexual activity to the missionary position.[105] If the merits of such a dismissal seem obvious to Finnis, it is only because of his unquestioning and inflexible conservative theology. His almost offhand disregard for the feelings and experiences of so many human beings – which are valuable and important to their holders – implies a complete lack of concern for the diversity of human experience and a blind determination to fit the world, whatever the consequences, into a narrow set of dogmas: into reality, as 'objectively' constructed.[106] One rather wonders how Finnis would respond if a government blithely chose to enact laws restricting public expressions of the Catholic faith (although not expressions in 'secret') on the grounds that they were 'an illusion' or a 'threat' and that 'in reality', religious salvation could only be found in a different faith altogether.[107]

The only evidence, in Finnis's work, of an attempt to consider the consequences of his arguments for lesbians and gays is a short aside, in a 1987 article, in which he claims that laws which are hostile towards members of 'immoral' minority groups may in fact be seen as upholding their human dignity by discouraging them from engaging in immoral conduct.[108] One wonders how, in the light of this comment, Finnis would respond to the US Government-commissioned *Report of the Secretary's Task Force on Youth Suicide*, discussed in chapter 3.[109] The report concluded that young lesbians and gays were two to three times more likely to attempt suicide than other young people in the USA, and that the widespread existence of hostile laws and social attitudes was a strong contributory factor in promoting this result. It is difficult to see how anyone with a genuine concern for the well-being of others could seriously claim, in the light of these findings, that laws like the failed Colorado constitutional amendment could truly be described as an expression of concern for the dignity of lesbians and gays. At best, such laws are a flawed attempt to impose an imaginary moral order on a world which is too diverse for such regulation; at worst, they are an expression of hatred and contempt for a minority towards whom 'Christian charity' is deemed to be too generous a gesture.

To summarize: it has been argued that Finnis's justification is internally inconsistent, in that he claims to present an argument for the use of law which is of a secular, 'constitutional' nature, when in reality his arguments make little or no sense unless one supports a conservative interpretation of Catholic sexual morality. This conservative interpretation – which lies at the root of Finnis's justification – is unattractive on its merits, given its debatable understanding of human sexuality (leading to an exaggerated vision of the efficacy of law in regulating behaviour) and its broad lack of concern for human feelings and emotions. If religious believers choose to apply such a morality to their own lives, so be it – but it cannot and should not form the basis of a justification for the use of law.

Other 'inherent wrongfulness' justifications

Two other 'inherent wrongfulness' arguments (both of which assume that the state is empowered to legislate against 'wrongful' activities) must now be considered. The first suggests that same-sex sexual acts may be morally condemned as 'wrongful', 'wrongful' being equated with 'unnatural' or 'perverse'; the second claims that such acts may be categorized as 'unnatural' for biological reasons. Both arguments are open to attack on substantive attractiveness grounds; and the 'biological' argument can also – if taken at face value – be criticized for internal inconsistency. For this reason, the 'biological' argument will be considered first.

A classic argument of the 'biological' variety is the claim that human beings are biologically 'designed' for some types of intercourse but not others – an obvious example being the assertion that the vagina is 'designed' to receive the male sex organ, but that the anus is not – prompting the demand that the law should not tolerate 'unnatural' acts. Arguments of this sort were deployed by some opponents of a reduction in the UK age of consent for homosexual acts during the 1994 House of Commons debate on the topic. Sir Nicholas Fairbairn MP suggested that 'heterosexual activity is normal and homosexual activity, putting your penis into another man's arsehole, is a perverse —'.[110] Sir Nicholas's argument was cut off at this point, but was echoed in spirit elsewhere in the debate.[111]

The internal consistency difficulty with such claims is that there is no agreed scientific basis on which they can be sustained – for any claim about 'natural' uses of parts of the body must be normative or evaluative to a degree, since it depends for its force on some theory of appropriate human capacity.[112] As Thomas Nagel has suggested, in order to categorize something as 'perverse' or 'unnatural', one must first have a clear idea about what is 'normal' *and why*.[113] Unless supporters of 'biological' arguments can supply a theory of sexual morality explaining why certain acts are 'unnatural' and therefore 'wrongful', or why – as a matter of justice and political morality – the state must intervene to prohibit or restrict them, then their argument will be seeking to advance a conclusion without proper analytical support. Such a conclusion could not be justified by the very limited premise of its supporting argument, and would therefore fail for internal inconsistency.

If a moral account of what is 'natural' is proposed, however, then further difficulties quickly arise. For a start, James Brundage has drawn attention to the wide range of possible interpretations of what is 'natural' (some of which claim to be more 'biological' than others) and suggests that:

> What is 'natural' often means whatever is thought (correctly or not) to be the usual practice of the majority. Thus heterosexual marital intercourse at night in the missionary position is identified as 'natural' for human beings and hence morally acceptable. Other coital positions in other circumstances are [according to this view] morally dubious or wrong. But 'natural', in this context, is ambiguous, and medieval writers used the term as inconsistently as unreflective moralists still do.[114]

This highlights a problem which particularly affects 'biological' theories – namely that, since it is difficult to advance any genuinely 'scientific' basis for such theories (that is, a basis which does not depend to an extent on moral evaluations of sexuality), they can easily collapse into an account of what *most people* consider 'natural': in which case the argument ceases to concern 'inherent wrongfulness' and slides instead into a 'populist morality' approach. And, as Thomas Nagel points out, such an approach may – in many societies – lead to the conclusion that even heterosexual adultery is 'perverse', given the social disapproval which it has traditionally attracted.[115]

Another difficulty is that even if genuine 'biological' proof could be produced to show why certain acts were 'unnatural' or 'perverted', it would still be necessary to show why – as a matter of justice and political morality – it was necessary for the law to prohibit or strongly to regulate them.[116] And, in deciding whether such an argument should prevail, it would still have to be weighed against the moral claims made by justifications sympathetic to greater legal tolerance, and may therefore – as will be argued in chapters 6 and 7 – remain open to challenge on substantive attractiveness grounds.

Given the difficulties of 'biological' theories, the conservative philosopher Roger Scruton has developed a more consistently moral account of 'perversion'. This is based on the concept of gender distinctions which, 'while necessary, are also socially constructed'.[117] Gender distinctions are a feature of all societies, Scruton argues, even if they vary in character from society to society.[118] Scruton claims that gender is a morally significant property of whoever possesses it,[119] and that human sexual acts are moralized by conceptions of gender.[120] Gender distinctions thus confer 'a certain mysterious quality' on the opposite sex, so that:

> in the [hetero]sexual act, the sexes confront each other through an experience that is opaque to their enquiry, involving perceptions and stratagems which are inseparable from the gender-identity of the subject who possesses them. In awakening the other's sexual feeling, you take responsibility for a transformation whose inner workings are in an important sense unknowable to you.[121]

It follows, Scruton argues, that it is a feature of sexual maturity to open yourself to the mystery of another gender; by so doing, you are exposing yourself to something you do not fully understand, which can help produce mutual commitment. Thus:

> In the heterosexual act ... I move out *from* my body *towards* the other, whose flesh is unknown to me; while in the homosexual act I remain locked within my own body, narcissistically contemplating in the other an excitement that is the mirror of my own.[122]

In a same-sex relationship:

> Without the fundamental experience of the otherness of the sexual partner, an important component in erotic love is ... put in jeopardy. For the homosexual, who knows intimately in himself the generality that he finds in the other, there may be a diminished sense of risk. The move out of the self may be less adventurous, the help of the other less required. In an important sense it is open to the homosexual to make himself less vulnerable and to offer, because he needs, less support.[123]

A perversion, Scruton claims, involves a failure to recognize – in and through sexual desire – the personal existence of the object of desire (a moral failing).[124] In consequence, he suggests that:

> homosexuality is perhaps not in itself a perversion, although it may exist in perverted forms. But it is *significantly* different from heterosexuality, in a way that partly explains, even if it does not justify, the traditional judgement of homosexuality as a perversion.[125]

It may be the case that gender distinctions are, as Scruton claims, a fundamental feature of all sexual acts – after all, it does seem plausible to suggest that a person's sex or gender (the two concepts are not synonymous) is a crucial definitional element in their attractiveness to others. The suggestion that one 'moves out' from one's body 'towards' another only in the heterosexual act is distinctly implausible, however. In any society where social hostility is directed at lesbians and gays – especially the young – it is clear that a far greater 'risk' is involved in 'coming out' and forming relationships with others of the same sex than is involved in pursuing the 'safe' route and liaising only with persons of the opposite sex. Far more may therefore be at stake for the participants, socially, in a homosexual act than in any heterosexual act. In addition, whether a sexual act is 'narcissistic' – that is, concerned only with the self and not the other partner – must depend on the individual parties to the act rather than any quality allegedly intrinsic to the act itself. Heterosexual acts can surely be just as narcissistic as any others. It is the personalities and motives of those involved in the act itself – rather than their sexual orientations – which will determine how narcissistic or how giving they are. Scruton's claim simply turns on unsupported – and arguably unattractive – generalizations, a point underlined in his discussion of the 'differing' sex drives of men and women. For Scruton paints a caricature of the sexes whereby – again, without supporting authority – men are disposed to be more promiscuous than women, who in turn seek men for protection.[126]

Scruton's account of the 'perverse' is clearly shaped by his own assumptions about the role of the sexes, and may clearly be challenged from alternative moral perspectives.[127] As Edwina Currie MP observed during the House of Commons debate on ages of consent: 'one person's sexual perversion is another person's preferred sexual practice'.[128] The enormous room for disagreement about what counts as 'natural' and as 'perverse' is shown if we contrast Scruton's account of perversion with that presented by Thomas Nagel. For Nagel claims – quite contrary to Scruton – that for an activity to be classified as perverse, it must distort the development of a capacity which a person potentially possesses. Sexual desire should involve some form of human interaction, so activities such as necrophilia might be classified as perverse because they preclude any interaction. There is nothing to say that homosexual intercourse involves the type of distortion necessary to warrant an accusation of perversion, however, if we assume that it is part of a person's natural capacity. It may entail a departure from social norms – but then so do many types of heterosexual intercourse.[129]

It has been argued that any claim that same-sex sexual acts are 'unnatural' or 'perverse' will involve a theory of sexual morality – for purely neutral, 'biological' accounts of what is 'natural' are impossible. Any decision to support (or reject as unacceptable) the arguments considered in this section of the chapter will therefore entail a preference for one view of sexual morality over another. Further accounts of sexual morality will be considered in chapters 6 and 7. For the time being, it should be clear that the justifications considered in this section of the chapter will fail since their distinctions between the 'natural' and the 'perverse' are so vague and unsettled.

The 'populist morality' approach

Lord Devlin's attempted rebuttal of the Wolfenden Committee's arguments – originally presented in his 1959 Maccabaean Lecture in Jurisprudence – must constitute the classic example of a 'populist morality' justification. It was suggested earlier that as a general matter, the first stage of such a justification will involve the claim that either a majority of members of society view same-sex sexual acts as immoral, or that the average member does so (although these two claims will usually amount to much the same thing in practice); and that the second stage must invoke theories of justice and political morality to explain why these moral perspectives should be enforced through the law. Lord Devlin's arguments can certainly be interpreted in this way – something which will be attempted here before a criticism of his justification is developed. It should be noted that while the main focus of Devlin's justification was on the criminal law, his arguments could just as easily be used to counter proposals to bring lesbians and gays within the scope of anti-discrimination laws, proposals to repeal overtly hostile laws (section 28 of the Local Government Act 1988 in the UK, for example), and proposals to allow same-sex marriages or the adoption or rearing of children by same-sex partners.[130]

Devlin's justification

Devlin's critique of the Wolfenden Committee's proposals was framed in terms of three questions: first, is society entitled at all to pass judgement on matters of morality, or are morals always a matter for individual or private judgement? Second, if society is entitled to pass judgement, is it also entitled to use law to enforce it? And third, if society is so entitled, ought law to be used in all cases of immorality, or only in some?[131]

Devlin's answer to the first question rested on his interpretation of how a society works. Devlin insisted that '[w]hat makes a society of any sort is a community of ideas, not only political ideas but also ideas about the way its members should behave and govern their lives; these latter ideas are its morals.'[132] Furthermore:

> If men and women try to create a society in which there is no fundamental agreement about good and evil they will fail; if, having based it on common agreement, the agreement goes, the society will disintegrate. For society is not something that is kept together physically; it is held by the invisible bonds of common thought. If the bonds were too far relaxed the members would drift apart. A common morality is part of the bondage. The bondage is part of the price of society; and mankind, which needs society, must pay its price.[133]

Devlin acknowledged that the answer to the first of his three questions virtually dictated the answer to the second, which clearly turned on his theory of political morality. For Devlin claimed that since a recognized morality is as necessary to a society as a recognized government, the state was entitled to use the law to protect morality in the same way that it can use law to protect anything else essential to its existence.[134] Law could be used to protect society from immorality in any area of life, just as it could protect society from treason.[135] The *content* of the moral code of any particular society was, however, unimportant – the fact that a society had what others would see as the wrong morality would not stop it from being a society and therefore entitled to enforce that morality. Under Devlin's theory, the mere *existence* of a shared morality was what helped distinguish a society from a group of unconnected individuals: morality was a 'glue' holding societies together.

In response to his third question, however, Devlin suggested that society had only a *prima facie* entitlement to use law to enforce morality – that is, one which could be rebutted by other factors.[136] For Devlin only opposed hard and fast *theoretical* limits on the use of law, such as the Wolfenden Committee's idea of a realm of privacy in which the law should have no business.[137] Devlin believed that some balance needed to be struck between society's moral judgements and the ability of individuals to control their own lives, and argued that a series of loose principles – which would guide rather than restrict the legislature – should be used in deciding whether to enact any particular law which enforced its morality (sexual or otherwise).[138] While society was entitled to use law to enforce morality, 'the decision about what particular cases it should be used in is essentially a practical one'.[139]

The three loose principles which Devlin suggested were as follows. First, the limits of a society's tolerance – in the sense of the extent to which it would tolerate departures from its shared moral standards – tended to shift from generation to generation. However, a society's laws – especially those based on morals – are less easily moved; the law should therefore be slow to act in response to any alteration in morality since that alteration might soon be reversed, leaving a revised law without moral backing.[140] Second, privacy should be respected as far as possible.[141] Devlin was hazy about how far this qualification could go. On the one hand, he stated that the qualification could apply in only a limited range of cases and not all private immorality could be excluded from the scope of the law. On the other hand, he suggested that where everyone involved in an immoral activity had consented, and the act was done in private, the public interest in morals might be balanced against respect for privacy. Devlin also surmised that, since the gravity of a crime was an important consideration, 'a distinction might well be made in the case of homosexuality between the lesser acts of indecency and the full offence'.[142] Third, the law is concerned with the minimum acceptable standards of conduct, not the maximum; society can therefore disapprove of practices morally without such judgements always being enforced by the law.[143] Devlin went so far as to describe this point as 'the biggest thing to be remembered'.[144]

The first loose principle – that there should be toleration of the maximum individual freedom which is consistent with the integrity of society – brought into play the most notable aspect of Devlin's argument, which is his definition of the morality – in this particular context, the sexual morality – which the law should enforce. At an abstract level, Devlin's view of the nature of morals was fairly orthodox: they were, he argued, rooted in a belief 'in the advance of man towards a goal' and were concerned with '[t]he distinction between virtue and vice, between good and evil so far as it affects our actions'.[145] However, when deciding what was to be defined as immoral for the purposes of legal prohibition – what the law was to treat as good and as evil – the relevant standard was 'what every right-minded person is presumed to consider to be immoral'.[146] An activity was therefore immoral if the right-minded person – the famous 'person on the Clapham omnibus' – considered it to be so. Furthermore, the right-minded person was not to be confused with the rational person – instead, she or he was 'not expected to reason about anything and [their] judgement may be largely a matter of feeling'.[147] The law was, therefore, to enforce common or popular morality,[148] and Devlin cited with approval Dean Rostow's description of popular morality as 'a blend of custom and conviction, of reason and feeling, of experience and prejudice'.[149]

This argument was further developed in Devlin's explanation of what counted, for the purposes of his first *ad hoc* principle, as the maximum individual freedom which could be tolerated. Devlin asserted that: 'Nothing should be punished by the law that does not lie beyond the limits of tolerance. It is not nearly enough to say that a majority dislike a practice; there must be a real feeling of reprobation.'[150] In determining whether a 'real feeling of reprobation' existed, widespread disgust about a particular practice was, apparently, 'a good indication that the bounds of toleration are being reached'.[151] If the genuine feeling in any society was that homosexuality was 'a vice so abominable that its mere presence is an offence' then that society could not be denied the right to eradicate it.[152] No society, Devlin declared,

> can do without intolerance, indignation, and disgust . . . matters of [morality] are not determined by rational argument. Every moral judgement, unless it claims a divine source, is simply a feeling that no right-minded man could behave in any other way without admitting that he was doing wrong. It is the power of common sense and not the power of reason that is behind the judgements of society.[153]

In writing the preface to *The Enforcement of Morals*, some years after these arguments were originally presented in his Maccabaean Lecture, Devlin attempted to revise his reasoning in two relevant ways. First, he suggested that the reasonable person was *not* expected to hold irrational beliefs; an example of an irrational belief, given modern knowledge, would be the Roman Emperor Justinian's reported assertion that homosexuality caused earthquakes. However:

> when the irrational is excluded, there is [sic] . . . a number of conclusions left for all of which some good reasons can be urged. The

exclusion of the irrational is usually an easy and comparatively unimportant process. For the difficult choice between a number of rational conclusions the ordinary man has to rely upon a 'feeling' for a right answer. Reasoning will get him nowhere.[154]

As this passage makes clear, Devlin still left considerable room for 'feeling': indeed, the only example we have of a belief which Devlin would exclude for irrationality – the Emperor Justinian's view about earthquakes – is so irrational that it could rightly be described as preposterous.[155] Devlin's suggestion that the reasonable person would not hold irrational beliefs is also difficult to reconcile with his earlier warning against confusing the reasonable person with the rational – for the obvious implication of this earlier warning is that the reasonable person *may* sometimes hold irrational beliefs (an implication supported by Devlin's favourable view of Rostow's argument). It may be possible that Devlin was categorizing a much wider range of beliefs as 'irrational' in the original lecture than he did in the preface – but there is no reference in the preface to such a shift in position. Devlin's preface may therefore simply contradict his earlier views. In any event, the range of beliefs which Devlin's later account would exclude for irrationality still seems too narrow to amount to much of a concession.

Devlin reiterated in the preface that he believed society's intolerance, indignation and disgust at a particular practice could justify the use of law to prohibit it. His second revision, however, was to suggest that for this prohibition to be justified, society's feelings had to be the product of calm and dispassionate assessment rather than hot-headed reaction. Devlin was confident both that intolerance and disgust could emerge from calm analysis and that 'the average Englishman' was capable of reacting in this way.[156]

All three of Devlin's questions involve what was described earlier as the second stage of reasoning in 'populist morality' justifications – that is, they turn on assertions of political morality (which in turn rest on certain sociological claims about the nature of a society) which seek to explain why society has the right to enforce its common morality. None of the three questions could, however, be applied – as a matter of logic – to same-sex sexual acts unless it was clear that the average, 'right-minded' person thought that such acts were wrong as a matter of sexual morality. Any such demonstration would clearly be of an empirical nature – for if the views of the average, 'right-minded' person were to be enforced, some sort of statistical selection would be necessary to show who counted as such a person, and how many such people there were.

A critique of Devlin's justification

Criticism of Devlin's justification may be developed using consistency and substantive attractiveness criteria. Under the substantive attractiveness heading, the plausibility of Devlin's claims about the effect of failing to enforce populist conceptions of sexual morality through law can be called into question – as can the acceptability, at a level of justice and political morality, of the type of sexual morality which he wished to see enforced. The exact criticisms which can be made will to an extent vary according to the interpretation placed on Devlin's arguments. When considering these criticisms, however, it should be remembered that Devlin's challenge to the idea that law should not be used to enforce morality is, as we saw in chapter 4, generally sound. Justifications for existing law or for law reform are always based on considerations of political morality, and justifications which specifically concern sexual behaviour (whether such justifications are progressive or restrictive in nature) will almost always, as a matter of logic, entail the enforcement of some view about sexual morality. The objection, in relation to Devlin's justification, goes to the populist sexual morality which he wished to enforce.

Let us start by asking whether Devlin's arguments are plausible. It is important here to distinguish between Devlin's *description* of a society as entailing a shared morality, and his *assertion* that departures from the shared morality will damage that morality and eventually lead to the collapse of the society itself. The description is, on its own, relatively uncontroversial. A society is, after all, more than just a collection of people who occupy the same physical space: it is first necessary for other important linkages and shared understandings to exist, one such linkage invariably being a set of notions about right and wrong ways of behaving – in other words, a morality. The very notion of a society implies a shared awareness of ideas, values and experiences, which form a backdrop against which the members of that society tend to interpret the world. Not every member of a society need accept all or even any of the linkages or shared understandings; most members need, though, to accept some. Such elements might include understandings of family relationships, of friendship and its boundaries, of work and notions of poverty and wealth and, at a very abstract level, of notions of right and wrong. Members of a society are also likely to feel some obligation towards each other, for example by believing that the society's political institutions should attempt to assist or to rescue members of the society in trouble abroad. Devlin's description of a society as entailing some form of shared morality is therefore plausible.

Devlin's assertion – focusing on how a society actually *works* – is somewhat less satisfactory, however. As Professor Hart has pointed out, it is unclear from Devlin's argument which of two different reasons he was relying on to justify the legal enforcement of a society's morality.[157] Hart labelled one possible reason the 'disintegration thesis', and the other the 'conservative thesis'. Elements of both 'theses' are vulnerable to attack on substantive attractiveness and internal consistency grounds, although it may be fair to say that criticism of the first 'thesis' will focus more strongly on internal consistency and plausibility issues. Criticism of the second will, by contrast, focus more strongly on its acceptability given that it rests on a distinctly unattractive theory of justice and political morality. More broadly, both 'theses' involve questionable assertions about whose view of sexual morality the law should enforce.

If Devlin's justification rests on the 'disintegration thesis', then it turns on the claim that since a shared morality is essential to a society's existence and since that society would be threatened by a breach of its shared morality, breaches may rightly be punished since society can use its laws to preserve its existence.[158] This justification is forward-looking – legal enforcement of morality can be justified because of the bad consequences which would follow if it were not.[159] As Hart observed, however, this thesis could only properly justify the use of law to enforce a society's shared morality if there were evidence – most obviously, empirical evidence – to *prove* that departures from the shared morality had the consequences which Devlin claimed. Enforcement of morality without evidence would at best be arbitrary. Devlin's justification contained no satisfactory evidence, leading Hart to suggest that the argument for enforcing a shared morality could not be sustained unless Devlin produced evidence to support the 'disintegration thesis'.[160] In other words, if Devlin's argument for the enforcement of a shared morality relied on the 'disintegration thesis' alone, it could be rejected for internal inconsistency due to a lack of sufficient analytical support in the form of empirical data.

The 'disintegration thesis' could also be criticized – under the substantive attractiveness heading – for resting on an implausible understanding of what a society is and how it works. Devlin's 'disintegration' arguments bear a strong resemblance to Professor Finnis's views concerning the 'threat' posed by male homosexuality to the institution of marriage – views which we have already dismissed as implausible. For any conventional understanding of the workings of a society would accept that not every practice which the majority of members of that society view as immoral threatens its existence. As Professor Hart has made clear, the 'disintegration thesis' is sustainable only if we adopt an artificial view of how a society works, based on the proposition that a society is *coterminous with* its popular morality at any given moment in history, so that a change in that society's morality is tantamount to its destruction and replacement by a new society.[161] Not only is this view absurd in practice (a point reinforced by Devlin's failure to provide any hard evidence to support a 'disintegration' argument), but it also assumes that it is justifiable for a society to preserve itself by force regardless of the acceptability or otherwise, objectively speaking, of its shared morality.

In a footnote to his original Maccabaean Lecture, added when it was reprinted in *The Enforcement of Morals*, Devlin attempted to rebut this criticism by arguing that he did not believe that a society's existence was threatened by *any* one specific deviation from its shared morality. Instead, deviations were *in their nature* capable of threatening a society's existence and so could not, in principle, be put beyond the reach of the law. This was clearly a dilution of Devlin's original view – as Ronald Dworkin put it, Devlin's concession 'tells us that we must understand . . . the crucial claim that society has a right to enforce its public morality by law – as [being] limited to a denial of the proposition that society never has such a right'.[162] Devlin also challenged Hart's critique of his view of how a society works by claiming that whether changes in its morality resulted in the disappearance of one society and its replacement by another really depended on the nature and extent of the changes – it was all, in other words, a matter of degree.[163] While this sounds like a sensible concession, however, it still leaves the 'disintegration thesis' unsupported by the empirical evidence which would be necessary for it to be viewed as capable of justifying the enforcement of a society's shared morality by law. We are also left to accept the implausible assertion that the commission of a homosexual act in private between consenting adults is something which is capable – in its nature – of threatening the moral structure of a society. If Devlin's justification rests on the 'disintegration thesis', it must surely be seen as implausible and therefore substantively unattractive.[164]

These particular criticisms might be deflected if Devlin's justification is instead read as resting on the second and more extreme argument, which Hart labelled the 'conservative thesis'. According to this argument, which Ronald Dworkin (who labels it 'society's right to follow its own lights') believes underpinned much of Devlin's later writing, the legal enforcement of morality is a good thing in and of itself, regardless of its consequences; a society may enforce its morality by law since the majority of its citizens are entitled to follow their moral conviction that their moral environment is valuable and should be protected from change.[165] This interpretation of Devlin's justification – if correct – is, however, clearly open to challenge on the ground that its underpinning theory of justice and political morality is unacceptable. For Devlin would be claiming that the state should enforce the moral convictions of the majority of its citizens (or of the average and reasonable citizen, depending on interpretation) regardless of the effects this would have on individuals. Such an argument would be wholly relativist – for it amounts to the claim that something is right in a given society just because members of that society say so (see chapter 4).[166] Members of unpopular social groups could thus be deprived of any entitlement to protection against the majority (or popular) view, and their treatment could not permissibly be criticized from outside the society. This is clearly not a position with which many would feel comfortable – for (even given Devlin's three loose principles) individuals would have no solid entitlements save that their moral views be taken into account in any determination of their society's shared morality.

The consequences of reasoning of this sort are all too apparent in the USA. For something akin to the 'conservative thesis' would seem to have been present in the majority's judgment in *Bowers v. Hardwick*, where the Georgia anti-sodomy law was found to survive constitutional scrutiny under the Due Process Clause. Justice White suggested that the Supreme Court would not declare 'a fundamental right to engage in homosexual sodomy' to exist – for it could not be said to be deeply rooted in the nation's history and tradition, nor implicit in the concept of ordered liberty.[167] Furthermore, the Court could not accept the argument that a belief – if held by the majority of citizens – that homosexual conduct was immoral was an insufficient basis for supporting the constitutionality of an anti-sodomy law.[168]

The general criticism of Devlin's theory of justice and political morality can be reinforced if we consider what he actually counted as the 'morality' which the law is to enforce. For, regardless of whether the 'disintegration thesis' or the 'conservative thesis' provides the better interpretation of Devlin's justification, it can be seen as substantively unattractive because of his suggestion that morality can encompass views based on prejudice, intolerance and disgust. The enforcement of feelings such as these – which both of the 'theses' seek to justify – could clearly have disastrous consequences for the well-being of unpopular social minorities. Given the implausibility of Devlin's 'disintegration' claims, it is not even as though he offers any strong reason why these consequences might be a price worth paying for the enforcement of populist moral views. As Ronald Dworkin succinctly put it: 'What is shocking and wrong is not [Lord Devlin's] idea that the community's morality counts, but his idea of what counts as the community's morality' in relation to sexual activity.[169]

Devlin's suggestions in his preface – that some beliefs may be excluded from consideration because they are irrational or have not resulted from calm and dispassionate analysis – are actually of little help in moderating his argument. For, while stressing the importance of calm and dispassionate analysis, Devlin nevertheless reasserted his belief that intolerance and disgust could give rise to a legitimate use of law. This is clearly inconsistent – for it is hard to see how feelings of intolerance and disgust can *ever* give rise (at least consistently) to calm and dispassionate analysis. A society's feelings of intolerance and disgust are most likely to spring from its shared morality[170] – and, as we have seen, Devlin appeared to believe that prejudices form one chunk of that morality. A reaction which is rooted even to a minor extent in prejudice is, however, hardly the sort of thing which springs to mind as an example of calm and dispassionate analysis. (Even if it were possible to square this particular circle, Devlin in any event never made clear in the preface what he meant by calm and dispassionate analysis.)

This inconsistency is compounded if we remember that very few beliefs would be excluded for irrationality on the view adopted by Devlin in his preface, giving a very wide scope for law-makers' 'feelings' in the creation of new law. Given that 'feelings' could be, on Devlin's definition, much the same thing as intuitions, it again seems difficult to envisage the role they could serve in calm and dispassionate analysis. Since Devlin mentioned calm and dispassionate analysis in his original lecture, it is possible that his position was, in some way, always more moderate than critics have assumed.[171] If this was so, however, Devlin made little attempt to highlight the fact. In assessing Devlin's view of the sexual morality which the law should enforce, we are therefore left with a choice between his earlier clearly populist notions and the later incoherent explanations of them. Neither account seems particularly appealing in substantive attractiveness terms given that both would allow the law to ride roughshod over the freedoms of unpopular minority groups.

If the 'disintegration thesis' account of Devlin's justification is favoured, another internal inconsistency problem arises due to the respect for privacy principle which, according to Devlin, should influence individual decisions whether to enforce morality through law. For, given the weight which the 'disintegration thesis' placed on the harm which immoral acts allegedly inflict on society, it is not clear why even a limited privacy qualification should be supported. If an allegedly immoral act is intrinsically likely to contribute to the decay of a society's common morality, it is hard to see why it should make any difference whether it occurs in public or private: at best, any difference could only be one of degree. It is also unclear how far Devlin intended the privacy qualification to extend in relation to homosexual acts: where, for example, did he envisage a line being drawn between 'lesser acts of indecency' and 'the full offence'? If 'the full offence' is supposed to be buggery, and 'lesser acts of indecency' any intimate physical contact short of this (including oral sex), it is certainly difficult to see why one act should bring the 'disintegration thesis' and the criminal law into play, while the other should not. It is arguable whether people who are generally disgusted at the idea of sex between men would feel *significantly* greater revulsion at the thought of one type of act than the other.[172]

On balance, then, Devlin's justification must be rejected. First, it contains too many loose ends and points which are arguably contradictory – however it is interpreted – bringing the internal consistency criterion into play. Second, if the 'disintegration thesis' is the preferred interpretation of Devlin's arguments, then his arguments must be rejected (under the substantive attractiveness heading) for implausibility. Third, if one is concerned to protect the entitlements of minority groups, then *any* theory of justice and political morality which sanctions the enforcement of populist morality can be rejected as unacceptable (under the substantive attractiveness heading). This is especially true of Devlin's theory – whether the 'disintegration' or the 'conservative thesis' is adopted – because of the type of sexual morality which he would be happy to see enforced: that is, 'feelings' based on ill-informed prejudice. Even if Devlin's later revisions are taken into account, his justification could still have deleterious consequences for the legal entitlements of members of unpopular minority groups. Indeed, members of any minority group (including racial and religious minorities) could legitimately be penalized under Devlin's justification since his argument was not confined to the enforcement of sexual morality. Devlin's justification cannot plausibly be adopted in any society with a serious concern to safeguard the basic liberties of its members.

Conclusion

We have seen that 'inherent wrongfulness' and 'populist morality' justifications are open to serious objection, both because they contain internal inconsistencies and because they rely on arguments which are implausible, *prima facie* unacceptable on their merits, or both. It may well be felt that these failings are sufficient on their own to disqualify such justifications from serious consideration. It is important to remember, however, that disqualifying hostile justifications does not amount to endorsing a more sympathetic legal regime for lesbians and gays. Such a regime requires a positive justification of its own – and it is this for which we shall search in chapters 6 and 7.

Notes

1. Patrick Devlin, *The Enforcement of Morals* (Oxford: Oxford University Press, 1965), p. 9.
2. Cf. Thomas Nagel's suggestion that assessments of 'perversion' are evaluative, but do not necessarily have to be of a moral character – *Mortal Questions* (Cambridge: Cambridge University Press, 1979), pp. 51–2.
3. An example of such a justification, in the constitutional law context, can be found in Richard Duncan's article 'Who wants to stop the Church: Homosexual rights legislation, public policy, and religious freedom' (1994) 69 *Notre Dame Law Review* 393. Duncan's misunderstandings of the workings of anti-discrimination law are too considerable – and too profound – to list here.
4. John Finnis, 'Law, morality, and "sexual orientation"' (1993–4) 69 *Notre Dame Law Review* 1049 at 1055.
5. *Ibid.* at 1055.
6. For analysis and defence of 'new natural law' thinking, see Robert George, 'Recent criticism of natural law theory' (1988) 55 *University of Chicago Law Review* 1371.
7. Finnis, 'Law, morality, and "sexual orientation"'.

8. See further chapter 2.
9. Principally in 'Natural law and unnatural acts' (1970) 11 *The Heythrop Journal* 365; *Natural Law and Natural Rights* (Oxford: Clarendon Press, 1980); 'Legal enforcement of "duties to oneself": Kant v. Neo-Kantians' (1987) 87 *Columbia Law Review* 433; *Moral Absolutes: Tradition, Revision, and Truth* (Washington, DC: Catholic University of America Press, 1990). Also relevant is Finnis's 'Personal integrity, sexual morality, and responsible parenthood' (1985) 1 *Anthropos: Rivistadi di Studi Sulla Persona e la Famiglia* 43. In this respect – as in many others – Andrew Sullivan's treatment of the issues is both sketchy and inadequate: see *Virtually Normal: An Argument About Homosexuality* (London: Picador, 1995), ch. 3.
10. John Finnis, 'Is natural law theory compatible with limited government?' in Robert George (ed.), *Natural Law, Liberalism and Morality* (Oxford: Clarendon Press, 1996).
11. Finnis uses the word 'immoral' on many occasions – see, e.g., 'Legal enforcement of "duties to oneself"' at 445, n. 60; 'Law, morality, and "sexual orientation"' at 1052.
12. *Ibid.* at 1076.
13. Finnis, *Natural Law and Natural Rights*, pp. 29, 33.
14. *Ibid.*, p. 23.
15. *Ibid.*, p. 22.
16. *Ibid.*, pp. 85–97.
17. *Ibid.*, pp. 64–73.
18. *Ibid.*, pp. 23, 103.
19. *Ibid.*, p. 101.
20. *Ibid.*, pp. 126–7.
21. *Ibid.*, pp. 103–26.
22. Finnis, 'Natural law and unnatural acts' at 384.
23. *Ibid.* at 385, emphasis added.
24. Finnis, *Natural Law and Natural Rights*, pp. 86–7.
25. Cf. Finnis, 'Natural law and unnatural acts' at 373.
26. *Ibid.* at 381.
27. *Ibid.* at 382.
28. *Ibid.* at 383.
29. *Ibid.* at 384.
30. *Ibid.* at 384–5.
31. See, generally, Finnis, 'Law, morality, and "sexual orientation"' at 1064–7. Finnis briefly mentioned, at the end of the 1970 article, the role of the good of friendship in sexual activity – 'Natural law and unnatural acts' at 387.
32. Finnis suggests, in *Natural Law and Natural Rights*, pp. 90–2, that the list of seven basic goods is not exhaustive. For the treatment of marriage as a basic good, see Finnis, 'Law, morality, and "sexual orientation"' at 1070–1; 'Is natural law theory compatible with limited government?' at 4, 13–14.
33. Robert George and Gerard Bradley, 'Marriage and the liberal imagination' (1995) 84 *Georgetown Law Journal* 301 at 310–12.
34. Finnis, 'Law, morality, and "sexual orientation"' at 304–5; see also 'Is natural law theory compatible with limited government?' at 14.
35. *Ibid.* at 302.
36. *Ibid.* at 314.
37. George, 'Recent criticism of natural law theory' at 1429.
38. Finnis, 'Law, morality, and "sexual orientation"' at 1065.
39. *Ibid.*
40. *Ibid.* at 1066.
41. *Ibid.* at 1066, n. 46.
42. *Ibid.* at 1067.
43. George and Bradley, 'Marriage and the liberal imagination' at 302, n. 5.
44. Finnis, 'Law, morality, and "sexual orientation"' at 1067.
45. *Ibid.* at 1066–7.
46. *Ibid.* at 1067–8.
47. *Ibid.* at 1070.
48. *Ibid.*
49. See further Finnis, 'Is natural law theory compatible with limited government?'.
50. *Ibid.*; Finnis, *Natural Law and Natural Rights*, pp. 150–3.
51. *Ibid.*; see also pp. 147–50. See, however, 'Is natural law theory compatible with limited government?' at 5 (sharing in married life as a *common* good).
52. Finnis, 'Law, morality, and "sexual orientation"' at 1071.

53. Finnis, *Natural Law and Natural Rights*, p. 146.
54. Finnis, 'Law, morality, and "sexual orientation"' at 1072.
55. *Ibid.*
56. *Ibid.* at 1073–4, 1076.
57. *Ibid.* at 1074.
58. *Ibid.* at 1075.
59. The conservatism of Finnis's religious outlook is made clear in his book *Moral Absolutes*, both in his arguments concerning contraception and the pill, and in his more general attack on 'proportionalism'. In *Natural Law and Natural Rights*, p. v, Finnis (rightly) accepts that the labels 'ethics', 'political philosophy', 'philosophy of law' and '[J]urisprudence' cannot be treated as referring to disciplines which are analytically distinct.
60. Finnis, 'Law, morality, and "sexual orientation"' at 1055. Finnis's question appears to be invoking the spirit of Justice Blackmun's dissent in *Bowers v. Hardwick*: 'The legitimacy of secular legislation depends ... on whether the State can advance some justification for its law beyond its conformity to religious doctrine' (1986) 106 S Ct 2841 at 2855.
61. Finnis, *Natural Law and Natural Rights*, p. 49; see also the preface and ch. 13.
62. Finnis, 'Law, morality, and "sexual orientation"' at 1063–76.
63. *Ibid.* at 1063. Finnis had earlier published, with Joseph Boyle and Germain Grisez, a book titled *Nuclear Deterrence, Morality and Realism* (Oxford: Clarendon Press, 1987) – a theological interpretation of the morality of nuclear deterrence.
64. Finnis, 'Law, morality, and "sexual orientation"' at 1073.
65. Finnis, *Natural Law and Natural Rights*, p. vi.
66. Finnis, 'Law, morality, and "sexual orientation"' at 1063; see, more generally, the argument at 1055–63.
67. Martha Nussbaum, 'Platonic love and Colorado law: the relevance of ancient Greek norms to modern sexual controversies' (1994) 80 *Virginia Law Review* 1515.
68. Cf. Finnis, 'Law, morality, and "sexual orientation"' at 1073.
69. David Richards, 'Kantian ethics and the harm principle: A reply to John Finnis' (1987) 87 *Columbia Law Review* 457 at 468. A useful example may be seen in Finnis's book *Natural Law and Natural Rights*, p. 86, where the author appears to allow for the possibility that a range of human goods, including play, may be involved in sexual acts; in fact, as some of Finnis's more 'esoteric' writings reveal, his true opinion is very much narrower.
70. See n. 9 above.
71. Finnis, 'Legal enforcement of "duties to oneself"' at 445, n. 60.
72. Finnis, 'Natural law and unnatural acts', at 376, 377.
73. *Ibid.* at 372–87.
74. Finnis, *Moral Absolutes*, p. 10.
75. *Ibid.*, p. 106.
76. Cf. Sullivan, *Virtually Normal*, ch. 1.
77. Finnis, *Moral Absolutes*, pp. 8–9.
78. Cf. Roger Scruton, *Sexual Desire: A Philosophical Investigation* (London: Phoenix, 1986), p. 287.
79. G. E. M. Anscombe, 'Contraception and chastity', in Michael Bayles (ed.), *Ethics and Population* (Cambridge: Schenkman, 1976), p. 147.
80. G. E. M. Anscombe, 'You can have sex without children: Christianity and the new offer', in *Collected Philosophical Papers Volume 3: Ethics, Religion and Politics* (Oxford: Basil Blackwell, 1981), pp. 84–5.
81. Although cf. Bernard Williams and Michael Tanner, 'Discussion of contraception and chastity', in Bayles (ed.), *Ethics and Population*, p. 155. For a similar – if less expert – defence of Catholic teachings, see Michael Buckley, *Morality and the Homosexual: A Catholic Approach to a Moral Problem* (London: Sands & Co., 1959), pp. 132–5, 197–9.
82. George and Bradley, 'Marriage and the liberal imagination' at 307.
83. *Ibid.* at 310.
84. For more liberal Christian argument, see, e.g., Pim Pronk, *Against Nature: Types of Moral Argumentation*

Regarding Homosexuality (Michigan: Eerdmans Publishing, 1993); compare, more generally, the historical argument in James Brundage, *Law, Sex, and Christian Society in Medieval Europe* (Chicago: University of Chicago Press, 1987).

85. This question grows out of the assumption, discussed in chapter 4, that talk of justifications for law and law reform presupposes the existence of a democratic state. A theocratic state need not, as a matter of logic, be totalitarian. The government of a totalitarian state claims that its laws are justified because it says so. In a truly theocratic state, by contrast, laws are justifiable when – and because – they implement the word of the official deity. This is just a logical argument, though: most nominally theocratic states could fairly be described as totalitarian in practice.

86. Cf., however, E. Clinton Gardner, *Justice and Christian Ethics* (Cambridge: Cambridge University Press, 1995), esp. ch. 7.

87. Richards, 'Kantian ethics and the harm principle' at 471 (emphasis added); Richards' general views on the place of religious argument are outlined in his *Sex, Drugs, Death, and the Law: An Essay on Human Rights and Overcriminalization* (Totowa: Rowman & Littlefield, 1982), pp. 48–9. For a related critique, see Brundage, *Law, Sex, and Christian Society*, esp. p. 595.

88. An analogous argument can be found in Ronald Dworkin's discussion of a 'moral position' – *Taking Rights Seriously* (London: Duckworth, 1977), pp. 248–53. Note, however, Richard Posner's doubts about Dworkin's argument: *Sex and Reason* (Cambridge, MA: Harvard University Press, 1992), pp. 230–2.

89. See further the discussion in chapter 4.

90. Richards, 'Kantian ethics and the harm principle' at 468.

91. H.C. Deb., 21 February 1994, Column 114.

92. Buckley, *Morality and the Homosexual*, pp. 197–9.

93. See materials cited in chapter 1. Cf. also the arguments of Tristan Garel-Jones MP concerning the 'moral climates' of countries where law reform has occurred – H.C. Deb., 21 February 1994, Column 109.

94. See, e.g., 'Family matters' (a debate between journalists Polly Toynbee and Melanie Phillips), *Prospect*, June 1996, p. 20.

95. Cf. Stephen Macedo, 'Homosexuality and the conservative mind' (1995) 84 *Georgetown Law Journal* 261 at 285–91. For further criticism of the 'threat to marriage' argument, see Richards, *Sex, Drugs, Death, and the Law*, p. 56.

96. Cf. Macedo, 'Homosexuality and the conservative mind' at 291–2; Richards, *Sex, Drugs, Death, and the Law*, p. 46.

97. For comparable examples (from related, but not identical political and theological standpoints to Finnis's), see Anna Marie Smith, *New Right Discourse on Race and Sexuality* (Cambridge: Cambridge University Press, 1994), ch. 5.

98. Finnis, 'Law, morality, and "sexual orientation"' at 1062. See, by contrast, Richards, *Sex, Drugs, Death, and the Law*, p. 40.

99. Finnis, 'Law, morality, and "sexual orientation"' at 1052. The inverted commas surrounding 'sexual orientation' are a reflection of this perspective.

100. *Ibid.*

101. *Ibid.* at 1069.

102. *Ibid.* at 1053.

103. *Ibid.* at, e.g., 1055, 1061, 1062, 1069, 1070.

104. *Ibid.* at 1061.

105. A point mirrored by Tony Blair MP (then Shadow Home Secretary) during the 1994 House of Commons debate concerning ages of consent – H.C. Deb., 21 February 1994, Column 99.

106. See Macedo's similar criticisms, 'Homosexuality and the conservative mind' at 284–5, 292–3, and Williams and Tanner's criticisms of Anscombe,

'Discussion of contraception and chastity', pp. 159-61.
107. Cf. Robert Wintemute, *Sexual Orientation and Human Rights: the United States Constitution, the European Convention, and the Canadian Charter* (Oxford: Clarendon Press, 1995), p. 252.
108. Finnis, 'Legal enforcement of "duties to oneself"' at 437 – echoing Finnis's earlier comment in 'A bill of rights for Britain? The moral of contemporary jurisprudence' (1985) *Proceedings of the British Academy*, vol. LXXI, 303 at 325. See also Finnis, 'Is natural law theory compatible with limited government?' at 23, n. 42.
109. *Report of the Secretary's Task Force on Youth Suicide: Volume 3. Prevention and Interventions in Youth Suicide* (US Department of Health and Human Services, 1989).
110. H.C. Deb., 21 February 1994, Column 98. See, in similar vein, the reported comments of Conservative MP Terry Dicks – 'Homosexuals are perverts and [spending money on information about safer sex] is just . . . sending more perverts round to tell them how to do it better' – *Guardian*, 3 August 1996, p. 6 ('Anger over gay sex workers ad').
111. Cf. H.C. Deb., 21 February 1994, Columns 79, 98 (Bill Walker MP), 113 (Rev Ian Paisley MP).
112. Cf. Scruton, *Sexual Desire*, p. 305; Thomas Nagel, *Mortal Questions*, p. 51.
113. Scruton, *Sexual Desire*, p. 284.
114. Brundage, *Law, Sex and Christian Society*, p. 7.
115. Nagel, *Mortal Questions*, p. 40.
116. Cf. Macedo, 'Homosexuality and the conservative mind' at 265-71.
117. Scruton, *Sexual Desire*, pp. 309, 311.
118. *Ibid.*, p. 266.
119. *Ibid.*, pp. 275-6.
120. *Ibid.*, pp. 277-9.
121. *Ibid.*, p. 306; see also p. 283.
122. *Ibid.*, p. 310. Scruton pursues this argument (while accepting that the law should not necessarily be used to prohibit consenting same-sex sexual acts) in 'Gay reservations', ch. 8 in Michael Leahy and Dan Cohn-Sherbok (eds), *The Liberation Debate: Rights at Issue* (London: Routledge, 1996).
123. Scruton, *Sexual Desire*, p. 307.
124. *Ibid.*, p. 289.
125. *Ibid.*, p. 305.
126. *Ibid.*, pp. 261-5. See, in similar vein, Martha Nussbaum's critique of Scruton, in 'Lesbian and gay rights: Pro' and 'Nussbaum's reply', chs 7 and 9 in Leahy and Cohn-Sherbok (eds), *The Liberation Debate*.
127. Posner, *Sex and Reason*, pp. 228-30.
128. H.C. Deb., 21 February 1994, Columns 77-8.
129. Nagel, *Mortal Questions*, pp. 39-51.
130. For Devlin's own views on the ambit of his theory, see *The Enforcement of Morals*, chs 2-4.
131. *Ibid.*, pp. 8-9.
132. *Ibid.*, p. 9.
133. *Ibid.*, p. 10; see also p. 120.
134. *Ibid.*, p. 11.
135. *Ibid.*, pp. 12-14.
136. *Ibid.*, p. 11.
137. *Ibid.*, chs 4 and 6.
138. *Ibid.*, pp. 15-16.
139. *Ibid.*, p. 20; see also pp. 21-2.
140. *Ibid.*, p. 18. See further Devlin's arguments about appropriate judicial and legislative approaches to law reform: 'Judges and lawmakers' (1976) 39 *Modern Law Review* 1.
141. Devlin, *The Enforcement of Morals*, pp. 18-19.
142. *Ibid.*, p. 19.
143. *Ibid.*, pp. 19-20. Devlin seems to be echoing Lon Fuller's distinction between moralities of duty and moralities of aspiration – cf. H. L. A. Hart, 'Lon L. Fuller: The Morality of Law', essay 16 in *Essays in Jurisprudence and Philosophy* (Oxford: Clarendon Press, 1983), pp. 344-5.
144. Devlin, *The Enforcement of Morals*, p. 19.
145. *Ibid.*, p. 120.
146. *Ibid.*, p. 16.
147. *Ibid.*, p. 15.
148. *Ibid.*, pp. x, 89-92, 94.

149. Dean Rostow, 'The enforcement of morals' (1960) *Cambridge Law Journal* 174 at 197; cited in Devlin, *The Enforcement of Morals*, p. 95.
150. *Ibid.*, pp.16–17.
151. *Ibid.*, p. 17.
152. *Ibid.*
153. *Ibid.*
154. *Ibid.*, p. viii.
155. See Dworkin's analysis of this point in *Taking Rights Seriously*, p. 254, esp. n. 3.
156. Devlin, *The Enforcement of Morals*, p. ix.
157. H. L. A. Hart, *Law, Liberty, and Morality* (Oxford: Oxford University Press, 1963), pp. 48–52; 'Social solidarity and the enforcement of morality', essay 11 in *Essays in Jurisprudence and Philosophy*; Ronald Dworkin, 'Liberty and moralism', ch. 10 in *Taking Rights Seriously*.
158. Hart, 'Social solidarity and the enforcement of morality', pp. 248 *et seq.*
159. Paul Roberts, 'Consent and the criminal law: Philosophical foundations', Appendix C to Law Commission C Consultation Paper 139, *Consent in the Criminal Law* (1995), at paras C.73 and C.74, goes so far as to suggest that this makes it inaccurate to describe the 'disintegration thesis' as 'moralistic'. Instead, he argues, it turns directly on an appeal to the harm principle, the harm consisting in the threatened disintegration of society as a result of immoral practices. This argument need not affect the classification employed in this chapter, however, since a 'disintegration'-driven account of Devlin's theory still *justifies and entails* the enforcement of populist conceptions of morality – the factor which is crucial in placing it within our 'populist morality' category. If, furthermore, Devlin's theory is interpreted according to the 'conservative thesis' (see below), then Roberts's argument becomes superfluous.
160. Hart, 'Social solidarity and the enforcement of morality', p. 250.
161. Dworkin, *Taking Rights Seriously*, p. 244 – paraphrasing Hart, 'Social solidarity and the enforcement of morality', pp. 51–2. It should be noted, however, that Dworkin's presentation of Hart's argument puts something of a gloss on the original.
162. Dworkin, *Taking Rights Seriously*, p. 244.
163. Devlin, *The Enforcement of Morals*, p. 13, n. 1; see also pp. 115–16.
164. See also Dworkin's argument – *Taking Rights Seriously*, pp. 244–6.
165. Hart, *Law, Liberty, and Morality*, p. 50; 'Social solidarity and the enforcement of morality', p. 249; Dworkin, *Taking Rights Seriously*, pp. 246–8.
166. Cf. Robert George's analogous argument: *Making Men Moral: Civil Liberties and Public Morality* (Oxford: Clarendon Press, 1993), pp. 71–82.
167. *Bowers v. Hardwick* at 2844.
168. *Ibid.* at 2846–7.
169. Dworkin, *Taking Rights Seriously*, p. 255. For analogous criticism, see Richards, *Sex, Drugs, Death, and the Law*, pp. 43–9. More generally, see Sheldon Leader, 'The right to privacy, the enforcement of morals, and the judicial function: An argument' (1990) 43 *Current Legal Problems* 115. For broader criticism of majoritarian theories of justice and political morality, see Ronald Dworkin, 'Liberal community' (1989) 77 *California Law Review* 479 – and, from a conservative perspective, Finnis, 'A bill of rights for Britain?' at 312–14.
170. Cf. Posner, *Sex and Reason*, p. 230.
171. Devlin, *The Enforcement of Morals*, pp. 17, 22.
172. Devlin had, however, proposed just such a distinction when giving evidence to the Wolfenden Committee – at the time, he was a supporter of law reform: *ibid.*, p. vi.

6

Justifications for Legal Protection: Immutability, Respect for Privacy, and Liberationism

> *Many . . . conservative moralists defend a 'Maginot Line' strategy with respect to sexual morality which suggests that to concede any territory at all [to the claims of lesbians and gays] is to give up on the very project of drawing moral distinctions. But . . . why on earth is that the case? Can we not draw more fine-grained distinctions at retail? Why must we dispose of this vast, diverse, and in many ways poorly understood aspect of human existence on the basis of the most abstract and sweeping claims?*
>
> — Stephen Macedo[1]

Introduction

It was argued in chapter 5 that the justifications for various degrees of hostile legal treatment of lesbians and gays were presumptively unsound. In consequence, laws which depend for their moral legitimacy on those justifications may be seen as *prima facie* illegitimate. In this and the following chapter, we need to take things one stage further by asking what substantive justifications can be advanced for law reform measures – or for existing laws – which meaningfully entitle lesbians and gays to engage in consenting sexual acts with adults of the same sex, to be free from discrimination in the workplace and other public areas of life, and so on.

There is a strong pragmatic reason for dividing up consideration of hostile and sympathetic justifications in this way. In a society where liberty is valued, rebuttal of the justifications considered in chapter 5 should show that intrusive or hostile legal regulation of lesbian and gay sexuality is illegitimate. This conclusion – resting on the idea of a presumption in favour of liberty – may be of limited practical help in a hostile social climate, however. It will vindicate by default – for those who support the presumption that the law should respect individual liberty – the introduction or maintenance of a more tolerant legal regime, given that it would show us why hostile laws could not properly be defended. To offer a convincing argument for more openly sympathetic legal treatment of lesbians and gays, however, we need to go one step further and show why such laws would be positively good and desirable. After all, any argument is – and will appear to be – stronger if it contains positive claims in its favour, rather than just negative rebuttals of opposing arguments.

A strong, convincing justification for a more sympathetic legal regime should not, therefore, be content with showing what is bad in its opponents. Instead, it must demonstrate that there is an appealing moral good (as a matter of sexual morality) in same-sex sexual acts, relationships and sexuality generally – which the law should seek to respect.[2] Logically, this means that there will be a corresponding moral wrong in laws which are hostile towards lesbians and gays – a wrong which can be defined as the failure to respect the moral good involved in lesbian and gay sexuality, sexual acts, etc. It is only by demonstrating a clear moral good that the sought-after legal regime can be securely justified.[3]

In this and the next chapter, we will examine what have been, in recent years, the four most popular justifications for a sympathetic legal regime – immutability, respect for privacy, liberationism, and equality. Each of these justifications will be found wanting – as, by implication, are related justifications. At the end of chapter 7, an alternative – and, it will be argued, preferable – empowerment-based justification will be proposed. It should be stressed that these justifications by no means exhaust, between them, the scope for debate about the social position of lesbians and gays.[4] Since the subject-matter of this book is the *legal* regulation of sexuality, however, our argument can meaningfully be restricted to theories which can most easily be applied to the law itself. It should also be noted that in day-to-day political campaigning, advocates of a more sympathetic legal regime frequently rely on a mixture of the different justifications: privacy is sometimes combined with equality, or equality with immutability, for example.[5] These combinations are logically possible, so long as the same theory of justice and political morality is assumed to underpin the justifications which are combined. Combinations may, however, appear more confusing than a single justification standing alone, and will therefore be avoided. And, since we are concerned with practical law reform issues, it seems pointless to discuss *every* possible justification or interpretation of the four most popular justifications – a task of near infinite proportions. Since we are concerned with justifications which will be useful in practice, we can sensibly confine debate to those which, in the recent past, have been most popular with campaigners. The fallacies of these justifications can, in any event, be related to any alternatives – driving us back to the need to develop a new justification.

Six general points should be made at this stage. First, none of the justifications – at least as presented here – draws a strong distinction, in terms of sexual morality, between sexual acts which occur in the course of committed emotional relationships and those which occur on a casual basis. This might at first seem surprising. After all, the *participants* in sexual acts are likely to experience different feelings and emotions depending upon whether their liaison is of a committed or casual nature, and this will affect the value and significance which they attach to it. Equally, people often have strong feelings about the *comparative* moral status of sexual acts committed on either basis.[6]

For a justification to distinguish between casual and committed sexual acts, however, it – and the laws which it seeks to underpin – would have to provide answers to questions such as what constitutes a committed emotional relationship as opposed to a casual encounter (a question to which no two people are likely to offer exactly the same reply), what constitutes intercourse as opposed to heavy petting, and how participants in sexual acts should deal with their own and their partner's feelings and desires. Merely by concerning itself with difficult and intensely personal questions of this sort, a justification raises the possibility that it will trigger intrusive legal regulation of people's sexual lives. For the law could only provide relatively general answers to these questions, and would inevitably end up overriding some or many people's choices concerning their sexual behaviour – regardless of the degree of regulation of casual sexual encounters which it actually sought to impose. Furthermore, unless the justification was deliberately slanted against lesbians and gays – in which case it would be open to the types of criticism deployed in chapter 5 – it would intrude upon the sexual behaviour of all adults, regardless of sexual orientation. For heterosexual *and* same-sex relationships often evolve from initially casual sexual encounters, which play a role in the lives of (certainly young) adults of all sexual orientations.[7] Supporters of laws which would grant at least some sexual freedom to lesbians and gays are unlikely, therefore, to be sympathetic to this sort of legal regime, and would seek to challenge it using the privacy, liberationist and empowerment justifications (equality justifications do not seek to distinguish between casual and committed sexual acts, but could not be used to challenge a regime which did so provided that regime was neutral between persons of different sexual orientations[8]).

This begs the question of how any justification distinguishes between situations where the law should – and should not – intervene to regulate sexual behaviour. An example may help in clarifying the matter. Hostile theorists sometimes raise the spectre of promiscuity among gay men, implying that this is a relevant issue in any moral evaluation of sexual acts between men considered as a category. Supporters of the justifications to be considered in this chapter would agree that they are concerned with whether and how the law should regulate or support same-sex sexual acts *as a category of sexual act*. They would claim that they are not, however, concerned with the motives of the parties involved in individual sexual acts – and it is the parties' motives which provide the basic means of distinguishing between casual and committed encounters. For supporters of the sympathetic justifications, the parties' motives may raise questions of personal sexual etiquette, but this can provide no reliable guide to the moral status of same-sex sexual activity considered as a category.

This point can be underlined using a related example. Most of us would feel that it is in some way immoral to drive recklessly, given the danger this poses to other road users and to pedestrians, and we would doubtless condemn as morally culpable a driver who killed someone during an episode of reckless driving. We would surely see it as unreasonable, however (at least unless we were Luddites), to jump from the claim that *some* people drive in an immoral way to the claim that driving is an immoral activity *per se* because pedestrians are sometimes killed by reckless drivers. The first claim concerns the morality of some drivers' actions considered individually, while the second is an evaluation of the nature of driving in general. Just as unreasonable a jump is involved, however, when using assumptions about the alleged individual sexual behaviour of some gay men as a basis for condemning all homosexual acts. Saying that a particular person's sexual behaviour is immoral is not (even if that claim were true) the same thing as suggesting that a certain type of sexual act is in and of itself immoral. The fact that X behaves in a promiscuous, selfish or unfeeling way may affect our assessment of X's morals and the quality of his sexual encounters – but that is a separate issue from the inherent moral status of the types of sexual act which X, among many others, just happens to engage in.

Some types of motive for participating in sexual acts do, however, bring even the sympathetic justifications into play (save, perhaps, for immutability). For, in identifying something as an act of rape – a type of sexual act which all the justifications would regard as immoral and properly punishable by law – it is the parties' motives (in the sense of their reasons for acting as they do) that are crucial. The victim only succumbs to the assailant's demands because they are forced to – whether through physical restraint or fear of the consequences if they refuse – and the assailant is either indifferent to the victim's suffering or actually enjoys it. It is each justification's background theories of justice and political morality – and of sexual morality – which ultimately provide the key to distinguishing acts which may entail problems of personal sexual etiquette from acts which clearly merit the legitimate use of law. According to Lord Devlin's hostile justification, for example, same-sex sexual acts are not simply a matter of etiquette, given the justification's background theories of justice and political morality. Equally, the exact reason why supporters of sympathetic justifications believe that an act of rape may properly be condemned by law will vary according to their background theories of justice and political morality.

The second general point is that the essentialist/constructionist debate concerning the nature of sexuality – initially discussed in chapter 3 – will be relevant when assessing the comparative merits of each justification. We concluded in chapter 3 that a moderate constructionist account – which maintains that the direction of a person's sexual orientation may well be fixed from society to society and age to age (there have thus always been men who have been attracted to men, women who have been attracted to women, women who have been attracted to men, and men who have been attracted to women) – but that the social meanings attached to these attractions may well vary (people who are attracted to others of the same sex will not always have been categorized, or even have seen themselves, as lesbian or gay, in the same way that those whose direction of attraction is to the opposite sex will not always have been categorized, or have seen themselves, as heterosexual).[9] It was also suggested in chapter

3 that any justification which rested on an essentialist account of sexuality – that is, on an account which claims that sexual categories are fixed across time, so that it is possible to identify 'lesbian' or 'gay' members of any society – would therefore be unsound. Using the substantive attractiveness assessment criterion set out in chapter 4, it can now be added that any such justification is in fact unsound because it is implausible, since the account of human sexuality on which it rests is flawed; it may also be irrelevant in the society to which it is applied. Within this framework, it should nevertheless be stressed that a viable justification for law reform should seek to unite the supporters of as many different views about the nature of sexuality as is feasible – for to fail to do this would detract from its appeal in the society to which it is addressed.

This brings us neatly to the third point, which is that a justification for existing law or law reform must make sense in the circumstances of the society to which it is addressed, if it is not to fail for irrelevance. To be successful, a justification should therefore be fairly easy to understand – it must make sense, as an argument. To appear convincing, a justification must be capable of comfortably sustaining all the practical demands which it claims to underpin: the enactment of anti-discrimination laws as well as the removal of excessively regulatory criminal laws, for example. If a justification cannot sustain the whole range of law reform demands – at least without being stretched to the point of artificiality – then it may be safer simply to abandon it rather than to say that it can still underpin some law reform claims provided that it is coupled with a second, apparently separate justification which will deal with the others. Such a coupling would most likely appear confusing, especially if there is room for clashes between the two justifications adopted.

The fourth point is that we are concerned to show why a sympathetic legal regime is justifiable philosophically – rather than as a matter of constitutional law in a particular legal system. This distinction is relevant given that some of the philosophical justifications which we shall consider – in particular, respect for privacy – have also been put forward in the USA as constitutional grounds for protecting the proposed or actual legal entitlements of lesbians and gays; argument concerning the legal right to privacy was, for example, the central constitutional issue in *Bowers* v. *Hardwick*.[10] When used in US constitutional law, however, respect for privacy has to be clothed in precedent and layers of reasoning which are specific to that context; when used as a philosophical argument, by contrast, no such constraints exist.[11] While the literature concerning constitutional rights can be helpful in highlighting arguments surrounding related philosophical justifications, therefore, arguments for or against a particular constitutional law position should not be seen as a definitive guide to how any justification should be assessed philosophically.[12]

Fifth, each justification is capable of remedying a different selection of the legal issues presented in chapter 2, and of doing so for different reasons. When doing so, each justification will – as suggested in chapter 3 – imply its own notion of what should be described, in campaigners' terminology, as 'lesbian and gay rights' issues (even if, historically speaking, the supporters of the justification concerned did not use such language themselves). Rejecting a particular justification may affect the range of issues which we can place within the 'lesbian and gay rights' bracket – something which is entirely sensible analytically, since we need a reason for classifying any law reform question in this way and it is difficult to think of a better reason than a sound law reform justification. Any other style of reasoning would most likely mean the sacrifice of purity of analysis to political sloganizing. Other implications of particular justifications are, however, relevant in assessing that justification's desirability: equality-driven justifications are, for example, either assimilationist or Balkanizing in their effect – if applied, they will either support the complete identification of lesbians and gays with moral values which prevail among heterosexuals, or a strong social separation of lesbians and gays into distinct 'minority' groups.

Finally, it should be stressed that while certain arguments will be rejected as philosophical justifications for law reform in this context – equality, for example, or respect for privacy – this does not mean that such concepts have no value when used in other ways. So, while we will rebut the argument that the need to respect and foster people's personal identities as lesbians or gay men can be the unit of comparison underpinning a sound law reform justification, it is certainly not being suggested that lesbian or gay identities – in all their forms – are not morally valuable. As we will see in chapter 7, identity is simply being rejected as an element in law reform justifications. A similar point can be made about respect for privacy: while it will be argued that this cannot amount to a sound law reform justification in the present context, this does not mean that there are not strong arguments for recognizing a legally enforceable right to privacy as a matter of English – or US constitutional – law more generally.[13] When considering each possible justification, it should therefore be recalled that we are concerned with producing sound, concise arguments for law reform or for existing, sympathetic laws *as they affect lesbians and gays*. We will now turn to the first justification – immutability.

Immutability

It is sometimes claimed, both as a matter of popular argument and under US constitutional law,[14] that people should be entitled to engage in consenting sexual acts with adults of the same sex, and should be protected from discrimination in employment and public aspects of life more generally, if it can be shown that human sexual orientation is immutable. Immutability refers to the idea that a person's sexual orientation is either biologically predetermined,[15] or is at least fixed at such an early stage in life that they cannot be held morally responsible for it.[16] As a consequence of this immutability, the argument runs, the law cannot require a person to alter their sexual orientation without imposing an inhumane burden upon them. Immutability arguments were used (unsuccessfully) to oppose the enactment of section 28 of the Local Government Act 1988 in the UK. In the House of Commons debate on what became section 28, Chris Smith MP – opposing the ban on the intentional 'promotion of homosexuality' – argued that:

> We are what we are. It is impossible to force or encourage someone into a different sexuality from that which pertains to them. What is needed is not to be involved in changing, persuading, forcing, encouraging people into different sexualities. What is important is to enable people to understand the sexuality that they have, and that cannot be changed.[17]

Supporters of immutability claims would maintain that it is thus impermissible for the law to penalize a person because of their sexual orientation, and arguably to penalize expressions of it in the form of sexual activity. The law does not penalize people due to accidents of birth such as their sex or race, and even seeks to prevent them from being discriminated against on this basis in employment and related contexts – and it would surely be morally arbitrary to treat people unfavourably because of a characteristic which they have acquired via an accident. In consequence, the law cannot consistently – and should not – treat people unfavourably where an analogous accident such as their sexual orientation is in issue.

Close scrutiny soon reveals that while this argument may make intuitive sense, it carries little moral weight on its own. For we do regard it as legitimate – and very far from morally arbitrary – to judge people on the basis of *certain* immutable characteristics. A person's intelligence is viewed as a proper basis for selection for a university place or an academic job, for example, just as innate physical strength is viewed as a qualification for employment as a wrestler. We all have immutable features by which we are judged, yet the law only steps in to preclude judgement on the ground of certain immutable traits and in certain circumstances. As Janet Halley rightly suggests, an additional factor of moral (or legal) significance is *always* necessary to determine the boundary between cases where judgement by reference to an immutable factor is permissible – a decision not to employ persons who have been blind since birth as driving instructors, for example – from those cases where it is impermissible – such as a decision only to employ white males. We need, Halley suggests, to find 'a principled way of distinguishing the many discriminations based on immutable characteristics that we do not find normatively or legally troubling'.[18] An immutability argument may well be used to help humanize perceptions of lesbians and gays in popular debate, but it is analytically incomplete either as an explanation of what is wrong with hostile legal regulation or as a justification for law reform.[19]

If immutability is to be used as a justification for law reform, we would also need to be clear about what it is, exactly, that is 'innate'. Talk of a person's sexual orientation is usually taken to refer to the *direction* of their sexual attraction – that is, to whether they are in principle attracted to males, to females, or to both. In order properly to claim that each person's direction of attraction was 'innate', we would therefore need conclusive proof that it was predetermined or fixed at an early age. At present, however, the limited scientific data available is far from conclusive, and does not attract the support of a majority of lesbian and gay theorists.[20] Furthermore, even if clear proof could be found, theorists would still need to produce a separate moral account of why this *particular* immutable characteristic was not a valid basis for judging or regulating a person's life.[21] It seems quite likely that any such 'separate' account would collapse into one of the other justifications, given that it is hard to see why a complex claim of this sort should be preferred to the simpler argument – available using other justifications – which focus solely on the moral good involved in lesbian and gay sexuality. Also, if the 'innate' factor is taken to be the direction of a person's sexual attraction, this is insufficient by itself to explain why it is wrong to discriminate against people for actually *engaging* in same-sex sexual acts – as we saw in chapter 2 in relation to the US cases concerning military employment. If, by contrast, we believe that it is a person's *identity* as a lesbian or as a gay man which is innate, then a justification based on such a claim would face the same difficulties as those faced by equality justifications which invoke identity as their unit of comparison – an issue which we will consider in chapter 7.

Even if a conclusive explanation of the 'origins' or 'causes' of human sexual orientation could be produced, together with a sound moral reason for distinguishing blameworthy from neutral immutable characteristics, the immutability argument would still be undesirable on its merits. For when applied to people's behaviour, all that it boils down to is the rather spineless claim that 'I can't help it' – which is just about the weakest defence a person can offer for an action which annoys or injures others.[22] A compulsive rapist or child molester might, for example, make such a claim – yet few would regard their activity as any more morally defensible as a consequence. Immutability arguments offer no suggestion that there is any positive moral good in lesbian and gay sexuality. Indeed, it might plausibly be claimed that immutability arguments have the effect of presenting a lesbian or gay sexual orientation as an unfortunate disability – at least if we are talking about *accidents* of birth – which should attract sympathy and understanding, rather than as something which large numbers of people see as a healthy and valuable aspect of their lives. Immutability even raises the repellent possibility of eugenics – for if sexual orientation is biologically predetermined, it may become possible for parents-to-be to discover the sexual orientation of their child before it is born, leading to the possibility of anti-lesbian and gay parents seeking to abort non-heterosexual foetuses.[23]

Immutability arguments are, therefore, unhelpful and perhaps even harmful. The potential slipperiness of any 'human nature'-based argument should be clear from the discussion in chapter 5 of hostile justifications which rely on this factor. On their own, observations about 'human nature' count for nothing: they only become important – whether as hostile or sympathetic arguments – once coupled with a moral stance through which they can be interpreted.[24] Given the weak and potentially adverse features of 'immutability' claims, it would therefore seem sensible to treat discussion of the 'causes' of human sexual orientation as just an interesting piece of scientific speculation – leaving argument about the moral significance of particular sexual orientations to alternative law reform justifications.

Respect for privacy

Respect for privacy is the longest-standing justification to have been employed by would-be law reformers. Its original – and perhaps most famous – appearance in this context occurred in the Wolfenden Report in 1957, where it was used as the basis for the Committee's proposal partly to decriminalize male homosexual acts in England and Wales.[25] As we saw in chapters 4 and 5, the Committee attempted to place a limited range of sexual activities beyond the legitimate reach of legal regulation. It tried to justify this with the argument that:

> Unless a deliberate attempt is to be made by society, acting through the agency of the law, to equate the sphere of crime with that of sin, there must remain a realm of private morality and immorality which is, in brief and crude terms, not the law's business. . . . to emphasise the personal and private nature of moral or immoral conduct is to emphasise the personal and private responsibility of the individual for his own actions, and that is a responsibility which a mature agent can properly be expected to carry for himself without the threat of punishment from the law.[26]

Private, consenting sexual acts between adult males came, according to the Committee, within this protected realm.

A diluted version of the Committee's decriminalization proposal was only enacted as law in 1967,[27] but supporters of reform continued during the intervening period to stress the need to protect the *privacy* of people whose sex lives would otherwise be a matter for the criminal law.[28] A similar respect for privacy argument was at the centre of the reformist case in Canada, where partial decriminalization occurred via an amendment to the Criminal Code in 1969. Pierre Trudeau, as Justice Minister, had quipped that 'The state has no place in the bedrooms of the nation', and in presenting for Parliamentary approval the proposal to amend the Code, Trudeau's successor John Turner argued that:

> we believe that the law and morals are two separate philosophical

propositions ... that there are aspects of human life and relationships between people which ... ought better be left to private morality than subject to public order within the strictures of the criminal law ... as between two consenting adults in private ... homosexual acts particularly – ought not to be within the purview of the criminal law.[29]

Respect for privacy arguments seem, in fact, to have been invoked by law reform campaigners on just about every occasion when attempts have been made to overturn criminal laws which totally prohibit same-sex sexual acts (and, while reform of laws enforcing unequal ages of consent tends to be advocated via versions of the equality justification, Edwina Currie MP employed a respect for privacy argument in this context during the 1994 House of Commons debate on the subject[30]). In *Bowers* v. *Hardwick*,[31] as we saw in chapter 2, the US Supreme Court upheld by a majority the state of Georgia's anti-sodomy law, which had been challenged on the basis that sexual acts between persons of the same sex came within the privacy protections of the Due Process Clause of the US Constitution. Justice White, for the majority, was clear that there was no 'right of privacy that extends to homosexual sodomy'.[32] By contrast, Justice Blackmun suggested in his dissenting judgment that the case implicated the constitutional right to privacy in its decisional aspect – protecting the fundamental interest of individuals in controlling the nature of their intimate associations with others – and in its spatial aspect, which gave special protection to the intimacy of the home.[33]

Similarly, the main argument in European Court of Human Rights cases concerning total prohibitions on same-sex sexual acts – *Dudgeon* v. *United Kingdom*,[34] *Norris* v. *Ireland*[35] and *Modinos* v. *Cyprus*[36] – has turned on whether such prohibitions breach Article 8 of the European Convention on Human Rights, which lays down the individual's right to respect for his or her private life. The Court ruled in all three cases that complete criminal prohibitions violated Article 8, and in the *Norris* case, a particularly wide interpretation was offered of the meaning of privacy within that Article. The complainant himself had never been prosecuted for consenting homosexual activity, so there had been no direct physical violation of his privacy. The Court nevertheless found that the constant risk which he stood of being prosecuted, with the social anxiety and guilt this created was, when considered against the backdrop of the considerable social prejudice against gay men in Ireland, sufficient to make him a 'victim' who was entitled to complain, under the Convention, that Irish law had violated his privacy.

These examples relate, of course, to constitutional rather than philosophical arguments. Respect for privacy claims were probably at the centre of the pro-reform arguments in *Bowers* v. *Hardwick* and the Convention cases simply because they happened to be available under the constitutional instrument concerned – a matter of chance so far as the litigants were concerned, rather than the deliberate philosophical support for privacy which underpinned the Wolfenden proposals. The constitutional cases are nevertheless important for two reasons. First, the fact that a respect for privacy claim was available at all under the constitutions concerned is testament to the widespread popularity and resonance of such claims in human rights contexts. Second, the contrast between *Bowers* v. *Hardwick* and the European Convention cases highlights the considerable scope for argument about the meaning of respect for privacy – an uncertainty which also affects privacy when considered as a philosophical justification. For a central task for respect for privacy theorists is to explain how, exactly, a certain area of life is to be demarcated as private – and why it is right, as a matter of justice and political morality, for the law to abstain from regulating it.

Before exploring some possible explanations, we should consider a preliminary objection to respect for privacy as a justification. In the quotations from the Wolfenden Report and the Canadian Parliamentary debates, set out above, the importance of respect for privacy was seen as flowing from – and integrally bound up with – the claim that legal regulation of certain types of morality is impermissible. These respect for privacy arguments are therefore anti-perfectionist in nature. Since we dismissed anti-perfectionist arguments in chapter 4 – claiming instead that the realms of law and morals are not readily separable – it might be thought that respect for privacy immediately collapses as a justification. This is not in fact the case, since only some respect for privacy arguments are anti-perfectionist. There are certainly general objections which apply to all respect for privacy claims, but the anti-perfectionist objection is only fatal to arguments – like those made in the Wolfenden Report and in the Canadian Parliament – which actually rest on the assumption that law and morals are readily separable. We will return to this point when analysing individual respect for privacy arguments which have concerned themselves with same-sex sexual acts.

Let us now consider how respect for privacy might be used to defend such acts from legal regulation. Judith Jarvis Thomson memorably suggested that, 'Perhaps the most striking thing about the right to privacy is that nobody seems to have any very clear idea what it is.'[37] The classic definition of privacy is that it consists in the 'right to be let alone'.[38] It is difficult, however, to argue that any human being can – or should, as a member of a community – be 'let alone' entirely. In consequence, there has been considerable constitutional and philosophical argument about how, exactly, respect for privacy should be understood.[39] At a philosophical level, it has been interpreted in at least three ways, each interpretation having, as Justice Blackmun's dissent in *Bowers* v. *Hardwick* implies, rather different consequences for the range of laws which a respect for privacy justification could support. The first interpretation maintains that certain physical spaces – usually the home – should be free from legal regulation. The second interpretation suggests that certain activities or relationships should be free from regulation. The third interpretation maintains that certain types of information about an individual should be protected from revelation.[40]

Exactly which activities or information should in fact be protected using *any* of these three interpretations will depend upon the theory of justice and political morality which is seen as underpinning and explaining the interpretation concerned. A wide variety of theories have been offered. Ruth Gavison, for example, argues that privacy protects secrecy, anonymity and solitude, and should be regarded as an aspect of individual liberty.[41] Charles Fried, by contrast, sees privacy as connected with a person's control over information relating to themselves, and suggests that it rests on the moral concept of respect for human personality and personhood.[42] In the context of sexual behaviour, three distinct respect for privacy arguments have been advanced – two of which are nominally anti-perfectionist, and the third apparently perfectionist. We will critically examine each of these, before considering the problems faced by *all* types of respect for privacy claim.

The first argument has been developed by David Richards, who claims that respect for privacy rests on a basic moral vision of people as autonomous and entitled to equal respect.[43] Autonomy, Richards suggests, turns on the idea that people have a range of capacities enabling them to act on and to develop plans of action in their lives, and to evaluate their lives according to principles of ethics to which they have given their rational assent.[44] Each person's capacity for autonomy should, Richards argues, be viewed as being of equal value – hence the notion of treating people as equals.[45] Respect for privacy is (as a matter of US constitutional law):

> associated with and intended to facilitate the exercise of autonomy in certain basic kinds of choice that bear upon the coherent rationality of a person's life plan. . . . Certain choices in life are taken to bear fundamentally on the entire design of one's life, for these choices determine the basic decisions of work and love, which in turn order many of the subsidiary choices of human life.[46]

Richards' justification thus sets out to be anti-perfectionist in nature: the state should not itself enforce moral goods through law, but must instead respect people's autonomy by deferring to their choice of basic goods to pursue.[47]

Richards brings sexual activity into the picture via the assertion that:

> Sexual experience is, for human beings, a profoundly personal, spontaneous, and absorbing experience in which they express intimate fantasies and vulnerabilities which typically cannot brook the sense of an external, critical observer. That humans require privacy for sex relates to the nature of the experience . . .[48]

Sexual autonomy is, Richards suggests, central to the idea that a person is free. Sexuality has a powerful role as an independent force in a person's imaginative life and general development, and sexual affection may be a crucial ingredient in forming lasting, loving relationships. The absence of any form of love would make a person's life empty, deformed and twisted.[49] Sexuality is not 'a spiritually empty experience that the state may compulsorily legitimize only in the form of rigid, marital procreational sex, but one of the fundamental experiences through which, as an end in itself, people define the meaning of their lives'.[50] Given the value of autonomy, this self-definition extends to the sex of the person(s) with whom one has sexual relations. Richards is thus interpreting privacy as something applicable to certain activities (here, sexual acts) rather than to physical spaces – and it is the general sexual autonomy argument which allows Richards to rebut the hostile justifications considered in chapter 5.[51]

Richards' discussion of the positive value of sexual activity certainly sounds plausible, but it also exposes his justification to the charge of internal inconsistency. To see why this is so, we need to consider two other comments made by Richards. These are, first, the claim that:

> The constitutional right of privacy cases typically arise in areas where there is a strong conventional wisdom that certain conduct is morally wrong and where the justice of that wisdom is under fundamental attack.... the constitutional right to privacy is, in part, to be understood in terms of a transvaluation of values: certain areas of conduct, traditionally conceived of as morally wrong, and thus the proper object of public regulation and prohibition, are now perceived as affirmative goods the pursuit of which does not raise serious moral questions and which thus is no longer a proper object of public critical concern.[52]

And second, the argument that:

> The right to privacy does not merely signify that it is no longer not morally wrong to do certain things [i.e. that a 'neutral' position of mere toleration exists], but that there is an affirmative moral right to do them which it is, by definition, a transgression of moral duty to violate.[53]

As Robert George suggests, both passages convey the strong impression that Richards believes that same-sex sexual acts should be permitted, not because they are 'moral evils which, for moral reasons, the law must nevertheless refrain from prohibiting' – the classic anti-perfectionist position – but instead because they are 'valuable aspects of people's lives ... [which] far from being evils which we must reluctantly tolerate, are "positive moral goods" that we should treat as subjects of fundamental human rights'.[54] This is especially evident in the 'not morally wrong'/ 'affirmative moral right' distinction contained in the second passage cited above. If George's interpretation is correct, however, then Richards' justification cannot be seen as anti-perfectionist – as seems to have been intended – but must instead be viewed as perfectionist. For legal tolerance of same-sex sexual acts, under Richards' right to privacy, would spring from the need to respect autonomy, which is manifested (in this context) in the *positive* value of human sexuality.

This leaves Richards' justification in an impossible position. If George is wrong and the justification is in fact anti-perfectionist, it will fail because of the implausibility of the 'separation of law and morals' position – the idea of a 'neutral' justification being unbelievable. If George's interpretation is right and Richards' justification veers clearly into perfectionism, however, then it must be dismissed for internal inconsistency – for it sets out to be one type of theory and ends up as quite another.[55] George also claims that even if Richards' argument is anti-perfectionist, it can still be dismissed for internal inconsistency since it relies on an interpretation of autonomy which is inconsistent with the Kantian understanding of the term which Richards claims to invoke.[56]

A second, ostensibly anti-perfectionist justification has been advanced by Ronald Dworkin in the wake of the US Supreme Court decision in *Bowers* v. *Hardwick*.[57] Dworkin's argument is not openly couched in the language of privacy, but clearly does rely, as Philip Selznick has suggested, 'on a favourite gambit of liberal theory – the separation of [public and private] spheres'.[58] Dworkin's central claim is that while a political community has certain collective moral interests – the success or failure of which helps to determine whether individual citizens' lives are good or bad – the range of interests which assume such a role, and which are therefore the subject of legitimate community concern, is inherently limited.[59] Dworkin therefore supports the 'ethical primacy of the community's life' – the notion that individual citizens do identify with, and to an extent depend upon, the success of their community as an important part of their individual lives – while rejecting any idea that the political community can be seen as a sort of 'super-person', the collective life of which 'embodies all the features and dimensions of a human life'.[60]

As a consequence, Dworkin believes that the political community's communal life includes 'only the acts treated as collective by the practices and attitudes that create the community as a collective agent'.[61] Dworkin draws an analogy with the functioning of an orchestra: the communal life of an orchestra is limited – by the practices and attitudes which designate it as an orchestra – to the production of music. Thus:

> The musicians treat their performances together as the performance of their orchestra personified, and they share in its triumphs and failures as their own. But they do not suppose that the orchestra also has a sex life, in some way composed of the sexual activities of its members. Or that it has headaches, or high blood pressure, or responsibilities of friendship . . .[62]

In similar fashion, Dworkin claims, a distinction can be drawn between 'the collective life of a political community' – which 'includes its official political acts: legislation, adjudication, enforcement, and the other executive functions of government' and which 'should be taken to exhaust the communal life of a political body, so that citizens are understood to act together, as a collective, only in that structured way' – and the personal sex lives of individual citizens.[63] It is nonsensical, he claims, to think of a political community (as much as an orchestra) having a collective sex life. But it is only by supposing that the sex lives of individual citizens somehow combine into a collective sex life, capable in itself of moral evaluation (in the way that the performances of individual musicians combine into the performance of an orchestra, or the acts of citizens and officials in a political community combine in legislation) that one may suppose that one citizen's sex life can be defiled by the sexual practices of others, and that the community has a legitimate interest in prohibiting these latter practices.[64] One can therefore support the primacy of the political community's true, limited communal life without 'abandoning or compromising liberal tolerance and neutrality about the good life' – including individual sexual practices.[65]

A welcome feature of Dworkin's argument is that he does take care – unlike many liberal theorists – to recognize the crucial role played by a person's community in defining and shaping their life and character. His argument thus avoids the 'atomistic' criticisms of liberal theories discussed in chapter 3.[66] In three important respects, however, Dworkin's justification is flawed – and must therefore be viewed as implausible.[67] First, Bernard Williams has pointed out that there is an important gap in Dworkin's argument – for he fails to explain exactly *which* acts of individuals are relevant to the community, and which are not.[68] Dworkin seems simply to assume that a distinction between collective and individual can unproblematically be drawn, based around the 'practices and attitudes' of the society concerned. Given that there is, in reality, no consensus relating to this issue (as our discussion in chapters 3 and 4 revealed), Dworkin needs to supply some further explanation. Dworkin's broader political philosophy implicitly provides some possible answers, but Dworkin fails to turn these into a concrete analysis of the limits of the 'collective'.

This ties in with a second problem, which is that Dworkin's bald assertion that legislation can in and of itself be seen as 'collective', rather than 'individual', must be mistaken. For the whole purpose of Dworkin's argument is to show why anti-sodomy *statutes* – the product of state legislatures – are illegitimate because of their consequences for individuals.

Merely defining legislating as a 'collective' activity cannot be plausible if the whole purpose of the moral debate is to determine whether some presumptively 'collective' activities are in fact impermissible because they violate important 'individual' interests. Again, this boils down to a failure adequately to distinguish between 'collective' and 'individual'.

The third, related argument has been developed by Philip Selznick, who points out that while sexual preferences and actions are individual, the norms which govern our sex lives are usually collective.[69] If we take this as meaning that the ways in which people understand, speculate about and go about involving themselves in sexual acts varies from society to society, this is undoubtedly true. In some societies, polygamy has been seen as a social 'norm'; in others, monogamous marriage is the standard. In some societies, sexual unions are arranged by the participants' parents; in others, by the participants themselves. How we understand what comes within Dworkin's realm of 'individual' interests may therefore depend upon our prior, 'collectively'-determined assumptions – making a straightforward distinction between 'individual' and 'collective' impossible.

Having examined some problematical aspects of the Richards and Dworkin justifications, we must now consider two broader objections to anti-perfectionist respect for privacy theories generally. First, such theories may well be unattractive on their merits. While the Richards and Dworkin justifications attach a positive value to – or are at least neutral about – the morality of same-sex sexual acts, anti-perfectionist justifications are equally compatible with moral hostility towards such acts, allowing for grudging legal tolerance only. They may just as easily be underpinned by conservative theories of justice and political morality as by the liberal theories advocated by Richards and Dworkin. When anti-perfectionist respect for privacy arguments were advanced in the Parliamentary debates in Britain and Canada in the 1960s, for example, most supporters of decriminalization were careful to stress their personal distaste for and moral disapproval of homosexual acts.[70] And, when the Sexual Offences Bill finally passed through the House of Lords in 1967, its sponsor, Lord Arran – in a speech described by Jeffrey Weeks as 'hardly a trumpet-call to freedom'[71] – demanded that:

> those who have, as it were, been in bondage and for whom the prison doors are now open [should] show their thanks by comporting themselves quietly and with dignity. . . . Any form of ostentatious

behaviour now, or in the future, any form of public flaunting, would be utterly distasteful and would . . . make the sponsors of the Bill regret that they have ever done what they have done. Homosexuals must . . . remember that while there may be nothing bad in being a homosexual, there is certainly nothing good.[72]

There would thus appear to be some truth in Michael Sandel's argument that anti-perfectionist privacy claims can leave 'wholly unchallenged the adverse [social] views of homosexuality itself. Unless those views can be plausibly addressed, even a Court ruling in their favor is unlikely to win for homosexuals more than a thin and fragile toleration.'[73] Indeed, the possibility of combining respect for privacy with moral condemnation of same-sex sexual acts is neatly illustrated by John Finnis's argument, discussed in chapter 5, that such acts should be permitted so long as they occur 'in secret'.[74] This clearly reinforces Kendall Thomas's powerful argument that in US constitutional litigation:

> the rhetoric of privacy has historically functioned to perpetuate the oppressive politics of the 'closet': privacy is the ideological substrate of the very secrecy that has forced gay men and lesbians to remain hidden and underground. . . . There is no reason to think that we can rid privacy of its sedimented history.[75]

The second objection goes to internal consistency – and illustrates the general point made in chapter 4 about the practical impossibility of creating a set of laws which do not enforce morality to some degree. This objection concerns the fact that anti-perfectionist respect for privacy justifications are concerned to protect *consenting* sexual activity only. No anti-perfectionist respect for privacy justification would deem rape, sexual harassment or child molestation to be valid expressions of the rapist's or harasser's autonomy, meriting immunity from legal prohibition for this reason (this is true of both activity-based and geographical interpretations of privacy). This means that anti-perfectionist privacy justifications must implicitly be relying on an additional moral factor – most likely the need to protect the autonomy of the rape or harassment victim – to place sexual acts which are procured by coercion *outside* the zone of privacy, however this is defined. Any discussion of privacy thus presupposes legal respect for some additional moral value which will be crucial in separating private, protected sexual acts from those which are impermissible – thereby preventing any justification from being consistently anti-perfectionist.

Perfectionist respect for privacy justifications are confronted by a related problem – something which is neatly illustrated by the third relevant, apparently perfectionist privacy justification advanced by Richard Mohr.[76] To understand this problem, we first need to examine Mohr's arguments as a whole. Mohr implies that his analysis is of a philosophical character, although it is in fact largely an interpretation of privacy as a matter of US constitutional law.[77] He underpins his arguments with intermittent philosophical remarks, however. These seek to tie the law reform demands which are advanced to the notion of respect for human dignity – which, Mohr clearly believes, the law should respect. Mohr suggests that 'the basic [moral] evil of [anti-]sodomy laws is that they are an affront to dignity'.[78] This is because they fail to respect a person as a 'chooser – a subject conscious of herself as an agent with plans, projects, and a view of her own achievements'.[79] They also violate two important human entitlements: first, the entitlement to equal respect, in that anti-sodomy laws do not treat a lesbian or gay person's desires, plans, aspirations and values as worthy of social care on a par with that offered to others; and second, the entitlement to respect as a moral agent – that is, that one be judged according to one's individual merits or accomplishments, rather than by reference to 'widely irrelevant features' such as one's sexual orientation.[80] In similar vein, Mohr claims that anti-discrimination laws may be justified since discrimination fails to show respect for persons as equals.[81]

These assertions are in fact open to challenge, given that Mohr's philosophical argument is rather vague.[82] The argument is not presented as a cohesive whole, and the suggested definition of dignity is rather loose. Mohr does not acknowledge, for example, that people can have widely differing views of what constitutes an 'irrelevant feature' when assessing or characterizing someone in moral terms. A conservative might well believe that a person's lesbian or gay sexual orientation *is* a relevant reason for treating them unfavourably. We can certainly argue that this view is wrong – but this is not the same as claiming that, so long as one holds a conservative view, sexual orientation will not seem relevant. There really is no morally neutral way, at least in this context, in which a human characteristic can be marked out as 'relevant' in the way that Mohr appears to believe is possible. In addition, Mohr fails to explain exactly how his notion of 'entitlement to equal respect' would work: for there clearly *are* human desires, plans and aspirations which can rightly be treated less favourably than others – a desire or plan to become a torturer or a mass murderer, for example. Loose talk about 'equal respect' is an insufficient foundation for coherent philosophical analysis.

The crucial issue, for present purposes, stems from the fact that Mohr rests his respect for privacy argument – when dealing with laws prohibiting same-sex sexual acts – on this dignity-based analysis. Mohr interprets privacy as relating to activities – here, sexual acts – rather than to physical spaces,[83] and argues that sexual activity by its very nature excludes all but the participants, for whom ordinary perceptions of the rest of the world diminish during intercourse. Sexual acts are thus, Mohr claims, inherently private.[84] Furthermore, sexual activity plays a fundamentally important role in most people's lives, and it is certainly not something which they can readily forego.[85] Invasions of sexual privacy are thus attacks upon dignity. Mohr deals with the issue of consent by suggesting that a sexual act cannot count as private unless the participants have freely engaged in it, a suggestion which presumably relates back to his underlying notion of dignity.[86] He also claims – in a way which supporters of a physical space interpretation of privacy might find implausible – that sexual activity between consenting adults in 'cruising areas' (parks, toilets, etc.) to which the public have access can, potentially, be protected as private because they fall within the activity-related interpretation of the term.[87]

The central problem is that whatever one thinks of Mohr's claims, they clearly show that in a perfectionist theory, respect for privacy is in practice redundant as a distinct philosophical argument. For, while Mohr's justification is dressed up in the constitutional language of privacy, this is simply a vehicle for the deeper notion of respect for human dignity – the idea which acts as the philosophical driving force behind the justification. Privacy is, for Mohr, really just the label under which dignity is promoted in the area of sexual activity. A similar conclusion is possible if we imagine, for a moment, what an openly perfectionist version of David Richards' justification might look like. Such an argument would have to claim that the need to respect sexual autonomy is a positive moral good, which demands that the law – no longer neutral between different conceptions of the moral good – respects consenting sexual acts under a constitutional right to privacy. The law would be charged, under this theory, with respecting autonomy as a moral good, privacy being reduced to the label under which autonomy just happened to be protected constitutionally. In fact, the conclusion that privacy is being used as a label for a deeper moral value can be levelled at just about any perfectionist privacy theory, for they all derive the value of privacy, in relation to consenting sexual acts, from a deeper, background moral good. Given the importance of being clear about which moral good the law is charged with enforcing under a perfectionist justification (a justification which claims to enforce one moral good while in fact enforcing another will fail for internal inconsistency), it may therefore be more straightforward to abandon talk of privacy as the essence of any such justification, and to focus instead on the underlying moral value – whatever it is – as the basis for the laws or law reform measures concerned.

To those familiar with the philosophical and constitutional literature on privacy, few of the problems affecting the perfectionist and anti-perfectionist privacy justifications should really come as a surprise. Apart from the term's uncertain meaning, debate has long persisted about whether privacy is a specific good in itself – and if so, why – or whether it protects a set of distinct goods which are just grouped together under the heading 'privacy' for the sake of convenience.[88] The rivalry between perfectionist and anti-perfectionist privacy theories in the area of sexual behaviour rather parallels this debate. Perfectionists maintain that consenting sexual behaviour entails a background moral good and should be protected under the privacy heading for this reason, while anti-perfectionists see same-sex sexual acts as 'private' because of some underlying characteristic which they just happen to share with other acts falling within the privacy bracket. It almost seems inevitable that respect for privacy justifications are the subject of so much debate about their meaning and ambit.

There is, in addition, one major problem which affects both perfectionist and anti-perfectionist arguments. This problem – which counts against the substantive attractiveness of privacy justifications – relates to the notion of 'lesbian and gay rights' which they entail. For, while Richard Mohr has challenged the claim (highlighted in the quotation from Kendall Thomas) that privacy justifications merely protect secrecy about sexuality – that they keep lesbian and gay sexuality 'in the closet', in other words[89] – it *is* fair to say that privacy arguments are only capable of supporting law reform demands which concern the sphere of sexual behaviour. Given contemporary demands for anti-discrimination laws and other positive legal protections, privacy arguments thus seem somewhat old-fashioned – whether privacy is interpreted as respect for certain physical spaces, respect for certain relationships, or respect for control of information.[90] It would look distinctly implausible to advance a demand for anti-discrimination protections in employment using a privacy justification, for employment is commonly felt to come within the public or market sphere of life. It might, of course, be possible for those who favour privacy justifications for reforming the criminal law to claim that they support another justification entirely – equality, for instance – for creating anti-discrimination laws. A claim of this sort is, however, likely to involve such a complex mixture of moral goods – and such a complex explanation of why certain things count as 'lesbian and gay rights' issues – that it would make little sense to a possibly sceptical public, damaging the case for the legal reforms concerned.

More fundamentally, it may be the case that by focusing on sexual activity, respect for privacy justifications present a radically discontinuous picture of lesbian and gay life. For privacy-based justifications can only understand the notion of a sexual orientation in terms of sexual desires or contacts, when in reality, a person's sexual orientation is likely to affect their personality, outlook and experiences in every aspect of their life, at least in societies where that person's sexual orientation may be viewed unfavourably. As the editors of the *Harvard Law Review* have suggested, respect for privacy is:

> especially ill-suited to the affirmation of [lesbian and] gay rights, because it assumes that homosexuality is merely a form of conduct that can take place in the privacy of the bedroom at a specified time, rather than a continuous aspect of personality or personhood that usually requires expression across the public/private spectrum.[91]

Respect for privacy fails, in short, to capture the nature either of lesbian and gay sexuality, or of the types of social discrimination faced by those who are lesbian or gay.

On balance, therefore, respect for privacy justifications are not very strong. The basis on which they seek to overcome hostile arguments about the morality of lesbian and gay sexual orientations and same-sex sexual acts is haphazard at best. In anti-perfectionist form, they are open to the standard objection that it is in reality impossible to disengage law from the substantive enforcement of certain types of morality, and they are worryingly easy to combine with hostile views of the morality of lesbian and gay sexuality and same-sex sexual acts. In perfectionist form, respect for privacy justifications are little more than labels – often, just constitutional law labels – for deeper moral views about the status of lesbian and gay sexual orientations and acts. In neither form are respect for privacy justifications capable of supporting arguments for anti-discrimination laws or for any improvements to the legal position of lesbians and gays outside of areas directly concerned with sexual behaviour. Respect for privacy justifications are both internally inconsistent and substantively unattractive. If we are concerned with lasting and meaningful law reform, some other justification must therefore be found.

Liberationism and queer theory

Liberationist thought had its practical origins, logically enough, in the emergence of the gay liberation movement – originally discussed in chapter 3. It has been argued that the long-term origins of the gay liberation movement lay in the radicalization of youth culture at the end of the 1960s.[92] The immediate trigger for the birth of the New York Gay Liberation Front in June 1969 was, however, a police raid on a crowded gay bar, the Stonewall Inn in Christopher Street, New York. The ensuing riot, in the words of John D'Emilio,

> has come to assume mythic proportions among gay men and lesbians. The image of drag queens rioting in the streets and engaging in combat with helmeted officers of New York City's tactical police inverted the stereotype of meek, limp-wristed fairies. It was a wonderful moment of explosive rage in which a few transvestites and young gay men of color reshaped gay life forever.[93]

As an organized force, the Gay Liberation Front was relatively short-lived – groups were set up in some US and Canadian cities and in London but, at least in their original form, most collapsed fairly quickly. Historians of lesbian and gay politics tend to argue that the Front's significance lies in the campaigning energy which it unleashed (certainly in the USA and Canada), and in the theorization which it offered of the adverse treatment of lesbians and gays in western societies.

Two points should immediately be stressed. First, it is simplistic to see liberationism as a single, neatly definable theory. There are many strands of liberationist argument, with a variety of roots, the most recent such arguments being grouped under the heading of queer theory. Since we are concerned only with the legal implications of liberationist arguments, it seems sensible to focus our discussion on the classic account of gay liberation offered by Dennis Altman.[94] Second – and unlike respect for privacy – the central focus of liberationist theory is not on the law itself. Liberationism (in whatever form) entails a much broader political and sociological outlook, and aims at the radical reconstitution of society as a whole. This broader outlook merely has certain implications for how, if at all, the law should operate. Since law is not central to the liberationist enterprise, its role and uses have not been considered in much depth by liberationist thinkers, and it is fair to say that liberationism offers at best a rather unclear picture of the role and possible uses of law and law reform. One exception to this is provided by Carl Stychin, who has recently sought to develop an account of queer legal theory, which we will consider at the end of this section of the chapter.[95] Before examining the liberationist treatment of law, it is necessary to consider some of the broader elements of liberationist theory.

For Dennis Altman, the root of liberationist thought lies in the claim that humans are, in Freudian language, polymorphous perverse at birth: that is, they enjoy an undifferentiated ability to derive sexual pleasure from all parts of the body, and have an essentially bisexual sex drive.[96] As infants develop, this potential is repressed due to the climate of sexual oppression prevalent in modern western societies, in which the moral worth of sex is still linked with reproduction.[97] This pattern of oppression has removed the erotic from large areas of life – confining it to those commonly viewed as explicitly sexual – and has denied the inherently bisexual, mutable nature of human sexual capacity.[98]

A liberated society would, by contrast, recognize bisexuality as the norm, together with the wide potential for erotic experience which is truly open to each human being.[99] Altman thus suggests that 'the theory of sexual liberation . . . rests on a belief that it is possible through the removal of at least some of the restraints on human eroticism to develop a greater sense of warmth, affection, and community between people'.[100] With liberation, Altman claims, homo- and heterosexuality would no longer be seen as separate conditions, but would instead be viewed as component strands of each individual, given that all humans are polymorphous perverse.[101] Altman thus suggests that 'the vision of liberation that I hold is precisely one that would make the homo/hetero distinction irrelevant'.[102] Liberation would therefore mean an end to the nuclear family and to monogamy as a social norm,[103] and the disappearance of masculinity and femininity as sharply differentiated social categories.[104]

Liberationism is a much more all-encompassing approach than respect for privacy, given that it offers – as part of its general concern for sexual freedom – such a complete moral/sociological theorization of human sexual capacity. It is also much more radical. First, the notions of polymorphous perversity and sexual oppression prompt the demand for a fundamental change in the ways in which society understands sexuality and the sexual act – in contrast to respect for privacy's rather more modest demand for greater legal tolerance of particular types of sexual act which society already categorizes as homosexual. Second, liberationism is not concerned merely with law reform within existing civil society and its legal system: unlike respect for privacy, it aims to promote fundamental changes in these forms of social organization.

It is here that a crucial uncertainty becomes apparent in Altman's account of liberationism: for it is not clear how fundamental a social change is actually envisaged. More specifically, it is also unclear whether liberationism sees the law as serving a role – and if so, what role – within a fully liberated society. Altman's argument certainly has radical potential, which shows through in his suggestion that:

> gay liberation advances beyond the civil rights liberalism of . . . earlier groups. . . . No longer is the claim made that gay people can fit into American society, that they are as decent, as patriotic, as clean-living as anyone else. Rather, it is argued, it is American society itself that needs to change.[105]

He also stresses that the required social change will need to amount to 'a total transformation' in order to free the sexually oppressed. Unfortunately, it is not made clear quite what this will entail, beyond the dismantling of the sexual categories of heterosexual/straight and homosexual/gay and lesbian.[106]

In addition, while Altman argues that civil rights-oriented law reform is insufficient, he does seem to envisage that law reform will play *some* role in creating a liberated society. For example, he states that:

> Liberation implies more than the mere absence of oppression. Obviously there is a need to end laws which discriminate against homosexuals, to proscribe police harassment. . . . Yet to remove the obvious forms of oppression is only an immediate necessity, rather than a sufficient step towards liberation . . . [which] will come only with a new morality and a revised notion of 'human nature'.[107]

And, in similar vein, that:

> it is important to change laws. . . . But that does not add up to liberation. We are freeing ourselves through the way we live, and as long as homosexuals are oppressed, walking arm-in-arm with one's lover down the street is as much a political act as campaigning for law reform.[108]

Both passages beg the (unanswered) question whether, once a fully liberated society is achieved, law would simply become redundant in dealing with sexuality, or whether some form of minimal regulation (to penalize rape, for example) would be required.[109] The answer appears almost certainly to be 'yes', although this is not spelt out in liberationist theory. Altman maintains that monogamous, married heterosexual relationships should no longer be privileged in terms of the legal benefits available to the participants, but this is just about his only detailed reference to how the law should operate.[110] Many liberationist campaigners have certainly assumed that law would play some role in a liberated society. As we saw in chapter 3, the Male Representatives of National Gay Liberation suggested, in the US, that all modes of sexual self-expression deserved legal protection,[111] while the London Gay Liberation Front demanded the rights – presumably the legal rights – to publicly express love and affection and to behave in public and in private in any way they chose, so long as others were not thereby harmed.[112] The strong implication is that liberationists tend to see law as serving some continuing role.[113] It therefore remains meaningful to talk of a liberationist justification *for law reform* – underlining the perceptiveness of Jeffrey Weeks' observation that the London Gay Liberation Front's revolutionary arguments were sometimes a cover for aims which might potentially be achievable within a liberal society.[114]

Objections can obviously be made to the theory of sexuality – the notion of inherent mutability and bisexuality – on which Altman's account rests.

Theories of sexuality have already been discussed in detail in chapter 3, where the radical constructionist view – which seems to lie behind Altman's notion of inherent bisexuality – was rejected.[115] If the argument of chapter 3 is correct, it follows that liberationist theories cannot be relied upon if they rest, like Altman's, on such a view. It will nevertheless be useful to highlight some deeper difficulties facing liberationist theories at the level of justice and political morality.

The crucial – if understandable – weakness lies in liberationism's uncertain attitude to practical law reform. It is understandable for the following reason. We noted in chapter 1 that law reform campaigners seem to be repelled by the coercive power of law in dealing with consenting sexual activity, yet also to see law as a useful way of entrenching the protections which they seek against social discrimination. The liberationist uncertainty is possibly just a reflection of this, albeit in acute form. For the liberationist attitude to law can perhaps best be categorized as cautiously pragmatic: law reform is seen as one, tactical step towards a sexually liberated society, rather than as an end in itself. This being so, liberationists may well assume that the social importance of law will diminish in a liberated society – at least in the area of sexuality – making detailed, principled speculation about its future role slightly superfluous. Altman notes, for example, that liberation may more profitably be regarded as a process than an attainable end-goal[116] – suggesting that discussion of the ideal role for law may just seem impractical or excessively abstract from the liberationist standpoint.

This unwillingness to speculate is, however, crucial since it leaves liberationists open to criticism even when using law on a pragmatic basis. For it could be claimed that since law is one of the principal means of enforcing state power, it is inconsistent with liberationists' avowedly revolutionary aims to engage with it at all. The political commentator Andrew Sullivan has suggested, in relation to liberationist campaigning groups in the USA, that 'For a politics designed to subvert existing structures, participating in the very instrument of state power is a nonsensical political objective.'[117]

Any assessment of how seriously this argument should be taken would probably turn into a debate about day-to-day political strategy. The argument does, however, expose a real problem in the liberationists' approach to law. For, given that liberationist theory offers no clearly spelt out, principled basis for dealing with day-to-day questions of law reform (as opposed to, say, deconstructing the notions of power and sexuality embodied in such questions), liberationists have left themselves without much ammunition for rebutting Sullivan's argument. The absence of a clear principled position about how far it is right – as a matter of justice and political morality – to use law reform as a pragmatic tactic on the road to sexual liberation also confronts liberationists with the dangerous possibility that their strategy may degenerate into a tacit co-option of the liberal, reformist agenda epitomized by the respect for privacy and equality/identity justifications. By failing to lay down any principled limits, liberationists have no coherent means of assessing the desirability of particular political tactics – including law reform – in the light of their background theories of society and sexuality. This must open any liberationist argument about law to the charge of internal inconsistency.

Even if they did speculate more extensively at a level of principle, liberationists would in any event be vexed by difficult arguments about perfectionism and anti-perfectionism. Liberationism is often felt to be libertarian in character, that is, it assumes that as a matter of justice and political morality, the state should play a minimal role in regulating sexual (or indeed any) areas of life, with individuals being free to define and to live out their lives exactly as they choose, subject only to the constraint that they should not harm others.[118] If this is so, then liberationism could claim to be strongly anti-perfectionist in approach: subject to the harm constraint, choices between moral goods are left entirely to private citizens. Altman suggests, for example, that 'Because homosexuality cannot find its justification in procreation nor in religiously sanctioned marriage, it represents an assertion of sexuality as an expression of hedonism and love free of any . . . social ends.'[119] Society (and its laws) should nevertheless respect people's freedom to engage in homosexual behaviour: 'liberation', Altman says, 'demands a renunciation of the traditional puritan ethic'.[120]

However, Altman's argument faces the same difficulty – when applied to law reform – as David Richards' respect for privacy claim. For it is not clear whether a law reform justification based on Altman's assertions would be saying that there is no moral good in same-sex sexual acts, but that they should be allowed since the state has no role in dictating people's sexual behaviour – an anti-perfectionist argument; or that there is some moral good ('hedonism and love', however people choose to define these terms) which should be respected *because it is* a moral good – a perfectionist argument. Altman's reasoning seems insufficiently detailed to offer a basis for a perfectionist justification, and a justification based solely upon hedonism may be unpopular.

If, as seems more likely, any justification would be anti-perfectionist, then it would be undermined by the general objections to such theories, discussed earlier. Given that it would depend upon a libertarian theory of justice and political morality, it could also be rejected because of the unattractiveness of such theories.[121] For libertarians seek to maximize individual choice (save where a choice would cause tangible harm to others), choice being seen as a paramount value. This position, however, boils down to saying that the statement 'I want X' or 'I choose to have X' offers a valid moral reason why I should have X – something which is plainly nonsensical. It might be claimed that I should have X because my wanting it – and getting it – recognizes my autonomy in making decisions affecting my life. But, as Joseph Raz has argued, our lives are not improved simply by the number of choices open to us.[122] Instead, a person's quality of life depends upon the range of morally valuable options from which they can choose – and, to be a morally valuable option, something must rest on a moral good of its own. This, of course, is completely contrary to the libertarian approach.

This discussion of Altman's arguments may be concluded with two observations. First, liberationist theories are clearly internally inconsistent when applied to questions of law reform, and are implausible if they rely on a radical constructionist notion of sexuality. Given their probable anti-perfectionist nature, Altman's arguments are also open to the type of objection which can be levelled at any libertarian theory of justice and political morality. The second point is, however, more positive. For liberationist theories make a useful contribution by recognizing the importance of our second central question: how helpful, in practice, is law and law reform in promoting the type of society in which we wish to live? Reformist campaigning groups often fall down by failing to ask this question – law is simply assumed to work some sort of social magic. By coupling a coherent and principled approach to law reform – currently lacking in liberationist thought – with a preliminary response to the second central question, we will hopefully end up with a much stronger analysis of law reform issues.

Carl Stychin's analysis of law from the standpoint of queer theory offers some clarification of the first, internal consistency point, but in doing so, introduces further loose ends of its own, relating to how a queer legal theory will develop. To understand these loose ends, we must first consider Stychin's view of 'queerness', which turns, not on a polymorphous perverse conception of the sex drive, but on a theory of sexual categorizations. Stychin defines 'queerness' as a refusal to accept dominant understandings of sexuality, including sexual categories such as gay, lesbian and heterosexual. Being 'queer' therefore turns on how a person sees *themselves* (negatively) in relation to conventional understandings of sexuality, rather than on how society would categorize them using socially constructed labels like lesbian or gay.[123] For to identify oneself as queer is to challenge the very idea that people can be divided neatly into conventional sexual categories. A 'queer' identity – for those who would adopt it for themselves – lacks any essential content: it is at best provisional, all sexual categorizations being seen as shifting and fluid.[124] In an era of postmodernist analysis, Stychin claims, it cannot plausibly be claimed that identity categories (whether lesbian, gay, straight or any other) are held together by fixed, essential truths:

> Central to a queer identity is the problematisation of categories of sexual identity and boundaries of sexual propriety, as they have been historically constituted. Queerness in part suggests an unwillingness to fix difference in any ultimate literality. . . . Queerness thus suggests the 'subversion of identity' at the same time that a category of identity is tenuously constructed.[125]

Underpinning this discussion is the notion that any identity usually defines itself in relation to some outside 'other', which is usually portrayed as dangerous, and used to reinforce the identity category concerned. Thus, Stychin suggests, ideas of national identity are usually reinforced by the idea of the enemy alien trying to creep into and undermine the nation concerned.[126] Ideas of heterosexual, lesbian or gay sexuality entail pictures of what they are *not* as much as what they are. And, in his discussion of the possibility of constituting a queer (as opposed to a lesbian or gay) identity, Stychin asks rhetorically whether, 'in constituting itself, an identity can avoid creating a series of exclusions through a set of boundaries by which the identity is coherently constituted'.[127] If the answer to this question is indeed 'no', as Stychin hints, then an interesting new light is cast on the currently popular notion of a 'lesbian and/or gay identity'. This observation does, however, raise a question for Stychin's own theory, which will become clear shortly.

According to Stychin, a queer *legal* theory rests on the apparent tension between law's repressive power and its ability to contribute to the development of oppositional identities – such as queer – by generating resistance to its requirements. A queer response will exploit these tensions by recognizing the importance of 'deploying categories of identity while, at the same time, maintaining an awareness of the provisional character of their use'.[128] Such a response will therefore serve to expose the constructed, fluid and queer character of sexual categories. As a practical matter, Stychin suggests that a liberationist approach to 'rights' may be adopted by campaigners. Under this approach, the language of rights could be employed on a pragmatic basis, depending on the political experience and history of the area and group concerned.[129] Rights are thus to be used as a political means for empowering the marginalized – 'a localised use of [rights] terminology which is anchored in an appeal to the specificity of a subject's location' – rather than as an abstract expression of universal entitlement.[130] The right publicly to articulate a marginal sexual identity can therefore be deployed to challenge attempts to restrict representations of non-heterosexual sexuality, including gay and lesbian literature, art, and pornography.[131]

These arguments certainly show that a liberationist/queer approach to law is possible, and they go some way towards clarifying how such an approach might work. They involve a series of loose ends, however, which ultimately make Stychin's theory unsatisfactory. First, it is not made clear how *any* reliance on identity is possible without co-opting the unified, essentialist model which Stychin rejects. While Stychin's queer strategy involves the pragmatic use of identity, he does not explain how far this can go without collapsing into a conventional privacy or equality approach. Second, Stychin accepts – as we have seen – that some people may well be excluded by a queer identity, which can imply a notion of the 'other'.[132] While a queer identity excludes far fewer than do conventional identity categories, it is unclear how many would have to be excluded before the desirability of queer legal theory becomes questionable. A third, related puzzle is what would happen if a still queerer analysis were to evolve: would queer theory fight it (a process which would surely entail an assertion of norms of some sort) or collapse? These questions expose a central uncertainty about where – and how far –

Stychin's queer theory can take us. Given its role in *reacting* to established categories, perhaps it is just impossible to think ahead. As Stychin argues: 'the tension between the assertion and deconstruction of identity categories is irresolvable and should be understood as a continuing contestation'.[133]

Given that we are concerned with the practical question of justifications for law reform, it is necessary to base our argument on more than just reaction to existing social norms. While queer theory may well be interesting as a form of social analysis, it cannot – at least as presently constituted – take us very far in our search for an adequate justification. The various loose ends in Stychin's account suggest that without further clarification, his theory risks becoming internally inconsistent by co-opting the very types of categorization which he claims to reject. Stychin's account is a welcome addition to the classic liberationist arguments, therefore, but ultimately brings us no nearer to an answer to our first central question.

Conclusion

Immutability, respect for privacy and liberationism must therefore fail as justifications, for a variety of reasons ranging from internal inconsistency to substantive unattractiveness. It is unclear whether the immutability argument focuses on sexual acts or particular sexual identities. Whichever is the case, additional moral reasoning is always needed to explain why the allegedly immutable attribute deserves protection. Even then, immutability would still be a weak argument, since it boils down to the claim that people should not be penalized because they cannot help the immutable feature – hardly a strong defence in a hostile society.

Respect for privacy arguments are also weak. In anti-perfectionist form, they are fatally undermined by the implausibility of any assumption that law should not enforce morality of some sort, and by their apparent compatability with hostile views of lesbian and gay sexuality. In perfectionist form, they turn out to be little more than a cover for deeper moral arguments based on notions of dignity or autonomy. Whether perfectionist or anti-perfectionist, privacy is, in any event, too narrow a base on which to rest the contemporary range of lesbian and gay law reform demands.

The third justification, liberationism, including queer theory, is far too vague when applied to practical questions of law reform. In particular, it is unclear how far liberationists are prepared to work with the established legal system, and to what extent queer theory's use of the idea of sexual identity entails the co-option of more traditional, unified identity categories. It is hard to see how liberationist theory could fail, in practice, to operate in an internally inconsistent fashion. We have seen, however, that liberationism does have some valuable observations to make concerning the relationship between law reform and social change – observations which it is important for any justification to take into account. We will return to this point in chapters 7 and 8.

Notes

1. Stephen Macedo, 'Reply to critics' (1995) 84 *Georgetown Law Journal* 329 at 337.
2. This chapter therefore employs what Michael Sandel has described as the 'naïve' style of argument for legal reform – 'Moral argument and liberal toleration: Abortion and homosexuality' (1989) 77 *California Law Review* 521. It may also be seen as an attempt to answer the question posed by conservative critic Hadley Arkes in his 'Questions of principle, not predictions: A reply to Macedo' (1995) 84 *Georgetown Law Journal* 321 at 324.
3. Cf. Sandel, 'Moral argument and liberal toleration' at 536–7.
4. US queer nationalist arguments are, for example, left on one side.
5. Several examples of this strategy were seen in the 1994 (UK) House of Commons debate concerning the appropriate age of consent for sexual acts between males – see H.C. Deb., 21 February 1994, Columns 74–86, 95–100, 104–13.
6. An argument which appears partly to employ such distinctions is Stephen Macedo's 'Homosexuality and the conservative mind' (1995) 84 *Georgetown Law Journal* 261.
7. If the justification purported to be neutral between different sexual orientations, then how large a role – in the case of each orientation – should be unimportant.
8. See chapter 7.
9. See chapter 3.
10. (1986) 106 S Ct 2841.
11. See also Michael Moore's warnings against confusing the philosophical and the constitutional: 'Sandelian antiliberalism' (1989) 77 *California Law Review* 539.
12. It should be added that those who support law reform using a particular philosophical justification might sometimes need, as a matter of necessity, to present their argument in analogous – but not identical – constitutional/legal terms. This is a potentially messy solution, but it is sometimes better than no solution at all. Paul Roberts clearly misses this point in his (mis)interpretation of my argument concerning the status, in English law, of consenting sado-masochistic sexual acts (see his 'Consent and the criminal law: Philosophical foundations', Appendix C to Law Commission Consultation Paper 139, *Consent in the Criminal Law* (London: HMSO, 1995), para. C.13, responding to Nicholas Bamforth, 'Sado-masochism and consent' [1994] *Criminal Law Review* 661). My argument was that such acts should be permitted using the empowerment justification presented in chapter 7 of this book, and that in consequence, a special exemption from criminal liability should be created for them. In an ideal legal system, no special exemption would be necessary – the

justification would be embodied in the very structure of the criminal law. As it is, however, an exemption is necessary as a practical matter – given the law reform options potentially available – in order to give effect to the justification. Roberts overlooks this (regrettably necessary) distinction between means and ends.

13. In English law, contrast Basil Markesinis, 'Our patchy law of privacy – Time to do something about it' (1990) 53 *Modern Law Review* 802, 'The Calcutt Report must not be forgotten' (1992) 55 *Modern Law Review* 118; Peter Prescott, '*Kaye v. Robertson* – A reply' (1991) 54 *Modern Law Review* 451.

14. See, e.g., the immutability limb of the equal protection analysis employed in *Watkins v. U.S. Army* (1988) 837 F 2d 1428 at 1347–8.

15. In US constitutional law, cf. Harris Miller, ' An argument for the application of Equal Protection heightened scrutiny to classifications based on homosexuality' (1984) 57 *Southern California Law Review* 797 at 818–21 (although note the slight doubt entertained here as to questions of 'causes').

16. In US constitutional law, cf. Note, 'The constitutionality of laws forbidding private homosexual conduct' (1974) 72 *Michigan Law Review* 1613 at 1625–6.

17. H.C. Deb., 8 May 1987, column 1007.

18. Janet Halley, 'Sexual orientation and the politics of biology: A critique of the argument from immutability' (1994) 46 *Stanford Law Review* 503 at 519 (Halley's comment refers to constitutional litigation, but the point is equally relevant to philosophical argument); see also Richard Mohr, *Gay Ideas: Outing and Other Controversies* (Boston: Beacon Press, 1992), pp. 248–50 (although note that, as elsewhere in his work, Mohr radically misunderstands the notion of social constructionism).

19. Halley, 'Sexual orientation and the politics of biology' at 567.

20. Halley offers a sceptical account of the surveys to date – *ibid.* at 525, 529–46, and predetermination would clearly be repellent to supporters of the liberationist perspective. For debate about the 'scientific' issues, see further Walter Bodmer and Robin McKie, *The Book of Man: The Quest to Discover Our Genetic Heritage* (London: Abacus, 1995); Dean Hamer and Peter Copeland, *The Science of Desire: The Search for the Gay Gene and the Biology of Behavior* (New York: Simon & Schuster, 1994).

21. The same is true of the analytically related argument that a person's sexual orientation is an illegitimate basis on which to judge them because it is 'irrelevant' to their ability to live a meaningful and worthwhile life, to fill a particular position in employment, etc. Any such argument would require a proper normative distinction between 'relevant' and 'irrelevant' attributes of a person's character.

22. See also John D'Emilio's argument in *Making Trouble: Essays on Gay History, Politics, and the University* (New York: Routledge, 1992), pp. 187–8.

23. See also Halley, 'Sexual orientation and the politics of biology' at 521–6. Abortion was openly suggested in the British tabloid press when the various surveys highlighting the possibility of biological predetermination were first published.

24. Cf. Dennis Altman's related argument in *Homosexuality: Oppression and Liberation* (London: Serpent's Tail, 2nd edn, 1993), p. 26.

25. *Report of the Committee on Homosexual Offences and Prostitution*, 1957 Cmnd. 247.

26. *Ibid.*, para. 61.

27. See the Sexual Offences Act 1967. The Wolfenden Committee supported the decriminalization of homosexual acts committed in private between consenting males aged twenty-one or over; a more restrictive definition of 'in private' was, however, introduced (together with other restrictions)

during the Bill's passage through Parliament – see Antony Grey, *Quest for Justice: Towards Homosexual Emancipation* (London: Sinclair-Stevenson, 1992), pp. 103–4, 108–9, 127, 240.

28. Stephen Jeffery-Poulter, *Peers, Queers, and Commons: the Struggle for Gay Law Reform from 1950 to the Present* (London: Routledge, 1991), chs 2–4, esp. pp. 51, 53, 81–9; Grey, *Quest for Justice*, chs 3–9.
29. Gary Kinsman, *The Regulation of Desire: Sexuality in Canada* (Montreal: Black Rose Books, 1987), pp. 163–72.
30. H.C. Deb., 21 February 1994, Columns 75, 77.
31. *Bowers v. Hardwick* (1986) 106 S Ct 2841.
32. *Ibid*. at 2843.
33. *Ibid*. at 2850–6.
34. (1981) 4 EHRR 149.
35. (1989) 13 EHRR 187.
36. (1993) 16 EHRR 485.
37. Judith Jarvis Thomson, 'The right to privacy' (1975) 4 *Philosophy & Public Affairs* 295 at 295.
38. The classic private law exposition of this sense of privacy remains Samuel Warren and Louis Brandeis's 'The right to privacy' (1890) 4 *Harvard Law Review* 193.
39. For examples of divisions of privacy, cf. Justice Blackmun's dissent in *Bowers v. Hardwick*, n.10 above; Kendall Thomas, 'Beyond the privacy principle' (1992) 92 *Columbia Law Review* 1431 at 1443–60; David Richards, *Sex, Drugs, Death, and the Law: An Essay on Human Rights and Overcriminalization* (Totowa: Rowman & Littlefield, 1982), pp. 33–4.
40. David Bedingfield, 'Privacy or publicity? The enduring confusion surrounding the American tort of invasion of privacy' (1992) 55 *Modern Law Review* 111.
41. Ruth Gavison, 'Privacy and the limits of law' (1980) 89 *Yale Law Journal* 421, esp. at 428, 451, 459.
42. Charles Fried, 'Privacy' (1968) 77 *Yale Law Journal* 475, esp. at 478–86. See also Jeffrey Reiman, 'Privacy, intimacy, and personhood' (1976) 6 *Philosophy & Public Affairs* 26, and Charles Fried's reply, Correspondence (1976) 6 *Philosophy & Public Affairs* 288. The notion of personhood is usefully criticized by Jeb Rubenfeld in 'The right to privacy' (1989) 102 *Harvard Law Review* 737 at 752–82.
43. Richards, *Sex, Drugs, Death, and the Law*, chs 1 and 2, esp. pp. 33–4. See also Louis Henkin, 'Privacy and autonomy' (1974) 74 *Columbia Law Review* 1410.
44. Richards, *Sex, Drugs, Death, and the Law*, p. 8.
45. *Ibid*., p. 9.
46. *Ibid*., p. 50.
47. *Ibid*., pp. 8–9; see, more broadly, Richards' article 'Kantian ethics and the harm principle: A reply to John Finnis' (1987) 87 *Columbia Law Review* 457.
48. Richards, *Sex, Drugs, Death, and the Law*, p. 38.
49. *Ibid*., pp. 52–3.
50. *Ibid*., p. 52. Note the similarity with H. L. A. Hart's argument in *Law, Liberty, and Morality* (Oxford: Oxford University Press, 1963), p. 22.
51. Cf. Richards' critique of the hostile justifications – *Sex, Drugs, Death, and the Law*, pp. 36–49.
52. *Ibid*., p. 35.
53. *Ibid*., p. 50.
54. Robert George, *Making Men Moral: Civil Liberties and Public Morality* (Oxford: Clarendon Press, 1993), p. 142.
55. *Ibid*., p. 146.
56. *Ibid*., pp. 146–56. For Richards' discussion of 'Kantian' autonomy, cf. *Sex, Drugs, Death, and the Law*, ch. 1.
57. Ronald Dworkin, 'Liberal community' (1989) 77 *California Law Review* 479. For earlier arguments advanced by Dworkin, see his 'Taking rights seriously', ch. 7 in *Taking Rights Seriously* (London: Duckworth, 1977) and 'Do we have a right to pornography?', ch. 17 in *A Matter of Principle* (Oxford: Clarendon Press, 1986).

58. Philip Selznick, 'Dworkin's unfinished task' (1989) 77 *California Law Review* 505 at 505.
59. Dworkin, 'Liberal community' at 491–2.
60. *Ibid.* at 495.
61. *Ibid.*
62. *Ibid.* at 495–6.
63. *Ibid.* at 500.
64. *Ibid.* at 497.
65. *Ibid.* at 500.
66. See chapter 3.
67. See also George, *Making Men Moral*, pp. 102–8.
68. Bernard Williams, 'Dworkin on community and critical interests' (1989) 77 *California Law Review* 515 at 518–20.
69. Selznick, 'Dworkin's unfinished task' at 506.
70. Kinsman, *The Regulation of Desire*, pp. 164–72; Jeffery-Poulter, *Peers, Queers and Commons*, pp. 81–2.
71. Jeffrey Weeks, *Coming Out: Homosexual Politics in Britain from the Nineteenth Century to the Present* (London: Quartet, rev. edn, 1990), p. 176.
72. Cited in Grey, *Quest for Justice*, pp. 125–6.
73. Sandel, 'Moral argument and liberal toleration' at 537.
74. See chapter 5.
75. Thomas, 'Beyond the privacy principle' at 1510. See also Stephen Seidman, 'Identity and politics in a "postmodern" gay culture: Some historical and conceptual notes', in Michael Warner (ed.), *Fear of a Queer Planet: Queer Politics and Social Theory* (Minneapolis: University of Minnesota Press, 1994), p. 111.
76. The tone of chs 2–4 of Richard Mohr's *Gays/Justice: A Study of Ethics, Society, and Law* (New York: Columbia University Press, 1988) generally seems perfectionist (although p. 4 is rather vague); see also, however, Mohr's arguments against majoritarian views of morality – *Gay Ideas*, ch. 3.
77. Mohr, *Gays/Justice*, pp. 3–4. At pp. 81–2, Mohr rejects an interpretation of the US Constitution which is based overtly on 'political philosophy'.
78. *Ibid.*, p. 57.
79. *Ibid.*, p. 58.
80. *Ibid.*, p. 59.
81. *Ibid.*, pp. 141–51.
82. For criticism, see Leslie Moran, 'Justice and its vicissitudes' (1991) 54 *Modern Law Review* 146.
83. Mohr, *Gays/Justice*, pp. 104–6.
84. *Ibid.*, pp. 100–4.
85. *Ibid.*, pp. 109–12 (note also Mohr's criticism of David Richards' arguments – p. 109, n. 32).
86. *Ibid.*, pp. 105–6.
87. *Ibid.*, pp. 104–6.
88. Compare Thomson, 'The right to privacy' at 313; Thomas Scanlon, 'Thomson on privacy' (1975) 4 *Philosophy & Public Affairs* 315; Reiman, 'Privacy, intimacy, and personhood'; Fried, 'Privacy'; June Eichbaum, 'Towards an autonomy-based theory of constitutional privacy: Beyond the ideology of familial privacy' (1979) 14 *Harvard Civil Rights–Civil Liberties Law Review* 361; Rubenfeld, 'The right of privacy'; Mohr, *Gays/Justice*, pp. 94 *et seq.*
89. *Ibid.*, pp. 98–100.
90. Cf. Patricia Cain's discussion, 'Litigating for lesbian and gay rights: A legal history' (1993) 79 *Virginia Law Review* 1551 at 1639.
91. Note, 'The constitutional status of sexual orientation', (1985) 98 *Harvard Law Review* 1285 at 1290. See, in similar vein, Daniel Ortiz, 'Creating controversy: Essentialism and constructivism and the politics of gay identity' (1993) 79 *Virginia Law Review* 1833 at 1852.
92. For discussion, see D'Emilio, *Making Trouble*, ch. 20; Weeks, *Coming Out*, ch. 16; Jeffery-Poulter, *Peers, Queers and Commons*, pp. 98–108; Kinsman, *The Regulation of Desire*, pp. 179–82.
93. D'Emilio, *Making Trouble*, pp. 239–40; for general discussion of the Gay Liberation Front, see pp. 239–46; Weeks, *Coming Out*, ch. 16.

94. Altman, *Homosexual: Oppression and Liberation*. For a comprehensive survey of liberationist thought and tactics, see Barry Adam, *The Rise of a Gay and Lesbian Movement* (Boston: Twayne, 1987), ch. 5.
95. Carl Stychin, *Law's Desire: Sexuality and the Limits of Justice* (London: Routledge, 1995), esp. ch. 8.
96. Altman, *Homosexuality: Oppression and Liberation*, p. 83.
97. *Ibid.*, pp. 84–8.
98. *Ibid.*, pp. 90, 95.
99. *Ibid.*, p. 115.
100. *Ibid.*, p. 101.
101. *Ibid.*, p. 239.
102. *Ibid.*
103. *Ibid.*, pp. 110–11.
104. *Ibid.*, p. 115.
105. *Ibid.*, p. 128.
106. *Ibid.*, p. 129; see also pp. 134, 137, 244.
107. *Ibid.*, p. 80.
108. *Ibid.*, p. 143.
109. Cf. Altman's reference to autonomy – *ibid.*, p. 116.
110. *Ibid.*, p. 110.
111. Statement of Demands to the Revolutionary Peoples Constitutional Convention from the Male Representatives of National Gay Liberation; reprinted in D. Deitcher (ed.), *Over the Rainbow: Lesbian and Gay Politics in America Since Stonewall* (London: Boxtree/Channel Four, 1995), p. 30.
112. *The Gay Liberation Front Demands*, cited in Jeffery-Poulter, *Peers, Queers and Commons*, pp. 100–1.
113. For a recent interpretation, see Peter Tatchell, *We Don't Want to March Straight: Masculinity, Queers and the Military* (London: Cassell, 1995), esp. ch. 3.
114. Weeks, *Coming Out*, p. 205. See also Adam, *The Rise of a Gay and Lesbian Movement*, p. 150.
115. Cf. also Andrew Sullivan, *Virtually Normal: An Argument About Homosexuality* (London: Picador, 1995), pp. 73, 75.
116. Altman, *Homosexuality: Oppression and Liberation*, p. 116.
117. Sullivan, *Virtually Normal*, p. 86.
118. Cf. Keith Birch, 'A community of interests', in Bob Cant and Susan Hemmings (eds), *Radical Records: Thirty Years of Lesbian and Gay History* (London: Routledge, 1988), pp. 51, 57.
119. Altman, *Homosexuality: Oppression and Liberation*, p. 89.
120. *Ibid.*, p. 104.
121. The most prominent such theory has been advanced by Robert Nozick in *Anarchy, State, and Utopia* (New York: Basic Books, 1974); for criticism, see Thomas Nagel, *Other Minds: Critical Essays 1969–1994* (New York: Oxford University Press, 1995), ch. 13.
122. Joseph Raz, *The Morality of Freedom* (Oxford: Clarendon Press, 1986), pp. 373–8.
123. Stychin, *Law's Desire*, p. 146.
124. *Ibid.*, p. 153.
125. *Ibid.*, p. 141.
126. *Ibid.*, p. 105.
127. *Ibid.*, p. 147.
128. *Ibid.*, p. 156.
129. *Ibid.*, pp. 36–7, 74–5.
130. *Ibid.*, p. 36.
131. *Ibid.*, chs 1–3.
132. *Ibid.*, pp. 146–7.
133. *Ibid.*, p. 140.

7

Justifications for Legal Protection: Equality and Beyond

Introduction

Since the mid-1980s, law reform campaigns on both sides of the Atlantic have been conducted using the language of equality for lesbians and gays – who have been characterized as a legitimate sexual minority or minorities. As John D'Emilio has suggested, most US campaigning work concerning lesbian and gay issues has fallen into

> a familiar, well-established equal rights framework, deeply rooted in American history. This history has provided gay men and lesbians with several models of struggles employed by minorities in search of equality. Blacks, women, ethnic groups, and religious minorities seek this equality through social movements, legislative agendas, and litigation.[1]

Even liberationist campaigners – whose arguments nowadays fall under the heading of queer theory – have been known to employ the *language* of equality as a rhetorical device, while aiming at more radical results than the mainstream 'equal rights' agenda would envisage.

Equality-based arguments clearly have a powerful emotive appeal. Unlike fully fledged liberationist arguments, they cannot claim to be revolutionary in character, but they do rest on the strong claim that lesbian and gay sexuality (or some specified aspect of it) is just as good, morally speaking, as heterosexuality. In consequence, they lack the apparent defensiveness which undermines respect for privacy justifications, and in their strongest form can be used to justify a wide range of law reform demands, going far beyond just liberalizing the criminal law relating to same-sex sexual acts. Equality arguments can be used to justify prohibiting employment discrimination against lesbians and gays, creating partnership rights for same-sex couples and allowing them to adopt children: for it could be said that the absence of any such laws allows people to be treated unequally – whether socially or by the law itself – simply because of their sexual orientation (it should be noted that even where test cases brought in pursuit of these entitlements have employed non-equality-based *constitutional* arguments, equality is still invoked as the *political* justification for the entitlements concerned). In fact, equality arguments potentially identify as 'lesbian and gay rights' issues *all* situations where lesbians and gays are treated less favourably than heterosexuals.

The popularity of equality as a law reform argument was demonstrated by its adoption as the watchword of the 1994 campaign for an equal age of consent in the UK. During the House of Commons debate on the topic, Tony Blair MP (then Shadow Home Secretary) urged Members – during a powerful speech in favour of reform – to 'be clear about the issue before us tonight. . . . It is whether the criminal law should discriminate between heterosexual and homosexual sex. It is therefore an issue not of age, but of equality.'[2] This was reinforced by Chris Smith MP, who asserted that 'The kernel of tonight's debate is the argument about equality. . . . I believe in the fundamental principle that we are all equal before the law. At present, the law does not permit that in the case of young gay men.'[3] Both MPs were careful to draw parallels with race and sex discrimination. Tony Blair suggested that 'A society that has learned, over time, racial and sexual equality can surely come to terms with equality of sexuality. That is the moral case for change tonight.'[4] And, according to Chris Smith: 'This country has laws that say one may not discriminate on the grounds of race or gender. . . . But the law discriminates in respect of the relationships of young gay men. To my mind, that means that it should be changed.'[5] In similar vein, a major empirical survey in the UK, which concluded that lesbians and gay men were often treated unfavourably at work because of their sexual orientation, was headed 'Less Equal than Others'[6] – the implication being that employees deserve equality regardless of their sexual orientation – while campaigning literature for lesbian and gay civil rights groups typically asks readers to 'Join us in the fight for equality'.[7]

To properly understand and assess equality-based arguments, we need to explore the meaning of the word 'equality' in greater detail. For different interpretations of the word give rise to differently structured justifications for laws and law reform, which may be open to analysis using distinct grounds, some of which are of a philosophical nature, others of which are concerned with the political desirability or efficacy of equality claims. In the next section of the chapter, we will critically assess the various understandings of equality which are relevant to the legal entitlements of lesbians and gays. It will be suggested that while equality is a more sophisticated basis for law reform demands than immutability or privacy-based claims, arguments based solely on equality are not in fact sustainable, analytically, when used as a justification for law or law reform. Rather different rhetorical or statistical understandings of equality can, however, play a valuable role *if* they are coupled with a quite distinct justification, based on empowerment. The last section of the chapter will be devoted to considering the empowerment justification.

Analysing equality

All equality-based arguments entail some sort of comparison,[8] for the idea that any two things are or should be seen as equal assumes, by definition, that they can be placed at the same point on some agreed scale. Such a scale may be either quantitative or qualitative. The statement 'A is of equal weight to B' presupposes a crude, quantitative scale – that is, one which measures objects on a numerical basis; weight, for example, is measured in numbers of kilos or stones. We are not concerned with such basic measurements here. We are interested instead in claims like 'action C has an equal moral status to action D', or 'the Es and the Fs have morally equal lives' – qualitative claims which make sense only if we employ a more impressionistic, moral scale according to which C and D, or the Es and the Fs, are measured.

A qualitative scale clearly underpins certain statements – like 'lesbians and gays are equal to heterosexuals' – and demands, for example, for 'equality of sexuality'. These statements and demands beg two important questions about the meaning of 'equality' – as, indeed, does any equality argument which rests on a qualitative scale.[9] The first question is *what* the statement, demand or argument is comparing; the second is *why* it is assuming that the things being compared should be rated as morally equal. The distinction between each equality argument lies in the way in which it answers these two questions. If the answers are coherent, they can be used to found a law reform justification, provided that we also believe – as a matter of justice and political morality – that the law should treat like alike. Unless pro-equality justifications can supply a coherent answer to both questions, however, they are likely to prove unacceptably ambiguous. We will now consider each question in turn.

Conduct or status? The 'what' question

It is not uncommon for supporters of equality arguments to offer blurred answers to the question of what their argument is comparing. During heated political debate, the importance of precision can easily be overlooked, but if equality arguments are to be presented in their strongest form, we need to be clear about exactly what unit of comparison they entail. For example, at least two interpretations are possible of Tony Blair's and Chris Smith's comments about ages of consent: they might have been claiming either that lesbians and gays are morally equal – all-things-considered – to heterosexuals *as people*; or, more narrowly, that sexual intercourse between men is – considered as a *type of act* – morally equal to intercourse between a woman and a man. Each interpretation involves a different unit of comparison and allows, in consequence, for a different range of laws to be justified (depending upon the exact qualitative scale in play).

A similar ambiguity can be found in the difficult status/conduct distinction in US constitutional law (originally discussed in chapter 2). In the *Watkins*[10] and *High Tech Gays*[11] cases, the US Court of Appeals was required to consider whether military regulations penalizing lesbians and gays were permissible under the Equal Protection provisions of the US Constitution. The Court was able to reach different conclusions in each case – despite their close factual similarity – according to whether the relevant regulations were interpreted as penalizing an individual's *status* as a lesbian or gay person (that is, their sexual orientation), or the sexual acts which they engaged in with persons of the same sex (that is, their sexual *conduct*). Unequal treatment because of conduct was found to be permissible, but not unequal treatment because of status – despite the uncertain boundary between the two.[12] Given the close factual similarities between the cases, this result appears ambiguous, and has caused much uncertainty in US constitutional law about the distinction between permissible and impermissible legal regulation. The lesson is that unless we are clear about what any equality-based philosophical justification for law or law reform is comparing and claiming to be equal, similar confusions are likely to occur. Unfortunately, as the following analysis will suggest, neither of the obvious units of comparison – conduct and status – is particularly satisfactory.

A conduct-based interpretation of the House of Commons age of consent arguments would (once the second, 'why' question had been answered) maintain that all consenting sexual acts between people aged sixteen or over are – and should be treated as though they are – morally equal. This, however, is more of an argument for general sexual liberty than for equality. It has already been suggested that equality arguments entail comparisons. Usually, we think of a comparison as involving two or more things which are fairly precisely defined (how, otherwise, can they be compared?) and which may initially appear to be distinct. An equality argument which compared statuses would be measuring as equal two defined, apparently distinct groups of human beings – lesbians and gays on the one hand, heterosexuals on the other. Since a conduct-based interpretation would concern only types of behaviour, however, it would not in itself entail any comparison between distinct groups of people (at least unless we assume that the range of acts in which a person engages is synonymous with their status as a member of a group – something which is not, as we shall see below, a particularly plausible claim in relation to sexual orientation).

Given that a conduct-based interpretation has no secure group-related mooring, it can therefore potentially require us to draw a comparison between the sexual acts of an entire society – all such acts being ranked as equal so long as they involve people aged sixteen or over who have consented. This 'comparison' is so general – involving the behaviour of almost every adult in the society concerned – that it more closely resembles a general statement about the morality of all sexually active adults, rather than a comparison of distinct groups in the sense described above. An issue which concerns all (or nearly all) members of a society is more easily seen as a general liberty issue, rather than a narrower, comparative, equality issue, for things are usually described as liberties only when they are capable of affecting everyone (or at least everyone who falls within a wide class, such as citizens). A conduct-based interpretation might therefore be attacked as internally inconsistent, since it claims to work as an interpretation of equality although it is better seen as liberty-driven.

A conduct-based comparison would also be likely to appear unattractive on its merits, if used as part of an equality-driven law reform justification: for, while such a justification could offer a wider range of protections than a privacy argument, its reason for granting them would be controversial. It would allow lesbians and gays to be protected from employment discrimination, but only because such discrimination would be seen as an impermissible response to their actual or perceived sexual behaviour – the impermissibility stemming from the assumption that all consenting sexual acts must be treated equally. The reason for legal protection would thus be one which, like privacy, interprets lesbian and gay sexuality as a range of sexual encounters and no more – an interpretation which was dismissed in chapter 6 as unattractive. All things considered, a conduct-based approach to equality must therefore be seen as unhelpful.

In fact, it seems far more likely that the reformist speakers in the 1994 House of Commons debate favoured the use of status as their unit of comparison. For this would fit neatly with the perception – implicit in the comments made by Tony Blair and Chris Smith – of lesbians and gays as a sort of socially persecuted 'ethnic minority' group, with sexual orientation discrimination being conceptually similar to sex and race discrimination. Such a perception has been popular with campaigners for much of the 1980s.[13] As Steven Epstein suggests, lesbians and gays have nowadays come

> to conceptualize themselves as a legitimate minority group, having a certain 'ethnic' status, and deserving the same protections against discrimination that are claimed by other groups in our society. To be gay . . . [has become] something like being Italian, black, or Jewish.[14]

The 'ethnic minority' approach fits neatly with the use of a status-based unit of comparison for the following reason. If someone is a member of a socially disfavoured minority group, it is this status – rather than their individual behaviour – which can be seen, at root, as the basis for the social discrimination they experience. An individual's behaviour may sometimes fuel the perception (held either by themselves or by others) that they are part of a particular group, or that they are an aggressive member of that group. Perceived group membership cannot usually be lost, however, by abstention from the acts which are typically associated with the group – or even by repudiation of the group itself. In a hostile social environment, a celibate gay man who is open about his sexual orientation is just as likely to be attacked as a promiscuous gay man, for example, in the same way that a black woman who is ashamed of her social and ethnic origins is just as likely to be abused by racialist whites as one who is proud. In both cases, it is the victim's *perceived* status as a member of a despised group which counts, rather than their own individual behaviour or attitudes to the group concerned. It follows logically that an equality-based response to social discrimination should fasten primarily on the victim's social *status*, rather than their behaviour. We might, of course, reasonably argue that the types of sexual act in which individual X willingly engages are relevant to our overall moral assessment of X considered as a person (has X taken care to avoid exploiting their sexual partner/s, physically or emotionally, for example?) — but this is relevant when assessing X's personal morality, rather than the reach of equality-based law reform justifications.

If equality arguments are to turn on status, then we need to know how people can be classified as being within the lesbian and gay 'ethnic minority'. For it is only possession of such a status which will entitle them, subject to a satisfactory answer to the 'why' question, to equality-based protection. Lesbians and gays have nothing as visible as a shared skin-colour to unite them, so campaigners have tended to associate their would-be 'ethnic' status with the possession of a lesbian or gay *identity*. Diana Fuss has argued that the notion of 'identity politics' now has

> notably wide currency in gay and lesbian communities. In common usage, the term . . . refers to the tendency to base one's politics on a sense of personal identity — as gay, as Jewish, as black, as female. . . . Identity politics has been taken up by gay activists as something of a rallying cry to stimulate personal awareness and political action.[15]

Jeffrey Weeks suggests that identity is

> about belonging, about what you have in common with some people and what differentiates you from others. At its most basic it gives you a sense of personal location, the stable core to your individuality. But it is also about your social relationships, your complex involvement with others . . .[16]

Indeed, the sense of a common lesbian and gay identity was, Weeks argues, 'probably stronger at the end of the 1980s than at any previous time'.[17] This perhaps explains the current popularity, among campaigners, of equality-driven law reform arguments: since such arguments usually rely on the idea of a lesbian and gay identity as the underpinning for their status-based unit of comparison, support for equality arguments and a sense of identity can easily be felt to go hand-in-hand.

At a personal level, one's identity as a lesbian or gay man is undoubtedly valuable. As Jeffrey Weeks suggests:

> For many in the modern world . . . it is an absolutely fundamental concept, offering a sense of personal unity, social location, and even at times a political commitment. . . . to say 'I am gay', 'I am a lesbian' . . . is to make a statement about belonging . . .[18]

The whole idea of 'coming out' – originally inspired by liberationist thinking, and nowadays fundamental to the idea of a stable and successful life as a lesbian or gay man – is inspired by the belief that it is good to assert one's sexual identity, rather than hiding one's sexuality as a guilty secret. In stressing the clear personal value of identity, however, it is important not to lose sight of the broader political picture. For, when used as the basis for comparison underpinning any equality claim, lesbian and gay identity proves to be profoundly unreliable. Equality arguments which make use of the idea of lesbian and gay identity – in practice, any argument which invokes status as a unit of comparison – are fatally weakened by three problems. The first two relate specifically to the concept of lesbian and/or gay identity; the third also undermines personal identity-based justifications for laws protecting people from hostile treatment on the ground of race, sex, etc.[19] We will now discuss each problem in turn.

We encountered the first – and arguably the most fundamental – problem in chapter 3. Justifications for laws and law reform need to remain comprehensible and plausible for a long period of time, for any new law, once created, will almost inevitably be long-lasting. This being so, no worthwhile justification should seek to rely on a possibly short-term unit of social understanding. As we have already seen, however, the concept of a lesbian and/or gay identity has only recently come into general circulation as a way in which people who are attracted to those of the same sex understand themselves. Following the moderate constructionist account adopted in chapter 3, it is clear that the ancient Greeks had no lesbian or gay identity,[20] despite their frequent indulgence in what would now be called homosexual acts. The Victorian English would not have understood such an identity, and neither would those who were homosexually active in pre-1960s England. The word 'gay' only became a popular form of self-description with the rise of the Gay Liberation

Front, and after that, it was many years before the word was accepted by society at large as an appropriate label for people who were attracted to those of the same sex. Equally, the currently-popular idea of lesbians and gays as a form of ethnic minority – with a clear identity relating to this status – has only really been popular *among lesbians and gays* since the 1980s.

Obviously, most if not all social categorizations change over time. People now known as lesbians and gays have, however, been more prone to redefinition than most. This may well be an indirect consequence of the social hostility and legal sanctions which have long been directed – in western societies – at those who practice same-sex sexual acts. Given that greater social tolerance has only been seen in recent years – the situation still being far from full social and legal acceptance – it is perhaps inevitable that any identity category is, in this context, more changeable than in others. This point is perhaps underlined by the recent attacks on the idea of a gay identity mounted by those campaigning from the perspective of queer theory.[21] This suggests, however, that while the current idea of a lesbian and/or gay identity is a healthy, valuable ingredient in many people's lives, it is perhaps trusting too much to fortune to rely on it as a crucial ingredient in a justification which will need to remain comprehensible for a long time.[22] For present-day law reform measures designed to protect or improve the social position of lesbians and gays will need the support of a justification which will be comprehensible – or at least, comprehensible once adapted – years from now. Without such a justification, the apparent legitimacy of any reforms may disappear with time, leaving them politically exposed, especially given that social hostility towards lesbians and gays is unlikely to die out in the immediate future (a related question is whether it is even legitimate – as opposed to politically efficacious – to seek to entrench any current identity category in law, arguably stifling social development[23]). As Jeffrey Weeks observes, identities 'reflect the variety of individual and social needs in the modern world. Such needs are in constant flux, and change over time. They cannot be frozen by any moral system.'[24] It would thus be politically foolish to employ, as the unit of comparison on which a justification rests, an identity whose longevity has not been tested, and which may become otiose in the future. Indeed, only essentialists could coherently support the idea that an identity-dependent law reform justification would have guaranteed long-term validity – and the essentialist understanding of social categories was rejected in chapter 3.[25] In the langauge of chapter 4, reliance on an identity-based unit of comparison will cause a justification to fail for irrelevance.

The second problem is whether it is possible adequately – and acceptably – to define the lesbian and/or gay identity which is to be used as the unit of comparison in any equality justification. Steven Seidman suggests that 'The notion of a unitary gay identity has been fundamental to the evolving gay communities of the 1980s.'[26] Before relying on such an identity as the unit of comparison in an equality-based justification, however, it is clearly necessary to have a fairly precise idea of what it is (as well as what is meant by the heterosexual identity with which it is to be compared). Serious doubts have been raised, however, about whether any unified notion of a lesbian and gay identity is actually possible. Angelia Wilson stresses the 'inability of some groups to offer a coherent account of exactly who they are',[27] and suggests that:

> the lesbian, gay and bisexual 'community' – and the quotation marks are necessary here – may be loosely held together by a shared oppression experienced in our heterosexist society. But . . . [t]he fundamental tensions that arose in the early days of activism between gay men and lesbian separatists undoubtedly prove that we do not, and do not wish to, share a 'way of life'.[28]

The differences of outlook, aspiration and lifestyle among gay men and lesbians, and among subgroups within these categories, means – according to Wilson – that a unified notion of a common lesbian *and* gay identity is unrealistic.[29] In similar vein, Jeffrey Weeks – who, it was noted earlier, suggests that at the end of the 1980s, the sense of a common lesbian and gay identity was stronger than ever before – also believes that the composition of the lesbian and gay 'community'

> was more complexly varied than ever before. The development of the community provided a context in which individuals could define themselves more precisely around specific sexual needs and desires, and in terms of other common belongings, such as those related to race and ethnicity or disability.[30]

Weeks stresses the growing differences between lesbian and gay male subcultures and identities, the former being 'less commercial than the male, and less explicitly oriented around sexual pleasure'.[31] And, within lesbianism itself, splits have emerged since the early 1980s between those who see their sexuality as a purely sexual identity, those who see it as a mixed sexual–political identity, and those who see it as a purely political identity.[32]

These differences of outlook suggest that it is impossible readily to define any unified lesbian and gay identity. If we insist on relying on identity as the bedrock of an equality justification, we are therefore forced into one of two alternative methods of analysis. On the one hand, the apparently wide range of possible understandings of a lesbian and/or gay identity might be forcibly condensed into one amalgam, creating a concept which can more easily be compared with the heterosexual. Steven Seidman suggests that this is largely what happened in lesbian and gay identity-based political campaigns in the 1980s: campaigners invoked a unified identity which was white, male and middle-class, marginalizing the experiences of black and disabled lesbians and gay men.[33] 'Gay' came to signify 'the experience of a white, middle-class, urban culture organized around sex, consumerism, and civil rights'.[34] On the other hand, the full range of different lesbian and gay identities could be acknowledged and celebrated by campaigners – but at the risk, as Jeffrey Weeks suggests, that 'what people had in common would be lost through asserting differences, the moral merits of "multiple oppressions" and one's place in a hierarchy of oppression'.[35] Neither possibility seems particularly attractive: the experiences of very many lesbians and gays would either be discounted as part of a drive to assert a unified identity – a potentially oppressive approach – or differences could be celebrated, but at the cost of political coherence. An identity-based unit of comparison would lead either to substantively unattractive or to ambiguous or implausible results.

The third problem with the notion of lesbian and/or gay identity is that even if it could adequately be defined, it would be unrealistic to suppose that everyone who is sexually attracted to or has sexual relations with people of the same sex could necessarily be seen as possessing such an identity. As Jeffrey Weeks suggests:

> not all homosexually inclined people want to identify their minority status – or even see themselves as homosexual. Sexologists, at least since Kinsey, have pointed out that there is no necessary connection between sexual behaviour and sexual identity. . . . There are some people who identify as gay and participate in the gay community but

do not experience or wish for homosexual activity. And there are homosexually active people who do not identify as gay.[36]

An obvious example of this latter category of person is the married man who has occasional, secret sexual encounters with other men. Typically, such people cannot bring themselves openly to acknowledge their homosexual inclinations, and are often deeply ashamed of them. The whole idea of 'coming out' as lesbian or gay involves the shedding of such fears and inhibitions. To overlook the distinction between ways of acting and ways of identifying is to deny the importance of this basic step. Jeffrey Weeks succinctly notes that 'Identity is not a destiny but a choice.'[37] And, as John D'Emilio suggests, a sexual identity:

> has to be discovered and accepted. One can choose not to accept it, or one can choose to hide it. At the very least, this suggests that the history of lesbian and gay politics is as much the history of the creation and elaboration of a self-conscious community and culture as it is the story of a social movement.[38]

Same-sex sexual acts may always have occurred, but the modern lesbian and gay political movement could only emerge when individual lesbians and gays had created the idea of an identity for themselves. As D'Emilio observes: 'The idea that homosexuals were a minority, that they were the targets of unjust treatment, had to be disseminated and at least somewhat internalized throughout the culture.'[39]

This pinpoints the third difficulty with an identity-based equality justification – a difficulty which involves its being torn between artificiality and under-inclusiveness. As we already know, justifications should identify the moral wrong involved in the things or actions prohibited by the laws which they underpin. In logic, an identity-based equality justification will see the wrong involved in the adverse treatment of lesbians and gays as being the unequal treatment of persons of morally equal sexual identities. If this formulation is strictly applied, however, it leaves us with no basis for protecting people who engage in same-sex sexual acts (or who wish to) but who strenuously *reject* a lesbian or gay identity for themselves.

In reaching this conclusion, the crucial point to remember is that from the perspective of 'coming out' (and from that of lesbian and gay law reform campaigning) it is *personal* identity which is important – that is, a person's *self-definition* rather than a label which other people (or society as a whole) has attached to them. Clearly, a person's self-definition needs ideally to be understood by others, and will usually be constructed using common social concepts. Nevertheless, others cannot meaningfully say that X now has a personal identity of a particular sort unless X *actually subscribes* to the values or behaviour associated with that identity (and even then, it is unlikely that X will understand or relate to those values and behaviour in exactly the same way as Y, who shares the identity: otherwise, everyone with that personal identity would be effectively the same).[40] To say otherwise would be to discount the intensely personal nature and value of an identity, or the idea of 'coming out' to a lesbian or gay identity. It must follow logically that an identity-based unit of comparison cannot – at least in this context – embrace those who reject the identity concerned. There clearly *are* social situations where other people do ascribe an identity to individuals against their will – the small boy bullied at school for being 'queer' because he does not like sport, for example. The small boy may not yet have experienced a sexual desire, however, and may grow up to live a promiscuously heterosexual life. The 'identity' which his schoolmates attach to him is a derogatory social label, not the very *personal* sense of identity which lies at the root of the type of equality-based justification we are considering.

We might, of course, artificially broaden our understanding of a lesbian or gay identity to include people who personally reject it, thereby bringing them within the reach of an equality justification. Discarding our basic definition of identity would be to cast logic to the winds, however – a manoeuvre amounting to an abandonment of the search for a properly defensible law reform justification. In any event, ascribing an identity to someone when they positively reject it would be a dubiously authoritarian and unattractive way of trying to 'protect' them. We would effectively be saying that regardless of their own self-definition, a person could not legitimately secure legal protection *until* they accepted an identity or had it thrust upon them. People attach radically differing significance to their own race, gender or sexual orientation, and it may well be that many people possess a series of identities into which they slip depending on the social role they are currently filling. Stressing that a particular identity must *always* be seen as the crucial unit of comparison in an equality-driven justification is simply to blank out a crucial element of human individuality.

Alternatively, we might concede that a personal identity-based justification cannot be used to defend those who reject a lesbian or gay identity – like the married man arrested for public homosexual activity – but retain it for those who do possess one. In terms of legal protection, however, the results would be distinctly sporadic: for two identical actions (the dismissal of two employees suspected to be gay or lesbian, for example) would entail different moral wrongs according to the self-definition of the victim. This is difficult to reconcile with the argument, made earlier, that social discrimination generally hinges on the perceived status of the victim, rather than on their actual behaviour. For a person's perceived status – the social label sense of 'identity' – is, as we have seen in the small boy example, unlikely to be affected by something as imperceptible as self-definition – suggesting that a self-definition (i.e., personal identity)-based response is unlikely to be effective in challenging that discrimination. Such a response would probably produce morally arbitrary and implausible results anyway: for we would need to know how strongly someone had to appreciate a particular identity before it could be seen as their self-definition, what constituted the rejection of an identity (something which is likely to be highly dependent on circumstances), and so on. These arguments suggest that it is logically preferable to abandon personal identity as our unit of comparison. The idea of a lesbian or gay identity is clearly valuable for many people as individuals, but personal identity is just too variable a concept to be used as part of a *general* justification for protective laws or for law reform – that is, as part of the reason for saying 'it is *always* wrong to discriminate against lesbians and gays because . . .'.

This conclusion is reinforced by Janet Halley's discussion of the US cases involving challenges to the constitutionality of discharges from military service due to a person's actual or perceived lesbian or gay sexuality. Halley points out that those who tried to challenge their dismissal ranged from a man who had committed a homosexual act on a one-off basis and bitterly regretted it afterwards, through to a boldly open, self-affirming lesbian. To regard both these people as sharing a *common* sexual identity – something we would have to do if personal identity were the basic unit of comparison in an equality-based justification – is plainly artificial. Their only shared experience, Halley argues, is a life-altering rejection stemming from their treatment at the hands of the military authorities.[41] Halley thus rejects – rightly, it is submitted – 'doctrinal argument that defines who we are in ways that some of us object to and cannot, and will not, conform to'.[42]

This particular identity problem is not confined to cases involving adverse treatment due to a person's sexual orientation, as the facts of the well-known English case, *De Souza* v. *A.A.*, neatly illustrate.[43] The case was brought by a black secretary who had overheard her work manager using a racially abusive term to describe her to a colleague. The central legal issue was whether overhearing such a remark amounted to a 'detriment' under section 2(4)(c) of the Race Relations Act 1976, entitling the secretary to bring a claim for direct discrimination. The court controversially found that it did not, ruling that a reasonable coloured secretary would merely feel distressed rather than positively disadvantaged by such a comment.[44] Leaving aside the dubious validity of this observation, the important point for present purposes is *why* the secretary might have felt insulted by her manager's comment. On the one hand, it could certainly have undermined her pride in her personal identity as a black woman. It is also possible, though, that the secretary had no personal identity relating to her ethnic origins, or even that she believed in the integration of all ethnic groups into a homogenous culture and positively rejected the notion of an ethnic identity – in which case, an alternative description of her hurt would have to be found. The fact that we do not know how Ms De Souza felt or how she defined herself shows how unreliable it is just to assume that the moral hurt done to her related to her personal identity as a black woman, and to say, as a consequence, that any equality-driven justification for granting her a legal remedy must rest on that identity as its unit of comparison. This underlines the unreliable role of something as individual and variable as a personal identity in helping to provide a general justification for legal coercion.

Another aspect of this third identity-related problem concerns whether justifications can claim to be of universal or purely local validity. We concluded in chapter 4 that it was unduly arrogant to claim universal validity for any justification, given that social understandings change across cultures and across time, but that it was nevertheless useful to try to construct a justification which would be as widely comprehensible as possible, if only through dialogue with other cultures. The problem with an equality justification which depends upon the distinctly recent, distinctly local notion of a lesbian and gay identity is that it would make dialogue with other cultures difficult. For, if the idea of a lesbian and gay identity is not accepted among all lesbians and gays in the west, it is unlikely to have resonance in more authoritarian regimes elsewhere. One reason for rejecting an essentialist view of sexuality was that, by trying to interpret earlier eras in terms of current social concepts, it failed properly to understand or to represent them. A similar outcome is likely, in relation to any current political dialogue with or analysis of other cultures, if excess weight is placed on the idea of a lesbian and gay identity.[45]

The 'why' question

So far, we have seen that neither the conduct- nor the status/identity-based interpretations can provide a satisfactory answer to the question of *what* an equality argument is comparing. We must now consider *why* any equality argument should count certain things as morally equal. For the statement 'Y and Z are [morally] equal' tells us nothing without an explanation of why they should be seen as equal. Any explanation must invoke theories of justice, political, and sometimes sexual morality, which will provide the qualitative scale used to rank as equal the things being compared.[46] In his House of Commons speech concerning ages of consent, for example, Tony Blair MP pointed out that:

> the most basic civilised value is the notion of respect for other people. That is what creates and sustains any decent society. That is why crime is wrong; that is why violent and abusive behaviour is wrong; that is why racial abuse is wrong. It is also why it is wrong to treat a man as inferior because his sexuality is different.[47]

The moral theory underpinning Blair's equality argument seems to be the notion of mutual respect, which determines that consenting sexual acts between people aged 16 or over merit equal treatment by the law, whatever the sex of the participants – as do those who participate in such acts. As Blair himself suggested: 'That is the moral case for change tonight. . . . [equalizing the law] is our chance to do good, and we should take it.'[48]

Several other underpinning theories are possible, but we do not need to consider them individually here, for their very existence ultimately reveals a fatal flaw in justifications which claim to be based solely on equality. This will become clear if we consider Peter Tatchell's strongly worded liberationist attack on equality justifications, and possible responses to it. Tatchell suggests that any equality claim must be seeking 'conformity with the straight status quo. Instead of social transformation, it aspires to assimilation . . . much of the contemporary gay rights agenda is about queers adapting to hetero society.'[49] The centrepiece of Tatchell's argument is that:

> Winning law reform and equality with straights ... means little more than homo conformity with hetero society. *We* comply with *their* system. It is parity on heterosexual terms – equal rights within a framework determined and dominated by straights. Our worth should be measured on *our* terms, as opposed to the criteria laid down by heteros.[50]

Tatchell does not explain in much detail how equality amounts to assimilation, but his argument must, in logic, run as follows. Equality claims (status- *and* acts-based) involve a comparison between some relevant aspect of lesbian and gay sexuality (i.e., a person's status as a lesbian or gay man, or their participation in same-sex sexual acts) and an equivalent aspect of heterosexuality. The implicit message of this comparison is that the relevant lesbian and gay aspect is acceptable *only* so long as it has a clear heterosexual counterpart. Where the lesbian and gay aspect is accepted, therefore, it is not on its own terms, but because it is equivalent to something heterosexual; by contrast, anything about the lesbian and gay aspect which has no heterosexual equivalent falls outside the scope of things which can be compared, and cannot be protected using an equality argument. In both cases, the heterosexual – as the basis for the equality comparison – is taken as the unchallengeable social norm, showing equality claims to be both weak and conservative. Such claims are not, according to this view, saying that there is anything morally good in lesbian or gay sexuality *per se* (whether understood in terms of status or acts). Rather, protection is only granted where – and because – lesbian and gay sexuality is similar enough to heterosexuality (which does involve a moral good) that the two cannot consistently be treated differently.[51]

Supporters of the Tatchell critique might therefore suggest that equality arguments could have nothing to say about societies where the sex lives of *all* adults are equally repressed. They could not, for example, be used to support law reform in societies where people were only allowed to have sexual relationships with partners chosen by their local priest (so long as we assume that the priests picked roughly equal numbers of same-sex as opposite-sex partners); or where employers regularly dismissed their workers for kissing one another in the street (again, assuming the sex of those kissing did not affect the likelihood of dismissal); or where no one – male or female, lesbian, gay or heterosexual – was allowed to have sex until they were 25 (assuming that the police enforced this law just as strongly whatever the sex and sexual orientation of those who broke it). Since there is no inequality of treatment in these hypothetical examples, equality arguments would, according to the Tatchell view, have nothing to criticize, even though the societies concerned seem highly intrusive in their regulation of sexual behaviour. This suggests that the ways in which equality arguments can work as justifications – if they can work meaningfully as justifications at all – will depend entirely on the circumstances of the societies to which they are applied. This point, if true, means that equality arguments fail to match their objects up with any general, non-comparative moral good: the law is not required to protect consenting sexual acts, or to prohibit discrimination in the workplace, because of something which is independently good about lesbian or gay sexuality. Rather, these things only merit protection where a comparison with the treatment of heterosexuals – something which varies from society to society – dictates that they should. This must – if true – leave equality arguments as distinctly thin justifications for laws or law reform measures which support consenting same-sex sexual behaviour and the expression of lesbian or gay sexuality more generally. The usefulness of equality arguments as *general* justifications for laws or law reform would certainly be undermined.

A further implication of this argument is that equality justifications simply misconceive the social problem which lesbians and gays are trying to rectify via law reform and political campaigning. John D'Emilio, for example, observes that: 'Our movement may have begun as the struggle of a "minority", but what we should now be trying to "liberate" is an aspect of the personal lives of all people – sexual expression';[52] and that:

> the issue that gay men and lesbians are facing is not simply one of a minority struggling for civil rights or equality. The issue is sex and its place in society and individual lives. The call for minority rights is simply one way of framing part of this larger issue – an issue that taps into the deepest layers of human and social irrationality.[53]

How one categorizes the 'issue' is, of course, often heavily bound up with one's more general political views and one's perception of which law reform justification is appropriate. Given D'Emilio's apparently liberationist perspective, it is thus no surprise that he should see a 'minority rights' model as deficient. It might also plausibly be claimed, in response to D'Emilio, that while social and legal discrimination against lesbians and gays is undoubtedly part of the general social unease about sexual topics prevalent in many western societies, D'Emilio's own characterization fails to place sufficient weight on the burden of discrimination borne by lesbians and gays as a group.

D'Emilio's argument may contain a glimmer of validity, however. If we think once again of the society where no one were allowed to have sex until they were 25, it would surely seem strange to claim, on the basis that the imaginary society has an equal age of consent and does not discriminate on the basis of sexual identity, that a 17-year-old gay male would be better off there (assuming that the criminal law was rigorously enforced) than in the UK. For in the UK, the 17-year-old would only have to wait for a year before being allowed to have sex legally; in the imaginary society, he would have to wait eight years under a strongly enforced criminal law. The conclusion that the UK position is worse must, however, follow if we believe that inequality – however defined – is the key issue. A common-sense understanding of the imaginary society example would surely suggest, by contrast, that a purely equality-based focus is just too narrow to capture the real harm done by laws which regulate consenting sexual behaviour in such an intrusive fashion. The example highlights the very different understandings offered by perceptions which are equality-driven, and those which are driven by liberty, empowerment or some other value. This is surely testimony, however, to the limitations of a strict equality justification.

It is in fact possible to rebut Peter Tatchell's anti-assimilationist critique – but only at the price of underlining the fatal flaw in solely equality-based justifications. The means of rebuttal lies is the distinction developed by Ronald Dworkin – originally noted in chapter 4 – between the state treating people *equally* in the distribution of resources or opportunities, and treating them *as equals* in the sense that they are entitled to its equal concern and respect.[54] Dworkin's arguments about equality are based on his deeper, resources-based liberal political theory,[55] and they are relevant here because Tatchell's critique only carries weight when used against equality defined as equal treatment.

A crucial difference between Dworkin's ideas of equal treatment and treatment as equals lies in the type of comparison which each involves.

Equal treatment requires only a crude evaluation of whether two people or actions are sufficiently 'the same' that they merit identical treatment by the state. Dworkin does not develop the idea at length, but equal treatment would seem to involve bare, unsophisticated comparisons which turn on outward appearances, thus allowing existing social norms to be reinforced. Any justification which advocated unsophisticated equal treatment would therefore fall foul of the Tatchell critique.

Treatment as equals – for Dworkin, the truly meaningful sense of equality – is, however, fuller and more flexible. The question is not 'whether any deviation [from equal/identical treatment] is permitted, but what reasons for deviation are consistent with equal concern and respect'.[56] To treat people as equals, the state must have regard for their individual capacities, aspirations and circumstances. These vary from person to person, so the state may well end up treating people differently in crude material terms, while showing equal regard for them as individuals given their personal characteristics or social situations. Treatment as equals sometimes requires equal treatment, but not always. Dworkin thus suggests that where a limited amount of emergency relief is available for two equally populated areas damaged by flooding, treating the citizens of both as equals will involve giving more money to the more heavily damaged area.[57] This is not identical treatment, but it shows equivalent concern – in the light of their circumstances – for all who are affected. In similar vein, treating people as equals means that those 'with a lively sense of their own equal worth, and pride in their own convictions, can . . . accept certain grounds for carrying special burdens for the community as a whole'.[58]

Treatment of people as equals therefore tends to be comparative only in a very loose sense. People are not crudely compared with others to see whether they match up to hard social norms. Rather, the focus is on the ways in which the state is required to give individuals concern and respect in the light of their characteristics and circumstances. This explains Dworkin's reason for claiming that political decisions must generally avoid any concern to promote a particular vision of the good life (originally discussed in chapter 4), for people's conceptions of such a life will differ, and the state would not be treating them as equals if it preferred one view over another. Instead: 'government . . . must impose no sacrifice or constraint on any citizen in virtue of an argument that the citizen could not accept without abandoning his sense of his equal worth'.[59] Equality of concern and respect therefore allows people to live an unpopular life free from state interference[60] – and a lesbian or gay person would be forced to abandon their sense of equal worth if they were to believe that the community would be better if their sexual orientation were eradicated.[61]

The loosely comparative element of this conception of equality only really comes into play when the state is determining what type of – and how much – assistance to give particular citizens. Stephen Guest interprets Dworkin as suggesting that 'Treating a person as an equal means treating him in such a way as to give him maximum freedom to develop his life in accordance with his convictions.'[62] This being so, some people may need to have their potential freedoms pushed upwards towards the level enjoyed by the average person[63] – a measurement which must involve comparisons to determine what counts as the average level. More broadly, however, any legal attack on a person's sexual orientation would be understood – and criticized – in terms of the state's obligation to uphold that person's sense of equal worth.

Dworkin's idea of treatment as equals is clearly broad enough – and sufficiently independent of the circumstances of individual societies – to avoid falling foul of Tatchell's assimilationist critique. It leaves us, though, with a major problem. For the comparative element in Dworkin's theory is actually so weak – and so far from the heart of Dworkin's argument – that it seems wrong to describe treatment as equals as a genuinely equality-driven approach. Dworkin himself suggests that defining what is meant by treating people as equals is 'the *same question* as the question of what it means for the government to treat all its citizens as free, or as independent, or with equal dignity'.[64] Joseph Raz has therefore perceptively suggested that Dworkin is really using the word 'equality' as a rhetorical device, rather than as the analytical basis for his theory.[65]

To be genuinely egalitarian, Raz claims, an argument must relate to equality in a way absent in other principles, and must explain why equality is, in and of itself, a moral good.[66] In most equality arguments – including Dworkin's – however, the word 'equality' just gives added political appeal to moral goods which would be moral goods even if the word were taken away.[67] Tony Blair's House of Commons speech, discussed above, might be analysed in much the same way given the notion of 'mutual respect' on which it relies. Looked at analytically, Raz suggests, rhetorical arguments of this sort are not designed to promote equality but rather to promote the cause of those who qualify under independently valid principles . . . principles of equal respect or concern, etc., often amount to little more than an assertion that all human beings are moral subjects, to an assertion of humanism. Such principles can be expressed with equal ease without invoking equality. They are not designed to increase equality but to encourage recognition that the well-being of all human beings counts.[68]

The strength of this point is shown by the fact that even Stephen Guest – who seeks to defend Dworkin's theory against Raz – opts for just the same 'rhetorical' mode, leaving Raz's point about the analytical nature of equality arguments effectively unanswered. Indeed, Guest is happy to suggest that Dworkin's theory of treatment as equals may be seen in terms of ideas of 'common humanity' – some distance indeed from strict, analytical equality.[69]

The fatal flaw in equality-based justifications becomes clearer if we pursue Raz's reasoning a little further. The flaw lies in the fact – mentioned briefly earlier – that *all* equality justifications must, as a matter of logic, presuppose that the people, actions, or things they are comparing are in some way morally valuable: for otherwise, such comparisons would be pointless. To determine why the things being compared are morally valuable, however, we need to invoke some distinct scale of value.[70] For, while genuine equality arguments can stipulate what is to be compared – sexual acts, sexual identities, etc. – they cannot in themselves explain why such things are morally valuable. As Raz suggests:

> we only have reason to care about inequalities in the distributions of *goods* and *ills*, that is of what is of value or disvalue for independent reasons. There is no reason to care about inequalities in the distribution of grains of sand, unless there is some other reason to wish to have or avoid sand.[71]

To argue that it is wrong for the law to treat lesbians and gays more harshly than heterosexuals, therefore, we need first to assume that there is something independently good about lesbian and gay sexuality (defined in terms of acts or identity) which makes such inequality morally bad.[72] The statistical fact of the inequality cannot, in itself, supply us with any argument for law reform. If it could, then convicted rapists or child molesters might claim that it was wrong for the law to treat them unequally by comparison with adults who only engage in sexual relations with fully consenting parties. Of course, rape and child abuse are in fact prohibited for strong, independent moral reasons – which, it will be argued in the next section of this chapter, also explain why consenting sexual activity is or should be protected.

The fatal flaw in justifications which claim to be based, analytically speaking, on equality arguments is that they are internally inconsistent, for they claim to be advancing one good while in fact advancing whatever earlier, independent moral arguments they happen to presuppose. They can therefore be rejected. Ronald Dworkin's treatment as equals theory is perhaps best seen as an attempt to overcome this problem of prior moral goods, given that it seeks itself to supply the reason for why failure to offer equality of concern and respect is wrong. The difficulty here, though, is that the rhetoric of equality which the theory employs helps to disguise its true nature – something which is unhelpful in the area of justifications for law reform. As Raz suggests, '[t]he price we pay is in intellectual confusion', given that the theory is presented in a way which fails to explain its true structure.[73]

The failure of equality-based justifications does not mean, however, that there is no role whatever for equality in relation to lesbian and gay issues. In fact, it can play two useful roles – the first political, the second analytical. First, as Joseph Raz implicitly acknowledges, the invocation of equality is not a problem so long as it is used and seen as a purely rhetorical flourish which backs up a coherent independent justification, rather than as a justification in its own right. For appeals to 'equality' clearly have strong political appeal in modern western societies, and there is no harm in using equality – like appeals to 'lesbian and gay rights' – as a campaigning slogan, so long as it is made clear that it is no more than that.[74] Second, if an independent law reform justification works successfully, it is likely to produce some sort of equality, provided that 'equality' is understood as a loose, statistical label which roughly *describes* a desirable end-result (in the same sense that members of a society can be loosely described as 'happy' or 'friendly'), rather than as the justification for getting us to that position. In using the word 'equality' in either of these two senses, it will of course be necessary to avoid internal inconsistency by distinguishing between the true, independent ground of protection – the justification in play – and 'equality' as the slogan surrounding, or hoped-for statistical result of, that protection. It is to the substantive justification for legal protections which we now turn.

A new start: empowerment

In this section of the chapter, it will be argued that an empowerment-based justification can best support claims for the removal of intrusive criminal laws regulating lesbian and gay sexuality, for the creation of anti-discrimination laws, for the creation of rights publicly to express same-sex affection, and for the creation of full partnership and family rights. To be more precise, this justification identifies a distinct moral good in consenting human sexual behaviour (and sexuality more generally), and suggests that hostile laws and social practices violate this good by objectifying lesbians and gays in a dehumanizing sense by failing to treat them as choosing, feeling human subjects. An empowerment-based justification – supported by what will be characterized as a social democratic theory of justice and political morality – is therefore necessary to remedy this objectification and to protect the moral good associated with freely chosen sexual behaviour and conceptions of sexuality. If the laws which the justification legitimates can successfully counter the objectification of lesbians and gays (an issue which will be considered in chapter 8), hopefully this will result in a rough statistical pattern of equality of sexuality.

A more detailed examination of each aspect of this argument should make clear that the empowerment justification avoids the problems affecting the other justifications we have considered. Even if a convincing counter-argument could be raised against the empowerment justification, however, it is worthwhile remembering that this would not – in and of itself – entitle the state to regulate same-sex sexual acts and lesbian and gay sexuality in a hostile or intrusive fashion. For in a society where it is acknowledged that the state must show a sound justification before using law to regulate any area of life – many would call this a presumption in favour of liberty – the state cannot legitimately embark on an anti-lesbian or gay legislative programme without proper evidence that such a programme is necessary to counter some clear harm. Effectively, this means that two layers of philosophical argument can be deployed to counter the creation or application of hostile laws: first, there is the empowerment-based justification in favour of protecting and supporting lesbian and gay sexuality; and even if this justification could be rebutted, there is, second, the general presumption in favour of liberty, which militates against hostile laws in the absence of evidence that lesbian and gay sexuality entails some clear harm. And, as we saw in chapter 5, no convincing evidence of this sort exists.

The first element in the empowerment justification is the claim that sexuality – encompassing sexual desires, feelings, aspirations, emotions and behaviour – is of central importance for human beings, regardless of the ways in which sexual behaviour and sexual categories are interpreted from society to society. Sometimes, people value and desire sexual acts just as sexual acts; on other occasions, their value stems from their role as a central means of communicating affection and experiencing desire within a broader emotional relationship. Sexual freedom of action can thus be important either as a means (one of the most powerful means of expressing affection within an emotional relationship) or as an end (simple sexual communion and pleasure), and it is probably fair to say that most adults – especially in contemporary western societies – will have had a variety of sexual experiences in each category. As H. L. A. Hart observed as part of his defence of the Wolfenden Committee's proposals, sexual impulses form a strong part of each person's day-to-day life, and their suppression can affect 'the development or balance of the individual's emotional life, happiness, and personality'.[75] The expression of such impulses in the form of sexual activity can be a powerful means – and expression of – mutual and reciprocal sexual and/or emotional fulfilment. Sexual activity is thus an exchange – one of the strongest expressions of human interdependence, rather than just something of importance on an individual basis.

Why should sexuality – so conceived – be of such central value to each of us, however? The likeliest answer is that our individual sexual tastes, sexual and emotional encounters and attachments are probably the most centrally personal characteristics and experiences we have. Some people may, as a personal matter, value other activities more highly – playing the stock market or building tables, for example. Two factors mark sexual desire and activity out as *generally* more personal and valuable for most of us, however. The first is the unique degree of human interdependence which even the most casual sexual encounter involves. Initially, this interdependence may be purely physical; if a sexual encounter develops into a relationship, however, then the interdependence can become deeper and more emotional in character. The second factor is that sexual tastes vary almost infinitely – in terms of what we think makes someone a desirable sexual partner, or what makes something a pleasurable sexual act – and each person's tastes and fantasies go to the very heart of what it is, for them, to be the particular human being that they are. The modern notion of sexual orientation, in the sense of the sex of the person(s) to whom one is attracted, is just one aspect of this. Within the basic parameters of their sexual orientation, people are often able to conceptualize their ideal sexual tastes and fantasies more clearly than other types of taste or aspiration. Not everyone can fulfil their sexual ambitions, of course – but anyone can have aspirations. Each person's conception of sexuality is thus, in its way, unique and central to them.

The clear implication of this is, of course, that each person's understanding of what is, for them, desirable sexual and/or emotional contact should – with one clear exception – be respected.[76] The idea of sexual activity as definitionally 'private' fails properly to capture this idea, as does the notion that sexuality can be boiled down to a set of sexual encounters alone: for as we have seen, sexual activity can – according to circumstances – be important both as a means and as an end. A role can also be found for personal sexual identity here, although not the comparative role which the concept plays in status-based equality justifications. For, if personal sexual desire or fantasy is important and deserves respect, it follows logically that *each person's* understanding of their sexual identity deserves respect too. Some individuals may well choose to understand their sexual desires and behaviour in terms of a standard sexual identity – heterosexual, lesbian or gay; others may choose to define themselves in a more individual way. Since each individual's personal definition deserves respect in its own right – rather than as a standardized basis for comparison – the personal identity problems affecting status-based equality justifications are thus avoided. Obviously, these arguments run completely counter to the traditional Catholic view of the proper purposes and value of sexual intercourse, but such a view was rejected in chapter 5.

The clear exception to this notion of general respect for each person's conception of desirable sexuality and sexual activity concerns non-consenting sexual acts, epitomized by the act of rape. Of course, this is only an exception in so far as the rapist (who presumably regards the rape as a desirable – or at least an acceptable – means of attaining sexual satisfaction) is concerned. From the standpoint of the victim, the act lacks the value which attaches to freely chosen sexual activity, and it is this which helps explain why rapes are properly seen as illegitimate and wrong. It should be self-evident that for a sexual act to have value for a person, they must have freely chosen to participate in it, and to participate in the way they have – for without free choice, the second of the two factors explaining the value of sexual activity is missing.

Philosophically, we can gather these ideas together under the notion of a moral entitlement to autonomy. R. A. Duff has suggested that respect for a person as an autonomous subject requires respect for their integrity as a sexual agent, able to decide for themselves who to take as sexual partners.[77] Duff uses this moral argument to justify the criminal law's prohibition of rape, and it can be used just as strongly to explain why a person's sexual fantasies, aspirations and behaviour should be respected. Lack of consent obviously destroys the underlying reason for protection – namely, respecting people as autonomous sexual agents. If autonomy is to be taken seriously, however, then each individual's appreciation and definition of what is, for them, a valuable sexual act must be respected, so long as that definition encompasses only consenting sexual activity.[78] We will return to the notion of autonomy below – but for now, it should be clear that within the limits of consent, each person's conception and expressions of sexuality are important and morally valuable.

The second element of the empowerment justification is the argument that laws and social practices which are hostile towards lesbians and gays violate this sexual autonomy-related moral good. This argument can be developed both anecdotally and analytically. Anecdotally, it is useful to recall (from chapter 3) the *Report of the Secretary's Task Force on Youth Suicide* in the US – one of the clear conclusions of which was that laws prohibiting same-sex sexual acts or singling out lesbians and gays for special, hostile treatment can cause particular misery to lesbian and gay teenagers by helping to reinforce both their own lack of self-esteem and the idea that it is socially acceptable to deride and attack sexual minorities.[79] More basically, we also have H. L. A. Hart's observation that laws which prohibit same-sex sexual acts can *literally* frustrate people, for they 'may create misery of a quite special degree. . . . both the difficulties involved in the repression of sexual impulses and the consequences of repression are quite different from "ordinary" crime.'[80]

At a more general level, we can argue analytically that laws or social practices which target particular groups for unfavourable treatment work to objectify members of those groups. Group members are stigmatized as unworthy of full consideration as human beings because of a characteristic or characteristics which they are assumed to possess by virtue of their actual or perceived membership of the group. Characteristically, social sensitivity or controversy will attach to the group concerned, explaining why it has been singled out for hostile treatment. People are thus the victims of discrimination – whether socially or at the hands of the law – where they are treated as objects rather than as subjects, the objectification relating to their actual or perceived membership of the group in question and to characteristics which are assumed to attach to that group. Richard Mohr captures the normative aspects of this point rather less precisely in his suggestion that each person should be seen as 'a creature who has ends of his own, who can recognise others as having ends of their own, and so who is capable of respecting others . . . a subject conscious of herself as an agent with plans, projects, and a view of her own achievements'.[81]

In the context of lesbians and gays, the sexual autonomy argument considered above suggests that people are morally entitled to be considered as sexual subjects, and it is this which explains why social or legal hostility directed against lesbians and gays is morally wrong. Such hostility can, of course, assume many forms, ranging from direct physical assault through to legal regulation. Within the law itself, hostility may be overt and direct – the complete criminal prohibition of same-sex sexual acts, for example – or more indirect, as where employers are allowed to discriminate with impunity against lesbian or gay employees, or where public authorities can deny same-sex partners the right to succeed to a deceased lover's council property, or where same-sex couples are precluded from involvement in adoption or child-care. It is the social sensitivity surrounding lesbian and gay sexuality (or race, or gender) in many western societies which explains why hostile treatment because of a person's sexual orientation (or race, or gender) can count as objectification, whereas adverse treatment because of a non-sensitive characteristic – a person's intelligence, for example – may not.

Two points should be stressed in relation to this notion of objectification. The first – which concerns questions of identity – is that objectification does not depend, analytically, upon the idea of an individual's personal identity as a lesbian or gay man. Instead, society's objectification of lesbians and gays as a group involves the 'social label' sense of identity – which we discussed earlier (see p. 247). In terms of the present discussion, the objectification of lesbians and gays as a perceived social group involves the social categorization of individual lesbians and gays in terms of a demeaning social label type of 'identity' – they are, for example, assumed to be perverts, child molesters, and insatiable sexual predators. For, as was suggested earlier, discrimination turns as a social practice on the application of hostile understandings of a group's status to actual or perceived members of that group.

The second point is that the range of socially sensitive groups will vary from society to society and age to age, as will the sets of people who collectively count as groups to whom a social label sense of 'identity' can be attached. This is only to be expected, given the moderate constructionist position adopted in chapter 3. There cannot be any group, defined by an essential 'truth', which will *always* be deemed to need legal protection from discrimination in every society at every stage of history. This has important consequences for the range of legal entitlements – and for the notion of 'lesbian and gay rights' – which the empowerment justification is capable of supporting. The idea of respect for individuals as autonomous sexual subjects should always dictate that people must be free from criminal regulation of freely chosen sexual activity. Whether people are entitled to anti-discrimination protections to prevent employment or other social discrimination against them will, however, vary according to the degree and the direction of social hostility in the society concerned. As a current campaigning slogan in the UK and the US, 'lesbian and gay rights' claims can plausibly encompass calls for partnership rights and freedom from social discrimination, as well as demands for freedom from intrusive criminal regulation. If, in other societies, lesbians and gays are not identified as a group and there is no social or legal hostility relating to a person's sexuality, non-criminal law-related demands will be superfluous. If, by contrast, there is hostility towards those who practice same-sex sexual acts, but such people are not *defined* as members of a western-style 'lesbian and gay' social category, protective laws may well be justified, but the form of objectification involved will differ from that experienced in the UK and the US. The notion of objectification thus helps delimit the range of law reform demands which an empowerment justification can support in each society – and, given the role accorded to respect for sexual autonomy, without merely reflecting the circumstances of the society concerned (thus avoiding the assimilationist critique which can be directed against some equality arguments).

Objectification can be seen as a uniquely dehumanizing activity. People are treated as unworthy of consideration as human beings due to their possession of perceived group characteristic(s) – the most extreme manifestation of this being 'queer-bashing' attacks intended physically to eradicate individual lesbians and gays *as human beings*. Objectification is thus a particularly acute form of disempowerment. People may, of course, fall victim to other types of disempowerment, particularly to disempowerment which is economic in form. These usually fall short of the total, objectivizing form of dehumanization which lies at the heart of objectification and social or legal hostility, however, for they do not turn on attaching a derogatory social label sense of 'identity' to individuals.

This brings us to the third element of the empowerment justification: namely, the idea that the state is under a duty, as a matter of justice and political morality, to empower its citizens – in particular, by enhancing their autonomy and by remedying objectification-based attacks upon it. The strongest perfectionist liberal theory of autonomy is, of course, that developed by Joseph Raz.[82] While the empowerment arguments to be advanced here fit more straightforwardly within the Western European social democratic tradition, they are in no way hostile to the aims of Raz's theory of autonomy-based liberalism. As Neil MacCormick argues, however, the modern European sense of social democracy is more clearly 'a philosophy of the moderate left . . . of the political spectrum . . . an alternative to, rather than a form of "socialism"'.[83] This sense of social democracy rests, it is submitted, on a balance between community and individual responsibilities and entitlements. Community clearly plays a strong role in shaping people's conceptions of the world, and individuals cannot generally sustain a meaningful existence outside of a community of some sort. Nevertheless, human autonomy is valuable both in its own right – allowing people to be empowered by taking control of their lives – and for the common good, by allowing for individual enterprise and initiative. The primary duty of the state is thus to maximize the scope for individual autonomy – across all spheres of life – while preventing individual exercises of autonomy from unacceptably disempowering others. People's individual conceptions of autonomy and freedom are likely to be strongly affected by their social background. Social democratic political thought is thus driven, not by some absolute commitment to equality – economic or otherwise – but rather by the more flexible idea of individual empowerment within the context of a society with a mixed, but generally free-market economy. This will sometimes require state intervention through law – although the decision whether to use law (or taxation, or state subsidies) will often, within the context of empowerment, be a pragmatic matter – allowing for the ongoing development of social democratic strategy. Social understandings of autonomy and empowerment will also vary from age to age, although certain things – such as basic sexual freedoms – remain central to human individuality in any society.

While social democratic theories of the state rank autonomy as a central value, 'equality' arguments may sometimes be used to refer to a statistical end-goal, or in a rhetorical sense – the two valuable uses of 'equality' discussed at the end of the previous section of this chapter.[84] Thus, David Miliband talks of the need to forge a coherent relationship between equality and diversity, and of the 'need for an integration of public action and market decisions'.[85] David Held, meanwhile, appears to make use of the statistical sense of 'equality' in arguing for a social democratic

> politics of empowerment – a politics which aims at a free and equal citizenry. Such a politics takes as its *raison d'être* the creation of 'equal autonomy' for all citizens . . . [and] obliges us to address illegitimate asymmetries of power and opportunity.[86]

A democracy, Held argues, requires a 'principle of autonomy' whereby people should enjoy equal entitlements and obligations within the social framework which generates and limits the *opportunities* available to them. People should thus 'be free and equal in the determination of their own lives, so long as they do not use this framework to negate the rights of others'.[87] This requires, for Held, protection of autonomy across a whole series of 'sites of power' in life, 'encompassing realms which can be referred to as the body, welfare, culture, civic associations, the economy, regulatory and legal institutions, and organized violence and coercive recreations'.[88] A set of empowering entitlements is thus necessary to ensure equal participative opportunities within one's community, to provide 'the basis of a substantive and enduring settlement between freedom and equality', as opposed to strict egalitarianism.[89] It should be noted that it is the availability of the entitlements themselves which provides the empowerment here (and therefore any justification for the use of law), with the idea of a 'settlement' falling short of egalitarianism clearly involving the statistical idea of 'equality' as a rough end-pattern. All of this requires a strong commitment to notions of community solidarity.[90]

The role of individual initiative is stressed by Anthony Giddens, who suggests that 'an individual must achieve a certain degree of autonomy of action as a condition of being able to survive and forge a life; but autonomy is not the same as egoism and moreover implies reciprocity and interdependence'. The central issue is thus *'reconciling autonomy and interdependence* in the various spheres of social life, including the economic domain'.[91] Questions of life-chances and life-style become ever more central to political argument 'in a world where what used to be fixed by either nature or tradition is now subject to human decisions'.[92] This requires an active citizenry: individuals and groups should be empowered to make things happen for themselves, rather than things just happening to them at the instigation of the state.[93] Giddens also calls for an opening-up of greater dialogue and trust in the sphere of sexual relations.[94]

Where, then, does a social democratic political theory leave us in relation to the entitlements of lesbians and gays? When coupled with Held's analysis of sites of power, Giddens's discussion of life-chances and life-styles reinforces the notion – discussed earlier – of sexual autonomy as a central moral good in its own right. The following distinction can therefore plausibly be drawn. On the one hand, freedom from criminal regulation of sexuality and consenting sexual behaviour is *always* desirable in *any* society as a means of underpinning each person's sexual autonomy; it can therefore justifiably be protected by the laws of any society. On the other hand, it is only in particular societies that the need will arise to prohibit social and legal discrimination against persons of minority sexual orientations, to allow for the recognition of same-sex partnerships and child-care entitlements, and so on. Laws offering these types of protection and entitlement will only be important – and justifiable – in societies where their presence is necessary as a means of empowerment by combatting objectification, whether due to the notions of sexual orientation, family, autonomy or social hostility which prevail in the societies concerned. Freedom of sexuality and consenting sexual activity should *always* therefore be seen as crucially important moral entitlements – for *every* individual in *every* society, however people happen to define themselves sexually or to be defined by others in that society and in the era concerned. By contrast, exact notions of and reasons for disempowerment will vary from society to society, as will identities, whether of the personal or social label varieties. Unlike a purely equality-based justification, this social democratic approach can therefore encompass (within the limits of consent) both freedom of sexuality for everyone, and protection of whatever socially sensitive sexual minority groups there happen to be in any society at any given moment. It is thus compatible with the moderate constructionist approach to sexual categories adopted in chapter 3. It views 'lesbian and gay rights' as merely a current, localized campaigning slogan, acknowledging that it lacks a fixed meaning and is only of value in societies where 'lesbians and gays' are seen as a socially sensitive group.

Some supporters of legal protections for lesbians and gays will disagree with a social democratic theory of the state entirely, but if they do so, they will need to find a justification which both stems from an alternative theory of the state *and* is itself plausible. This may well be a difficult task, for as we have already seen, pure equality arguments – the product of standard liberal or socialist thought – are flawed, as are libertarian views of sexuality and the state. By contrast, the social democratic theory of empowerment specifies a clear moral good in sexuality and consenting sexual relations, and explains how that good is violated by social and legal hostility directed at lesbians and gays. It provides a reason for legal intervention which is sensitive to current social circumstances – so is unlikely to become irrelevant with time – and takes a sufficiently wide view of why each individual's sexuality should be valuable to them in modern western societies that it can justify anti-discrimination laws and partnership rights as well as basic freedoms from criminal regulation. The notion of disempowerment on culturally sensitive grounds provides a justification for combating social and legal discrimination because of race, sex and sexual orientation, and does so whether or not the victim of the discrimination feels that their personal identity has been attacked. In short, the empowerment justification can encompass all the problem cases excluded by equality and privacy theories, and avoids the troubled reasoning which lies behind immutability and liberationist arguments.

The empowerment justification, it is submitted, provides a satisfactory answer to the book's first central question. In chapter 8, we will search for an answer to the second.

Notes

1. John D'Emilio, *Making Trouble: Essays on Gay History, Politics, and the University* (New York: Routledge, 1992), p. 182.
2. H.C. Deb., 21 February 1994, Column 97.
3. H.C. Deb., 21 February 1994, Column 110.
4. H.C. Deb., 21 February 1994, Column 99.
5. H.C. Deb., 21 February 1994, Column 111.
6. Anya Palmer, *Less Equal than Others: a survey of lesbians and gay men at work* (London: Stonewall, 1993).
7. *Stonewall Newsletter*, June 1996 (front cover).
8. Cf. Peter Westen, 'The empty idea of equality' (1982) 95 *Harvard Law Review* 537 at 537 (although contrast p. 556).
9. A classic analysis of equality as a general concept can be found in Sir Isaiah Berlin's essay 'Equality', in his *Concepts and Categories: Philosophical Essays* (Oxford: Oxford University Press, 1980).
10. *Watkins v. U.S. Army* (1988) 837 F 2d 1428; (1989) 875 F 2d 699.
11. *High Tech Gays v. Defense Industrial Security Clearance Office* (1990) 895 F 2d 563.
12. For further analysis, see chapter 2.
13. Cf. Paisley Currah, 'Searching for immutability: Homosexuality, race and rights discourse', in Angelia Wilson (ed.), *A Simple Matter of Justice?* (London: Cassell, 1995), p. 59; Steven Seidman, 'Identity and politics in a "postmodern" gay culture: Some historical and conceptual notes', in Michael Warner (ed.), *Fear of a Queer Planet: Queer Politics and Social Theory* (Minneapolis: University of Minnesota Press, 1994), pp. 110–11, 117–27; D'Emilio, *Making Trouble*, chs 13 and 14; Jeffrey Weeks, *Sexuality and its Discontents: Meanings, Myths and Modern Sexualities* (London: Routledge, 1985), pp. 195–210.
14. Steven Epstein, 'Gay politics, ethnic identity: The limits of social constructionism', ch. 10 in Edward Stein (ed.), *Forms of Desire: Sexual Orientation and the Social Constructionist Controversy* (New York: Garland, 1990), p. 243.
15. Diana Fuss, *Essentially Speaking: Feminism, Nature and Difference* (New York: Routledge, 1989), p. 97.
16. Jeffrey Weeks, *Against Nature: Essays on history, sexuality and identity* (London: Rivers Oram, 1991), p. 184.
17. Jeffrey Weeks, *Coming Out: Homosexual Politics in Britain from the Nineteenth Century to the Present* (London: Quartet, rev. edn, 1990), p. 232.
18. Weeks, *Against Nature*, p. 68. See also Fuss, *Essentially Speaking*, pp. 97–8.
19. The latter three arguments can therefore be used to rebut John Gardner's autonomy-driven, but identity-dependent, justification for anti-discrimination laws: 'Liberals and unlawful discrimination' (1989) 9 *Oxford Journal of Legal Studies* 1.
20. Cf. David Halperin, 'Sex before sexuality: Pederasty, politics, and power in Classical Athens', in M. B. Duberman, M. Vicinus and G. Chauncey (eds), *Hidden from History: Rethinking the Lesbian and Gay Past* (London: Penguin, 1989).
21. Seidman, 'Identity and politics', pp. 127–37; Carl Stychin, *Law's Desire: Sexuality and the Limits of Justice* (London: Routledge, 1995), ch. 8.
22. For discussion of the rapidly changing character of identities in this area, see Weeks, *Against Nature*, chs 1–5.
23. In the lesbian and gay context, cf. D'Emilio, *Making Trouble*, p. 186.
24. Weeks, *Against Nature*, p. 194.
25. Cf. Fuss, *Essentially Speaking*, p. 97.
26. Seidman, 'Identity and politics', p. 121.
27. Angelia Wilson, 'Which equality? Toleration, difference or respect', in Joseph Bristow and Angelia Wilson

(eds), *Activating Theory: Lesbian, Gay, Bisexual Politics* (London: Lawrence & Wishart, 1993), p. 180.
28. *Ibid.*, p. 181.
29. See also Fuss, *Essentially Speaking*, pp. 98–9.
30. Weeks, *Coming Out*, p. 232.
31. *Ibid.*, p. 233. See, generally, D'Emilio, *Making Trouble*, ch. 20.
32. Weeks, *Coming Out*, pp. 233–4; see also Weeks, *Against Nature*, pp. 80–1.
33. Seidman, 'Identity and politics', pp. 110, 117–27; see also Stychin, *Law's Desire*, pp. 144–7.
34. Seidman, 'Identity and politics', p. 120.
35. Weeks, *Coming Out*, p. 237.
36. Weeks, *Against Nature*, p. 79; see also Weeks, *Sexuality and its Discontents*, pp. 196–7.
37. *Ibid.*, p. 209.
38. D'Emilio, *Making Trouble*, p. 237.
39. *Ibid.*, p. 108.
40. See also Bernard Williams' subtle account of identity: 'Identity and identities', in Henry Harris (ed.), *Identity* (Oxford: Clarendon Press, 1995), ch. 1, esp. pp. 7–11.
41. Janet Halley, 'Sexual orientation and the politics of biology: A critique of the argument from immutability' (1994) 46 *Stanford Law Review* 503 at 563.
42. *Ibid.* at 529.
43. [1986] IRLR 103.
44. This construction of 'detriment' is almost certainly inconsistent with the broader view adopted under the Sex Discrimination Act 1975 – see *Gill & Coote v. El Vino Co* [1983] IRLR 206.
45. Cf. Seidman, 'Identity and politics', pp. 126–7.
46. The underpinning theories of justice and political and sexual morality may well shape the operation of the 'what' question. For, by providing the qualitative scale by which attributes or actions are measured, they can determine the moral weight accorded to each object which is being measured, which will in turn determine when things can be ranked as 'equal'.
47. H.C. Deb., 21 February 1994, Column 100.
48. H.C. Deb., 21 February 1994, Column 100.
49. Peter Tatchell, *We Don't Want to March Straight: Masculinity, Queers and the Military* (London: Cassell, 1995), pp. 2–3.
50. *Ibid.*, p. 29.
51. For similar arguments, see Patricia Cain, 'Litigating for lesbian and gay rights: A legal history' (1993) 79 *Virginia Law Review* 1551 at 1639; Seidman, 'Identity and politics', p. 123; D'Emilio, *Making Trouble*, p. 187.
52. D'Emilio, *Making Trouble*, p. 12.
53. *Ibid.*, p. 187.
54. Ronald Dworkin, *A Matter of Principle* (Oxford: Clarendon Press, 1986), pp. 190–8, 205–13.
55. Originally developed in two articles: 'What is equality? Part 1: Equality of welfare' (1981) 10 *Philosophy & Public Affairs* 185 (Dworkin's rebuttal of welfarist liberal equality theories) and 'What is equality? Part 2: Equality of resources' (1981) 10 *Philosophy & Public Affairs* 283 (where Dworkin's own resources-based theory is defended).
56. Dworkin, *A Matter of Principle*, p. 209.
57. *Ibid.*, p. 190.
58. *Ibid.*, pp. 108–9.
59. *Ibid.*, pp. 205–6.
60. *Ibid.*, pp. 190–1.
61. *Ibid.*, p. 206.
62. Stephen Guest, *Ronald Dworkin* (Edinburgh: Edinburgh University Press, 1992), p. 256.
63. *Ibid.*, pp. 256–7.
64. Dworkin, *A Matter of Principle*, p. 191 (emphasis added); note, however, Dworkin's own interpretation of the concept of liberty: 'What is equality? Part 3: The place of liberty' (1987) 73 *Iowa Law Review* 1.
65. Joseph Raz, *The Morality of Freedom* (Oxford: Clarendon Press, 1986), pp. 217, 228.
66. *Ibid.*, p. 218. Raz's analysis of what might count as an egalitarian principle – set out in the rest of ch. 9

of *The Morality of Freedom* – actually is a little more complex, involving a comparison between principles which are diminishing and non-diminishing.
67. *Ibid.*, p. 220.
68. *Ibid.*, p. 218.
69. Guest, *Ronald Dworkin*, pp. 226–30, 271.
70. For contrasting views, see Bernard Williams, 'The idea of equality', ch. 6 in Peter Laslett and W. G. Runciman (eds), *Philosophy, Politics and Society* (Second Series) (Oxford: Basil Blackwell, 1962); Thomas Nagel, *Mortal Questions* (Cambridge: Cambridge University Press, 1979), ch. 8.
71. Raz, *The Morality of Freedom*, p. 235. See also Westen, 'The empty idea of equality', esp. pp. 542, 547–8, 557, 575, 577–81.
72. Going back to the earlier 'what' question, Bernard Williams makes the similar point that possession of a particular identity is not necessarily a good in itself – see his 'Identity and identities', p. 9.
73. Raz, *The Morality of Freedom*, p. 228.
74. See also Steven Epstein's discussion of the political uses of 'identity' in 'Gay politics, ethnic identity', pp. 289 et seq.
75. H. L. A. Hart, *Law, Liberty, and Morality* (Oxford: Oxford University Press, 1963), p. 22.
76. Another possible exception relates to sexual activity in a crowded public place – in a railway compartment or in a shopping street, for example. It could well be claimed that a person's own fantasies about having sex in the street should not be respected simply because of the nuisance such activity may cause passers-by. Unlike forced sexual activity, however, this possible exception cannot be explained in terms of our two factors marking out sexual activity as valuable – and it may be felt to present dangers of a 'slippery slope' leading towards excessive regulation of sexual behaviour.
77. R. A. Duff, *Intention, Agency and Criminal Liability: Philosophy of Action and the Criminal Law* (Oxford: Blackwell, 1990), pp. 167–73.
78. For a practical application of this argument, see Nicholas Bamforth, 'Sado-masochism and consent' [1994] *Criminal Law Review* 661.
79. *Report of the Secretary's Task Force on Youth Suicide: Volume 3. Prevention and Interventions in Youth Suicide* (U.S. Department of Health and Human Services, 1989).
80. Hart, *Law, Liberty, and Morality*, p. 22.
81. Richard Mohr, *Gays/Justice: A Study of Ethics, Society, and Law* (New York: Columbia University Press, 1988), p. 58.
82. Raz, *The Morality of Freedom*.
83. Neil MacCormick, *Legal Right and Social Democracy: Essays in Legal and Political Philosophy* (Oxford: Clarendon Press, 1982), p. 1. It should be noted that very different interpretations of the implications of Raz's theory are possible: contrast Gardner, 'Liberals and unlawful discrimination'; Robert George, *Making Men Moral: Civil Liberties and Public Morality* (Oxford: Clarendon Press, 1993), ch. 6.
84. For an argument which ends up pragmatically balancing equality and liberty (although without explicitly acknowledging that it is engaging in such a manoeuvre) see MacCormick, *Legal Right and Social Democracy*, ch. 1. John Gray's critique of social democratic arguments mistakenly views equality as a foundation stone of social democracy, as opposed to a pragmatic tactic or statistical end-goal – see John Gray, *After Social Democracy: Politics, Capitalism, and the Common Life* (London: Demos, 1996), pp. 24–8.
85. David Miliband (ed.), *Reinventing the Left* (Cambridge: Polity Press, 1994), p. 6.

86. David Held, 'Inequalities of power, problems of democracy', in Miliband (ed.), *Reinventing the Left*, p. 47.
87. *Ibid.*, p. 48.
88. *Ibid.*, p. 52.
89. *Ibid.*, p. 58.
90. Interesting discussion can be found in William Sullivan, 'Reinventing community: Prospects for politics', in Colin Crouch and David Marquand (eds), *Reinventing Collective Action: From the Global to the Local* (Oxford: Blackwell, 1995).
91. Anthony Giddens, 'Brave new world: The new context of politics', in Miliband (ed.), *Reinventing the Left*, p. 29.
92. *Ibid.*, p. 30.
93. *Ibid.*, pp. 31–2.
94. *Ibid.*, p. 33; see, however, Perry Anderson's critique of Giddens in his Comment 'Power, politics and the Enlightenment', in Miliband (ed.), *Reinventing the Left*, p. 43.

8

The Limits of Law and Law Reform

> *The [Canadian] Charter of Rights and Freedoms . . . has its advocates, its enthusiasts, its sceptics, and its denouncers. For some . . . [it] is the crowning glory in the firmament of liberalism. Other commentators represent the Charter as a most dangerous form of capitalist class rule while writers occupying a different point on the political spectrum have characterized it as a powerful weapon in the hands of self-seeking 'special interest groups'. Some people . . . take a pragmatic approach to the Charter – 'it's here, it's a tool, let's use it as best we can'.*
>
> — Didi Herman[1]

Introduction

In this chapter, we will examine our second central question, namely whether (and if so, how far) law reform measures are likely to help reduce or eliminate social hostility and discrimination directed at lesbians and gays. In the language of chapter 3, we are asking whether measures designed to create 'lesbian and gay legal rights' are also likely to generate sought-after social entitlements for lesbians and gays (what counts as a 'legal right' or a 'sought-after social entitlement' will depend, of course, upon the law reform justification in play). The importance of the question lies in the fact that there is, as noted in chapter 1, little point in campaigning for or creating new laws if they are unlikely to have some desirable social effect. If it cannot be shown that existing, punitive laws clearly harm lesbians and gays in everyday life (for example, by reinforcing social prejudices), or if it cannot be shown that protective laws will encourage the growth of social acceptance, then it may be the case that political campaigners would be better employed in outreach and educational work rather than in campaigns for law reform.[2]

If would-be law reformers are to be realistic in their campaigning, it is important to take proper account of the limitations of law reform. Failure to do so will lead to unrealistic expectations about the social effects of legal change. As Otto Kahn-Freund has warned:

> Many people have something like a magic belief in the efficacy of the law in shaping human conduct and social relations. It is a superstition which is itself a fact of political importance, but a superstition it is all the same. . . . where there are strong forces or traditions favouring a pattern or action . . . the role which the law can play in improving the situation, though not negligible, can never be decisive.[3]

There would certainly appear to be 'strong forces or traditions' – especially in the UK and the USA – which support 'traditionalist' notions of appropriate masculine and feminine gender roles and sexual behaviour, with heterosexuality as the approved social norm. Any law reform measure designed to improve the social position of lesbians and gays will therefore, as the quotation from Kahn-Freund implies, face an uphill task. This observation is reinforced by the poor record of legislation against racial discrimination – originally enacted in the UK in 1968 and in the USA in 1964[4] – given that such legislation might also be said to have been intended to challenge a 'strong force or tradition' in the form of oppression of ethnic minority groups. For it now seems clear that the mere existence of laws prohibiting racial discrimination in specified circumstances has not in reality resulted in the eradication of discrimination, or in anything approaching racial equality.[5]

As a side issue, it should be noted that the effectiveness of law and law reform has broader implications (beyond the scope of this book) for theories of political morality – for, as Roger Cotterrell has observed, law is seen in contemporary western societies as one of the primary instruments of state power.[6] As swathes of post-Second World War legislation show, law has been used by successive governments as a tool in their attempts to achieve many of their central policy goals.[7] If law is ineffective in achieving its social goals, doubt must be cast on its worth as an instrument of social policy.

It will be difficult to approach our second central question in an entirely neutral fashion. As Didi Herman implies in the passage cited above, one's background theories of justice and political morality affect one's assessment of how effective a particular piece of law, such as the Canadian Charter of

Rights and Freedoms, is in protecting lesbians and gays.[8] Herman identifies four possible perspectives on the effectiveness of human rights instruments such as the Charter, each perspective being based on separate theories of justice and political morality. Only the first three perspectives are concerned with the effectiveness of law as a means of *improving* the social entitlements of lesbians and gays, however. Herman describes the fourth perspective as reactionary, in that its supporters believe that individual rights litigation fragments society as a whole, involving a surrender of the power of the majority to what they categorize as undemocratic 'special interest groups', including lesbians and gays.[9] Supporters of this view are likely to favour one of the regulatory theories of justice and political morality discussed in chapter 5, and will be concerned that law may be an effective means for lesbians and gays to *challenge* the reactionaries' favoured regime, under which lesbian and gay sexual acts will either be prohibited, or treated as a second class form of sexuality which is only permitted so long as it is relegated to private situations.

Of the three perspectives which could be held by those who favour an improvement in the social entitlements of lesbians and gays, the first is that of the 'rights debunkers', who criticize the type of individualistic legal rights contained in the Charter (or other human rights instruments) as empty distractions from the truly worthwhile struggle, which is against the entire capitalist economic order. From this perspective, it is worthless – and possibly even a hindrance to radical social change – to spend time creating legal rights to protect lesbians and gays.[10] By contrast, 'rights promoters' – the supporters of Herman's second perspective – believe, in typical liberal fashion, that it is fundamentally important to secure legal rights for minority groups, such rights having a potentially transformative effect on the social situation. The securing of new legal entitlements to protect lesbians and gays would in itself be an important achievement for supporters of this perspective.[11] The third perspective is pragmatic, suggesting that the acquisition of legal rights for lesbians and gays is never an end in itself and is rarely decisive in countering social oppression, but may still serve some useful purpose as part of the broader struggle for social change.[12]

Each of these three perspectives rests on different background theories of justice and political morality and, as a consequence, entails a different understanding of what counts as an 'improvement' in the social entitlements of lesbians and gays. Herman's category of 'rights debunkers' will consist of radicals who wish to replace the existing political system altogether, and who would categorize law as a creature of the current governing class, explaining why they see law reform as useless. The only effective tactic for improving the social position of lesbians and gays, for 'rights debunkers', would be the downfall of the existing political system.[13] 'Rights enthusiasts', by contrast, are likely to be reformist liberals who believe in working within the existing political system, and who are likely to see the most effective strategy for improving the social treatment of lesbians and gays as bringing test cases through the courts and lobbying for legislative reform. As Herman implies, 'rights enthusiasts' are likely to support the equality/identity justification for law reform,[14] and will as such see the incorporation of lesbians and gays into the existing political order on equal terms to heterosexuals as an effective improvement in their social position. Supporters of the social democratic theory (and consequent justification for law reform) advocated in chapter 7 are, by contrast, likely to opt for what Herman calls the pragmatist perspective, given the importance placed by their theory of justice on the need to take account of day-to-day social circumstances.[15] What will count as an effective improvement in the social position of lesbians and gays will be, for pragmatists, something which is best calculated on a case-by-case basis: law reform will sometimes be seen as a useful step towards improvement; in other circumstances, alternative tactics may be preferable.

It follows that the discussion in this chapter will be conducted from a pragmatist perspective (something which was, perhaps, already evident given the way in which our second central question is phrased). We will, in other words, consider the effectiveness of law and law reform with a sceptical eye, searching for their limitations – for to do otherwise would be naïve. We will begin by considering some theoretical points concerning the general effectiveness of law in achieving social change, before considering some more specific examples relating to lesbians and gays. It will be argued throughout the chapter that while law reform is often a useful tactic in challenging and countering social oppression, any 'magic belief' in the power of the law to bring about social change would be misplaced.

In the analysis which follows, it is important to remember that the social effects of law in the UK may not exactly parallel those in the US or in Canada – it would seem fair to say, for example, that citizens of the USA are often more aware of their constitutional (legal) rights than are their British counterparts, suggesting that law plays a stronger role in the political consciousness of the US citizen. On the other hand, it may also appear plausible to claim that there is a greater incidence of *lawlessness* in US life, in the form of crimes of violence, than there is in the UK. The discussion will therefore begin at a rather general level, becoming more specific as we proceed.

Theories about the effects of law

Before considering the effect of rules of law – whether long-established or newly implemented via law reform measures – on social attitudes and social behaviour, we must briefly examine their effect within the legal system itself. This at first sight may seem unnecessary, given that it is often thought that a legal rule (whether embodied in statute or case law) will resolve authoritatively any dispute which falls within its scope, and that it will hence be clear what effect any rule will have when it is applied. Introducing a new rule or reforming an existing one would, on this view, directly affect the way in which disputes falling within the scope of the relevant rule are resolved in court, with the legal rights of the parties being determined according to the rule concerned.

This impression, however, is too blunt on its own, given that there is actually considerable controversy about how judges do (and should) decide cases – in other words, about how they apply rules in practice. Doreen McBarnet suggests, for example, that judges may well attempt to erode or qualify, through decisions in individual cases, broader rules of law which they dislike,[16] and it is certainly clear that many legal rules allow wide scope for judicial interpretation or manipulation. The mere existence of a rule is thus unlikely to have an automatic and decisive effect on the outcome of cases falling within its scope: rather, we must also take account of the effect of judicial interpretation of the rule in assessing its precise impact on the legal system concerned. Merely creating a law prohibiting discrimination against lesbians and gays would therefore be insufficient to ensure their protection in every case where it seemed likely that the law would, in theory, protect them – it would also depend upon how judges interpreted the rule in practice. This is to some extent a matter of drafting, in that the most likely candidates for judicial manipulation are rules which are ambiguous. However they are interpreted, rules of law nevertheless retain enormous importance within the legal system, given that judges always feel obliged to take account of them in their reasoning – whether the reasoning is designed to apply, extend, qualify or deny the relevance of the rule concerned.[17]

What effects, though, can law have within society as a whole? It is perhaps best to evaluate this question in terms of Yehezkel Dror's concept of social change. Dror suggests that:

> Society is always undergoing processes of change; human generations follow one another and different persons fulfil various social roles. The concept 'social change' does not refer to this constant change in the population of every society, but refers to changes in the society as such, including the various social institutions, roles and status definitions, accepted ideologies, value patterns, pattern variables and value-profiles. In other words, the concept of social change refers to changes in social structure or in culture.[18]

Bringing law into the picture, William Evan notes that:

> Law emerges not only to *codify* existing customs, morals, or mores, but also to *modify* the behaviour and the values presently existing in a particular society. The conception of law as a codification of existing customs, morals, or mores implies a relatively passive function. On the other hand, the conception of law as a means of social change, i.e., as a potential for modifying behaviour and beliefs, implies a relatively active function.[19]

Evan's argument is analytical rather than prescriptive, for he makes no attempt to lay down *which* modifications of behaviour and belief law should bring about in its 'active function'. As such, a law which encouraged greater social discrimination against lesbians and gays would, if successful, be acting as an agent of social change as much as a law which successfully discouraged such conduct. It is also important to notice that Evan's argument does not fall foul of Kahn-Freund's 'magic belief' objection, for Evan does not assume that a legal change *automatically* ensures a corresponding social change. Rather, law in its 'active function' is seen as having the *potential* for modifying behaviour and beliefs.

How, though, might law be thought – in theoretical terms – to be capable of modifying behaviour and beliefs, and what obstacles might stand in its way? If law and law reform can have some social effect, in other words, what form/s can this effect take? One way in which law might be thought to have a social effect is by guiding behaviour patterns outside the court room, and, as a general matter, 'technical' laws might be thought to have this effect as much as laws directly concerned with civil liberties. In the 'technical' area we might argue, for example, that the existence of rules laying down conveyancing formalities for the buying and selling of property – with penalties for failure to comply with the rules – encourages the use of the procedures approved by the rules.[20] In the civil liberties sphere, public order legislation could be said to enable citizens to distinguish lawful from unlawful forms of public protest.[21] From this perspective, a court case could often be seen as a device of the last resort: in general, for example, the aim of a law prohibiting discrimination in employment against lesbians and gays would be for people to obey its provisions without the need for actual enforcement, so that a court case – at least in an area where the law is clear – would amount to a failure of the law's guidance function.[22] It should be added that the social effect of law as a guidance device may often be affected by the clarity of the law concerned and the degree to which the public is aware of it. Another important factor is the degree to which a law is *actually* enforced by those with the power to enforce it, rather than, for example, simply providing a background for disputes to be resolved by negotiation and out-of-court settlements (see further below).[23]

The alleged social effect of law as a guidance device is concerned with law's effect on people's behaviour. What, however, of people's *beliefs*? Roger Cotterrell has suggested that 'educative' legislation is intended '*to change ideas* by influencing behaviour', an example being the original race relations legislation in the UK.[24] This is to be distinguished from 'symbolic' legislation which, he suggests, has no role in promoting social change, instead existing merely to 'placat[e] opposed interests of various sections of society while avoiding change'.[25] No realistic consideration may have been given, for example, to the possibility of enforcing symbolic legislation.[26] Such legislation might include general but unenforceable aspirations contained within a human rights code, the effect of which could be to dampen down demands for further change by giving the appearance of granting greater freedom to citizens – something akin to Herman's 'rights debunker' perspective.[27] We should note, however, that the failure of a piece of legislation to promote social change would not, in theory, prevent it from having a social effect, for the effect would be to curtail demands for further legal reform. In addition, it is not necessarily true to say that symbolic legislation is always *intended* to avoid change: a legislature which wished to make a statement of its support for human rights notions might introduce an unenforceable human rights code because it was worried by the political power which an entrenched Bill of Rights would confer on the judiciary. The code itself would be intended, in these circumstances, as a statement of support for human rights notions, and as a way of encouraging others to support them.

Theorists are much less clear about how, exactly, law is supposed to educate. Anthony Lester and Geoffrey Bindman, writing on the impact of race relations legislation, simply assert that, 'Contrary to the belief of some critics, legislation and education are not incompatible; legislation is a powerful form of education, and legislation and education depend upon each other.'[28] In similar vein, Evert van der Veen and Adrianne Dercksen have argued that social discrimination against lesbians or gays results from negative views of lesbian and gay sexuality conveyed, at least in European Community Member States, by legislation and prevailing religious and medical doctrines which marginalize or stigmatize them.[29] Unfortunately, the authors fail to explain how this process actually works.

Some writers have been slightly more precise. In attempting to explain what he describes as the 'active function' for law, William Evan suggests that:

> As an instrument of social change, law entails two interrelated processes: the institutionalization and the internalization of patterns of behavior. In this context, institutionalization of a pattern of behaviour means the establishment of a norm with provisions for its enforcement, and internalization of a pattern of behavior means the incorporation of the value or values implicit in a law. *Law . . . can affect behavior directly only through the process of institutionalization; if, however, the institutionalization process is successful, it, in turn, facilitates the internalization of attitudes or beliefs.*[30]

While being a little more exact about the mechanics of the educative process, this still fails to explain how the mere fact that something has been successfully established as a rule of law can alter people's attitudes or beliefs. A similar comment may be made about Peter Cicchino, Bruce Deming and Katherine Nicholson's observation, in relation to the enactment – after many unsuccessful attempts – of a Massachusetts Gay Civil Rights Bill in 1989, that:

with regard to changing public consciousness, law itself has an educative function. Whatever the failures of advocates of the [civil rights] bill in educating the public during the 17-year struggle for enactment, the very presence of such a statute, and the public awareness that gay and lesbian people can now invoke the power of the state for protection, can have a powerful impact on cultural perceptions of gay and lesbian people.[31]

In fact, the notion that law can, on its own, miraculously 'educate' a grudging or hostile populace seems almost as simplistic as popular assumptions about the alleged deterrent effect of law.[32] As mentioned earlier, recent literature has shown the lack of 'bite' which the race relations legislation has had, despite the optimism of writers such as Lester and Bindman in the early 1970s,[33] suggesting that law plays a less important role in people's day-to-day evaluations of how they should behave in social situations than is sometimes assumed. An obvious example is that despite the existence of well-publicized traffic speed limits, many – or most – drivers seem to disregard the limits on a casual and regular basis, without any moral qualms at the fact that they are thereby breaking the law. Equally, one suspects that most people's instinctive revulsion at the idea of intentionally killing another human being is not dependent solely on the existence of a law against murder. Popular reactions to news of an intentional killing tend to take the form of anger at the fact that the victim was killed. That the killing involved the law against murder being broken is rather beside the point.[34]

In short, blandly asserting that the creation or existence of law is capable of 'educating' people – in the sense of altering their beliefs – is a serious underestimation of the variety and the independence of human responses to the law. People's conceptions of moral right and wrong seem frequently to be shaped not by the present law, but by their assumptions about what one is socially and morally entitled to do – something which turns on their background theory of justice rather than the wording of the law itself.[35] For example, while sexual harassment at work contravenes the Sex Discrimination Act 1975 in the UK, it remains rife in the workplace.[36] This suggests that many male employees either feel that it is socially acceptable to treat women in this way, or assume that they can do so and escape unpunished – the assumption behind either state of mind being that male employees are socially entitled to harass women regardless of the law.

There are three other relevant factors in assessing the social effect of law. First, Yehezkel Dror has argued that 'whether law-enforcing agencies prosecute or refrain from prosecuting certain offenses affects the impact of the law on society, although the law itself is not changed'.[37] This argument can be developed to cover the enforcement of law more generally, including (if appropriate) decisions about whether to arrest and decisions as to the level of penalty, civil or criminal, to be imposed on an unsuccessful defendant (we will see below, however, that the mere non-enforcement of a law might not deprive it of all social effect).[38] Second, judicial emasculation of a law may blunt the social message which that law conveys, diluting its social effect.[39] Third, as Dror notes, 'Basic institutions rooted in traditions and values, such as the family, seem to be extremely resistant to changes imposed by the law.'[40] This ties in with the point made above about the danger of over-stressing the social importance of law: if we are concerned with institutions with a special place in our culture, such as the family, popular views about morality are particularly unlikely to be altered by the mere existence of a law. These three factors are, of course, mutually reinforcing, in that popular prejudice will be engaged or affected even less by a law which is not effectively enforced.

There are, however, four reasons why it would be wrong to say that law or law reform lacks any social effect. First, it *is* clear – despite the sceptical tone employed above – that law is often important in people's instant reactions to events: the oft-heard assertion that 'there ought to be a law against it', 'it' referring to any practice of which the speaker disapproves, suggests that people do think of law, at least sometimes, as having a practical and/or moral role. Indeed, if law did not have this importance, then law reform debates, at least where sensitive social issues such as ages of consent or anti-discrimination laws are concerned, would not assume the significance which they do, whether for supporters or opponents of the law reform measures being debated. Second, in the *Dudgeon* and *Norris* cases (see chapter 2), the European Court of Human Rights accepted that law can have social effects. The Court agreed that the mere existence of a law which singled out lesbians and/or gays for unfavourable treatment may, even if it is not enforced, nevertheless affect those penalized under it to the extent that they can claim to be 'victims' under Article 25 of the Convention, with standing to litigate.[41] This reinforces what is, for many lesbians and gays, an almost intuitive feeling – that where laws mark out lesbians and gays (or any other socially disfavoured group) for special, hostile treatment, this can reinforce existing prejudices against them, as well as existing feelings of social isolation which many lesbians and gays (especially those who have not 'come out') tend to feel. This suggests that the notion of symbolic legislation can be taken further, and deployed less cynically, than Roger Cotterrell would suggest. Cotterrell admits that his notions of symbolic and educative legislation 'cannot always be clearly separated'.[42] The European Convention cases suggest that even if not enforced, hostile laws might have a symbolic social effect. This suggests that law *can* sometimes stigmatize or, if deployed for positive social purposes, empower members of the social groups – such as lesbians and gays – which it covers.[43]

Third, Kendall Thomas has developed a strong argument in his analysis of the legal and social position of lesbians and gays in the USA. While avoiding any claim that the widespread US legal prohibitions on oral and anal intercourse – which were legitimated, as we saw in chapter 2, by the Supreme Court's ruling in *Bowers* v. *Hardwick*[44] – directly *cause* homophobic attacks, Thomas nevertheless suggests that they tend to *legitimize* such violence. Thomas asserts that:

> homosexual [anti-] sodomy statutes express the official 'theory' of homophobia; private acts of violence against gay men and lesbians 'translate' that theory into brutal 'practice'. In other words, private homophobic violence punishes what homosexual sodomy statutes prohibit.[45]

Under this theory, criminal prohibitions on homosexual behaviour contribute to the development of a social climate in which homophobic violence is accepted and even celebrated.

This argument is reinforced by the 1989 US *Report of the Secretary's Task Force on Youth Suicide*, considered in chapter 3.[46] The report, it will be recalled, concluded that young lesbians and gays were two to three times more likely to attempt suicide than other young people in the USA, a major cause of this phenomenon being poor self-esteem, depression and fear induced by social discrimination against and oppression of lesbians and gays. The drafters of the report were convinced that existing hostile laws had an impact on the behaviour of young lesbians and gays – as would, more positively, the introduction of anti-discrimination laws. Having drawn attention to the current legal restrictions (see chapter 2), the report observed starkly that 'Gay and lesbian youth see this and take it to heart.'[47] And, in calling for the introduction of anti-discrimination laws, it was suggested that 'Laws can help to establish the principle of equality for lesbians and gay men and define the conduct of others in their interactions with them.'[48]

The fourth argument for the view that law can have a social effect is that not even the strongest critics of the weakness of existing anti-discrimination laws have advocated their repeal. For, while such laws may have little positive social effect at the moment, repealing them could suggest that members of social minority groups are no longer worthy of the protection of the state, and should no longer have the chance to obtain a legal remedy of any type when faced with discrimination. Repeal could, in short, send a symbolic message of a disastrous variety.[49]

The analysis in this section leaves us, then, with an apparently contradictory picture. On the one hand, the notion that law, acting alone, can have a social effect as an educative agent is clearly too simplistic, and we can see that law plays a much smaller role in popular moral evaluations than some theorists have tended to assume. On the other hand, law is popularly perceived as having some role, we have indications that it can play a symbolic role or a role which reinforces the social disempowerment of lesbians and gays, and people tend intuitively to feel that law reform is an important political issue.[50] We will now attempt to clarify the picture a little by conducting a more detailed examination of legislators' and judges' stated feelings about law reform as it affects the position of lesbians and gays.

Legal regulation of lesbian and gay sexuality

In this section, we will consider views about the significance of law reform held by those involved, whether as supporters or opponents of law reform campaigns. We have already seen, at a general level, that there are great difficulties in the view that law can encourage or educate. Many of the opinions expressed in the law reform debates considered in this section not only support this, but also help provide an answer to some of the problems considered in the previous section.

In the UK, the richest source of material on political attitudes to the likely social effect of law and law reform in the lesbian and gay context can be found in the 1957 Wolfenden Committee Report;[51] in the

Parliamentary debates and the reactions to the proposals enacted as the 1967 Sexual Offences Act and section 28 of the 1988 Local Government Act; and in the House of Commons debate on the age of consent sections of the 1994 Criminal Justice and Public Order Act (originally discussed in chapter 1). In 1957, the Wolfenden Committee believed that it was unlikely that partial decriminalization of sexual acts between men would bring about a substantial increase in their occurrence. Such an argument, the Committee felt, 'seems to us to exaggerate the effect of the law on human behaviour'.[52] And Lady Gaitskell, during the House of Lords debate on what became the 1967 Act, argued that: 'I do not believe that the present laws keep homosexuality in check, and I do not believe that homosexuality would be increased if the laws were liberalised.'[53]

Similarly, during the House of Commons debate on what became the 1994 Act, Edwina Currie MP asserted that 'one cannot make men moral by law, that all that one can do is criminalise their preferences'.[54] Conversely, as Stephen Jeffery-Poulter has pointed out, in every Parliamentary debate on what became the 1967 Act, 'even the most fervent of the Bill's supporters had repeatedly asserted that they did not wish to suggest that Parliament was encouraging or approving of homosexual activity by removing criminal sanctions against it'.[55] This is reinforced by the history of the period after the passage of the 1967 Act, during which time the growth of organized gay clubs, cafes, helplines and associations occurred very slowly, being met with ongoing hostile reactions.[56]

This suggests two things. First, a characteristic as central to a person as their sexual orientation will not be altered by the law, and its actual incidence, as opposed to openness about its incidence, is unlikely to be altered dramatically. Law might encourage people to hide or even to ignore their sexual orientation for fear of being caught, but it cannot alter it or snuff it out. This constitutes an in-built limitation on the social effect, if any, of law.[57] Second, it is not the mere fact that the law has been altered which will bring about a change in public opinion, i.e. have an educative effect. To expect it to do so, especially in an area where the majority of the population is hostile to the law reform measure concerned, is to take a very simplistic view of human nature. The process is in fact much more subtle, and varies from case to case and from society to society. The debate surrounding any change in the law will clearly be important, for this enables both lawmakers and members of the public to express opinions which would not otherwise be heard. This openness can, in turn, encourage members of the public to rethink their attitudes, regardless of the actual success or otherwise of the law reform measure concerned, and may encourage those who, in social life, wish to assert their own lesbian or gay sexual orientation more openly. At a more indirect level, the visibility of the topic created by the public debate may mean that lesbian and gay sexuality will come to seem more understandable (perhaps even more human) to a heterosexual population which still remains largely ignorant about it. One of the greatest causes of human prejudice is, after all, ignorance, and by presenting hard data and argument on a topic, it is harder for opinions based on ignorance to be sustained.[58] Bigotry is always likely, to some extent, to remain – another in-built limitation on the social effect of law and any debate surrounding its alteration – but the impact, extent and social tolerance of bigotry may diminish.

This argument about the relevance of debate can be supported by two examples. First, Edwina Currie MP was clear that one effect of the House of Commons debate on the 1994 Act was that 'The taboo of silence that has denied the sexuality of young gay men has been decisively broken. Tonight's debate establishes the question as a matter of conscience – as it should be',[59] and that 'It is interesting that once respondents know a gay man, attitudes change dramatically and bigotry disappears.'[60] Second, in a courageous letter which appeared in the *New Statesman* in 1960 (i.e., prior to partial legality in England and Wales), three gay men – Roger Butler, Raymond Gregson and Robert Moorcroft – making what Stephen Jeffery-Poulter describes as one of the earliest gestures of 'coming out' in the British press, welcomed the then debate about the Wolfenden Committee proposals because:

> Over the past few years an enormous amount has been spoken and written about the homosexual situation. Most of it has been realistic and sensible, some has been vicious and ill-informed. But whatever its form we welcome it because we must welcome anything which brings this topic, for so long taboo, into open discussion. Only in this way can prejudice, which is born of fear and ignorance be overcome.[61]

Three examples suggest, however, that law sometimes does have a symbolic social impact, in the sense discussed at the end of the last section. First, the authors of the 1960 letter were clear that homosexuality, at the time, was 'a problem only because of the prevailing attitude towards it, and because the law encourages such an attitude and hinders every attempt to overcome it'.[62] Second, we must remember the point – which we characterized as concerning the symbolic effect of law – developed by the European Court of Human Rights when it was considering laws directed against gay male sexual activity in the *Dudgeon*, *Norris* and *Modinos* cases.[63] For the Court was clear that laws marking out lesbians and gays (or other socially disfavoured groups) for special, hostile treatment can reinforce how other people see lesbians and gays, and how lesbians and gays see themselves – regardless of whether the hostile laws are actually enforced. Third, as Didi Herman's analysis of lesbian and gay law reform campaigns in Canada suggests, it would also seem likely that campaigning work affirms a sense of self-worth for many lesbians and gays.[64] In the UK, prior to the debate over the age of consent provisions of the 1994 Criminal Justice and Public Order Act, the lesbian and gay community itself organized the campaign which produced and influenced that debate, via the lesbian and gay press and several pressure groups. It is clear that without such a campaign – i.e., without lesbians and gay men *themselves* feeling sufficiently affected by the existing legislation that they decided to do something about it – no such debate would have happened. Also relevant here is Chris Smith MP's assertion in the 1994 House of Commons debate that a higher age of consent for homosexual than for heterosexual acts

> automatically means that young gay men will be set apart from society. If we remove that discrimination from the statute-book, it may go some way towards giving young gay men the self-respect and the self-dignity to which they are entitled and should have.[65]

On balance, it would therefore seem that the crucial issue is to distinguish between situations when law is and is not likely to have a symbolic and/or educational effect, and which segments of society are likely to feel that effect.

The material considered so far prompts some tentative conclusions. The central suggestion must be that the social effect of law and law reform is, in reality, somewhat lopsided. It seems that law reform *alone* is, in the main, unlikely to have much impact, educationally or otherwise, on the bulk of the population. *Debate* about law reform may, however, have an educational effect, although this will depend on the subject and the degree to which the listener's prejudice is in-built or encouraged by the surroundings; the impact here is, anyway, likely to be felt only gradually. Equally, in areas of life where certain moral reactions are simply taken for granted – for example, people's usual moral reaction to an intentional killing, or to exceeding a speed limit – the existence of a relevant law has little or no role to play.

The key to law's social effect would seem to lie in the reactions – respectively of lesbians and gays, and of the rest of the population – to laws which could be seen as empowering lesbians and gays and to laws which are identified as weakening their social position still further. The important feature is the sensitivities which the role of lesbians and gays raises within popular culture. For a group which raises sensitivities of a particularly acute sort in the popular imagination – and lesbians, bisexuals and gay men certainly fall into this category – the existence of a law which marks them out for special, hostile treatment can help in reinforcing existing attitudes.[66] The law itself, in this situation, is an ingredient of popular culture. Equally, the mere existence of that law, when set against a prevailing background of social prejudice, will have a strong symbolic impact for those who are aware that they are lesbian or gay – hence the ongoing UK campaign to equalize the age of consent. In similar vein, reform of the law to the advantage of a disempowered group such as lesbians and gays may have the effect of giving them greater confidence and making them more assertive. We should note, however, that the introduction of new, hostile laws has also galvanized lesbians and gays into political action as much as campaigns to change the existing law: the lesbian and gay community's campaign against section 28 of the 1988 Local Government Act in the UK, or against the Colorado constitutional amendment in the USA, are clear evidence of this.[67]

What this suggests is that the social effect of law, law reform or debate about these topics can never be divorced from the relevant social background, and that, while law may reinforce existing prejudices against lesbians and gays,[68] debate and information – which might be associated with a move to alter the law – can help in eradicating social sensitivities and consequent prejudice. Even then this will be a slow process, and the extent to which debate surrounding the process of law reform impacts upon a particular society will clearly vary depending on the strength of pre-existing feelings about lesbians and gays in the society concerned. Regardless of the social effect of law in this sense, however, its mere existence can clearly contribute at a symbolic level to feelings of disempowerment among its victims, and an alteration in the law in favour of groups such as lesbians and gays could assist, as Chris Smith MP suggested, in making them feel more socially accepted. Law thus seems to have a variety of social effects which vary, depending upon the existing social background against which any law reform proposal is introduced, or against which an existing law operates.

A further qualification must be made. This is that it is perhaps artificial to attempt to scrutinize individual laws for their social effect. Particular, well-publicized law reform issues – and debate surrounding law reform by case law can do this as much as law reform by legislation[69] – may focus attention on an area of social sensitivity more generally. But outside this particular forum, it is likely to be the whole body of laws, or laws of which the public is aware, which will produce any social effect. The House of Commons debate about ages of consent during the passage of the 1994 Act enabled positive images of gay men to be presented, yet the existence of section 28 of the 1988 Local Government Act still attaches a strong stigma to lesbian and gay sexual orientations in the UK. It will be interesting to see whether, with hindsight, the social effect of the debate over the 1994 Act comes to be identified as positive, in that it enabled favourable arguments about gay male sexuality to be heard (especially since these concerned the particularly sensitive area of sexual activity and young men), or as negative, in that a regime of unequal treatment was reaffirmed.

Some pragmatic conclusions

What can we learn from the above arguments about the value of law reform exercises in eradicating social discrimination directed against lesbians and gays? How, in other words, is our second central question to be answered?

The answer seems to be that law reform, whether by legislation or case law,[70] can sometimes have a positive, empowering effect in terms of the sense of security and self-worth held by lesbians and gays. Where this happens, law is assuming a symbolic social role. Debate about law reform may also have some effect, in an educative sense, on heterosexuals; this cannot, however, be taken for granted, and any effect is likely to be over the long term. This seems to suggest that the reasons for law reform must be spelt out very clearly, and that education of the public, via outreach programmes and the like, is probably the more important element in any programme designed to eradicate anti-lesbian and gay discrimination as a matter of social practice. Among possible law reform measures, those which convey a clear message are also to be preferred over those which are ambiguous. It will take time – and judicial decisions – before the exact meaning and strength of the legal entitlements protected by law reform measures become clear, and still further time for this to filter down into popular consciousness. It is likely that the social effect of a law reform measure designed to assist lesbians and gays will also depend, to an extent, on the level of social sensitivity which already surrounds the entitlement/s which the new law claims to protect. It is unlikely, for example, that a population (or a judiciary) which is largely hostile to lesbians, bisexuals and gays will suddenly be converted to their cause by the creation of new legal entitlements to protect them: it is likely instead that considerable educational work would need to be done for the new provisions to have a beneficial social effect.

Our conclusion here must therefore be that if we believe that lesbians, bisexuals and gays are morally entitled to respect for and freedom to follow and express their sexual orientations, then protecting these entitlements through law is unlikely, on its own, to eradicate social discrimination. This should not be taken as a reason for resisting law reform proposals – for the law reform process may still, as suggested above, play some useful social role. Rather, it is an argument for placing law reform campaigns in proper perspective: as a sometimes, but not inevitably useful – and by no means the only – tactic in combating discrimination as a matter of everyday social practice. For the reasons highlighted in the previous sections, law sometimes has effects, both social and legal, and to this extent, law reform may be a useful device. Law and law reform are not, however, guaranteed to generate respect, in day-to-day social life, for the people and entitlements which they claim to protect. Given that the social and legal effects of a law reform measure are likely to be complicated and variable, it seems fair to conclude that we cannot rely on law alone if our background theory of justice suggests that lesbians and gays deserve some improvement in the (weak) social entitlements which they currently hold. So, although we have discussed a number of law reform justifications which advocate, with varying power, the idea that improvements in the legal entitlements of lesbians and gays would be commendable, it would be foolish to believe that any law reform measure is an end in itself. In fact, law reform is but a first step towards ensuring substantive justice for lesbians and gays in everyday life.

Notes

1. Didi Herman, 'The good, the bad, and the smugly: Perspectives on the Canadian Charter of Rights and Freedoms' (1994) 14 *Oxford Journal of Legal Studies* 590 at 590.
2. This issue cannot, as the word 'better' implies, be divorced entirely from background theories of justice or political morality, for some may believe, for example, that it is better as a matter of principle to use educational work rather than law in the absence of strong evidence, as opposed to mere suspicion, that the use of law will achieve the desired social goals.
3. 'Industrial relations and the law: retrospect and prospect' (1969) 7 *British Journal of Industrial Relations* 301 at 311. For a view which assumes the efficacy of law, at least in co-operative societies, see A. M. Honoré, 'The dependence of morality on law' (1993) 13 *Oxford Journal of Legal Studies* 1, and 'Necessite oblige', ch. 6 in *Making Law Bind: Essays Legal and Philosophical* (Oxford: Clarendon Press, 1987).
4. In the UK, see the Race Relations Acts 1968 and 1976; in the US, see the Civil Rights Act 1964.
5. See, e.g., Laurence Lustgarten, 'Racial inequality and the limits of law' (1986) 49 *Modern Law Review* 68; Derrick Bell, 'An allegorical critique of the United States civil rights model'; and Bob Hepple, 'Have twenty-five years of the Race Relations Acts in Britain been a failure?', chs 1 and 2 in B. Hepple and E. Szyszczak (eds), *Discrimination: the Limits of Law* (London: Mansell, 1992).
6. Roger Cotterrell, *The Sociology of Law: An Introduction* (London: Butterworths, 2nd edn, 1992), p. 45.
7. The introduction of laws in attempts to resolve perceived labour relations and public order problems are examples of this.
8. See, generally, Herman, 'The good, the bad, and the smugly'. Perhaps the clearest examples of the interconnection suggested by Herman can be seen in economic justifications for the use of law – see, generally, Richard Posner, *Sex and Reason* (Cambridge, MA: Harvard University Press, 1992).
9. Herman, 'The good, the bad, and the smugly' at 596-8.
10. *Ibid.* at 593-4.
11. *Ibid.* at 594-6.
12. *Ibid.* at 596. See further Herman's *Rights of Passage: Struggles for Lesbian and Gay Legal Equality* (Toronto: University of Toronto Press, 1994), pp. 57-60.
13. It would not therefore be possible, using Herman's terminology, to place the gay liberationists fully within the 'rights debunker' category, given their apparent support for legal reform as a stepping stone on the path to social transformation (see further chapter 3).
14. Herman, 'The good, the bad, and the smugly' at 597.
15. Some supporters of the social democratic theory may of course be 'rights enthusiasts', and some liberals may be pragmatists; the correlations suggested here are simply those which are more likely to be obvious.
16. Doreen McBarnet, 'Legal form and legal mystification: An analytical postscript on the Scottish Criminal Justice Act, the Royal Commission on Criminal Procedure, and the politics of law and order' (1982) *International Journal of the Sociology of Law* 409, esp. at 414. For broader theoretical debate, compare Ronald Dworkin, *Law's Empire* (London: Fontana, 1986); J. A. G. Griffith, 'Judicial decision-making in public law' [1985] *Public Law* 564; Sir John Laws, 'Law and democracy' [1995] *Public Law* 72; Lord Woolf, 'Droit public – English style' [1995] *Public Law* 57.
17. The impact on a legal system of rules which are not directly enforceable in domestic courts may be much more sporadic – for an example, see Leo Flynn, 'The significance of the

European Convention on Human Rights in the Irish legal order' (1994) *Irish Journal of European Law* 4.
18. Yehezkel Dror, 'Law and social change' (1959) 33 *Tulane Law Review* 787 at 788; see also Roger Cotterrell, *The Sociology of Law*, pp. 47–8.
19. William Evan, 'Law as an instrument of social change', ch. 22 in A. W. Gouldner and S. M. Miller (eds), *Applied Sociology – Opportunities and Problems* (Glencoe, IL: The Free Press, 1965), p. 286. The model proposed by Evan at pp. 288–92 is clearly artificial – see Laurence Lustgarten, 'Racial equality and the limits of law' at 70, n. 11. Lord Devlin's (conservative) discussion in 'Judges and law-makers' (1976) 39 *Modern Law Review* 1, might be seen as invoking the likely normative aspects of Evan's passive function.
20. Cf. Law of Property Act 1925; Land Registration Act 1925; Land Charges Act 1972.
21. Cf. Public Order Act 1986; Criminal Justice and Public Order Act 1994.
22. A good example is the Highway Code: the sections with a statutory basis are capable of enforcement in the courts, but potential motorists are tested on the Code before being issued with a full driving licence. Such a test would be superfluous unless it were intended that the motorists' knowledge of the relevant sections would subsequently guide their driving and *prevent* them from breaking the law. The Wolfenden Committee were clearly of opinion that the criminal law played a preventive role in the field of sexual offences – *Report of the Committee on Homosexual Offences and Prostitution* (1957 Cmnd. 247, reprinted 1968), para. 213.
23. See Peter Cane, *Atiyah's Accidents, Compensation and the Law* (London: Butterworths, 5th edn, 1993), ch. 10 for discussion of disparities between rules of Tort law and methods of out-of-court settlement pursued by insurance companies in Tort cases.
24. Cotterrell, *The Sociology of Law*, p. 55 (my italics); see also Bob Hepple, 'Have twenty-five years . . .', pp. 27–8; A. Lester and G. Bindman, *Race and Law* (London: Longman, 1972), pp. 85–7.
25. Cotterrell, *The Sociology of Law*, p. 54; see also pp. 102–6. For a more optimistic treatment of 'symbolic' law, see Eric Heinze, *Sexual Orientation: A Human Right* (Dordrecht: Martinus Nijhoff, 1995), ch. 5.
26. Cotterrell, *The Sociology of Law*, p. 54.
27. Another example could be the Consumer Protection Act 1987.
28. Lester and Bindman, *Race and Law*, pp. 85–6.
29. Evert van der Veen and Adrianne Dercksen, 'The social situation in the Member States', ch. 4 in K. Waaldijk and A. Clapham (eds), *Homosexuality: A European Community Issue* (Dordrecht/Boston/London: Martinus Nijhoff Publishers, 1993), pp. 137–40, 142, 159.
30. Evan, 'Law as an instrument of social change' at 286–7 (my italics).
31. Peter Cicchino, Bruce Deming and Katherine Nicholson, 'Sex, lies and civil rights: A critical history of the Massachusetts Gay Civil Rights Bill', reproduced in Didi Herman and Carl Stychin (eds), *Legal Inversions: Lesbians, Gay Men and the Politics of Law* (Philadelphia: Temple University Press, 1995), ch. 7 at p. 157.
32. See Andrew Ashworth's discussion in *Sentencing and Criminal Justice* (London: Butterworths, 2nd edn, 1995), pp. 62–6.
33. Lester and Bindman, *Race and Law*.
34. Although the legal term 'murder' has an emotive appeal which 'manslaughter' does not; equally, both terms are the creatures of law rather than popular imagination.
35. While different assumptions prevail in different social groups within any society, the parameters of such groups turning on factors such as employment hierarchy, sexual

orientation, notions of social class, etc., the political cultures of the UK and USA tend to be influenced by a particular set of assumptions epitomized by morally laden phrases like 'family values'. No hard-and-fast rule can be laid down concerning which assumptions are likely to be most dominant in particular circumstances, although the assumptions of stronger social groups would seem to start from an advantageous position in influencing people who do not feel themselves to be in any way distinct from the social mainstream.

36. *Strathclyde R.C. v. Porcelli* [1986] IRLR 134; *Bracebridge Engineering v. Darby* [1990] IRLR 3.
37. Dror, 'Law and social change' at 794. See also Cotterrell, *The Sociology of Law*, p. 56.
38. Cf. *ibid.*, pp. 105–6.
39. Although see McBarnet, 'Legal form and legal mystification'.
40. Dror, 'Law and social change' at 801. See also Kahn-Freund, 'Industrial relations and the law' at 311; Evan, 'Law as an instrument of social change' at 287–8.
41. *Norris v. Ireland* (1989) 13 EHRR 187 at 194–6; *Dudgeon v. United Kingdom* (1981) 4 EHRR 149 at 160–2; see also the analogous argument in *Modinos v. Cyprus* (1993) 16 EHRR 485 at 493–4.
42. Cotterrell, *The Sociology of Law*, p. 54.
43. Cf. Cicchino, Deming and Nicholson, 'Sex, lies and civil rights', pp. 157–9.
44. (1986) 106 S. Crt. 2841.
45. Kendall Thomas, 'Beyond the privacy principle' (1992) 92 *Columbia Law Review* 1431 at 1485–6; the thesis is developed at 1435, 1475, 1477, 1485–6 (esp. n. 194), 1490–2 (esp. n. 206), 1508, 1514.
46. *Report of the Secretary's Task Force on Youth Suicide: Volume 3. Prevention and Interventions in Youth Suicide* (U.S. Department of Health and Human Services, 1989) (contained in Gary Remafedi (ed.),

Death By Denial: Studies of suicide in gay and lesbian teenagers (Boston: Alyson Publications, 1994)).
47. *Ibid.*, p. 42 (emphasis added).
48. *Ibid.*, p. 55.
49. Nicola Lacey, 'From individual to group?', ch. 7 in Hepple and Szyszczak (eds), *Discrimination: The Limits of Law*, p. 121. Reading Derrick Bell's 'An allegorical critique of the United States civil rights model' in the same volume provides a good test of the importance one attaches to the social role of legislation.
50. For a theory about the value of law for socially disempowered groups, see Valerie Kerruish, *Jurisprudence as Ideology* (London: Routledge, 1991), esp. chs 6 and 7.
51. *Report of the Committee on Homosexual Offences and Prostitution.*
52. *Ibid.*, para. 58. See also para. 59.
53. Stephen Jeffery-Poulter, *Peers, Queers and Commons: the Struggle for Gay Law Reform from 1950 to the Present* (London: Routledge, 1991), p. 89.
54. H.C. Deb., 21 February 1994, Column 76.
55. Jeffery-Poulter, *Peers, Queers and Commons*, pp. 81–2.
56. Cf. *ibid.*, chs 5–10; Robert Wintemute, 'Sexual orientation discrimination', in Christopher McCrudden and Gerald Chambers (eds), *Individual Rights and the Law in Britain* (Oxford: Clarendon Press, 1994).
57. For discussion of law's ineffectiveness in some spheres of life, see Roger Cotterrell, *Law's Community: Legal Theory in Sociological Perspective* (Oxford: Clarendon Press, 1995), pp. 266–7. An interesting feature of the present context is the subtle shift in argument, between 1967 and 1994, on the part of those opposed to, respectively, partial decriminalization and reduction in the age of consent to 16. In 1967, opponents' arguments looked at the direct message which they believed a change in the law

would give, i.e. that of moral approval. In 1994, the main argument was that law should 'protect' an alleged group of young men, uncertain of their sexual orientation, from exploitation *by others* who sought to 'convince' them.

58. This being so, it is interesting to note that the lesbian and gay campaigners who pushed for the introduction of the Massachusetts Gay Civil Rights Bill believed that it was best to confine debate, so far as possible, to the state legislature, and were anxious to resist putting the measure to any sort of popular test via a state-wide referendum – see Cicchino, Deming and Nicholson, 'Sex, lies and civil rights'.

59. H.C. Deb., 21 February 1994, Column 74.

60. H.C. Deb., 21 February 1994, Columns 75–6.

61. *New Statesman*, 4 June 1960. Reprinted in Jeffery-Poulter, *Peers, Queers and Commons*, pp. 66–7.

62. *Ibid*. For contemporary evidence, see Gordon Westwood, *A Minority – A Report on the Life of the Male Homosexual in Great Britain* (London: Longmans, 1960), pp. 144–7.

63. See n. 41 above.

64. Herman, *Rights of Passage*, ch. 4.

65. H.C. Deb., 21 February 1994, Column 111.

66. See Kendall Thomas's analysis of the US position – 'Beyond the privacy principle'.

67. Cf. Jeffery-Poulter, *Peers, Queers and Commons*, ch. 11; Wintemute, 'Sexual orientation discrimination' pp. 507–10; Carl Stychin, *Law's Desire: Sexuality and the Limits of Justice* (London: Routledge, 1995), pp. 48–9, 53. Another example may be the widespread protest – among many strands of youth culture – during the passage through Parliament of the then Criminal Justice and Public Order Bill 1994, due to its restrictive public order and trespass provisions. A reverse example would be the galvanization, in Canada, of 'Christian' right groups in the face of proposals to extend anti-discrimination legislation to protect lesbians and gays – a move felt to be hostile *by the right-wingers* – cf. Herman, *Rights of Passage*, chs 5 and 6.

68. Cf. Marc Burke, 'Homosexuality as deviance: The case of the gay police officer' (1994) 34 *British Journal of Criminology* 192, esp. at 196–7, for further analysis of this point.

69. Marital rape is perhaps an example.

70. An example of law reform by case law can be seen in the redefinition, in *R v. Birmingham City Council, ex parte Equal Opportunities Commission* [1989] 1 AC 1155 and *James v. Eastleigh B.C.* [1990] 2 AC 751, of the meaning of direct discrimination within section 1(1)(a) of the Sex Discrimination Act 1975, a consequence of which was an apparent widening in the range of groups potentially able to claim protection under the Act – see Nicholas Bamforth, 'The changing concept of sex discrimination' (1993) 56 *Modern Law Review* 872; 'Sexual orientation and dismissal from employment' (1994) *New Law Journal* 1402.

Bibliography

Adam, Barry. *The Rise of a Gay and Lesbian Movement*. Boston: Twayne, 1987.

Allan, T. R. S. 'Citizenship and obligation: Civil disobedience and civil dissent' [1996] 55 *Cambridge Law Journal* 89.

Altman, Dennis. *Homosexuality: Oppression and Liberation*. London: Serpent's Tail, 2nd edn, 1993.

Anderson, Perry. 'Power, politics and the Enlightenment', in David Miliband (ed.), *Reinventing the Left*. Cambridge: Polity Press, 1994.

Angelo Corlett, J. 'The problem of collective moral rights' (1994) 7 *Canadian Journal of Law and Jurisprudence* 237.

Anscombe, G. E. M. 'Contraception and chastity', ch. 8 in Michael Bayles (ed.), *Ethics and Population*. Cambridge: Schenkman, 1976.

Anscombe, G. E. M. 'You can have sex without children: Christianity and the new offer', in *Collected Philosophical Papers volume 3: Ethics, Religion and Poltics*. Oxford: Basil Blackwell, 1981.

Arkes, Hadley. 'Questions of principle, not predictions: A reply to Macedo' (1995) 84 *Georgetown Law Journal* 321.

Ashworth, Andrew. *Principles of Criminal Law*. Oxford: Clarendon Press, 2nd edn, 1995.

Ashworth, Andrew. *Sentencing and Criminal Justice*. London: Butterworths, 2nd edn, 1995.

Ayer, A. J. *Freedom and Morality and Other Essays*. Oxford: Clarendon Press, 1984.

Bamforth, Nicholas. 'The changing concept of sex discrimination' (1993) 56 *Modern Law Review* 872.

Bamforth, Nicholas. 'Sado-masochism and consent' [1994] *Criminal Law Review* 661.

Bamforth, Nicholas. 'Sexual orientation and dismissal from employment' (1994) 144 *New Law Journal* 1402.

Bamforth, Nicholas. 'Sexuality and law in the new Europe' (1995) 58 *Modern Law Review* 109.

Bamforth, Nicholas. 'Setting the limits of anti-discrimination law: Some legal and social concepts', in Janet Dine and Bob Watt (eds), *Discrimination Law: Concepts, Limitations and Justifications*. Harlow: Longman, 1996.

Barendt, Eric. *Freedom of Speech*. Oxford: Clarendon Press, 1985.

Bartlett, Peter. 'Another sodomitical erection', unpublished paper presented at the Lancaster University 'Legal Queeries' conference, September 1995.

Bayles, Michael (ed.). *Ethics and Population*. Cambridge: Schenkman, 1976.

Bedingfield, David. 'Privacy or publicity? The enduring confusion surrounding the American Tort of invasion of privacy' (1992) 55 *Modern Law Review* 111.

Bell, Daniel. *Communitarianism and its Critics*. Oxford: Clarendon Press, 1993.

Bell, Derrick. 'An allegorical critique of the United States civil rights model', ch. 1 in B. Hepple and E. Szyszczak (eds), *Discrimination: the Limits of Law*. London: Mansell, 1992.

Berlin, Sir Isaiah. 'Equality', in *Concepts and Categories: Philosophical Essays*. Oxford: Oxford University Press, 1980.

Birch, Anthony. *The Concepts and Theories of Modern Democracy*. London: Routledge, 1993.

Birch, Keith. 'A community of interests', in Bob Cant and Susan Hemmings (eds), *Radical Records: Thirty Years of Lesbian and Gay History*. London: Routledge, 1988.

Bodmer, Walter and McKie, Robin. *The Book of Man: The Quest to Discover

Our Genetic Heritage. London: Abacus, 1995.

Boswell, John. *Christianity, Social Tolerance, and Homosexuality: Gay People in Western Europe from the Beginning of the Christian Era to the Fourteenth Century*. Chicago: University of Chicago Press, 1980.

Boswell, John. 'Categories, experience and sexuality' in Edward Stein (ed.), *Forms of Desire: Sexual Orientation and the Social Constructionist Controversy*. New York: Garland, 1990.

Bradley, David. 'Homosexuality and child custody in English law' (1987) 1 *International Journal of Law and the Family* 155.

Bristow, Joseph and Wilson, Angelia (eds). *Activating Theory: Lesbian, Gay, Bisexual Politics*. London: Lawrence & Wishart, 1993.

Brundage, James. *Law, Sex, and Christian Society in Medieval Europe*. Chicago: University of Chicago Press, 1987.

Buckley, Michael. *Morality and the Homosexual: A Catholic Approach to a Moral Problem*. London: Sands & Co., 1959.

Burke, Marc. 'Homosexuality as deviance: The case of the gay police officer' (1994) 34 *British Journal of Criminology* 192.

Cain, Patricia. 'Litigating for lesbian and gay rights: A legal history' (1993) 79 *Virginia Law Review* 1551.

Campbell, Tom. *The Left and Rights: A Conceptual Analysis of the Idea of Socialist Rights*. London: Routledge, 1983.

Cane, Peter. *Atiyah's Accidents, Compensation and the Law*. London: Butterworths, 5th edn, 1993.

Cant, Bob and Hemmings, Susan (eds). *Radical Records: Thirty Years of Lesbian and Gay History*. London: Routledge, 1988.

Cicchino, Peter, Deming, Bruce and Nicholson, Katherine. 'Sex, lies and civil rights: A critical history of the Massachusetts Gay Civil Rights Bill', reproduced as ch. 7 of Didi Herman and Carl Stychin (eds), *Legal Inversions: Lesbians, Gay Men and the Politics of Law*. Philadelphia: Temple University Press, 1995.

Colvin, Madeleine and Hawksley, Jane. *Section 28: A Practical Guide to the Law and its Implementation*. London: National Council for Civil Liberties, 1989.

Cook, W. W. (ed.). *Fundamental Legal Conceptions*. New Haven CT: Yale University Press, 1923.

Cooper, Davina. *Sexing the City: Lesbian and Gay Politics Within the Activist State*. London: Rivers Oram, 1994.

Cotterrell, Roger. *The Politics of Jurisprudence: A Critical Introduction to Legal Philosophy*. London: Butterworths, 1989.

Cotterrell, Roger. *The Sociology of Law: An Introduction*. London: Butterworths, 2nd edn, 1992.

Cotterrell, Roger. *Law's Community: Legal Theory in Sociological Perspective*. Oxford: Clarendon Press, 1995.

Craig, Paul. *Public Law and Democracy in the United Kingdom and the United States of America*. Oxford: Clarendon Press, 1990.

Crane, Paul. *Gays and the Law*. London: Pluto Press, 1982.

Crouch, Colin and Marquand, David (eds). *Reinventing Collective Action: From the Global to the Local*. Oxford: Blackwell, 1995.

Currah, Paisley. 'Searching for immutability: Homosexuality, race and rights discourse', in Angelia Wilson (ed.), *A Simple Matter of Justice?* London: Cassell, 1995.

Deitcher, D. (ed.). *Over the Rainbow: Lesbian and Gay Politics in America Since Stonewall*. London: Boxtree/Channel Four, 1995.

D'Emilio, John. 'Gay politics and community in San Francisco since World War II', in M. B. Duberman, M. Vicinus and G. Chauncey (eds), *Hidden from History: Reclaiming the Gay and Lesbian Past*. London: Penguin, 1989.

D'Emilio, John. *Making Trouble: Essays on Gay History, Politics, and the University*. New York: Routledge, 1992.

Devlin, Lord. *The Enforcement of Morals*. Oxford: Oxford University Press, 1965.

Devlin, Lord. 'Judges and law-makers' (1976) 39 *Modern Law Review* 1.

Dine, Janet and Watt, Bob (eds). *Discrimination Law: Concepts, Limitations and Justifications*. Harlow: Longman, 1996.

Dror, Yehezkel. 'Law and social change' (1959) 33 *Tulane Law Review* 787.

Drucker, Peter. '"In the tropics there is no sin": Sexuality and gay–lesbian movements in the Third World' (1996) 218 *New Left Review* 75.

Duberman, M. B., Vicinus, M. and Chauncey, G. (eds). *Hidden from History: Reclaiming the Gay and Lesbian Past*. London: Penguin, 1989.

Duff, R. A. *Intention, Agency and Criminal Liability: Philosophy of Action and the Criminal Law*. Oxford: Blackwell, 1990.

Duncan, Richard. 'Who wants to stop the Church: Homosexual rights legislation, public policy, and religious freedom' (1994) 69 *Notre Dame Law Review* 393.

Dworkin, Ronald. *Taking Rights Seriously*. London: Duckworth, 1977.

Dworkin, Ronald. 'What is equality? Part 1: Equality of welfare' (1981) 10 *Philosophy & Public Affairs* 185.

Dworkin, Ronald. 'What is equality? Part 2: Equality of resources' (1981) 10 *Philosophy & Public Affairs* 283.

Dworkin, Ronald. *A Matter of Principle*. Oxford: Clarendon Press, 1986.

Dworkin, Ronald. *Law's Empire*. London: Fontana, 1986.

Dworkin, Ronald. 'What is equality? Part 3: The place of liberty' (1987) 73 *Iowa Law Review* 1.

Dworkin, Ronald. 'Liberal community' (1989) 77 *California Law Review* 479.

Dworkin, Ronald. 'Sex, death, and the courts', *New York Review of Books*, 8 August 1996, p. 44.

Eichbaum, June. 'Towards an autonomy-based theory of constitutional privacy: Beyond the ideology of familial privacy' (1979) 14 *Harvard Civil Rights–Civil Liberties Law Review* 361.

Epstein, Steven. 'Gay politics, ethnic identity: The limits of social constructionism', in Edward Stein (ed.), *Forms of Desire: Sexual Orientation and the Social Constructionist Controversy*. New York: Garland, 1990.

Evan, William. 'Law as an instrument of social change', ch. 22 in A. W. Gouldner and S. M. Miller (eds), *Applied Sociology – Opportunities and Problems*. Glencoe, IL: The Free Press, 1965.

Feinberg, Joel. *Harm to Others*, vol. 1 of *The Moral Limits of the Criminal Law*. New York: Oxford University Press, 1984.

Feinberg, Joel. *Harmless Wrongdoing*, vol. 4 of *The Moral Limits of the Criminal Law*. New York: Oxford University Press, 1990.

Feinberg, Joel. 'In defence of moral rights' (1992) 12 *Oxford Journal of Legal Studies* 149.

Finnis, John. 'Natural law and unnatural acts' (1970) 11 *The Heythrop Journal* 365.

Finnis, John. *Natural Law and Natural Rights*. Oxford: Clarendon Press, 1980.

Finnis, John. *Fundamentals of Ethics*. Oxford: Clarendon Press, 1983.

Finnis, John. 'A Bill of Rights for Britain? The moral of contemporary jurisprudence' (1985) *Proceedings of the British Academy*, vol. LXXI, 303.

Finnis, John. 'Personal integrity, sexual morality, and responsible parenthood' (1985) 1 *Anthropos: Rivistadi di Studi Sulla Persona e la Famiglia* 43.

Finnis, John. 'On "The Critical Legal Studies Movement"' (1985) 30 *American Journal of Jurisprudence* 21.

Finnis, John. 'Legal enforcement of "duties to oneself": Kant v. neo-Kantians' (1987) 87 *Columbia Law Review* 433.

Finnis, John. *Moral Absolutes: Tradition, Revision, and Truth*. Washington, DC: Catholic University of America Press, 1990.

Finnis, John. 'Law, morality, and "sexual orientation"' (1993–4) 69 *Notre Dame Law Review* 1049.

Finnis, John. 'Is natural law theory compatible with limited government?' in Robert George (ed.), *Natural Law, Liberalism and Morality*. Oxford: Clarendon Press, 1996.

Finnis, John, with Boyle, Joseph and Grisez, Germain. *Nuclear Deterrence, Morality and Realism*. Oxford: Clarendon Press, 1987.

Fitzgerald, P. J. *Salmond on Jurisprudence*. London: Sweet & Maxwell, 12th edn, 1966.

Flynn, Leo. 'The significance of the European Convention on Human Rights in the Irish legal order' (1994) *Irish Journal of European Law* 4.

Foucault, Michel. *The History of Sexuality – Volume 1: An Introduction*. London: Penguin, 1981, English translation.

Frazer, Elizabeth and Lacey, Nicola. *The Politics of Community: A Feminist Critique of the Liberal–Communitarian Debate*. Hemel Hempstead: Harvester Wheatsheaf, 1993.

Freeden, Michael. *Rights*. Milton Keynes: Open University Press, 1991.

Freeman, Michael. *Lloyd's Introduction to Jurisprudence*. London: Sweet & Maxwell, 6th edn, 1994.

Frey, R. G. (ed.). *Utility and Rights*. Oxford: Basil Blackwell, 1984.

Fried, Charles. 'Privacy' (1968) 77 *Yale Law Journal* 475.

Fried, Charles. Correspondence, (1976) 6 *Philosophy & Public Affairs* 288.

Friedman, David. 'A positive account of property rights', in Ellen Frankel Paul, Fred Miller and Jeffrey Paul (eds), *Property Rights*. Cambridge: Cambridge University Press, 1994.

Fukuyama, Francis. 'The end of history?' Summer (1989) 16 *The National Interest* 3.

Fukuyama, Francis. *The End of History and the Last Man*. New York: Free Press, 1992.

Fuss, Diana. *Essentially Speaking: Feminism, Nature & Difference*. New York: Routledge, 1990.

Gardner, E. Clinton. *Justice and Christian Ethics*. Cambridge: Cambridge University Press, 1995.

Gardner, John. 'Liberals and unlawful discrimination' (1989) 9 *Oxford Journal of Legal Studies* 1.

Gardner, John. 'Freedom of Expression', in Christopher McCrudden and Gerald Chambers (eds), *Individual Rights and the Law in Britain*. Oxford: Clarendon Press, 1994.

Gavison, Ruth. 'Privacy and the limits of law' (1980) 89 *Yale Law Journal* 421.

Gay Left Collective (eds). *Homosexuality: Power and Politics*. London: Allison & Busby, 1980.

Gearty, Conor and Tomkins, Adam (eds). *Understanding Human Rights*. London: Mansell, 1996.

Gellner, Ernest. 'Sauce for the liberal goose', *Prospect*, November 1995, 56.

George, Robert. 'Recent criticism of natural law theory' (1988) 55 *University of Chicago Law Review* 1371.

George, Robert. *Making Men Moral: Civil Liberties and Public Morality*. Oxford: Clarendon Press, 1993.

George, Robert (ed.). *Natural Law, Liberalism and Morality*. Oxford: Clarendon Press, 1996.

George, Robert and Bradley, Gerard. 'Marriage and the liberal imagination' (1995) 84 *Georgetown Law Journal* 301.

Giddens, Anthony. 'Brave new world: The new context of politics', in David Miliband (ed.), *Reinventing the Left*. Cambridge: Polity Press, 1994.

Gilligan, Carol. *In a Different Voice: Psychological Theory and Women's Development*. Cambridge, MA: Harvard University Press, rev. edn, 1993.

Glazer, Nathan. 'Individual rights against group rights', in his *Ethnic Dilemmas: 1964–1982*. Cambridge, MA: Harvard University Press, 1982.

Glendon, Mary Anne. *Rights Talk: The Impoverishment of Political Discourse*. New York, Free Press, 1991.

Gold, Marc. 'Comment: *Andrews v. Law Society of British Columbia*' (1989) 34 *McGill Law Journal* 1063.

Gomez, J. 'Out of the past', in D. Deitcher (ed.), *Over the Rainbow: Lesbian and Gay Politics in America Since Stonewall*. London: Boxtree/Channel Four, 1995.

Gouldner, A. W. and Miller, S. M. (eds). *Applied Sociology – Opportunities and Problems*. Glencoe, IL: The Free Press, 1965.

Grau, Gunter (ed.). *Hidden Holocaust? Gay and Lesbian Persecution in Germany 1933–45*. London: Cassell, 1995.

Gray, John. *After Social Democracy: Politics, Capitalism, and the Common Life*. London: Demos, 1996.

Greasley, Phil. *Gay Men at Work: A report on discrimination against gay men in employment in London*. London: Lesbian and Gay Employment Rights, 1986.

Green, Leslie. 'Two views of collective rights' (1991) 4 *Canadian Journal of Law and Jurisprudence* 315.

Greenawalt, Kent. *Conflicts of Law and Morality*. Oxford: Clarendon Press, 1987.

Grey, Antony. *Quest for Justice – Towards Homosexual Emancipation*. London: Sinclair-Stevenson, 1992.

Griffith, J. A. G. 'Judicial decision-making in public law' [1985] *Public Law* 564.

Guest, Stephen. *Ronald Dworkin*. Edinburgh: Edinburgh University Press, 1992.

Guthrie, Mark and Hamilton, Angus. *The Lesbian and Gay Rights Handbook*. London: Cassell, forthcoming.

Gutmann, Amy (ed.). *Multiculturalism: Examining the Politics of Recognition*. Princeton, NJ: Princeton University Press, 1994.

Hacker, P. M. S. and Raz, J. (eds). *Law, Morality and Society: Essays in Honour of H. L. A. Hart*. Oxford: Clarendon Press, 1977.

Haigh, Richard and Harris, Dai (eds). *AIDS: A Guide to the Law*. London: Routledge, 2nd edn, 1995.

Hall, Edmund. *We Can't Even March Straight: Homosexuality and the British Armed Forces*. London: Vintage, 1995.

Halley, Janet. 'The construction of heterosexuality', in Michael Warner (ed.), *Fear of a Queer Planet*. Minneapolis: University of Minnesota Press, 1993.

Halley, Janet. 'Sexual orientation and the politics of biology: A critique of the argument from immutability' (1994) 46 *Stanford Law Review* 503.

Halperin, David. 'Sex before sexuality: Pederasty, politics, and power in Classical Athens', in M. B. Duberman, M. Vicinus and G. Chauncey (eds), *Hidden from History: Rethinking the Lesbian and Gay Past*. London: Penguin, 1989.

Hamer, Dean and Copeland, Peter. *The Science of Desire: The Search for the Gay Gene and the Biology of Behavior*. New York: Simon & Schuster, 1994.

Harris, Henry (ed.). *Identity*. Oxford: Clarendon Press, 1995.

Harris, Neville. *The Law Relating to Schools*. London: Tolley, 2nd edn, 1995.

Hart, H. L. A. *Law, Liberty, and Morality*. Oxford: Oxford University Press, 1963.

Hart, H. L. A. *Essays on Bentham*. Oxford: Clarendon Press, 1982.

Hart, H. L. A. *Essays in Jurisprudence and Philosophy*. Oxford: Clarendon Press, 1983.

Hart, H. L. A. *The Concept of Law*. Oxford: Clarendon Press, 2nd edn, 1994.

Hartney, Michael. 'Some confusions concerning collective rights' (1991) 4 *Canadian Journal of Law and Jurisprudence* 293.

Heger, Heinz. *The Men With The Pink Triangle*, intro. by David Fernbach. London: GMP, 1972.

Heinze, Eric. *Sexual Orientation: A Human Right*. Dordrecht: Martinus Nijhoff, 1995.

Held, David. 'Inequalities of power, problems of democracy', in David Miliband (ed.), *Reinventing the Left*. Cambridge: Polity Press, 1994.

Held, David. *Models of Democracy*. Oxford: Blackwell, 2nd edn, 1996.

Henkin, Louis. 'Privacy and autonomy' (1974) 74 *Columbia Law Review* 1410.

Hepple, Bob. 'Have twenty-five years of the Race Relations Acts in Britain been a failure?', ch. 2 in B. Hepple and E. Szyszczak (eds), *Discrimination: the Limits of Law*. London: Mansell, 1992.

Hepple, Bob and Szyszczak, E. (eds). *Discrimination: the Limits of Law*. London: Mansell, 1992.

Herek, Gregory and Berrill, Kevin (eds). *Hate Crimes: Confronting Violence Against Lesbians and Gay Men*. Newbury Park: Sage, 1992.

Herman, Didi. 'Are we family?: Lesbian rights and women's liberation' (1990) 28 *Osgoode Hall Law Journal* 789.

Herman, Didi 'The good, the bad, and the smugly: Perspectives on the Canadian Charter of Rights and Freedoms' (1994) 14 *Oxford Journal of Legal Studies* 590.

Herman, Didi. *Rights of Passage: Struggles for Lesbian and Gay Legal Equality*. Toronto, University of Toronto Press, 1994.

Herman, Didi and Stychin, Carl (eds). *Legal Inversions: Lesbians, Gay Men and the Politics of Law*. Philadelphia: Temple University Press, 1995.

Hindley, J. Clifford. 'The age of consent for male homosexuals' [1986] *Criminal Law Review* 595.

Hohfeld, W. N. 'Fundamental legal conceptions as applied in judicial reasoning', ch. 1 in W. W. Cook (ed.), *Fundamental Legal Conceptions*. New Haven, CT: Yale University Press, 1923.

Honoré, A. M. *Making Law Bind: Essays Legal and Philosophical*. Oxford: Clarendon Press, 1987.

Honoré, A. M. 'The dependence of morality on law' (1993) 13 *Oxford Journal of Legal Studies* 1.

Ingram, Attracta. *A Political Theory of Rights*. Oxford: Clarendon Press, 1994.

Jarvis Thomson, Judith. 'The right to privacy' (1975) 4 *Philosophy & Public Affairs* 295.

Jarvis Thomson, Judith. *The Realm of Rights*. Cambridge, MA: Harvard University Press, 1990.

Jeffery-Poulter, Stephen. *Peers, Queers and Commons: The Struggle for Gay Law Reform from 1950 to the Present*. London: Routledge, 1991.

Jenkins, Roy. *Gladstone*. London: Macmillan, 1995.

Kahn-Freund, Otto. 'Industrial relations and the law: Retrospect and prospect' (1969) 7 *British Journal of Industrial Relations* 301.

Katz, Jonathan N. *Gay American History: Lesbians and Gay Men in the U.S.A.* New York: Meridian, rev. edn, 1992.

Kerruish, Valerie. *Jurisprudence as Ideology*. London: Routledge, 1991.

Kingdom, Elizabeth. *What's Wrong With Rights? Problems for Feminist Politics of Law*. Edinburgh: Edinburgh University Press, 1991.

Kinsman, Gary. *The Regulation of Desire: Sexuality in Canada*. Montreal: Black Rose Books, 1987.

Kymlicka, Will. *Liberalism, Community, and Culture*. Oxford: Clarendon Press, 1989.

Kymlicka, Will. 'Liberal individualism and liberal neutrality' (1989) 99 *Ethics* 883.

Kymlicka, Will. *Contemporary Political Philosophy: An Introduction*. Oxford: Clarendon Press, 1990.

Kymlicka, Will. *Multicultural Citizenship*. Oxford: Clarendon Press, 1995.

Lacey, Nicola. 'From individual to group?', in Bob Hepple and Erica Szyszczak (eds), *Discrimination: the Limits of Law*. London: Mansell, 1992.

Laslett, Peter and Runciman, W. G. (eds). *Philosophy, Politics and Society* (Second Series). Oxford: Basil Blackwell, 1962.

Law Commission Consultation Paper No. 139, *Consent in the Criminal Law*. London: HMSO, 1995.

Laws, Sir John. 'Law and democracy' [1995] *Public Law* 72.

Leader, Sheldon. 'The right to privacy, the enforcement of morals, and the judicial function: An argument' (1990) 43 *Current Legal Problems* 115.

Leahy, Michael and Cohn-Sherbok, Dan (eds). *The Liberation Debate: Rights at Issue*. London: Routledge, 1996.

Lester, Anthony and Bindman, Geoffrey. *Race and Law*. London: Longman, 1972.

Locke, Lawrence. 'Personhood and moral responsibility' (1990) 9 *Law and Philosophy* 39.

Lustgarten, Laurence. 'Problems of proof in employment discrimination cases' (1977) 6 *Industrial Law Journal* 212.

Lustgarten, Laurence. 'Racial inequality and the limits of law' (1986) 49 *Modern Law Review* 68.

Lyons, David. *Ethics and the Rule of Law*. Cambridge: Cambridge University Press, 1984.

McBarnet, Doreen. 'Legal form and legal mystification: An analytical postscript on the Scottish Criminal Justice Act, the Royal Commission on Criminal Procedure, and the politics of law and order' (1982) *International Journal of the Sociology of Law* 409.

McCloskey, H. J. 'Respect for human moral rights versus maximising good', in R. G. Frey (ed.), *Utility and Rights*. Oxford: Basil Blackwell, 1984.

MacCormick, Neil. 'Rights in legislation', in P. M. S. Hacker and J. Raz (eds), *Law, Morality and Society: Essays in Honour of H. L. A. Hart*. Oxford: Clarendon Press, 1977.

MacCormick, Neil. *H. L. A. Hart*. London: Edward Arnold, 1981.

MacCormick, Neil. *Legal Right and Social Democracy: Essays in Legal and Political Philosophy*. Oxford: Clarendon Press, 1982.

MacCormick, Neil. 'A moralistic case for amoralistic law?' (1985) 20 *Valparaiso University Law Review* 1.

McCrudden, Christopher and Chambers, Gerald (eds). *Individual Rights and the Law in Britain*. Oxford: Clarendon Press, 1994.

Macedo, Stephen. *Liberal Virtues: Citizenship, Virtue, and Community in Liberal Constitutionalism*. Oxford: Clarendon Press, 1990.

Macedo, Stephen. 'Homosexuality and the conservative mind' (1995) 84 *Georgetown Law Journal* 261.

Macedo, Stephen. 'Reply to critics' (1995) 84 *Georgetown Law Journal* 329.

MacIntyre, Alasdair. *After Virtue: A Study in Moral Theory*. London: Duckworth, 2nd edn, 1985.

MacIntyre, Alasdair. *Whose Justice? Which Rationality?* London: Duckworth, 1988.

Mackie, J. L. *Ethics: Inventing Right and Wrong*. London: Penguin, 1977.

MacKinnon, Catharine. 'Feminism, Marxism, method, and the state: An agenda for theory' (1982) 7 *Signs: Journal of Women in Culture and Society* 515.

MacKinnon, Catharine. 'Feminism, Marxism, method, and the state: Toward feminist Jurisprudence' (1983) 8 *Signs: Journal of Women in Culture and Society* 635.

MacKinnon, Catharine. *Feminism Unmodified: Discourses on Life and Law.* Cambridge, MA: Harvard University Press, 1987.

Malik, Maleiha. 'Communal goods as human rights', ch. 7 in Conor Gearty and Adam Tomkins (eds), *Understanding Human Rights.* London: Mansell, 1996.

Markesinis, Basil. 'The Calcutt Report must not be forgotten' (1992) 55 *Modern Law Review* 118.

Markesinis, Basil. 'Our patchy law of privacy – Time to do something about it' (1990) 53 *Modern Law Review* 802.

Marneffe, Peter De. 'Liberalism, liberty and neutrality' (1990) 19 *Philosophy & Public Affairs* 253.

Marshall, John. 'The politics of tea and sympathy', in Gay Left Collective (eds), *Homosexuality: Power and Politics.* London: Allison & Busby, 1980.

Midgley, Mary. *Can't We Make Moral Judgements?* Bristol: The Bristol Press, 1991.

Miliband, David (ed.). *Reinventing the Left.* Cambridge: Polity Press, 1994.

Mill, J. S. *On Liberty*, ed. Stefan Collini. Cambridge: Cambridge University Press, 1989 edn.

Miller, Harris. 'An argument for the application of Equal Protection heightened scrutiny to classifications based on homosexuality' (1984) 57 *Southern California Law Review* 797.

Mohr, Richard. *Gays/Justice: A Study of Ethics, Society, and Law.* New York: Columbia University Press, 1988.

Mohr, Richard. *Gay Ideas: Outing and Other Controversies.* Boston: Beacon Press, 1992.

Mohr, Richard. 'The perils of postmodernity for gay rights' (1995) 8 *Canadian Journal of Law and Jurisprudence* 5.

Moore, Michael. 'Sandelian antiliberalism' (1989) 77 *California Law Review* 539.

Moran, Leslie. 'Justice and its vicissitudes' (1991) 54 *Modern Law Review* 146.

Mouffe, Chantal. *The Return of the Political.* London: Verso, 1993.

Mulhall, Stephen and Swift, Adam. *Liberals and Communitarians.* Oxford: Basil Blackwell, 1992.

Nagel, Thomas. *Mortal Questions.* Cambridge: Cambridge University Press, 1979.

Nagel, Thomas. *The View From Nowhere.* Oxford: Oxford University Press, 1986.

Nagel, Thomas. 'Moral conflict and political legitimacy' (1987) 16 *Philosophy & Public Affairs* 215.

Nagel, Thomas. *Equality and Partiality.* New York: Oxford University Press, 1991.

Nagel, Thomas. *Other Minds: Critical Essays 1969–1994.* New York: Oxford University Press, 1995.

Narveson, Jan. 'Contractarian rights', in R. G. Frey (ed.), *Utility and Rights.* Oxford: Basil Blackwell, 1984.

Norrie, Kenneth McK. 'Symbolic and meaningless legislation' (September 1988) *Journal of the Law Society of Scotland* 310.

Note, 'The constitutionality of laws forbidding private homosexual conduct' (1974) 72 *Michigan Law Review* 1613.

Note, 'The constitutional status of sexual orientation' (1985) 98 *Harvard Law Review* 1285.

Note, 'Custody denials to parents in same-sex relationships: an Equal Protection analysis' (1989) 102 *Harvard Law Review* 617.

Note, 'Developments in the law – Sexual orientation' (1989) 102 *Harvard Law Review* 1508.

Nozick, Robert. *Anarchy, State and Utopia.* New York: Basic Books, 1974.

Nussbaum, Martha. 'Platonic love and Colorado law: the relevance of Ancient Greek norms to modern sexual controversies' (1994) 80 *Virginia Law Review* 1515.

Nussbaum, Martha. 'Lesbian and gay rights: Pro' and 'Nussbaum's reply', chs 7 and 9 in Michael Leahy and Dan Cohn-Sherbok (eds), *The Liberation Debate: Rights at Issue.* London: Routledge, 1996.

Ortiz, Daniel. 'Creating controversy: Essentialism and constructivism and the politics of gay identity' (1993) 79 *Virginia Law Review* 1833.

Ortner, S. B. and Whitehead, H. (eds). *Sexual Meanings: The Cultural Construction of Gender and Sexuality.* Cambridge: Cambridge University Press, 1981.

Padgug, Robert. 'Sexual matters: Rethinking sexuality in history', in M. B. Duberman, M. Vicinus and G. Chauncey (eds), *Hidden from History: Reclaiming the Lesbian and Gay Past.* London: Penguin, 1989.

Palmer, Anya. *Less Equal than Others: a survey of lesbians and gay men at work*. London: Stonewall, 1993.

Palmer, Anya. 'Lesbian and gay rights campaigning: A report from the coalface', in Angelia R. Wilson (ed.), *A Simple Matter of Justice?* London: Cassell, 1995.

Paul, Ellen Frankel, Miller, Fred and Paul, Jeffrey (eds). *Property Rights*. Cambridge: Cambridge University Press, 1994.

Peck, Dale. 'Making history', ch. 4 in D. Deitcher (ed.), *Over the Rainbow: Lesbian and Gay Politics in America Since Stonewall*. London: Boxtree/Channel Four, 1995.

Phillips, Oliver. 'Zimbabwean law and the production of a white man's disease'. Unpublished paper delivered at the Lancaster University 'Legal Queeries' conference, September 1995.

Plant, Raymond. *Modern Political Thought*. Oxford: Basil Blackwell, 1991.

Plant, Richard. *The Pink Triangle: The Nazi War Against Homosexuals*. Edinburgh: Mainstream Publishing, 1987.

Plummer, Kenneth (ed.). *The Making of the Modern Homosexual*. London: Hutchinson, 1981.

Polikoff, Nancy. 'We will not get what we ask for: Why legalizing gay and lesbian marriage will not "dismantle the legal structure of gender in every marriage"' (1993) 79 *Virginia Law Review* 1535.

Posner, Richard. *Sex and Reason*. Cambridge, MA: Harvard University Press, 1992.

Power, Lisa. *No Bath But Plenty of Bubbles: An Oral History of the Gay Liberation Front 1970–73*. London: Cassell, 1995.

Prescott, Peter. 'Kaye v. Robertson – A Reply' (1991) 54 *Modern Law Review* 451.

Pronk, Pim. *Against Nature: Types of Moral Argumentation Regarding Homosexuality*. Michigan: Eerdmans Publishing, 1993.

Rawls, John. *A Theory of Justice*. Oxford: Oxford University Press, 1972.

Rawls, John. 'Kantian constructivism in moral theory' (1980) *Journal of Philosophy* 77.

Rawls, John. *Political Liberalism*. New York: Columbia University Press, 1993.

Raz, Joseph. *The Morality of Freedom*. Oxford: Clarendon Press, 1986.

Raz, Joseph. *Ethics in the Public Domain: Essays in the Morality of Law and Politics*. Oxford: Clarendon Press, 1994.

Reece, Helen. 'The paramountcy principle: Consensus or construct?' (1996) 49 *Current Legal Problems* Part 2, 267.

Reece, Helen. 'Subverting the stigmatization argument' (1996) 23 *Journal of Law and Society* 484.

Reiman, Jeffrey. 'Privacy, intimacy, and personhood' (1976) 6 *Philosophy & Public Affairs* 26.

Remafedi, Gary (ed.). *Death By Denial: Studies of suicide in gay and lesbian teenagers*. Boston: Alyson Publications, 1994.

Richards, David. *Sex, Drugs, Death, and the Law: An Essay on Human Rights and Overcriminalization*. Totowa: Rowman & Littlefield, 1982.

Richards, David. 'Kantian ethics and the harm principle: A reply to John Finnis' (1987) 87 *Columbia Law Review* 457.

Roberts, Paul. 'Consent and the criminal law: Philosophical foundations', Appendix C to Law Commission Consultation Paper No. 139, *Consent in the Criminal Law*. London: HMSO, 1995.

Rorty, Richard. *Contingency, Irony and Solidarity*. Cambridge: Cambridge University Press, 1989.

Rorty, Richard. *Objectivity, Relativism and Truth*. Cambridge: Cambridge University Press, 1991.

Rorty, Richard. 'Human rights, rationality, and sentimentality', in Stephen Shute and Susan Hurley (eds), *On Human Rights*. New York: Basic Books, 1993.

Rostow, Dean. 'The enforcement of morals' (1960) *Cambridge Law Journal* 174.

Roth, Peter and Gryk, Wesley. 'AIDS and insurance', ch. 6 in Richard Haigh and Dai Harris (eds), *AIDS: A Guide to the Law*. London: Routledge, 2nd edn, 1995.

Rubenfeld, Jeb. 'The right to privacy' (1989) 102 *Harvard Law Review* 737.

Rubenstein, William (ed.). *Lesbians, Gay Men and the Law*. New York: New Press, 1993.

Russell, Frances. 'Soliciting discrimination' (1996) 146 *New Law Journal* 187 and 223.

Ryan, Alan (ed.). *Justice*. Oxford: Oxford University Press, 1993.

Sandel, Michael. *Liberalism and the Limits of Justice.* Cambridge: Cambridge University Press, 1982.

Sandel, Michael. 'Moral argument and liberal toleration: Abortion and homosexuality' (1989) 77 *California Law Review* 521.

Scanlon, Thomas. 'Thomson on privacy' (1975) 4 *Philosophy & Public Affairs* 315.

Scruton, Roger. *Sexual Desire: A Philosophical Investigation.* London: Phoenix, 1986.

Scruton, Roger. 'Gay reservations', ch. 8 in Michael Leahy and Dan Cohn-Sherbok (eds), *The Liberation Debate: Rights at Issue.* London: Routledge, 1996.

Sedley, Sir Stephen. 'Human rights: a twenty-first century agenda' [1995] *Public Law* 386.

Seidman, Steven. 'Identity and politics in a "postmodern" gay culture', in Michael Warner (ed.), *Fear of a Queer Planet.* Minneapolis: University of Minnesota Press, 1993.

Selznick, Philip, 'Dworkin's unfinished task' (1989) 77 *California Law Review* 505.

Sherman, Suzanne (ed.). *Lesbian and Gay Marriages: Private Commitments, Public Ceremonies.* Philadelphia: Temple University Press, 1992.

Shute, Stephen and Hurley, Susan (eds). *On Human Rights.* New York: Basic Books, 1993.

Smart, Carol. 'Feminism and law: Some problems of analysis and strategy' (1986) 14 *International Journal of the Sociology of Law* 109.

Smart, Carol. *Feminism and the Power of Law.* London: Routledge, 1989.

Smith, Anna Marie. *New Right Discourse on Race and Sexuality.* Cambridge: Cambridge University Press, 1994.

Stein, Edward. 'The essentials of constructionism and the construction of essentialism' in Edward Stein (ed.), *Forms of Desire: Sexual Orientation and the Social Constructionist Controversy.* New York: Garland, 1990.

Stein, Edward (ed.). *Forms of Desire: Sexual Orientation and the Social Constructionist Controversy.* New York: Garland, 1990.

Stychin, Carl. 'Essential rights and contested identities: Sexual orientation and equality rights Jurisprudence in Canada' (1995) 8 *Canadian Journal of Law & Jurisprudence* 49.

Stychin, Carl. *Law's Desire: Sexuality and the Limits of Justice.* London: Routledge, 1995.

Stychin, Carl. 'Novel concepts: A comment on *Egan and Nesbit* v. *The Queen*' (1995) 6 *Constitutional Forum Constitutionnel* 101.

Sullivan, Andrew. *Virtually Normal: An Argument About Homosexuality.* London: Picador, 1995.

Sullivan, William. 'Reinventing community: Prospects for politics', in Colin Crouch and David Marquand (eds), *Reinventing Collective Action: From the Global to the Local.* Oxford: Blackwell, 1995.

Tatchell, Peter. *We Don't Want to March Straight: Masculinity, Queers and the Military.* London: Cassell, 1995.

Taylor, Charles. *Philosophy and the Human Sciences: Philosophical Papers, volume 2.* Cambridge: Cambridge University Press, 1985.

Taylor, Charles. *Sources of the Self: The Making of the Modern Identity.* Cambridge: Cambridge University Press, 1989.

Taylor, Charles. 'The Politics of recognition', in Amy Gutmann (ed.), *Multiculturalism: Examining the Politics of Recognition.* Princeton, NJ: Princeton University Press, 1994.

Taylor, Nina (ed.). *All in A Day's Work: A report on anti-lesbian discrimination in employment and unemployment in London.* London: Lesbian Employment Rights, 1986.

The Report of the Committee on Homosexual Offences and Prostitution ('Wolfenden Committee'). Command Paper No. 247 (1957).

Thomas, Kendall. 'Beyond the privacy principle' (1992) 92 *Columbia Law Review* 1431.

Thomson, J. M. 'Crime, morality and unfair dismissal' (1982) 98 *Law Quarterly Review* 423.

Toynbee, Polly and Phillips, Melanie. 'Family matters', *Prospect*, June 1996, p. 20.

Trakman, Leon. 'Section 15: Equality? Where?' (1995) 6 *Constitutional Forum Constitutionnel* 112.

van der Veen, Evert and Dercksen, Adrianne. 'The social situation in the Member States', ch. 4 in K. Waaldijk and

A. Clapham (eds), *Homosexuality: A European Community Issue*. Dordrecht: Martinus Nijhoff Publishers, 1993.

Waaldijk, Kees and Clapham, Andrew (eds). *Homosexuality: A European Community Issue – Essays on Lesbian and Gay Rights in European Law and Policy*. Dordrecht: Martinus Nijhoff, 1993.

Walzer, Michael. *Spheres of Justice: A Defence of Pluralism and Equality*. Oxford: Basil Blackwell, 1983.

Walzer, Michael. *Interpretation and Social Criticism*. Cambridge, MA: Harvard University Press, 1987.

Warner, Michael (ed.). *Fear of a Queer Planet: Queer Politics and Social Theory*. Minneapolis: University of Minnesota Press, 1993.

Warren, Samuel and Brandeis, Louis. 'The right to privacy' (1890) 4 *Harvard Law Review* 193.

Watney, Simon. 'The ideology of the GLF', in Gay Left Collective (eds), *Homosexuality: Power and Politics*. London: Allison & Busby, 1980.

Watt, R. A. 'HIV, discrimination, unfair dismissal and pressure to dismiss' (1992) 21 *Industrial Law Journal* 280.

Weeks, Jeffrey. 'Discourse, desire and sexual deviance: Some problems in a history of homosexuality', in Kenneth Plummer (ed.), *The Making of the Modern Homosexual*. London: Hutchinson, 1981.

Weeks, Jeffrey. *Sexuality and its Discontents: Meanings, Myths and Modern Sexualities*. London: Routledge, 1985.

Weeks, Jeffrey. *Coming Out: Homosexual Politics in Britain from the Nineteenth Century to the Present*. London: Quartet, rev. edn, 1990.

Weeks, Jeffrey. *Against Nature: Essays on History, Sexuality and Identity*. London: Rivers Oram, 1991.

Westen, Peter. 'The empty idea of equality' (1982) 95 *Harvard Law Review* 537.

Westwood, Gordon. *A Minority – A Report on the Life of the Male Homosexual in Great Britain*. London: Longmans, 1960.

Williams, Bernard. 'The idea of equality', ch. 6 in Peter Laslett and W. G. Runciman (eds), *Philosophy, Politics and Society* (Second Series). Oxford: Basil Blackwell, 1962.

Williams, Bernard. 'Dworkin on community and critical interests' (1989) 77 *California Law Review* 515.

Williams, Bernard. *Morality: An Introduction to Ethics*. Cambridge: Cambridge University Press, 1993, Canto edn.

Williams, Bernard. 'Identity and identities', ch. 1 of Henry Harris (ed.), *Identity*. Oxford: Clarendon Press, 1995.

Williams, Bernard and Tanner, Michael. 'Discussion of contraception and chastity', ch. 9 in Michael Bayles (ed.), *Ethics and Population*. Cambridge: Schenkman, 1976.

Wilson, Angelia R. 'Which equality? Toleration, difference or respect', in Joseph Bristow and Angelia Wilson (eds), *Activating Theory: Lesbian, Gay, Bisexual Politics*. London: Lawrence & Wishart, 1993.

Wilson, Angelia R. (ed.). *A Simple Matter of Justice?* London: Cassell, 1995.

Wintemute, Robert. 'Sexual orientation discrimination', ch. 15 in Christopher McCrudden and Gerald Chambers (eds), *Individual Rights and the Law in Britain*. Oxford: Clarendon Press, 1994.

Wintemute, Robert. 'Discrimination against same-sex couples: Sections 15(1) and 1 of the *Charter*' (1995) 74 *Canadian Bar Review* 682.

Wintemute, Robert. *Sexual Orientation and Human Rights: The United States Constitution, the European Convention, and the Canadian Charter*. Oxford: Clarendon Press, 1995.

Woods, Chris. *State of the Queer Nation: A Critique of Gay and Lesbian Politics in 1990s Britain*. London: Cassell, 1995.

Woolf, Lord. 'Droit public – English style' [1995] *Public Law* 57.

Table of Cases

United Kingdom
B v. B [1991] 1 FLR 402 49–51, 52
Bell v. Devon & Cornwall Police Authority [1978] IRLR 283 61
Boychuk v. Symons Holdings [1977] IRLR 395 43–4
Bracebridge Engineering v. Darby [1990] IRLR 3 292
Buck v. The Letchworth Palace (1987, unreported) 61
C v. C [1991] 1 FLR 223 50, 62
Carrington v. Helix [1990] IRLR 6 18
Chief Constable of Hampshire v. Mace (1987) 84 Cr App Rep 40 59
Corbett v. Corbett [1970] 2 All ER 33 62
Council of Civil Service Unions v. Minister for the Civil Service [1985] 1 AC 374 61–2
De Souza v. AA [1986] IRLR 103 249
DPP v. Orum [1989] 1 WLR 88 59
Gill & Coote v. El Vino Co [1983] QB 425 59, 269
Harrogate B.C. v. Simpson [1986] 2 Family LR 91 62
James v. Eastleigh B.C. [1990] 2 AC 751 61, 293
Masterson v. Holden [1986] 3 All ER 39 58–9
P&S v. Cornwall C.C. [1996] All ER (EC) 397 45–6
Parkin v. Norman [1983] QB 92 59
Pepper v. Hart [1992] 3 WLR 1032 63
Re D [1977] AC 603 48, 50, 58, 62
Re P (1983) 4 FLR 401 49–50, 62
R v. Birmingham City Council, ex parte Equal Opportunities Commission [1989] 1 AC 1155 61, 293
R v. Bow Street Magistrates, ex parte Noncyp [1988] 3 WLR 827 63
R v. Brown [1994] 1 AC 212 32, 88, 105
R v. Chief Metropolitan Stipendiary Magistrate, ex parte Choudhury [1991] 1 All ER 306 139, 147
R v. Home Secretary, ex parte Brind [1991] 1 AC 696 59
R v. Kirkup (1993) 96 Cr App Rep 352 58, 59
R v. Knuller [1973] AC 435 29–30, 31, 54
R v. Preece [1970] Crim LR 296 58, 59
R v. Reakes [1974] Crim LR 615 28–9, 30
R v. Secretary of State for Defence, ex parte Smith [1995] 4 All ER 473 (Divisional Court), [1996] 1 All ER 257 (Court of Appeal) 18, 44–6, 61
R v. Wilson, The Times, 5 March 1996 59
S v. S (1980) 1 FLR 143 62
Saunders v. Scottish National Camps Association [1980] IRLR 174 (Employment Appeal Tribunal), [1981] IRLR 277 (Court of Session) 43–4, 105
Strathclyde R.C. v. Porcelli [1986] IRLR 134 292
T, Petitioner The Times, 20 August, 1996 62
Wallace & O'Rourke v. B.G. Turnkey Services (Scotland) Ltd (unreported, 9 July 1993) 61
West Midlands Passenger Transport Executive v. Singh [1988] IRLR 186 18
Whitehouse v. Lemon [1979] AC 617 63
Whitfield v. Whitfield (unreported, 4 November 1976) 50
Wiseman v. Salford C.C. [1981] IRLR 202 61

United States
A v. A (1973) 514 P 2d 358 63
Able v. U.S. (1995, unreported) 61
American Civil Liberties Union v. Echohawk (1993) 857 P 2d 626 63
Baehr v. Lewin (1993) 852 P 2d 44 46–7, 61

Table of Cases

Ben-Shalom v. Marsh (1989) 871 F 2d 454   55, 60, 61
Bowers v. Hardwick (1986) 106 S Crt 2841   24, 26–8, 37–43, 52, 60, 187–8, 192, 195, 201, 207–9, 212, 232, 282
Canfield v. State (1973) 506 F 2d 98   58
Carter v. State (1973) 500 SW 2d 3687   58
Chaffin v. Fyre (1975) 119 Cal Rptr 22   63
Citizens for Responsible Behavior v. Superior Court (1991) 2 Cal Rptr 2d 648   63
Collins v. Shell Oil (1991) 56 Fair Employment Prac. Cas. 440   61
Commonwealth v. Wasson (1992) 842 SW 2d 487   58
Conkel v. Conkel (1987) 509 NE 2d 983   63
Constant A. v. Paul C.A. (1985) 496 A 2d 1   63
D.H. v. J.H. (1981) 418 NE 2d 286   63
Dean v. District of Columbia (1995) 653 A 2d 307   62
Doe v. Doe (1983) 452 NE 2d 293   63
Doe v. Sparkes (1990) 733 F Supp 227   61
Equality Foundation v. City of Cincinnati (1994) 860 F Supp 417 (reversed by Court of Appeals, 1995, unreported)   60, 63
Gay Students Organization v. Bonner (1974) 509 F 2d 652   63
Gay Student Services v. Texas A. & M. University (1984) 737 F 2d 1317   63
G.A. v. D.A. (1987) 745 SW 2d 726   63
Hall v. Hall (1980) 291 NW 2d 143   63
High Tech Gays v. Defense Industrial Security Clearance Office (1990) 895 F 2d 563   38, 40–1, 60, 238, 268
Irish-American Gay, Lesbian and Bisexual Group of Boston v. City of Boston (1994) 636 NE 2d 1293   63
Jacobson v. Jacobson (1981) 314 NW 2d 79   63
L. v. D. (1982) 630 SW 2d 240   63
M.J.P. v. J.G.P. (1982) 640 P 2d 966   52, 63
Mabon v. Keisling (1993) 856 P 2d 1023   63
N.K.M. v. L.E.M. (1980) 606 SW 2d 179   63
National Gay Task Force v. City of Oklahoma (1984) 729 F 2d 1270   61, 63
Opinion of the Justices (1987) 530 A 2d 21   61, 63
People v. Superior Court (1988) 758 P 2d 1046   58
Pikula v. Pikula (1985) 374 NW 2d 705   62
Roe v. Roe (1985) 324 SE 2d 691   63
Romer v. Evans (1993) 854 P 2d 1270 (Colorado Supreme Court), (1996) 116 S Ct 1620 (US Supreme Court)   21, 37, 41–2
S.N.E. v. R.L.B. (1985) 699 P 2d 875   63
Shahar v. Bowers (1993) 836 F Supp 859   55, 62
Singer v. Hara (1974) 522 P 2d 1187   62
Singer v. U.S. Civil Service Commission (1976) 530 F 2d 247   62
State v. Morales (1992) 826 SW 2d 201, reversed at (1994) 869 SW 2d 941   58
Steffan v. Perry (1991) 780 F Supp 1, (1994) 41 F 3d 677   61
U.S. v. Carolene Products (1938) 304 US 144   60
Watkins v. U.S. Army (1988) 837 F 2d 1428, (1989) 875 F 2d 699   38–42, 60, 147, 231, 238, 268
Woodward v. U.S. (1989) 871 F 2d 1068   60

Canada

Andrews v. Law Society of British Columbia [1989] 1 SCR 143   60
Canada (Attorney-General) v. Mossop (1990) 71 DLR (4th) 661 (Court of Appeal), [1993] 1 SCR 554 (Supreme Court)   60, 62
Egan v. Canada (1993) 103 DLR (4th) 336 (FCA), [1995] 2 SCR 513 (SCC)   35–7, 47, 60
Haig v. Canada (1992) 9 OR (3d) 495   36, 60
Knodel v. British Columbia (Medical Services Commission) (1991) 58 BCLR (2d) 356   60
Layland v. Ontario (Minister of Consumer and Commercial Relations) (1993) 14 OR (3d) 658   62
Retail, Wholesale & Department Store Union v. Dolphin Delivery [1986] 2 SCR 573   60
Veysey v. Canada (Correctional Services) [1990] 1 FC 321, (1990) 109 NR 300 (FCA)   60

Australia

Australian Capital Television v. Commonwealth of Australia (1992) 177 CLR 106   61

International Covenant on Civil and Political Rights
Toonen v. Australia Communication (1994) 1–3 IHRR 97   61

European Convention on Human Rights
Dudgeon v. United Kingdom (1981) 4 EHRR 149   58, 207, 281, 286, 292
Laskey, Jaggard and Brown v. United Kingdom (109/1995/615/703–705), 19 February 1997   59, 105
Modinos v. Cyprus (1993) 16 EHRR 485   58, 207, 286, 292
Norris v. Ireland (1989) 13 EHRR 187   58, 207, 281, 286, 292
S v. U.K. (1986) 4 D&R 274   61

Index

Adam, Barry 64
Altman, Dennis 221–6
Anscombe, Elizabeth 166
anti-discrimination protections 5, 11, 12, 14, 16, 24, 33–46, 69, 139–40, 148, 151–2, 201, 216, 235, 258, 267
anti-perfectionism 134–6, 208–16, 218, 225–6, 229
anti-sodomy laws 25–8
Arnold, Sir John 49
Arran, Lord 32, 214
Ashworth, Andrew 30
autonomy 16, 209–12, 217, 229, 261–6

Bindman, Geoffrey 279, 280
Birch, Keith 64
Blackmun, Justice 209
Blair, Tony 236, 238, 240, 250, 255
blasphemous libel 54
blasphemy 139
Boswell, John 78, 81–3, 85
Bradley, Gerard 157, 159, 165, 167
Brundage, James 176
Brunetti, Circuit Judge 41
Buckley, Michael 170, 171
Burger, Chief Justice 27
Butler, Roger 285

Cain, Patricia 40
Callman, Judge 49–51
Canadian Charter of Rights and Freedoms 34–7, 47, 272–5
Canadian Criminal Code 206
Canadian Human Rights Act 36
Canby, Judge 40
Catholic theology 162–74, 260

censorship of political participation 33, 52–5
children 48–52, 56, 155–60
'Christian' right 54, 68, 134
Cicchino, Peter 279
Colorado State Constitution, Amendment 2 14, 25, 33, 37, 41, 43, 54, 107–9, 148, 154, 287
Colvine, Madeline 53
communitarianism 95–8, 113–17, 120, 124
consent, age of 3–4, 29, 30, 175, 178, 207, 236, 238–40, 250, 253, 284–6, 288
constructionism
 generally 15, 51, 65, 74–85, 200–1
 moderate 15, 79–82, 83, 200, 267
 radical 51, 79–82, 83, 200, 267
Cotterrell, Roger 273, 278, 282
Criminal Justice and Public Order Act 1994 3–4, 7, 29, 31, 33, 45, 284–6, 288
criminal law 1, 3–4, 12, 16, 24, 25–32, 148–9, 201, 206–7, 235, 253, 258, 267, 281
 in UK 28–32
 in US 24, 26–8, 37
 proper function of 125
Currie, Edwina 4, 178, 207, 284–5

D'Emilio, John 64, 76, 220, 235, 246, 252, 253
Defense of Marriage Act 1996 46–7
Deming, Bruce 279
Dercksen, Adrianne 279
De Souza, Ms. 249
Devlin, Lord 129–33, 136, 148, 149, 179–90, 200
dignity, respect for 216–17, 229

Dror, Yehezkel 277, 281
Duff, R.A. 261
Dworkin, Ronald 7, 37, 41, 42, 116, 117, 123, 135, 136, 186–8, 212–14, 253–5, 257

employment 37–46, 56, 205, 248–9
empowerment 16, 17, 88–91, 199, 237, 258–67
Epstein, Steven 76, 80, 240
equality 11–12, 16, 86–91, 115, 135–6, 197, 199, 202, 219, 235–57, 258, 266–7
   conduct-based view 238–40, 250, 256
   status-based view 238–9, 240–50, 256
Equal Treatment Directive 44–5
essentialism 15, 65, 74–85, 118, 200–1
European Convention on Human Rights 46, 207–8, 281–2
European Court of Human Rights 207, 281
Evan, William 277, 279

Fairbairn, Sir Nicholas 175
family and partnership rights 24, 33, 46–52, 56, 235, 258, 267
feminism 91–6
Fernbach, David 22
Finnis, John 14, 16, 107–9, 117, 128, 149, 150, 152–74, 186, 215
Frazer, Elizabeth 124
Freeden, Michael 72
freedom 255
Fried, Charles 209
Fuss, Diana 74, 75, 81, 241

Gaitskell, Lady 284
Gardner, John 72, 73
Gavison, Ruth 209
Gay Activists Alliance 64
Gay Liberation Front 64, 66, 67, 220, 223, 242–3
Gellner, Ernest 115–17
George, Robert 157–9, 165, 167, 211, 212
German Penal Code 22
Giddens, Anthony 265–6
Gilligan, Carol 96

Glendon, Mary Ann 95, 97
Glidewell, Lord Justice 50
Gregson, Raymond 285
Grisez, Germain 162
gross indecency 25
Guest, Stephen 255

Halley, Janet 204, 248
Halperin, David 77
Hardwick, Michael 26–8
harm principle 130–2
Hart, H.L.A. 90, 91, 107–10, 128–30, 132–4, 136, 185–7, 259, 261
Hawksley, Jane 53
Heger, Heinz 22
Held, David 265, 266
Herman, Didi 272–5, 278, 286
human nature 175–9, 205–6

identity 202, 227–8, 241–50, 260, 262–4, 267
immutability 197, 203–6, 237
'inherent wrongfulness' 149–79

Jeffery-Poulter, Stephen 284–5
Jurisprudence 7
justice, theories of 5–10, 12, 16, 108–43, 225, 273–5
justifications for law and law reform 5–10, 12, 13, 15, 16, 23, 55–6, 65, 70, 83–4, 86–91, 107–43, 196–230, 235–67
   conservative justifications 9, 14, 16, 148–90, 216
   consistency of 137–42, 161–7, 175–6, 188–90, 210–12, 215, 219–20, 226, 229–30, 257
   criteria for assessing 137–42
   operation of 198–203
   reach of 112–24, 142–3, 249–50
   substantive attractiveness of 137–42, 150, 167–74, 176–9, 184–8, 205–6, 211–12, 219–20, 229, 242–50

Kahn-Freund, Sir Otto 273, 277
Katz, Jonathan 1, 70
Kingdom, Elizabeth 94, 95, 98
Kinsman, Gary 94
Kymlicka, Will 96–8, 115, 135

Index

Lacey, Nicola 124
law reform, effects of 5, 10–11, 15, 16, 55, 118–19, 172–3, 272–90
Lester, Anthony 279, 280
liberalism 113–18, 123, 213, 264
liberationism 11–12, 16, 197, 199, 220–6, 229–30, 235, 242, 250, 252–3, 267
libertarianism 97–8, 226
liberty 196–7, 258
Local Government Act 1988 25, 33, 53–4, 148, 154, 179, 203, 284, 287–8

McBarnet, Doreen 276
MacCormick, Neil 5, 71, 72, 131, 136, 264
Macedo, Stephen 196
Male Representatives of National Gay Liberation 66, 223
marriage 171–2
  as basic good 157–60, 165–6
  same-sex 46–7, 179
Massachusetts Gay Civil Rights Bill 279
Massachusetts Governor's Commission Report 68–70
Miliband, David 265
Mill, John Stuart 130–2
Mohr, Richard 115–16, 216–18, 262
Moorcroft, Robert 285
moral relativism 112–24
morality
  descriptive 7–8
  evaluative 8
  legal enforcement of 110, 127–36, 179–90
  political 5–7, 10, 108–9, 126–36, 149–51, 153–75, 179, 225, 258, 273–5
  sexual 9–10, 125–36, 149–51, 153–75, 183, 197, 198, 200
Morris, Lord 29
Mugabe, Robert 112

Nagel, Thomas 175–8
Narvesen, Jan 72
National Gay and Lesbian Task Force 68
Nazi Germany 22–3

new natural lawyers 153–75
Nicholson, Katherine 279
Norrie, Kenneth 53
Norris, Circuit Judge 38–40, 42
Nozick, Robert 7, 9
Nussbaum, Martha 163

Obscene Publications Acts 1959 and 1964 54
Offences Against the Person Act 1861 32
Ormrod, Lord Justice 50

Padgug, Robert 78, 79
Paisley, Ian 4, 170
perfectionism 135–6, 211–12, 216–20, 225–6, 229
perversion 175–9
Phillips, Justice 43–4
philosophy
  legal 7, 13
  political 7, 13–14
Plant, Raymond 6, 114, 127
Plant, Richard 22
'populist morality' 149, 151, 176, 179–90
privacy, respect for 11–12, 16, 88–91, 115, 125, 197, 199, 201–3, 206–22, 225, 229, 235, 237
Public Order Act 1986 31

queer theory 220–1, 226–9, 235

Race Relations Act 1976 249
Raz, Joseph 90, 91, 131, 135, 226, 255, 257, 264
Reid, Lord 30
Reinhardt, Judge 40
Report of the Secretary's Task Force on Youth Suicide 68–70, 174, 261, 282–3
Richards, David 163, 168, 169, 209–12, 214, 217, 225
rights
  as entitlements 66–74
  interest theory 71–3, 97
  legal 66–7, 69–74, 85–6, 98–9, 223
  lesbian and gay 15, 64–99, 202, 218–19, 228, 257, 264, 267, 272–5
  moral 67, 70–4, 85–6, 98–9
  reach of 114

social 66-7, 69-74, 85-6, 98-9
will theory 71-2, 97
Roberts, Paul 131
Rorty, Richard 1, 118-20, 123, 124, 138
Rostow, Dean 182, 183
Rubenstein, William 28

sado-masochism 32, 87-8
Sandel, Michael 215
Scruton, Roger 176-8
Sedley, Sir Stephen 92, 121-4
Seidman, Steven 244, 245
Selznick, Philip 212, 214
sex discrimination 44-6
Sex Discrimination Act 1975 44, 93, 280
sexual harassment 280
Sexual Offences Act 1956 29
Sexual Offences Act 1967 28-32, 92-3, 214-15, 284
sexuality
  causes of 203-6
  role of 259-60
  theories of 15, 17, 51, 65, 74-85, 172-3, 221-6, 229-30, 235
Smart, Carol 91-5
Smith, Chris 3, 203, 236, 238, 240, 286, 288
social democracy 258-67, 275
society, nature of 184-8
Stein, Edward 81
Stonewall Riot 64, 220
Stychin, Carl 47, 78, 221, 226-9
Sullivan, Andrew 224, 225

Tatchell, Peter 250-2, 254-5
Taylor, Charles 95, 97, 120, 121
Thomas, Kendall 28, 215, 218, 282
Thomson, Judith Jarvis 209
totalitarianism 110-11
transcultural standards 115-24
transsexuals 45
Trudeau, Pierre 206
Turner, John 206

unfair dismissal 43-4, 89
United States constitution 34-5, 37-43
  Due Process clause 24, 26, 40, 187, 207
  Equal Protection clause 37-41, 54, 140, 238
  First Amendment 55

van der Veen, Evert 279
violence, anti-lesbian and gay 2, 262

Walzer, Michael 114, 115, 120
Watkins, Lord Justice 50
Watkins, Sergeant 38, 40
Weeks, Jeffrey 64, 76-8, 214, 215, 223, 241-6
Weld, William 68
White, Justice 27, 187
Whitehouse, Mary 54
Wilberforce, Lord 48
Williams, Bernard 121-3, 213
Wilson, Angelia 244
Wintemute, Robert 32
Wolfenden Committee Report 14, 77, 107, 125, 129-30, 133, 179, 180, 206, 208, 259, 284

Zimbabwe 112-15, 117